Take a Decade

A TRUE STORY

Mike,

Thank you for your support!

Stephen Mundy

Copyright © 2024 Stephen Mundy
All rights reserved
First Edition

Fulton Books
Meadville, PA

Published by Fulton Books 2024

ISBN 979-8-88982-405-3 (paperback)
ISBN 979-8-88982-406-0 (digital)

Printed in the United States of America

This book is dedicated to the one person who supported me and loved me no matter where I was and where I was going. To you, Mom. I love you.

1
CHAPTER

It's 2:00 a.m., and it was my time to take over the helm of the *Red Rhino*. The seas were not good, not good at all. The swells were ten- to fifteen-foot whitecaps, and the winds were blowing twenty-knot winds. It was miserable out there, and it was now my turn to steer this boat in the right direction. It would be a white-knuckle and stressful next four hours.

After grabbing my snack and a drink, which was water and a pudding, I entered the helm to find JD very glad to see me. The helm was about twenty feet long and six feet wide, and at this time of night, it was *dark*; the only real light coming off all the equipment was a light-green glare. The anchor was still banging on the side of the boat with every wave. That was getting really old to hear because we didn't want to lose our anchor or punch a hole in the hull. Neither option was beneficial to five guys delivering a boat across the Pacific Ocean.

My next four hours were already mapped out on the GPS; this was done in the morning by the captain using our charts, fuel consumption, and most importantly, the weather to make an educated guess on just how many miles we could cover that day. This shift, the 2:00 a.m.–6:00 a.m., was the last before our new stats. We were bringing this boat, an 85' × 40' steel-hull catamaran navy ship built in 1966 as a torpedo recovery vessel and now used for big-wave surfing dudes and as a tender for a submarine, to Subic Bay, Philippines, its new home. Our mission was to deliver it *safely* 5,300 miles from Oahu, Hawaii.

I took a look over at my little cup of chocolate pudding and thought, *Not yet*. It was too soon for my snack. Just then, like a snap of my fingers, I lost all power in the helm. GPS—gone, radar—gone, lights—gone, steering—gone. "Holy shit." That was exactly what I said. *What the heck do I do? I can't see or control the boat. Oh, shit.* The first thing I did was throttle down. I had to get control of it, and the only way I knew how was to slow it down. If you have ever worked or even been a passenger on a boat, when the boat slows down like this, it usually means one of two things: You've reached your destination, or something is wrong. We had not made it to our destination.

Within ninety seconds, the "official captain," Al, was standing there. Ninety-five seconds later, Joel, our chief engineer; 110 seconds later, Brian, our chief electrician; and 125 seconds later, JD, our chief navigator—they were all standing at the helm. All I could say was "Holy shit, I lost everything."

Captain Al told me to take the wheel. The wheel was actually just that, a three-foot-diameter golden boat wheel. But wait a minute, we had not once used this prehistoric device to steer the boat. All the steering had been done with our joystick and instruments. Without power, we had no idea which way we were heading, no idea of the direction of the rudders, and this was not good. So I grabbed the wheel and started turning it to the left, and a wave hit us hard. I turned to the right; now we were sideways on a wave, not at all where we wanted to be. To the left, we were turning, but with us throttled down ten knots to three knots, she was turning slow. Just then, the problem was determined: The helm battery backup alternator/recharging was broken. Al, Joel, JD, and Brian were all brainstorming. All I could think was, *Hurry the hell up!*

Joel said, "We need the battery in the engine room." Al came and took the wheel, and I breathed a sigh of relief. *I'm not at the wheel, and I'm not calling the shots. Thank God.* We were getting hit hard with waves; the boat was still all over the place. Our lives were definitely on the line for the first real time during this whole trip.

We needed that battery! Now this was not just your average car battery. It's a big-ass hard-core marine-grade battery that weighed 150 lbs. The real problem was that it was two flights down. The battery we needed was in our utility room, which was in front of the engine room. It's the floor below water, and we were two floors above the waterline.

Out of the helm, through the galley, down the steps, past the bunk rooms, through the entertainment room, down a hatch, and through a bulkhead door, there it was, hooked up for a backup bank for a generator. I said, "Okay, Joel, how are we going to do this?"

He said, "Grab that hoist and climb back out. Hook it to the top of the hatch." JD and I muscled it over to the bottom of the stairs. They strapped it up and yelled to start pulling. I pulled on the rope, and they balanced it from swinging back and forth. The pulley system was working slow and steady. We had to angle it a bit just so it would fit coming out of the metal bulkhead door that was on the floor; that's done by those two standing underneath this swinging time bomb. I grabbed it and pulled as hard as I could just to get it out of the floor bulkhead and onto the next level. We made it to the first floor. Now we had one more flight of stairs and then from one end of the boat to the other.

The next level was just old-school balls-to-the-walls muscle. The three of us picked it up somehow and carried it up the flight of stairs, getting knocked into the wall and doing everything we could to keep our balance and not drop it. We made it to the galley and took a quick break. We then made our way through the galley while the boat was getting rocked hard from the portside. That was the toughest part because we had nothing to hang on to or help balance ourselves. At least coming up the stairs, we had the walls to keep us balanced. *Can't drop this battery, we would be in a lot of trouble. Wait, wait, and wait for the wave to hit, and now slow and steady.* We made it to the helm. Al was frantically just trying to keep the boat from getting rocked, and Brian was ready to connect. We got it into place, and Brian did his thing, connecting the cables and getting the wiring all set up. This took about fifteen minutes, and he got the cables on and all connected. The switch was turned on. Oh my, *yes!* We had power. We had lights. We had our electronics. We were going to make this trip.

We all looked at one another with a "What the fuck was that?" smile and just started to laugh. Damn, that was a little on the scary side, and it had to happen when I was at the wheel. It was now about 3:30 a.m. We had gotten the boat back on course, and the guys left the helm to try and go back to sleep. Al turned and said, "Mundy, don't break anything else," with a smile.

"Roger that, Captain."

CHAPTER 2

Okay, okay, okay, we need to slow down and all get on the same page. My Name is Stephen Mundy, I'm 30 years old, 6,1" 185lbs, and this is my book. I've been called Steve, Stevo, Mundy, and a few other things. I'm writing this book because I think I have a good story to tell. It's about travel, adventure, love, death, and good old life. I've had the opportunities in my life to just go with the flow and see what the world has to offer. Situations have come my way, some good, some not so good.

I am going back in time but not to the beginning, not as far as the Ice Age—let's say we get this started around the year 2000, a nice even number and really the beginning of my adventure.

I had been living in Phoenix, Arizona, for the past seven years. The southwest, the wild, wild West. The home of the rattlesnake and the OK Corral. Desert and land that goes forever. My buddy and best friend, Murph, had arrived in Phoenix seven years earlier by taking a fifty-four-hour Greyhound bus ride cross-country from Baltimore, Maryland, to Phoenix, Arizona. A lot had happened in my life up until this time, but for who I am now and what I have accomplished, a huge part of who I am started here.

It was the first of March, Monday morning, and at this point in my career, I was not looking forward to going to work. Not much had changed in the last six months even though I had a great job as a financial representative for the Vanguard Group. I was just not sure this was for me. It was my fourth calendar year, and all I could say to myself each morning was "It's almost time." It was a cubicle job, a team job, making money for our investors and doing what it took to keep them happy. A shirt-and-tie position, security clearance with the SEC (Securities and Exchange Commission), basically it was Wall Street, just in the desert and not NYC.

But it had become just a paycheck. It was a way of life to do what I really enjoyed doing, and that was anything outside—hiking, camping, exploring, and hanging out by a pool with friends. However, I was not born with a golden spoon, so work it was and coming home to my two cats, Samsun and Ashbury.

I was single at this time in my life. I had ended a relationship with a beautiful, caring, loving person about six months prior. It was a very difficult decision to make as we were engaged and living together. The day I approached Sally about maybe postponing our wedding was the day that I went to pick up our mail, and the invitations, matchbooks, napkins, and all that other fancy stuff that was used for a wedding had arrived. I knew when I got that package I had to tell her. I left everything right in the container and walked back into the house. She was in the bathroom, and I walked up behind her and said, "We need to talk." We sat on the end of the bed, and I said, "Sally, something doesn't feel right about getting married. Can we, for now, just wait for a bit?"

She was devastated. We both cried and talked for about an hour. Now we had to tell our families. She called her parents; they kind of understood, and I called mine, and they kind of understood. Sally and I went to a marriage counselor for a few weeks and tried to make it happen, but my heart wasn't there. A few months later, she moved out.

Something I have learned about people is that everyone has a story, everyone has something to share, and everyone has a past. The fun part of life is meeting people and getting them to share their experiences and life's moments. You can learn a lot about yourself through other people.

What keeps people going to the same job day after day if they don't enjoy it? I did have a plan, a very exciting plan that started probably close to a year ago. It all happened around two o'clock one morning, and I was having one of those "What am I doing with my life?" conversations. You know the real annoying ones that you can't shut your mind off or stop thinking about bad things. All you want is to go to sleep so you don't have to think anymore. Then it happened. I had a plan; I knew exactly what I was going to do. I was going to backpack across Europe for three weeks. Yes, that is what I'm going to do. Wow, what a feeling came over me, going from "What I am doing with the rest of my life?" to "Now I know what I'm going to do with the next part of my life." It was such a needed boost in my life, and I thought it would be frigging fantastic to take three weeks and backpack through Europe. I slept like a baby, and the next morning, I woke up with a new outlook on my life.

It was just three months away. The plan was set, tickets were purchased, passport received, and bags were almost packed. At this point, work was work, and I went in and did my job every day to the best of my abilities. The best part of the day was the last five minutes of the day when it was time to punch out. I may have clocked into my computer late several times; I never once punched out late. At five o'clock, I was done.

Now life got fun again. It was a weekday, so it was time for Graydon, Jason, and I to meet at the gym. Monday was chest and biceps day, which was our favorite. It was time to add a little weight to the program and keep doing what I had been doing for the past three months: get stronger and get in better shape. I went from bench-pressing 150 lbs. to 260 lbs. My chest and arms were getting bigger and stronger, and this would help while traveling. Just about everything I was doing at this point in my life was for Europe.

Working out really started with Jason, who had transferred with a buddy of his from the PA office to the Phoenix office. The first time I saw him, I was like, This guy is huge, definitely likes going to the gym. He was about 6'4", 230 lbs., and a good-looking guy. He kind of had a slight look of being gay, but I soon found out he wasn't; this is because the next day, he hit on the same girl I was trying to get with. I didn't care for him at first because he did get the girl. Bastard! However, within a few days, we connected and began a great friendship. It also had a lot to do with Graydon, 6'2", 185 lbs., and also a good-looking guy. Graydon and I had been hanging out for a while. We both had the same love for the outdoors and having fun in life.

He was a very positive, laid-back, and easy-to-talk-to guy, and we felt the same way about work—it was just a way to keep having fun doing what we enjoyed. We had camped and hiked together many times before we started hanging out with Jason. It was when the three of us first hung out we realized we all had a dark side.

The three of us were three peas in a pod. We worked together, worked out together, did weekend camping trips, and hung out at each other's apartment: Jason's sister Michelle, Mike, Sara, Duce, Leah, and the three of us. Pool parties, the club scene, and camping out. We had a good time, worked hard and partied hard. At first, it was beers at the pool, Friday night happy hour, and any other reason to have a good time. Then we started to dabble in a few more things. One day, Jason asked Graydon and me, "Have you ever tried ecstasy?"

We said, "No, no, we have not." Now up to this time, I had tried cocaine, acid, mushrooms, and of course, marijuana. I did go to college for a really long time, so this is why I went to college for a really long time. We had a good time. I didn't miss too many parties those first few years. I had also seen the Grateful Dead twenty-five times.

So we were planning a night out, headed to the clubs. If you were near or around the club scene in Scottsdale, Arizona, around the late nineties, early 2000, this was a good place to be. The clubs were amazing, at least eight to ten great places to go and get crazy. Our first time we "rolled"—that is what you call it—we started at 10:00 p.m., and by 11:00 p.m., we were right in the middle of the dance floor, dancing to techno and having a whole-body experience. Your body is so relaxed, every touch feels amazing, the lights are the brightest colors you have ever seen, and all you can do is just smile. I'm sure not everyone in the clubs at this time was experiencing what we were, but more were than weren't. It was the thing to do and the place to do it. Then after the clubs closed, everyone would go to some person's house or mansion and just continue the party.

After a few months of this routine, things started to get a little boring. It was the same people out and same results every time. We decided to relax a bit, and that is when I happened across a guy who lived very close and sold cocaine. Now most things I've tried were all good and fun. This stuff, however, could change your world. It started as a once-a-week thing: Get a few people together and do some lines. Cocaine is the "solve all the problems in the world" drug. Your senses work overtime. You feel like you are about as good as it comes. Get five or six people, a couple of eight balls, a carton of cigarettes, and you can only imagine what life's problems can be solved. The problem with cocaine is you always want more. It's not like drinking where you can just pass out somewhere or like weed when you just end up falling asleep after eating a bunch of junk food. Coke will haunt you all night long. It is the *worst* feeling coming down. You feel like shit, and nothing else matters.

    Our partying increased from just on weekends to every other day. We would always come up with some excuse why today would be a good day to indulge. It usually didn't take much convincing. My problem was the guy was using my apartment to meet other people. I didn't mind; it just meant more for me and *free*. Now we were still going to work, and we were still working out four days a week. I wasn't selling things to get high or spending a ton of money on this; I'd always been very tight with my money. It was just our social activities that we enjoyed doing at this point in our lives. For me, however, it was all going to stop on June 10, my departure date for Europe. This was something I had been looking forward to doing for a while now, and nothing was going to get in my way.

    As the date got closer, my excitement grew. It was hard to even concentrate at work. All I wanted to talk about was things I was going to see and do in Europe. Each night, I was preparing a little bit more—changing clothes that I was going to bring, packing my bags, and continuing to read my *Lonely Planet's Guide* to traveling across Europe. The only other thing that I was looking forward to was our partnership bonus check. This year, my partnership was for $5,200. I could have a real good time and still have something in the bank when I got back. Well, this is what I thought at least.

    My last day of work was on Friday, and I was leaving Saturday. Now if I had not gone out Thursday with my friends and partied all night, I would have gone to work. However, I did go out with my friends, and we tore it up, the club, drugs, and women. It was one last big night for me, and I was going to miss my friends, so we had fun. The next morning was my last day of work, and I had so many things to do. That was the day we received our partnership money, and I still needed to buy a camcorder and camera and finish last-minute packing, and man, was I hurting. So I called in sick my last day. I went right back to sleep and woke up four hours later, finally ready to finish what I needed to do. But that night, I found out that my team was throwing me a going-away party, cake and everything. I really felt bad. That was kind of a shitty thing to do, but I really didn't know. That was the last bad thing that would happen to me because of partying, I promised myself.

Finally, it was the day I had been waiting to arrive for over a year now. I was going to be flying to Washington, Dulles, then to Heathrow, London. It was going to be a long day yet exciting. My roommate, Greg, who looked like a Rasta man, black with dreadlocks and who had a ten-foot African rock python as a pet, took me to the airport. At the airport, I made my last call in the United States to my mom and dad. Both were very supportive and excited for me. My mom was very nervous, I could tell, and very happy for me at the same time. She is and will always be my biggest supporter. My mother is still the most important person in my life. So after one more beer and a shot in the USA, I was on my way to Europe.

CHAPTER 3

The flight to Europe was awesome, free food and drinks the entire way. I ate well and yes, drank the entire time. I couldn't help my excitement. I was meeting one of my best friends, his name is Steve as well, so it made introducing us easier. Steve was 6'3 and 250lbs, a big guy, but athletic as well. He was flying from Baltimore to London and we would be getting to Heathrow airport about one hour before I did. When I made the decision to travel around Europe, Steve was in right away. He could go for 2 weeks; I would have 3 weeks to see how far I could get, we both wanted to see as much as possible.

We touched down and I found Steve right away. Big hugs and we both were so excited to actually standing on European soil. There had been months of planning, preparing, booking, and the hardest part was the waiting, but guess what it has all been worth it for this very moment. Stephen Mundy is in Europe.

London, England

Our first part of this journey started in London and there was so much to see and do. Those first few days of walking around and seeing the different architecture of the buildings. Just realizing that this part of the world is so much older than the states. The sounds of the street cars sounded different, especially the emergency vehicles. The cobble stone streets and walkways that we so admire are just the norm. The streets were narrow and of course they drive on the other side of the rode, so even crossing the streets was a little different. The smells of fresh food be prepared on the streets, the way people moved around, and every time you turn a corner there is something else amazing to see. It just seems so surreal that I'm actually here and loving every moment of it.

Life was different right from the beginning. We stayed at St. Simean's Hostel for our stay in London. Our room was half below the street and half above the street, which was more of an alley way then street. We could actually leave our room by going out our window. Shared bathrooms and a good old fashion English breakfast each morning, which was 2 eggs, a biscuit, small piece of ham, and really strong coffee. It never really filled us up, but got us started for the day. As far as our meals for the most part we usually found an outdoor pub of some sort to eat and enjoy a pint. I really enjoyed the home-made sandwiches with fresh meats and cheeses. Steve and I also both enjoyed the same drink, Grand Marnier and a cold pint of a local beer.

London is filled with things to see and do and we walked and used the Tube, the subway system to get everywhere we wanted to go. When you think of London, certain attractions always come to mind: Big ben and the Parliament building, which is one of London's most iconic symbols. The London Tower Bridge, which is a modern marvel suspension bridge and draw bridge that we walked over and had one of the best views of the city from the top. Kennington Palace, home to the royal family and the famous guards that protect the royal families and secure the grounds. We watched the changing of the guards and it was so impressive to see them move like they do. The Tower of London, once used as a prison where Elizabeth I and Sir Walter Raleigh spent time behind the dark walls. Of course, we could not come to London and not stop at Buckingham Palace and try and get a peak at the Queen, but she wasn't available for Steve and I to have tea with that day. This was just the start of what we had seen and so much more to come.

While walking around London we had a mission to find the London Bridge, this is the one used in the nursery rhyme we have all heard of. We though that the London tower Bridge was it, but we were wrong. We were given directions and I was actually standing on a small bridge and asked a guy walking by, "excuse me sir, can you tell me where the London Bridge is?" he looked at us and said "you're standing on it right now." What, this small bridge is it and he said yes. We felt very stupid for not knowing this, but hey we didn't know. The original London Bridge was disassembled and ship to Lake Havasu, Arizona in 196. The one we were standing on was made after the fact. It was still cool to have said we walked over the London Bridge, even though it wasn't the original.

One thing we stumbled upon was the London Dungeon and let me tell you it was worth it. The outside of the building was old and the lady working the booth was also old, which made it better for some reason. This was a historical timeline of the history of London. They use special effects and live people to describe everything this city has been through. It started with the wrath of Henry VII, public executions, the torture chambers, the Black Plaque, the Great Fire of London, jack the ripper, and anything else that might have happened. It was so worth the money and honestly, I had a much better understanding of what this city had been through over the past 1000 years after this tour. If you visit London, but this on your list.

One evening we had dinner and drinks at Piccadilly Circus, which is a junction for 5 major streets in the west end in the city of Westminster. It is like a combination of Time Square in NYC and Pier 39 in San Fransico. Great place to watch people and we enjoyed several drinks while we were there. It was just one big party and everyone was having a blast.

Our last night in London, we did something that was probably my favorite thing we did the entire time in London. Earlier that day we signed up to do a walking tour/pup crawl at night, it was called "A walk with Jack the Ripper." We meet at 10pm and our guide was dressed up just like they dressed back in the 1800's. He wore a big black hat and was carrying an old fashion lantern that actually worked.

We spend two hours walking around the White Chapel District. He took us to each of places that they had found a victim of "Jack the Ripper." It started in the autumn months of 1888 and a series of gruesome murders that held this area hostage for months. He killed prostitutes by slicing them from the groin to the neck, leaving the bodies to be discovered the next day. Even though there were suspects no one has ever been charged with these murders.

I believe we walked to about 7 different locations and each place had a pup nearby. Stop and talk about a horrible murder and then go have a shot, what else can you do. One other thing about this night was I met my first girl of the trip. Her and a friend were enjoying the same thing we were, we started talking at the first pub and never stopped. The four of us had another drink after the pub crawl and when we said our goodbyes, we stunk away and enjoyed a great farewell kiss. I almost got hit by a car when I crossed the street to get back to Steve, literally I was inches from getting smacked. Yes, this was my favorite night so far.

London was a great start to this adventure. Everything from the old buildings, historical attractions, the narrow streets, smoked filled pubs, The River Thames, and time with my friend. We had been taking as many pictures as we could and I also had a camcorder, so I was trying to get as much on video as I could. Unfortunately for Steve, he was the only one I could interview and that got old real fast for him. I found it hilarious and for the most part we had fun with it.

It was around the 5th day and we had our first travel day. Today we would be flying to Amsterdam and excited in so many ways. I love to fly, it was our 2nd country, which meant another stamp in my pass port and yes weed is legal where we are going. We both enjoyed "a good smoke" and this place was world known for its café's and so much more.

We started from the train station, which is where we got information on a cheap place to stay. As we walked out of the terminal, it was the number of bicycles all over the place that caught our eyes, I mean thousands lined up everywhere. We were walking, so they did nothing for us. We found our place, which was a basic room with the shower down the hall and it was perfect. Dropped off our bags and with the help of the guy who checked us in, he sent us to our first of many "cafés" named Amnesia.

It was a short walk and we were there. This was the first for both of us to actually walk into a place of business and smoke weed legally. What a treat and something I've made many people over the years very jealous of doing. We walked in, went to the bar and the bartender, who was hot, handed us a menu. Everything listed like a fine wine, priced by the gram and we placed our order. 2 grams of this, 1 gram of that, about $30 worth and two beers. We were set for a few days and sat down at a table and enjoyed our first of many experiences inside an Amsterdam Café.

It didn't take long to be feeling really good and time to start exploring. So far, we had seen London and all it had to offer and it was awesome. Amsterdam had something about it, that was different and absolutely beautiful and that was miles of canals that went around the whole city. They were used for transporting everything from product to people. The building that lined the canals were painted in brighter colors, even the street lights were old and unique looking. Let me tell you it wasn't just that we were high, everything looked so remarkable. The world went on around us and we just took it all in.

There were no wrong turns to make because every turn was a new street and something new and amazing to see. We also tried to go into as many cafés as possible, if not to at least pick something up for the road. We left with about 10 grams of different kinds from different places. There was Bulldogs, Blue Velvet, Doors, and my favorite 420. There are so many, that we just didn't have time. Walk around, sightseeing, stop for a bit to eat and drink, and just take in this beautiful European city.

Every day we were there it was wake up, have a smoke, enjoy our complimentary breakfast and wonder the streets of Amsterdam. Van Gogh Museum was a big hit for both us. He is the one artist that everyone has heard of and we were lucky enough to see a majority of his work. Great place to visit and would definitely recommend it to everyone. There was also Rembrandt's Museum there as well and it to was great, just for me I liked Van Gogh's work a little better.

After a few days wondering around the city, Steve was getting a little cranky and tired of just walking. He headed back to the room and I spent the first hours of being alone in Europe. It was no problem and I knew that in a week, Steve would be gone and it would be just me to make all of the decisions and plans. Kinda scary, but hey ill deal with that when it happened.

One other thing about this place and maybe it was because I was high most of the time. The people here are all beautiful, seriously! Even the girls sweeping the streets were attractive, both men and women all seemed to be well kept, healthy, and very happy. It had to be because Amsterdam is truly a beautiful city.

Our last night there and we still had to check out one area. The "Red-Light District," which is an area in Amsterdam that prostitution is legal. We approached the street and it was remarkable. It was rows of town houses and each unit had a large window facing the street, which was lined with "red lights." The girls would stand in the window and it was the best window shopping I have ever done. Trust me, they were not all "10's", that is for sure. However, they were all happy to see us and would do anything to us we had ever imagined. Steve was out from the beginning, but I had my eye on one girl, she was blond, beautiful, and a "10" in my book. I told Steve "Come on man, take one for the team". He said "not a chance in hell." I however went to go find my girl and as I approached her window, I guy about 65 years old walked out and that blew it for me. I wasn't going to touch her after he did. Oh well, maybe next time! We had a big laugh out of this and maybe the old guy saved my life!

Our time here flew by and we so hated to leave, however there was still so many things to see and do. After picking up supplies and contacting our families back home via e-mail, which was rather easy with Internet cafes all over the place. It was great to hear everything back home was going well. We filled in our families and friends on what we had seen so far and just kept them updated on our location. It was good to hear from my parents, I'm sure my mom was worrying.

This next leg of the trip would be our first of many bus trips and the first time we would use our Euro Rail Pass that we both purchased before we left the states. We each had 10 bus trips on our pass This trip would take us to Berlin, Germany with a layover in Dusseldorf. It took about 4 hours and all we did is laugh and stare out the windows and marvel at the Netherlands landscaping. The wind mills are all amazing and I don't think I saw two alike. All different and all different colors. It was such a relaxing and peaceful first bus trip. We did spend a majority of the trip sitting at the bar, which was at the back of the train. It had larger windows, a few small tables, and a few seats at the bar. It was a perfect place to pass the time.

Duesseldorf, Germany

We arrived at the train station in Duesseldorf, which was our first city entering Germany. We had a few hours to kill, so after getting our passports stamped, we headed to the closes place to grab something to eat and drink.

The place we choose will always be in my memory. From our table you could see this church with half its steeple blown off from the war. We were in a part of Germany the was a battle field during WW II. It was my first time actually seeing the destructions of something from WW II. It was something out of a history book and here it was right in front of me.

There was not a lot of touristy things to do here, more of an Industrial area, so we were back at the train station ready to get boarded soon we hoped. Let's just say our 2hr delay turned into a 8hr delay and we basically sat at the train station, hotter then hell and waited the entire time. We kept being told, it would be soon, just a little longer, well let me tell you my friends, we were not happy. It basically just decreased our time in Berlin. We were on a bit of a time frame and had 2 more stops before Steve leaves. If we had known it was going to be so long, we would have walked around the city a bit more. But hey we still had fun, we found a place to smoke!

Berlin, Germany

We Finally arrived in Berlin at 6:00am. It was early and we didn't have a lot of time here, one day. We were leaving at 8:00pm from Berlin to Munich, so we had to make it count. We got really lucky and they had storage lockers in the train station, so we didn't have to carry all our gear with us, it would have limited us on what we could do, for sure.

Now it was time to make "Time Count," the clock was ticking and we both wanted to see as much of Berlin as we could. However, we had to slow things down because hey, it was only 6am and nothing was opened, so after a long night of sitting we ended walking around the Berlin Zoo, and didn't see a single animal. We could hear them, but the walls were tall and hey they wanted us to pay, we would have if they were OPEN.

After things came alive around the city, we were able to make some plans for the day. We found one thing that would work well, not take the whole day and see some of the sights. It was a walking tour of Berlin. After breakfast, eggs and toast and a beer or two. we made our way to the meeting point. Our tour started at the Brandenburg Gate, which is a gate made with gigantic white pillars and has 4 horses pulling a man holding an Eagle, its Berlins best known landmark. The cameras came out and the picture taking began, of course I had my camcorder as well.

This was a very informational way to see the city. We just walked and our guide informed us of what we were seeing. We were in both East and West Germany, which is referred to now as East Central and West Central. We stopped at so many unbelievable and historical places: Former Soviet Union Embassy, Nazi Air Ministry, the Berlin Wall, Checkpoint Charlie, and even stood over Hitler's bunker. It was such a great day and I even got a small piece of the Berlin Wall and a stamp in my passport for Checkpoint Charlie, so cool!

After our tour it was time to get some supplies for the next trip and we were mighty thirsty after that walk. We found the perfect outdoor restaurant and I wanted a German kebab and a cold beer. This is what we ordered and our beers came out first, then our German kebabs. Well, the beers were right on and tasted great, our kebabs were just a small hotdog, that's it and it tasted just like a small hotdog. Oh well, we need to brush up on our German, for food ordering purposes.

After walking around a bit, picking up a bottle of Vodka for our next adventure, and finding a good spot to have a smoke, it was back to the train station. This day just flew by and I'm happy we made the most of our time. Our next adventure, which is getting to Munich.

It's more about how we are going to Munich and that is we have a "Sleeper Car" for this trip. It was a long overnight trip, so we decided to go in style. We will have a bed on this train, so excited.

The last thing I was able to do before we left and that was call my dad and wish him a Happy Father's Day. Besides the cost of a collect call from Europe, it meant a lot to him that I called him. He spent time In Germany, while in the Air Force and loved it. He was happy that I was seeing the world, something we often talked about. It was great to hear my parents' voices and they were happy we were having a great trip and THAT WE WERE.

Once on the train we found our rooms and it was bunkbeds, small closet, several shelves, and a small desk. I yelled out "I got top bunk." Steve said to me "yes you do, I'm not getting up there." We got settled in, made a drink, joked and laughed, and sat back while the train pulled out of the station. It too had a Bar Car, so we made our way back there and spent a good portion of the night there. Talked with others and watched the landscape go by, small towns would come and go, people in and out of the bar car, several Heinekens later, and life was good.

The rocking of the train was so relaxing, except for the walk back from the bar, I could have used a little less rocking, but I made it. We made it to our room, used the bathroom down the hall and crawled into my bunk. We joked and talk for a bit, then said our goodnights and I was out. Except for having to use the bathroom in the middle of the night, which was down the ladder, out the door, down the hall, back to the room, and back up the ladder, it was a great night and I slept like a baby.

Munich, Germany

We arrived in Munich around 6:30am and at this point not much is opened. Our plan was to spend 2 night/3 days here, then we would have a few days in Paris before he leaves. We were able to leave our main backs at the station, so all we had was our day packs to carry around for the next few days. We just had to pack our small bags for 3 days. After things opened up, we found a place for the next

2 night and made our way there for a well needed shower, it had been 3 long days. Our place was the usual, 2 beds, dresser, one chair, and shower down the hall $20 each, which has been the average per night for most of the trip. After we were cleaned up, out the door we went.

When coming to Munich you have to at least go to a beer garden for at least one. We decided to get this out of the way and go there first. To be honest, this was the only thing we wanted to do. Ha ha We found one and it was huge, the size of a football field, and it was packed. The German music was playing, the smell of food in the air, people were playing games or sitting at tables, and we walked right in and made ourself at home.

We walked around a bit and I asked this guy, "how does this work?" He said "just find a seat and they will find you." So, that is what we did and as soon as we sat down a German women asked us what we wanted. I pointed to the big cold beers and said "2 please" and she was gone. This place is awesome and the energy was very high and not one unhappy person.

She returned and let me tell you this women had some serious fore arms, carrying 3- 40oz size glass mugs in each hand. She definitely scared me, so I was supper polite. We got our beers, $5.50 each and was given a menu. We had our big cheers, "Here is to a great trip, so many things we have seen and experienced and it wasn't over yet." That first beer went down about as good as it gets. Here I didn't even look at the menu, I could see exactly what I wanted and the person right next to me was eating it. Finally, we had our German kebabs, 3x the size of the last one, covered in onions, cabbage, and mustard. It was so good and the beers keep coming. She didn't even ask if we wanted another one, she just keep bringing them to us when we were empty. *I love this place.*

I went to the bathroom, several times and found out that our beers are $5.50 and when you return the glass, you get $.50 back, that was smart. This way the bar maids don't have to get the empties. This place was amazing and you know how time flies, well guess what we spent the entire day there and by 8pm we were pickled. We somehow found our room and never left again that night. Maybe we could have done more here in Munich then sit at a beer garden all

TAKE A DECADE

day, but I say, "Why not spend a day at a beer garden?" It was a great day and I got some great footage on my camcorder, which is still my best friend.

The next morning, or should I say early afternoon, we had some food and started to feel better. We had a few things to do today, book our trip to Paris, which was easy and find a street here in Munich. Steve's last name is a name of a street here in Munich and we spent an hour walking around with our map looking for it. it was something he wanted to do and we found it and he got his picture under the sign, Landwehr Street! Then it was to a pup to celebrate this moment. We celebrated a lot of moments!

With our two things done for the day we had the rest of the day to explore more. So, guess what we found, it was another beer garden and spent some quality time drinking more big beers. It wasn't that we didn't want to see more, but hey we had been walking around Europe for days and this was FUN. Once we were nice and happy, I told Steve "I need to find a Barber Shop." He looks at me and said "What for, you always were a hat." I told him that I wanted to shave my head and that the time is now. I finally had built of the nerve and had enough booze in me to make this educated decision.

After about 5 hours at this beer garden, we now had a mission and we left, this time I kept one of the big mugs for a souvenir, I just wanted one and seemed like a good idea at the time. We left and just started walking, there has to be a barber shop somewhere around here and it didn't take long to find one. I walked in and sat down in one of the chairs. The guy didn't speak English at all, so I grabbed his clippers and motioned with the clippers, ALL OFF. I had Steve record this and the guy proceeded to shave my head bald. Wow, what I new look for me. I walked out rubbing my head and Steve was just laughing at me, but I told my friends I'm coming back looking different and that I did.

We had to celebrate this moment, so for the next few hours we enjoyed watching the ERUO 2000 soccer match at a local pup, which Germany won. It is an experience to watch such an important game with the locals. They cheered and drank like nothing I had seen before. We cheered and Bood when they did, so we didn't get our asses kicked. It was a fun "local experience."

I like to think we had a great time in Munich, even though a lot of the time was in a beer garden. We did what we wanted, so for us it was a huge success. Maybe next time I will check out the city a little more, but for now I'm a happy person.

Paris, France

We left early the next morning and I was a hurting unit. My head was pounding from 2 days of steady drinking with very little water. I was also still bald when I woke up and that was a bit of a shock when I looked in the mirror, something that will take a while to get use to. Once on the train, which was an ICE High Speed Train, I feel asleep and slept till we made it to the French border. We got our passports stamped, which was our 4th country and this would be Steve's last. In just a few days I would be doing all of this solo and I would be lying if I wasn't a little nervous. Steve has done so much of the arranging of things, directions, and keeping me alive. Let's hope I can do it on my own.

After another longer then expected delay, we finally arrived in the beautiful city of Paris. It was a place I wanted to see and experience the French culture. We had just one night here, Steve would leave the next day and I was go further south after this, so once again we had to make it count.

We both agreed on seeing one thing and that is the Eiffel tower. Can't come to Paris and not see this amazing structure, so we had a plan. From our room, we could see the tower in the distance and it looked small. Our plan was to make our way in that direction, take our time and get to the Eiffel Tower just as the sun is setting. I wanted to see the lights of the city from the top at night. We got ready, had a smoke and out the door we went.

This day was one of my favorite days. We just started walking in the direction of the tower, which looked about an inch tall when we started, and we see whatever we could along the way. We had a map of the area, which pointed out all of the historical and main attraction of the city, so we had an idea of a few things we would pass along the way. Days like this just wondering around a new city are so much fun, everything is new and exciting.

Paris is just a beautiful city to see and the first major attraction we came upon was Notre Dame. Just looking at this beautiful church was breathtaking. The time and attention that went into the building of this was amazing. This church was consecrated to the Virgin Mary and the best example of French Gothic architecture. It was spectacular to see. We both took several pictures of this, even though neither of us were Catholic. After this it was an outdoor bar, 2 beers and 2 grand marines, which has been the norm for most of the trip, however today was special so we had another shot.

After we were primmed and ready we set out again. Next was the Lovre Museum, if we had more time we would have gone inside, but it would have taken all our time just to see the Moana Lisa and we both were OK not doing this. Still, walked around the outside and took as much of it in as we could. I hated to pass an opportunity up like this, but hey we couldn't see everything. It was back to our mission and each time we had a view of the Eiffel Tower it was getting bigger and bigger.

It is amazing when you're just walking around a city for the first time and you never know what your going to find. Well, we happened to stumble upon the memorial for Princess Diana and there were still a bunch of beautiful flowers, pictures, and candles burning. It was near the tunnel that she was killed in and it brough back that day like it was yesterday. I'm blessed to say I was here and passed on my respect for someone that left this world way to early. Princess Diana was one of a kind and the city of Paris keeps her memory alive.

We had walked, stopped for drinks, spent time just people watching, filled our bellies with amazing food and just admired the beauty of this city. It was very romantic and the first time I wished Steve was a girl, Ha ha! It seemed that ever song we heard was another romantic song. All we saw were couples everywhere and they were having a time of their lives. Let me tell you, I would not change anything about this trip. Steve and I had a blast, he was a great travel buddy, and would be missed.

Timing is everything and we could not have time this any better. As soon as it was dark we made it to the park and looked up at one of the coolest things that I had ever seen, The Eiffel Tower, wow this is impressive. Just then, 5 sec later, someone through the switch on and the tower lite up like magic. Holy shit that was amazing. We could not have time that any better. We did it my friend! Now to the top, lets go and away we went to the ticket counter. The Eiffel Tower is the tallest structure in Paris, over 1000ft tall built in 1887–1889 and the elevator ride to the top is fun as well, it goes sideways. We get out on the view platform and there are no words to describe the beauty of this city with all the lights. The Arc De Triumph in the distance is a center point of the city and shines like a candle. We could see forever, everything we had seen that day was now viewable from here, it was amazing. This was definitely a highlight for me, something I always wanted to see!

We accomplished our mission for the day, we made it back to our room and it was time for Steve to get ready. We both were leaving, but he had to pack for a flight, which gave us both time to go through all of our goodies. I had bought and "kept" so many things that my bag was getting full. It was time to get ride of some things. By now I had a few articles of clothes that were ready for the trash, so I started with underwear and socks, didn't need them anymore. As the trip progressed many articles of clothes didn't make it back to the states. Remember, I now have a 40oz glass mug in my bag.......

That night we reminisced about our trip and all the fun we had. We had been traveling for 2 weeks and spent time in 4 countries and 6 cities. So many major attractions that we expected and many that just popped up for us. We laughed about everything and Steve said "Hope you don't get lost as soon as I leave." He had been the navigator for most of the trip, so we will see. We enjoyed a smoke together and a final shot of GM that night. Tomorrow, it will be a different world.

Steve's train left on schedule and it was a sad goodbye. He wanted to do just 2 weeks and by this time he was ready to go home. I know he had a great time and memories forever. For me, I was not ready to go home, I wanted to see more. I still have 7 more days and my final destination is Athens, Greece. This is where I have my return flight set for. The question is can I see everything I still want to see in one week. That my friends was the big question.

After Steve left I still had a few hours to walk around Paris before my train left for my next destination, which was Geneva, Switzerland. I made my way out of the station and with in about 10 minutes I was lost, Steve would get a good laugh about this. Seriously, I spent about 2 hours just trying to get back to the station. At first it was a little unnerving, but soon it became exciting because of the different things I was seeing. However, I was still lost and thought to myself, was this a good idea or should I have left when Steve did. Absolutely Not, I got this!

Geneva, Switzerland

It was a little nerve racking making that fist trip solo. At the train station in Paris, I realized that everything I do from now on I have to carry all my gear with me. With Steve, I could leave him with my bags, use the bathroom or get something to eat and not worry about them, now it's different I have them all the time. Bathroom stalls are small enough, 2 backpacks and yourself, tight fit let me tell you. Getting food and my train ticket meant carrying everything with me and no one was there to have my back. Traveling solo was different, it just means keeping a wider eye on your surroundings.

We arrived in Geneva at 9pm and it was close to dark. I had a lot to do in a short period of time: find a place to stay, find an ATM, stop and grab something to eat and drink in my room, and get information on what to do tomorrow. My plan was to stay here one night, get on a train tomorrow night and be in Nice, France the Mediterranean in 2 days. I was able to find a private room and money before I left the station. Tonight, I was getting my own room, just to get situated with traveling solo and not worry about anyone else. The cost of the room was a little more $25, which I was now dealing with the Swiss Franc as currency. Traveling through Europe before the Euro Dollar kicked in made things exciting. Each country things were priced differently, so you didn't know until you bought something. I usually would buy a beer first and that was a good indicator how expensive things might be. It worked for me.

Geneva was impressive, from what I could see was a beautiful lake surrounded by mountains. The sun set was stunning over the lake and this small city seemed easy to get around. I found my place and when I went inside it was impressive. Looked like something out of a European movie, wow and it only cost $25. Now for food and drink, so I made my way to the main street and made a choice right or left. I went right and found a store close by and grabbed some supplies. I cashed out and was shocked how much things cost. I didn't take a lot out of the ATM because I was only going to be here one day and I'm going to need more money. I get back to my room and it hit's me, my exchange rate and the actual exchange rate is different. I made a math error and realized that my room wasn't $25, it was $75, (today it would cost $275) holy shit that is way over my budget. No wonder this room is so nice, I guess I did spoil myself. Lesson learned and it won't happen again! Steve has been gone for less then 24 hours and I've gotten lost and miss calculated my money already. Glad I got those to things out of the way.

After my second shower since I had been there, I was going to get my monies worth for the room, it was time to check out the town. First thing was to check out the lake, which was the center of attraction for sure. It was gorgeous to see the reflection of the mountain's on the lake. The entire area looked like a painting. I took the gondola to the top and had a view of the city that was more spectacular. Had a conversation with a 90 year old man and I didn't understand one word he was saying, but he told one hell of a story. It was a picture-perfect moment.

Traveling solo did have its advantages and you could just go where ever you wanted, for as long as you cared to be there. I wonder the streets, took a local bus for a bit just to check out a few different things. Stopped when I was hungry or thirsty and spent a lot of time people watching. I walked over this bridge and it felt like I had gone back in time. The buildings were older and painted with amazing colors, streets narrower, and everyone seemed to be dressed a little different. This was the place to buy things. Found a Swiss clock for my mom, Swiss chocolate, and a Swiss army knife. This is what a love about traveling and that is wondering into a place like this.

Once again, I wish I had more time to see more, but time is ticking. I felt I got a real good overview of this beautiful place and hopefully someday I will return. For now, it is back to the train station and get ready for a night train to Nice. Once on board, I found my cabin and it was a small room with a sliding glass door, which was covered with a curtain. 4 seats on one side and 4 seats on the other side. I was the first one there, so I took a window seat, that was a no brainer. Got my bags situated and watched people walk by. About 10 minutes later, still no one had entered this room, and just then the train started to move. I sat there for another 5 minutes and came to the conclusion, I had this whole car to myself, that is awesome. I shut the door and sprawled out like I owned the place.

Once we were underway, I made my way to the bar car, thinking maybe there will be a hottie I can bring home, who knows. Well, I spent one hour, had a few drinks and left alone, I wasn't waiting any longer, her loss! Found the bathroom, got cleaned up and went to my "room." Luckily, I still had some smoke left, so I sat real close to the window and enjoyed a few puffs of the good stuff. Had a few more beers and spend time looking through some of the video I had taken with my video camera. At this point I had filled 8 tapes; it was fun looking back at our tip. Time to sleep, put my camcorder back in my big bag and put it under my seat. Used my day pack as a pillow, laid down on the seats, and with the rocking of the train it didn't take long to fall asleep. Nighty Night see you in the Morning.

Nice, France

It must have been the rocking of the train, but I woke up and I could see daylight from my window. It was morning and that meant we should be close. I open the curtain to my window and there it was right it front of me," The Mediterranean Sea." We were moving right along the sea and I had a great view. I have to get this on Video… Steve Mundy made it to the Mediterranean Sea.

I grabbed my backpack from under my seat, opened it up and I said to myself "Where is my camcorder?" I tore my big bag apart, then my other bag. I was not feeling any pain when I went to sleep, but I remember putting my camcorder in the top of my big back pack, just like I had for the last 2 weeks. It was gone and I was devastated. I had been robbed in the night and could not believe it. All I could think about was all the things I was about to see and won't be on video. I was pissed and nothing I could do about it. I spoke with the conductor and he could have cared less. Comes to find out people travel the trains with children and at night they send the kids into rooms to steal whatever they can. They are small and if they get caught, they lie and say they were lost. It was a scam and they got me.

This was my first day that things just didn't start out very good. I left my big bag in a locker at the train station, I planned on 2 nights here, and then to Italy, ASAP! Oh man was I bumped out about this whole thing, but I just had to get over it and move on, so I grabbed a few beers and made my way to the beach.

The Mediterranean Sea is right there and it looks beautiful, it is 75 degrees and sunny, almost perfect. The beach looks rather busy and as I walk along the beach, my spirits are lifted when I start seeing half naked women, topless women everywhere. OK, life isn't so bad now, glad I don't have my camcorder right now, Ha Ha! I found a spot on the beach, but it isn't a sandy beach, it is all small stones. Not exactly what I was hoping for, but hey I had a great view ALL AROUND.

After my first beer, I stood up and walked right into the sea. The water was warm, crystal clear, and as I dove in all my worries went away. I spent 10 minutes, in the Mediterranean Sea just in AWE of where I was! As I got out I got the attention of a couple that were sitting in front of me, and they asked "Where are you from?" I told them "I'm from the states, living in Arizona." Just like that our friendship started.

There names were Stein and Athela, both from Sweden. We hit it off right away and started talking about traveling and how beautiful this place was. Stein and I both looked at each other when the word BEAUTY came up! There were girls everywhere and why I choose to sit where I did was there was a girl behind me that really caught my eye and she was by herself. The three of us sat there for about 15 minutes, enjoying a beer and we all smoked cigarettes, so we had a few. I was staring at the sea and I feel a tap on my shoulder and it is the girl I was talking about. She knelt down and ask if I had a lighter, I said "YES I DO." I properly lit her cigarette and I asked her "What is Your Name?" She replied, "My name is Vienna, from the Netherlands." Beautiful face, 5'6" 120lbs, brunet, and did I mention yet that she was topless? Sorry about that!

We hit it off right away. Within a few minutes she went and gather her stuff and joined our little group. Vienna was working on her 2nd degree, while leaving here in Nice. So, just like that I had friends and we sat there for hours talking and laughing like we had known each other for years. We were all out playing in the sea and I gave Vienna a little kiss. She smiled and said "I like You." My day was definitely getting better.

The four of us decided to have dinner together and after an amazing sunset, my first for the Mediterranean, we packed up from the beach and walked towards town. We decided on sea food and Vienna knew a spot not far. By this time, we were holding hands, just 2 couples going out to dinner. The sea food was amazing, I had a sea food pasta, absolutely loaded with sea food. We had drinks, laughed, and enjoyed a great meal. I thought to myself, just 2 days ago if Steve had not left, he would be sitting here. Now, I'm sitting here with 3 new friends and it is great feeling to know I can meet people.

Towards the end of dinner, Stein asked me where I was staying. I said "Holy shit, I got caught up in the day and never booked anything yet. There has got to be something close." Stein and Athela were staying at a hostel, but it was full. Just then Vienna spoke up and told me that I could stay at her place. Wow, I didn't expect that or see that coming, but I said "sure, Thank You."

We went our separate ways after dinner. We had made plans to meet up on the beach tomorrow and maybe check a few things out. We waved goodbye and Vienna and I walked hand and hand back to her little flat. It was a small studio, with a shower and that is what I needed. When I came out of the bathroom, I could tell my night was going to get better. Vienna was lying on the bed and this time she had nothing on. This is a family book, so I'm not getting into detail, sorry! I can say this; My day started out horrible with my camcorder incident and ended just about as good as it gets!!!

The next morning, we were up and out the door by 8am, she had a class to attend. We kissed goodbye and made plans to meet up after. I made my way back to the beach and enjoyed a few hours to myself. Thinking that I can't wait to tell Stein about my night. The other thing I was thinking is I'm supposed to be flying out of Athens in 5 days. I still want to see parts of Italy, spend time on a Greece Island, and not rush in doing so. I just need more time.

At that point, sitting on the beach, staring at the sea, I decided that I'm not cutting this trip short. I'm here and I want to see as much as possible: Leaning tower of Pisa, the Roman Colosseum, and maybe Venice. I'm going to call my employer and let them know I'm going to be a little late getting home. Just like that I had given myself more time and it felt good.

They showed up and after a few hours on the beach we decided to go sightseeing. Vienna did show up, but was really busy that day and said she would meet up with us later, we kissed goodbye and I never saw her again. We had a great night and sometimes that is all you need.

The 3 of us decided to check out more of the French Rivera. We hoped on a bus and spend a good portion of the day hanging out with the rich and famous near Monte Carlo. Wow, is one word to describe this place or picture-perfect works as well. The entire area of this section of the French Rivera is breath taking. From the homes high up on the cliffs to the million-dollar Yachts in the harbor there is really nothing bad to look at. It was 80 degrees, slight breeze from the sea, and the smell of money everywhere.

We spent the day walking around, stopping to have a drink and snack from time to time. We tried to go inside the Monte Carlo casino, but without a sports coat, we could not go in. I wanted to place one bet at the same casino the James Bond 007 had been. Oh well, next time I'll know. It was a great day seeing how the rich and famous people survive. Those poor people!

We made our way back to their hostel and luckily, they had a room for me. I needed one-night and then off to Italy. I did get a chance to make my phone call to my employer. I left a message "Sorry to inform you, but due to a train strike, I'm unable to get to my final destination on time. I'll have to change my flight, I will get back to you ASAP. Sorry for the late notice." That was it and I now had more time, how much time, that I didn't know yet.

After we all got situated and had a shower the three of us started parting in their room. They had a balcony and we were just hanging out when the door next to us opened and 3 girls walked out. All attractive, but one stood out to me. She was Asian, but grew up in the states. They all had just graduated from college and this is where they wanted to go, which was good for me. Her name was Laura and she was Korean and a cute little thing. We hit it off right away.

The 6 of us started having a great time and all of a sudden, the door on the other balcony opened and 3 guys and 1 girl walked out. Now we had a party and a party it turned out to be. I went from being solo to having a group to hang out with. We left the hostel, about 10 of us and went to a club for some drinks. This place was going off... CRAZY BUSY. Dance music was load, dance floor was packed, the lights, packed with people and we all fit right in. We found a table and we all proceed to get shit faced. We danced and drank like a group of friends that have known each other for every. I talked with everyone, shared stories, and we danced as one big group. It was a great night out on the town!

About 2am we made it back to the hostel and continued the party for a while. By now Laura and I had at least kissed, so I new she liked me a little. I told her I needed to get something out of my room, so she followed. We get to my room and I turned around and kissed her, this time it didn't stop. We never made it back to the group that night, she spent the remainder of the night with me and yes, it was ANOTHER GREAT NIGHT.

We were woken up at 8am, check out time! This is the earliest check out time I had ever had. After last night, all I needed was more sleep, the 3-4 hours I got was not enough. It was also hard getting out of bed with a beautiful naked girl with you, but we had to go.

We were all leaving that day for somewhere, so we all headed to the train station and said our goodbyes. I walked Laura to her gate and we kissed and hugged like we had been together forever. It was my first real ROMANIC moment of the trip. Then goodbye to my 2 new friends Stein and Athela, thank you for everything. It they had not said hello to me on the beach, none of this would have happened. The Butterfly effect…you never know.

Pisa, Italy

I was the last to go, no one there to say goodbye to me and that was Ok. What an experience traveling solo these last few days, minus the camcorder, everything has been a LOT OF FUN. It is up to me and only me to keep the good times going. It was now time to travel to Italy, first stop Pisa.

At the train station I could tell right away that this was not going to be a luxurious train ride. The train was old and looked about 100 years old, oh well it is the only way to my next spot. I get on board and no seats in the first car, no seats in the second car, and moving forward no seats available in any car, NOT ONE EMPTY SEAT on this train. As I walked between 2 cars, I noticed people sitting on the floors, between the cars, the area that holds the cars together and decided to grab a spot while I could. So, the next 5 hours I sat on the floor of this train, between 2 cars and tried to just sleep, it was a rough ride!

We get to Pisa and it is dark and late, all I want is a shower and a bed, it has been a very long 3 days with little sleep, and a rough ride here. At the station I find a place, in walking distance about 1 mile, for $30 a night. At this time, I found an ATM and withdrew some money, now I was using the Lire for currency, which is my 6th exchange. Before getting to my place I stopped in and grabbed a few snacks and a couple of Italian Peroni's, for the room. After cashing out, I was like this is cheap, beers cost $.60. My money is going to go far here and that is good because I'm spending it.

Get to my room and it is amazing, marble everywhere. The floors, the bathroom, even part of the lamp was all marble. It was an

Italian suite as far as I was concerned. The best part was that I had it all to myself. The sad part was after my shower, which felt so good and probably the nicest ever, I feel asleep and didn't wake up till 10am, check out time. I can say that I had and enjoyed a really nice room, for about 1 hour.

It was out the door with all my bags on my back and I was going to see something amazing today. The walk wasn't bad at all because I really saw more then I expected, they are more then one leaning towers in this area, I think I saw 4. It is when you enter the Cathedral Square, home to the Cathedral Pisa a magnificent church and see *THE Leaning Tower Of Pisa* it is remarkable. The tower is 184 ft tall, started building it in 1173 and finished in 1372. It had already started to lean even before they finished it. It was built with marble and the ground around it just wasn't strong enough to support it, so guess what it started to lean. I spent most of the day looking at this from all angles and enjoyed sitting on the grass by myself while watching others enjoy this as well. No pictures can describe seeing this with your own two eyes, very cool piece of history.

Rome, Italy

My train from Pisa left at 5pm and at least time I had an actual seat. It was in a train car, just like the one that I got robbed in. Just this time I wasn't alone. I shared it with a grandfather and granddaughter. They spoke no English and me no Italian, but I watch them interact together until she fell asleep on his lap. He was a good man and loved his granddaughter, you could tell.

We arrived at midnight and I was in Rome, Italy. *Wow someone pinch me.* I could believe I was actually here; this was one of the big places I wanted to go. Unfortunately, the tourist booth was closed so it was up to me to find a place to stay. All I could do was load up my gear and hit the streets. I walked out the door and started down this street and about 5 minutes down a guy comes up to me, grabs my bags and said "you need a place?" I said "No, I'm good" and picked up my pace. One block further and it happened again, this guy looked rougher then the last. It was actually a little scary for me.

This is not a good part of town and I either need to hide somewhere until the sun comes up, or get a place quickly. About 5 minutes longer and things are just looking worse, garbage all over the street, the smell of sewer or piss, not sure and no HILTON in sight. Just then a guy standing on a step asked me the same question "You need a place?" he looked better then the others and at this point I need to get off these streets.

I handed him $10 and he showed me to my room. It was nasty, some rooms just had blankets for doors, the clientele here was below average for sure. This was an hour rental whorehouse or drug hotel or something. I actually had a door to my room, with paper thin walls, I heard a few things that night that brought shivers done my spine. This place was the worse place I had ever stayed in, by far! Once in my room, I used the chair to secure and door and slept in all my cloths. Kept my bags backed right next to me on the bed, and tried not draw any attention. Somehow, I did fall asleep and by 8am I was out the door and alive, thank God!

It didn't take long to find a much nicer place to stay for the next 2-3 days. Still had not booked my return flight home, so time was on myside. After getting situated and educating myself as much as I could on the area, how to get around, I grabbed my bag and left to explore Rome. I'm beyond excited to be here in ROME!

I came here to see one thing and that was the Roman Colosseum, so this was my first mission. Once I figured out the subway system, which was easy, I hoped on and enjoyed the ride. I came up out of the tunnel and I'm looking and I don't see it at all, could I have gotten off to early, I check my map and it says it is here, well Dum ass turn around. There it was and it was incredible to actually see this in real life. It could hold 50,000 to 80,000 people at a time. It is listed as one of the New Seven Wonders of the World and attracts 7.5 million visitors a year. The sheer size of it was over whelming.

The coolest thing was that I walked around and semi-joined this tour group. I was listening to everything just didn't pay the $25 fee. So, when they all went inside, I joined the group and they never said anything. It was interesting to hear all the history about this place, look it up sometime. I'm just in awe that I'm actually inside the colosseum. I did my own thing once inside and it was amazing to see how it all worked so many years ago. This was a big thing for me and I know that I will return someday.

After taking care of the most important thing, everything else was a bonus. While in Rome it is so easy to just walk the streets, stop at an outdoor café and have a bit to eat, and admire your surroundings. There is not a bad view in Rome, that is for sure. While just walking around I came across the Spanish Steps and this guy told me about a Pup Crawl. It was a walking tour, check out the sites, and have a few drinks. This sounded like fun, even though I was by myself.

The Pup Crawl started in a few hours, so I went back to my room to get cleaned up and then dinner. I found an outdoor café, ordered a plate of pasta and a bottle of Chanti. This would be my meal every night I was in Rome. It was Pizza for lunch and pasta for dinner. Beer at lunch and wine at dinner. I can tell you I never had a bad meal and after every meal came the gelato (ice cream.) if it had not been for the walking, I would have gained 10 pounds easily.

We started the pup crawl at The Spanish Steps, which is something to see and a common meeting place for Italians. I met a few guys from the states. They were younger, but cool to hang out with. They were doing the same thing I was and checking out all the girls and the sights, of course. That night we walked and saw so many historical things; The Trevi Fountain (I made a wish,) Piazza Navona (Famous square in Pome,) oldest building in Rome, different embassies, and so much more. We would walk, see something and then into a pup for a shot, then back on the street and we did this for about 3 hours.

At the last pub of the night, a slice of pizza was needed and it tasted so good. Just then this girl walked up to me and introduced herself. She was not part of the pub crawl, just happened to be at this bar. Her name was Lauren, traveling solo for a week before she started her job. She was a cute little Jewish girl, with glasses from the states. We had a drink together and talked for about 15 minutes before I said something about getting out of here, It was after midnight. "Do you want to go to my place and hang out for a while?" She looked at me, reached up and gave me a kiss, "Sure lets go."

We got to my place and the kissing continued. I told her it had been a long hot day and needed a shower. I walked into the bathroom and started to get undressed, turned around and she was doing the same. We enjoyed a nice shower together, which gave us time to get to know each other.

We woke the next morning, had sex again and decided to enjoy each other's company another day. She was a very easy person to warm up to. When we were walking out the door, the guy who ran the place told me I had to pay extra because I had a quest. It was another $25, which didn't make me happy, but what could I do. Lauren spoke up and said, it cost me twice as much for my place, lets move into together and save money. I said "why not, sounds good to me." We grabbed her stuff that morning and Just like that I had a live in girlfriend.

For the next 2 days, we walked around Rome as a couple and it was so much fun. The first thing we did was take the train to the other side of the city, which is nicked named "pick pocket alley." I did witness and helped a man from getting robbed by a women and 2 little kids. It was an experience for the guy and myself. We arrived safely with all our possessions and made our way to the Vatican and Vatican city.

This place was overwhelming, just amazing place to see. Being the Home to the Pope, it better be nice. To be inside and see the Greek statues, the pristine gardens, the Sistine Chapel, which was painted by Michelangelo himself, and all of the Greece history was over whelming. We walked around for a few hours, and still didn't see everything. We both felt privileged to have seen what we did.

Then to St Peter's Basilica, which still to this date the most impressive church I have ever seen. 450ft high and 720ft long. The statue of St Peter and that of Mary holding Jesus is about as good as it gets. These were just 2 of about 1000 sculptures and pieces of art work that lined the church. Something can't be described easily with words and this place is one of them. Unforgettable is all I can say.

We had a great day together and enjoyed another wonderful night together. My time was up in Rome and she too was heading home. Both of us left around the same time and it was again a sad goodbye. Just 3 days ago I arrived and knew no one, now I'm back hand in hand with my new friend. We had spent about 48 hours together, yet it felt like a life time. I thank her for a wonderful time and wiched her nothing but the best. She boarded her train and we waved goodbye to each other as the train pulled away.

It has been a crazy week, not stop action and adventure. By this point traveling solo is no problem, you have to admit I've been doing pretty good. Steve would be proud. The stories that will come from this will be endless…

Ok, time to get back on track. I have a choice to make and its either travel to Venice or Florance. Both places have their appeal and things to see. By this time, I had met and talked with a lot of people, some local, some tourist. I had 3 nights 4 days left before heading to Greece. Many people said that after a day in Venice, you have seen it all. However, it could take a week to see everything in Florance. All I could do was flip a coin, which I actually did, Florance it was.

Before leaving Rome, I did finally book my return ticket home. It is ironic, but it was this day that I should have been flying home, oh well. Now, the clock was ticking again. I had bought my self another 10 days. Made the phone call to my employer and once again was only able to leave a message with my boss. "This is Steve Mundy, I have a returned flight book, should be in the office in 12 days." That was it, short and sweet. Of course, I contacted my family and friends to give them a heads up on my itinerary.

Florence, Italy

The train to Florence took about 3 hours, which all I did was enjoy the scenery and relax. We arrived at the train station and I could tell this place was special. I spent 3 nights here and had to move all three nights. One night in a small hostel, then another night with a family, which was different and something I won't do again. It wasn't until my third night I found a great place to stay, a hostel full of fun people. But hey, I'm getting ahead of myself.

Florence is the capital of the Tuscany region of Italy. It was the birth place of the Renaissance so we are talking about buildings that have been around before Rome was even built. There was a difference in the architecture of the building. Here they seemed more Gothic and ancient. The amount of detail on some of the building was absolute amazing. Each one different than the one next to it. The streets were narrow and filled with people sight seeing and working. After about the first hour of being here, I knew I made a good choice.

The first few days was all about walking around, stopping for a meal and drink, just what I have been doing for the last 3 weeks. Taking in as much as I could and enjoying every second of it. Most of my time was spent near the Uffizi Square, which was the center of town. I would take a different street each time and each time I would just walk upon something amazing to see. There were so many different vendors selling just about everything, however leather goods were the biggest selling item I saw. From coats, boots, gloves, and even sexy lingerie all for sale right on the street. Some of it was real and legal, then there was some that was fake and illegal. I did get to watch the cops do a sweep and arrest a few people, that was cool to see. All I knew was I needed none of it, just looking.

One main attraction is the Duomo or Cathedral of Florence. It took 200 hundred years to build and was finished in 1436. This cathedral is the centerpiece to the city of Florence. The Duomo includes the Baptistery, which is a religious building that was constructed between 1059 and 1128. This structure makes the entire area the oldest structure in Italy. Again, words can't describe what this looks like. The fact I was standing in a church that was almost 1000 years old, remarkable is all I can say.

Again, my first few days were fun and I just spent time by myself. I had walked up and down as many streets as I could find. Never ate at the same place, always had pasta and a bottle of Chanti, and every meal had been outside. Life was good and how can it get any better.

TAKE A DECADE

Well, it did get better and that was when I got to my third place to stay. Like I said before, wish I had found this place first. It was a hostel and when I got there it didn't look like much. Got checked in and the guy showed me to my room. It was a big room with 10 beds, 5 on each side. This was not exactly what I wanted, but it would work. He left and I choose the only open bed.

Now, this is why I wish I had found this place first. Sitting in chairs at the end of the room were 4 people. They said hello as I was getting situated and said "hope you don't mind, but we are going to SMOKE." I looked up and I said "Not a problem, I have some stuff from Amsterdam, Mind if I join you?" They all laughed and right then and there I had another group of friends. They were from the states: James, Pete, Joe, and Christina. All had just graduated college.

From that point on, we were now a group of 5. I was welcomed with open arms and we got along right away. They had been here for a week and basically seen it all. The only thing they had not seen yet was the David, another famous Michelangelo sculpture, which was the one thing I still needed to see. It just wasn't going to be today. They had found out about a public pool nearby that anyone could go to. They had been busy and wanted to have a down day and do nothing. They asked if I wanted to join them and I said "Absolutely, I'm good at doing nothing."

We found the pool, paid the daily fee of $5.00 and began a great day. We did stand out a little, I don't think a lot of tourists came here, however we fit right in. The beers got ordered and they never stopped coming. In and out of the pool, play a little pool basketball, relax on the chairs, and just really had fun with my new friends. We ordered a bunch of appetizers, shared everything and spent a well needed day, not walking, and not sight-seeing.

We made it back to the hostel and the party just kept going. We all did take time to shower and freshen up a bit and around 8pm we were ready to eat. It wasn't hard finding a place, a new place for all of us. Seriously, you could eat a meal for a year and not eat at the same place. We all enjoyed pasta, and this time I got 2 bottles of Chanti, they too were fans. It was great having people to hang out with. We made it back to our room and by 1am we were all ready to call it a night. It had been a long day in the sun and I had plans for the morning.

One reason I wanted to make it to this part of Italy was the wine. I was told of a small town nearby that was famous for their wines. It was a little get away for me, time outside of a busy city. The past 3 weeks have all been about cities and people, so a nice quite day was well needed.

Instant of a train, I took a bus, which was nice as well. Sit back and enjoy the scenery of the Tuscany Valley. It was rolling hills, grape vines everywhere, and small little towns in the foothills of the mountains. The town I went to is called San Casciano de Bagni, located in the heart of the Tuscany region. It was a small town, once off the bus I could see one end of the town to the other end. At least I can't get lost here.

First thing was getting lunch and a drink. I found a little café, outdoor seating and order pasta and this time a cold beer. It was hot and beer sounded good. My plan was to buy a few bottles of wine and mail them back home while I was here. It would be so cool to have a few bottles of wine from Italy to share with my friends back home. That was my plan and a dam good one at that.

After lunch I walked around this small town, watched a little dog chase a ball up and down the street (so cute,) got a feel for a very laid back Italian environment, it seemed everyone moved a lot slower. There wasn't a building over 3 stories, all with an old fashion Italian look to them, and I walked around the entire town in 30 minutes.

The town was small, yet had several places to buy wine. The first place I went into was small, yet he had a good selection. Somewhere covered in dust, which I figured would be out of my budget. The old Italian guy, at least 70, very weathered from working the vineyards all is life, offered me a few samples. I'm not sure what they were because I don't speak Italian. I could tell he loved them by the way his arms were swaying back and forth. I bought a few bottles from this guy and had the same experience in several more shops. In total I bought 6 bottles about $100, nothing crazy. Now to find a post office.

It didn't take long, remember very small town. I walk in, set the bottles on the counter, and tell him I would like to mail these back to the USA. He looked at me and asked for my permit/license to ship wine internationally. "What are you talking about?" He explained to me that I needed a permit/license to ship wine. I could take a few bottles back on the plane, but not through the mail. "Well that sucks." I just bought 6 bottles of wine and now what do I do?

My bag going back to Florence was a lot heavier, 6 BOTTLES of wine, oh my! Well, when I got back to the hostel, I became a HERO! It was so cool, everyone was hanging out in the courtyard, beautiful night, and just relaxing. They all said hello as soon as I walked in, that felt good they were happy to see me. At least 10 people hanging out and I proceeded to tell everyone what had happened that day. So, I told them, "Guess what, I can take them with me, anyone have a wine opener!" They all laughed and I started handing out bottles. We sat there until midnight drinking wine and having a great evening with new friends.

It was about this time that Pete asked me if I was interested in parting a little harder. I asked what he had in mind and said "cocaine?" He had a connection, $100,000 Lire for a ball, split 3 ways it would cost like $10 each. It was midnight, we had been drinking for hours, we were getting up early to see the David, I should have said NO, but at the point in the night, of course I was IN.

He got the stuff and Pete, Christina, and I took off. We spent the next 6 hours walking around Florence at night, just about as happy as you can get. We stood on bridges and just admired the lights around the city, the streets where quite, and we had the whole city to yourselves. We walked and talked until the sun came up and knew at the point that it was going to be a long day. It was a blast and a night to remember.

We get back and everyone is up and ready to see the David. They were all well rested and ready for the day. The 3 of us had pulled an all nightery, so it would catch up soon. After the David, i'm on a train north to Milan to catch a flight to Greece. It is going to be a long, rough day, and trust me it was.

We waited in line for 2 hours and the 3 of us, no sleep and coming down, are hurting. We did eat a little, but nothing tasted good, just water. It was already a hot day and just waiting was taking a toll on me. Finally, we are in view of the David and it was worth the wait. Michelangelo's famous marble sculpture, 17ft tall and 6.5ft wide. All out of one piece of marble. It was impressive to see and I don't usually admire other naked men, but he was worth it. There were so many other things to see as well in this museum, definitely worth the wait.

After all the fun I had had, great new friend's that I had meet, it was time to go. Again, I know I made the right choice to come here. It was a blast and I hope to return. We said our goodbyes and I was back at the train station right on time. It was going to be 3 hours, so hopefully I can get some sleep.

Milian, Italy

To be honest with you, I felt like I had gone through time travel. Got on the train, found a seat and went to sleep. BOOM… we are here. That was needed and I felt a little normal again. Now, to the airport for a night flight to Greece. I have a ticket, which I bought before I left from "another company." Well, I get to the airport and my ticket is a FAKE and they won't take it. I'm pissed, tired and now hungry. Well, to make a long story short, Ha Ha I had to spend the night in Milian because they had no other seats available. Plus, it cost me $300 for a one-way ticket. It was not what I needed, but hey, Shit happened!

I found the cheapest room, grabbed something to eat, spent more money then I should, and was back at the airport by 7am with a ticket. At least I felt well rested!

Athens, Greece

This was my first flight as a foreigner. No really, I was the only English-speaking person on the flight. Everyone was talking, but couldn't understand a word they were saying. It was cool. I just sat back, enjoyed free food and drinks and a great flight.

Going to Greece was a choice I made when booking this trip. Do I go to "Spain or Greece?" I chose Greece because I wanted to spend time on a few of the Greece Islands. There were things in Athens,

TAKE A DECADE

The Acropolis, that I wanted to see, it was just something about the Greece Islands I thought would be fun. When the plane landed and I got my final stamp in my passport, I now had 7 stamps! Wow, that seemed so unbelievable that I have made it to my final country.

First thing is finding a tourist's office and see what I can book. I loaded up my bags and headed out of the train station. It was at least 90 degrees and sunny. It didn't take long to start sweating. I walk about a mile, up and down a few streets, and still know tourist office. Just then this 50-year-old Greece guy asked if I needed help? "Yes, I'm trying to book a trip." He actually owned a travel agency, just didn't see the sign. We sat at his office, told him I had 6 days left and wanted to see as much as possible. He was able to book everything right there. 2 nights Mykonos, 3 nights Santorini, and 1 night in Athens. Ferries, transfers, hotels, etc.... all for $450. He was a little on the pushy side, "Do I trust Him," I wasn't sure, but he was able to take care of everything, so I agreed and paid him in cash $450.

Now it got interesting. He invited me to have a drink with him, he also owned a bar. Sounded good, I was hot and thirsty. We walk around the corner and enter his "BAR." It is a room about 15ft by 20ft and there were 2 girls there, that is it. he tells them to grab us a beer, we cheer and it taste great. He then says "Do you want to buy the girls a drink?" Now, that is weird. "Um sure I guess, "so they made a drink. I wanted one beer and just get out of there. Well, I had another one handed to me even before I finished the first and the girls had another. "OK, Buddy, I have to go." He then hands me a check for the drinks $60. This is when I lost it. Fuck you buddy, I just wanted a couple of beers. "You agreed to buy the girls a drink, now pay me." You son of a bitch, I just gave you $450 and now you want $60 more. All I had left was about $20 bucks, tried to hand it to him and he said $60 or I'll call the cops. "I know you have more money," is what he said. I had a travelers check for $100, he wouldn't take it, but escorted me to a bank and stood there while they cashed it. We get outside, give him money and I tell him that if my tickets are fake, I'll be back and happily spend time in prison kicking your ass, "YOU FUCKING PIECE of SHIT," and walked away.

Out of my entire trip this was the second time, I wasn't happy. I walked to the harbor, just grinding my teeth, if they don't let me on that boat, I'LL KILL HIM. It was now really hot with the sun and my blood pressure. Well, life got better when my ticket was good and walked on the boat. I found a spot on the top deck, laid out my blanket on a flat area, and started to enjoy my first day in the Greece. What had happened with that guy was over it was time to be happy again, and with a cold beer in hand, Life was good!

The ferry boat was 200ft long 40 ft wide, hauling people, cargo, and vehicles, so she was a good size boat. The boat sounded and we pulled out of the port. I had an amazing view now of Athens, I could see the Acropolis and everything. While walking around and a cab ride to the port, I felt Athens to be a very busy, unorganized, dirty city. My time in the city had been only 5 hours, but from what I've seen I wasn't a fan. However, from the Aegean Sea, which is the body of water, the city looked remarkable. As old as it gets and still standing. My last day, will hopefully be better then my first.

I sat on the top deck, sprawled out on my blanket, enjoying a cold beer, watching the Greece island's go by. The sea was turquoise blue and as I stood watching the ways hit the boat we were met with a few dolphins. It just doesn't get any better. It was the most relaxing, scenic, part of this trip so far. "Wow, Stephen Mundy is in the Greece Islands!"

Mykonos, Greece

We arrived at the harbor and the island looked like something from a magazine, the sun was just setting, so the view was breath taking. My ride was suppose to be here, but I didn't see anyone, so I got a cab to my hotel. Comes to find out he was there, I just didn't look, next time I will be Patient.

My room was perfect and the location was un real. It was dark when I got there, but the sea was right there. I could throw a rock into the sea, that's how close I was. All my windows were opened and I could hear the sea from my room. By this time, I really needed just a good night sleep. It had been a long 3 days with little sleep. This is the party island, so I need to get my strength back. "Boy did I ever."

I guess I was tired because I didn't get up till, 12 noon. Little later then I had expected, buy hey my body needed it. It was time to find a beach. Luckily for me there was a bus stop right across the street and I had a map of the area. I walked to the bus stop and 2 guys were waiting, we started talking, and we were all going the same direction. Tony and John, one Italian and one Asian, both from the states. We talked for about 5 minutes and just like that I had friends again.

We get to the beach and it is a white sandy, beautiful crystal clear water, palm tree swaying all around, it was PARADISE. The three of us had the same thing in mind, find a spot near a few good looking girls, of course most of them were topless, so it wouldn't be tough. We checked out the whole beach and wondered toward the end and all of a sudden it was all naked GUYS, "You can sit here, one guy said to us," and we politely declined and made our way back to the women.

We set up shop at the perfect spot, near 3 girls from the states. We started talking and instantly we hit it off. The 5 of us spent the rest of the day in and out of the water, drinking beers and having a blast. One out of the 3 girls, named Allisa was gorgeous and also topless. 5'3" 115lbs blond, absolutely beautiful. Her and Tony had started talking and I was happy for him. If he needed a wing man I was there. At least we could all look at her. Well, we had an amazing day, the sea was warm and every time I went swimming I just couldn't believe I was here.

By the end of the day, we all decided to meet up later and have dinner. The 3 of us headed back to our place, Tony and John were staying at the same place I was, that is why they were at the same bus stop. We relaxed for an hour, took showers and met the girls around 8 for dinner. Tony and Allisa set together, which I figured he would. We all head a great meal, more sea food and several more drinks. Now it was time to check out the night life.

We were told to check out this club, so after dinner we headed that way. It was 10pm and the place was dead, nobody was in there.

Well, that sucked we thought this was a party island. We decided to walk around and ended up by the ocean, enjoying the view and having a few beers. By midnight, we were all getting tired. We decided to stop by the club, see if anything is going on, if not, call it a night. Well, let me tell you, in 2 hours later and that place had come alive. It was wall to wall people, music blaring, and this was a GREECE PARTY.

Once inside, which took a few minutes, I went to the bar and ordered a screw driver. Guess what, they don't sell individual drinks, I had to buy a bottle of Vodka and picture of OJ. Not a problem, at least I won't have to fight the crowd for a drink the rest of the night. Between the 5 of us we had 3 bottles of booze. This is when the night got fun. Dancing, laughing, and enjoying this beach side club. We danced together, did shots together, and partied with at least 200 other people.

After about 3 hours, I noticed Tony is not making his move, DUMB ASS! So, I start dancing with Allisa and we get a little closer and soon enough, I took the chance and gave her a kiss. I made the right move. We danced together for a while and soon I noticed that Tony and Joe had split and her 2 friends had left, oh well. At this point I asked if she wanted to get out of here, she said "YES." "CHECK PLEASE.

We took a cab back to my place and right out of the cab I I carried her into my room, she was wearing a mini skirt and halter top, and her blond hair was around her Sholder. Once inside I told her I really needed a shower and if she wanted to, she could join me. I'll never forgot this as long as I live. She took het top off and said "You have seen these, but you haven't seen this and pulled her skirt and panties down!" All I could say was "No, I have not, but I'm very happy seeing that now." This night was my favorite so far, I know I keep saying that, but she was one of the best hook-ups I ever had. What A night in Mykonos, one for the book!

The next morning my phone rang at 8am, guy is here to take me to the port for my transfer. My head is pounding and I just wanted to lay naked next to this girl, FOREVER! It took everything I had to get up, but I had to move on. My driver gave her a ride home, nice kiss and she was gone. I have to say it one more time, "What a Night."

I'm back at the port and time to move on to Santorini, 3 nights and my last spot. It was crazy to think that this was coming to and end. All I knew was I was going to make the most of it. Once at the port, I had 30 minutes before we left, so food was needed. As I'm walking towards this café, near the port, I see this short dark hair girl. She catches my eye and I walk right over to her. This is too good to be true, I've met 4 girls in the past 2 weeks and is this number 5. Her name was Deanna 5'5" maybe 120lbs and we started talking. Both of us were heading in the same direction and both staying at the same place. How convenient is that. Well, I'm going to burst your bubble right now, nothing happened with Deanna, except a had a great person to hang out with. She informed me quickly, she had a boy friend and very happy. I never tried anything with her, she was a good girl!

Santorini, Greece

It was another 3 hours to get there, Deanna and I grabbed a drink and enjoyed the view from the top deck. We passed many small islands, watched the birds fly around the boat, enjoyed the sun on our skin, and got to know each other. I had a story to tell and so didn't she. Deanna had finished Grad school and was starting a new job when she got back. She was smart, good looking, and easy to talk to.

We get there and I have a ride waiting for me, she does not. The town is on the top of the island and it is a mile hike straight up. Now, I'm working on 3 hours sleep, and the last thing I wanted to do was climb this mountain. Guess what I did, I followed her up the mountain, just about threw-up half way, but I made it. When we got to the top we were both exhausted from carrier our bags, but the view was worth it.

Santorini is one of the furthest islands from the main land. It is known for its white washed building with blue roofs. It is one of those photos that every Travel Agency would have hanging in their office. It truly is a one-of-a-kind place. We are staying in Thera, "The

Town" which is a great place to watch the sun set, so we had been told. We found our hotel, got checked in to our separate rooms, and decided to check out the town. The streets were so narrow, very few vehicles, the buildings looked like they had been just painted, everything was so clean, a ton of plants hanging out of windows, and everyone seemed so happy. There was a gentle breeze coming from the sea and the sun was hot.

We found a place to have dinner and sat outside this open-air café. There was not a bad seat in the house. We had drinks and watched this quant little town operate. We enjoyed a great meal, we both got authentic Greece dishes and shared with each other. Finished up at the perfect time and made our way to the end of the island. There must have been 200 people doing the same thing. Slowly watching the sun disappear into the sea. That is exactly what it looked like and the colors were unforgettable. The best sun set of my life, so far! We stood there for an hour until it was all over, everyone clapped and the camera equipment was put away.

After this amazing performance from mother nature, we headed back and swam in our pool at the hotel. It felt good to cool off and we planned our next day. We got information on this tour: Ancient City, Volcano, Hot Springs, Island town, and back for another beautiful sun set. It fit our schedule, budget, and the best thing about it was it was also a booze cruise. After our swim, we walked back intown, booked our tour, and had one more drink before we called it a night. Tomorrow would be fun.

It was up early, around 8am, meeting Deanna, quick breakfast, grab supplies for lunch and then to the port. The weather was perfect, 75 degrees and sunny. We met up and found a place to grab a few pastries, water, a sandwich and a few beers. We were set for the day and we had time so we walked to the port, much easier going down.

We loaded up on a 40' boat, about 20 people and all got settled in. They told us about the trip, handed out drinks, and we were on our way. We started at a city called Akrotiri, the first settlement on the island around 1500's, walked around and we could see a few remaining structures., but the place was destroyed during a volcanic eruption. Then we travel to the volcano, now extinct, but still cool. The ground was hot, the color of the sand was red, and it was very cool to see. It was a great view and we walked around as much as we could. Next was the hot springs and my favorite place. We docked outside this small cove and all jumped in the water. It was only 4 ft deep and 15 degrees warmer. The sand on the bottom was "therapeutic" so, we all rubbed sand all over our bodies. We all looked like something out of a horror movie. All of us swam around and had a bit of fun with a little mud throwing fight, good times, but we had to leave. Last was a small fishing village, we walked around, not a lot to see, so we found a small beach and took a nap. The horn went off, we were back on the boat and 45 minutes later back to the island. It was a great day all around.

Once back on land, we had a bus take us to the top this time, so much easier. Then back to our rooms to clean up and get ready for the sunset. We had dinner at the same place, it was a cool place, and close to everything. Watched another amazing sunset, which would never get old. It looks like a cartoon almost. The colors on the water and the reflections' off the sea, you can't take your eyes away from it.

That night was a lot of the same, just wonder around, swim in our pool, enjoy a few drinks and plan the next day. Oh my, tomorrow is my last day, then one more day in Athens. It is really sinking in that it is almost over. I'm going to make the most of my last day here and rent a jeep and check out the rest of the island. I also can say I drove in Europe, "not really though."

We picked up my Samuria Suzuki Jeep the next morning, picked up a few supplies for the day and set out to see the island. Santorini looks a lot like Arizona, dry and very little vegetation. It is a much older island that has had issues with volcanoes. Mykonos was more tropical, which I prefer, but this was beautiful as well. We had a map and there were a few things to see. The streets, more like paths, were rough and I'm glad I had a jeep. It was a open jeep, so we had the fresh air and sunshine all around us, the entire day.

We ended up going to this small town about 20 miles away that had a Black Sand beach. It was beautiful and "yes" the sand was black. We rented snorkel gear and spent a good portion of the day right there on that beach. Food was brought to us, the sea was beautiful and a ton of fish for snorkeling, a few drinks and it was perfect. We could have stayed there the entire time, but we wanted to see more of the island.

All we did was take different roads, not really paying attention to the map. When I road ended, we just turned around and tried another. We spent about 3 hours just exploring the island. Stopped in a few shops, grabbed a snack, and away we would go. I never got stuck and every time I left the road, I never hit one thing. It was a blast and a great last day.

That night we celebrated and thanked each other for the great companionship and awesome experience. Deanna didn't want to do shots, so I did 2 shots of Grand Marnier. It seemed only fitting to have this as my last drink. Steve and I started with GM and I'm going to end with GM. I'm sure this is not my last drink, but hey you get the picture. We ended the night, gave her a hug, said our goodbyes, and this was it, WOW!

The next morning, I was up and out the door by 7am. My ride was waiting and back to the port. The ferry was ready and about the same size as the first one. It took about 4 fours to get here, so I'm assuming the same to get back. I find a spot on the top deck, spread out my blanket, and sat back and enjoyed the ride. With the sun warming me up, the rocking of the boat, it didn't take me long to fall asleep. When I woke up, 3 hours had gone by. Wow, that was quick. I had one more hour and we would be there. I spent time updating my journal and just staring out at the sea, can't believe I was able to see this.

Around 4 hours into our trip, there is really no sign of land at all. I go downstairs, use the bathroom and found a crew member and asked" how much longer?" This guy said "3 more hours." It only took 4 hours to get here, why so long to get back. He then informed me that I traveled 3 hours to Mykonos, then 4 hours to Santorini, total of 7 hours. it all made sense and I told him I was in no rush, take as long as you want. So, it was back to my spot on the ship, a few beers in hand and I'll sit back and watch this all day long.

TAKE A DECADE

ATHENS, GREECE

We arrived back in Athens and reality had set in; this was my last night in Europe. Now I had to find my last accommodations, Hotel Amazon. It was not easy to get to either, 20 minute dirty subway ride, 15 minute walk through the hood, and I finally found it. It seemed to be in a rough part of town, but hey maybe this is the good part, I really didn't know. My room was clean and she had a few beers sent right to my room, "Now, that is what I'm talking about." Got settled and all I wanted to see was The Acropolis.

I grabbed my day pack because I still wanted to pick up a few souvenirs. It was hotter than hell, so I grabbed a few extra waters. Stopped at the front desk and ask how to get to the Acropolis? First thing she said was "It is closed today because of the heat; it was over 100 degrees." What are you talking about, how can this be closed. She said "you can still walk around and see the structures, just can't go inside." Well, at least I'll be able to see it, so she gave me directions and I was off.

When she it was closed due to heat, I can understand. Just walking on the sidewalks and streets along with the pollution, made for a long 30-minute walk. My water was gone before I even got there, which just meant I had to buy more. 4 bottles of water that day, most of any other day on this trip, by far! Ha Ha

As I got closer, The Acropolis was enormous, you couldn't miss this, that is for sure. It looked like all the photos I had ever seen, just much larger. How they constructed something so tall, with such heavy material was stunning. The main structure, the Parthenon, stuck out the most. Completed in 437 BC this was the most important building in classic Greece. I spent time just walking around the outside and imagined what it was like back in the day. It was the place to be, that is for sure. After an hour in the direct sun, I was done. I didn't get the full tour, but I saw it and that is enough.

It was starting to get dark and I still needed to get a few things. On my way home, I wondered in to this souvenir shop and the guy says "what a shot of Ouzo?" I said "sure, sounds good." We had a drink and I started looking around. He talked the entire time, but not pushy like my first guy. I picked up a few things and he gave me another shot. I found a few more things and he gave me another shot. I was in the shop for an hour, found everything I needed and then some, and left with a really nice Buzz. If only we did this more in the states. He was a really nice guy, gave me a few things, including a small bottle of Ouzo for later. He was the total opposite from my first guy I met when I arrived, Thank You!

With everything done, it was time to pack for the last time. By this time, I had very few clothes left from the beginning of my trip. I had bought a few things and recycled the old. My bags were packed with a lot of great memories. Can't wait to share them with my Family and Friends.

THE FINAL DAY

It was a restless night; "I just didn't want to leave." If I had more money, I would have just kept going. However, it was time to get back home, make more money, see my family and friends and who knows where I could go next. Time will tell.

The taxi ride to the airport was the fastest and scariest ride ever. There is no order on the streets, just go when you can. We made it safely and it was time to say goodbye to EUROPE. When the plane took off, I honestly teared up and couldn't believe it was over. I still had to fly to Munich, then to Washington DC, and then to Arizona, but for me, THE JOURNEY was over.

This trip to Europe was my first international travel experience, 7 countries and 16 major cities. It was an eye-opening experience and I thank everyone that I met for an amazing time. Special thanks to Steve, for getting me started and being there in the beginning. It truly was an EPIC JORNEY!

4
CHAPTER

How Life Changes

It seemed like I was still on the plane flying at thirty-five thousand feet, or was it just where my head was at? I was still on cloud nine from such an amazing adventure. Murph, my best friend picked me up at the airport, and I was back to reality. He looked at me and said, "Nice haircut." He was the first person to see the new and improved Stephen Mundy. Now I was bald and very tan by this point and still in good shape with all the walking and carrying my backpacks. The big difference with me now is that I had an attitude. Yes, an attitude, I was now a worldly person. I had stamps in my passport to prove it, and I was very happy to show everyone.

It was Wednesday night by the time I got back to my apartment, and technically, I should be going back to work tomorrow. It had been over a month with an extended period off, and I was sure they were ready for me to come in. However, I was not going into work tomorrow; I needed a day off to unwind and see my friends. I'd go back Friday, and then I'd have two days off. Yes, that is what I would do, take a day and go back Friday. This was a good idea.

On Thursday, I slept and I slept. I contacted my mom and let her know that I was safe and sound and back in the States. I could tell in her voice that she was so relieved that I was back home and alive. I'm not a mom and will never be a mom, but let me tell you they are the most important person in every son's life. She loves me, and I love her unconditionally.

That night, after they got done work, Jason and Graydon stopped by to see me. I couldn't wait to see them and give them their gifts. I got both of them a soccer jersey from a local team in Europe. It was so much fun seeing the two of them that night. I got to tell them about everywhere I experienced and about all the girls I had a chance to be with. This is what they wanted to hear: the sex, drugs, and rock 'n' roll version of my trip. My family would get another version of my trip, which would be great as well. There are just some things you tell your buddies, and there are some things you tell your mother.

The guys filled me in on everything I had missed and all about work. It turned out they were not really happy about my extended time off. So at that point, which was Thursday night, I decided not to ruin my weekend. I decided I would just go back to work on Monday. Yes, that made more sense than starting back on a Friday. Basically, I would have made any excuse not to go back to work. It was going to be a long five months with absolutely no time off. I had used all my vacation days for the entire year. It would be five days a week for the next five months without anything to look forward to at all; it would suck big-time.

Jason and Graydon both commented on how good I looked—the new bald-headed, very tan Mundy—and I felt like a million bucks. The three of us enjoyed the night, and it was so good to see them. The plan was a mellow weekend: Try and see a few people like Mike and Michelle and get back in the gym on Monday after work. I asked these guys if they had been partying, and I was glad to hear that they had been good as well, and we had just a few drinks.

I was also able to spend more time with Murph and Kari, Murphy's wife, who started at Vanguard the same day I did. This also gave me time to fill them in on my trip and give them the gift I had brought back for them. It felt great to be back with a feeling that I had really accomplished something, and this made me happier than I had been in several years.

On Sunday, we spent the day at the pool, and again, the topic was Mundy's trip. How could it not be? We had fun that day and of course talked about work. They said it had been okay, nothing major happening except that my name and situation had been the talk of the town. We would see what happened tomorrow morning when I went back to the reality of work. It was really hard to get a grip on this after being so free and happy for the past several months.

The night ended, and my alarm was set for the usual time, 7:30 a.m. I was tired after the weekend of seeing everyone and getting unpacked. I did my laundry in an actual washing machine, which was a treat, something I had not been able to do in a while. It did feel great to sleep in my own bed.

Buzz, buzz, buzz. Holy shit, it's Monday morning, and I have to get up. I have to get up, shower, put a long-sleeved shirt on, nice pants, polished shoes, and a tie. I lay there for about five minutes, and my mind was working overtime and I had just woken up. I asked myself one very important question while I lay there, and that was "Do you like doing what you are doing, Steve? Do you like your job?" It wasn't that I hated my job. I liked the people I worked with. It was just the repetitiveness. *Can I go back to sitting in a cubicle, talking on the phone to investors, with a tie around my neck? Can I go back to my same life after what I had just experienced?* The answer came rather quickly, and at that time, I decided to shut my alarm off and go back to sleep. *I'm not going to do it. I don't know what I'll do, but my life and state of mind is more important. Sorry, Vanguard, but I quit.*

I finally woke up at around 11:00 a.m. and made the call. Actually, it was so easy. All I had to do was leave a message with my team leader. "Sorry to inform you this way, but you didn't answer your phone. I've decided *not* to come back to work. After all I have seen and done in the past month, my eyes are opened to the world and I want to see more. I am sorry for such short notice. However, there is no easy way to do this except to just say thanks for everything and the experience. I just want more out of my life!"

That was it, and I was now unemployed. What was I going to do now with the rest of my life? There were so many questions, and absolutely none of them had to be answered right now. I did call

Murph, Jason, and Graydon with my new decision, and they were shocked. "How can you just quit without having anything lined up, and what will you do for money?" they all asked. "How can you just quit a job like this?"

I said, "It is really easy. Just *do it* and don't look back." My mind had been made up, and I was going to make things work out one way or the other. My parents, however, were not really impressed with my decision to quit my job. I explained that I wanted to travel more, and I just didn't want to wait another year before I could go somewhere again. I had been on my own for many years, and this decision would affect me and only me.

It was the middle of July, and my life was now different then it had been for the past four years. The big thing was, of course, money and I did have a few thousand in the bank, which was money from my paychecks. It wasn't a lot, and I knew with rent and bills that would not last long. However, I did get a nice surprise for the next three pay periods, and that is I still got a paycheck from Vanguard. I quit so abruptly that they did not get my name out of the system, and they still paid me for not even being there. This was absolutely awesome, and it just keep my vacation going longer and longer.

The next few months were very lazy and fun. The day I spent lounging by my pool and playing golf. It was fun not having to go to work but lonely as well. All my friends had their *jobs* to go to each day and couldn't hang out with me. Oh well, I survived and occupied my time. We did still meet up at the gym a few days a week, but by five o'clock, I had already had a few drinks, and lifting weights just wasn't as appealing as it was before I left. For me, during this period, it was all about what was next in my life. My wheels were spinning, and I was trying to figure out what I could do next.

That came to me one day about a month or so home from Europe. I had been home all day and went to the pool for a few hours. I had a few beers and smoked a little of the funny stuff, and I was sitting on my couch, and I had an idea. In my living room, I had a globe of the world and walked over and grabbed it. I sat down with it on my lap and said, "Okay, Arizona is here, and if I wanted to go to the other side of the planet, where could I go?" As I looked at the globe of the world and calculated the other side of the world, it was my next journey. At that point, sitting on my couch without a job or anything else stopping me doing this, my decision had been made. I was going to fly to Japan and spend a month traveling around that country. *Why not?* I said to myself. *You can do this, and it will be a blast.* That was it, and I had made up my mind on my next adventure.

What another great day, making such a great choice to travel to the Orient. It was time to celebrate. All my friends were happy with my decision yet concerned for my financial status and really just didn't understand what traveling meant to me. It wasn't their place to worry about my financial situation; all I wanted was for them to support me. I then called my parents and gave them the good news. "Where are you going?" my mom said. "You are going alone. Are you sure about this?"

"Absolutely, I'm sure of this decision, and it will be a great experience." She didn't have the same enthusiasm as I did, but as always, she was my biggest supporter.

The next month was all about getting prepared and packed. I purchased my plane ticket for November 2, 2000, which was my birthday. What a great present to myself, a trip to Japan. I had been a good boy this year and really did deserve this opportunity. During this time, I was very careful where I spent any money. I didn't go out and didn't buy anything I did not need. The only real thing I had to buy before this trip was a new camcorder. I wasn't going without one. The rest of my money was for my trip.

This trip would be very different from Europe. First, I was going to be solo the entire time. Second, this area was completely different from Europe, which means I would stand out more. And third, I would be on a much stricter budget. The first thing I did was buy the book *Lonely Planet's Guide to Japan*. These books are great for anywhere in the world you want to go. They are written by travelers for travelers. It's all about traveling on a shoestring to get the most out of our trip.

In the weeks prior to departure, I read this book and came up with a bit of a game plan. Besides my plane ticket, the only thing I did purchase before I left was my first two nights in Japan. This was peace of mind for me to have a place to go the first night I arrived in Tokyo. It was time to get packed and gear up again for another big adventure.

The day before I left, my friends had a little party for me. They all had nothing but good things to say and, of course, good words of encouragement. They had also asked to bring them something back, of course.

The day had come, Nov 2, and after a good conversation with my family back home, it was time to head to the airport. Murph took me to the airport, which was nice to have him be the last person I said goodbye to. He has always been a great friend, and we have always had each other's back. It was now time for me to do this on my own, solo, and fulfill my dreams.

5
CHAPTER

The Other Side of the World

The flight to Japan was long, about twelve hours and covered about 5,777 miles from airport to airport. We had a short flight to Los Angeles, and while there, we just changed passengers, and I never had to get off the plane. I had a front-row seat, which was great because I had more leg room, and when the door closed, I realized I had all three seats to myself. It doesn't get much better than this while flying. The airline I had chosen was China Air, and what a wonderful experience. Most were female and all very polite and respectful. As soon as I could have a drink, I had a cold beer and not a Budweiser, which is what they first brought me, and a Grand Marnier. I had this combination for a good part of my trip. It was free, and I was going to have a good time. After our first movie, the food service started, and everyone got a hot towel to clean their hands and face before dinner. Then they walked up and down the aisle with wine. This was about as close to the first class as I had ever had. After we were served our meal, which was chicken, rice, veggie, and a roll, more wine followed. Then after dinner, they brought another warm towel and, would you know it, more wine. I was feeling pretty damn good by now. By this time, I was ready for a nap, and it was so easy to get comfortable with all three seats. So I stretched out using all three seats and enjoyed a quick nap for about an hour. Then it was up for more food, more drinks, and another movie. To be honest, I would have just stayed on this plane for the next month.

When the pilot came over the speaker and announced our landing in fifteen minutes, I got a little nervous. *Here goes nothing.* I was fifteen minutes away from setting foot in a country that I didn't know a lot about. I didn't have someone meeting me at the airport. I didn't know a single soul who lived here, and I didn't speak Japanese. All I could do was pray that all would go well, and this is what I kept saying to myself: *It will all work out.* The plane landed, and it was time to start the next journey in my life.

My first experience with Asian culture was at Narita Airport, which is one of the largest in Asia. Oh man, it was busy, people everywhere moving fast. This was going to be my way of life for the next month. As I went to get my bags, it was apparent that I looked different than 90 percent of the people. I'm 6'2" and bald, and oh yes, I'm white.

I retrieved my bags and found the train station, which was somewhere here in the airport. The other thing I needed was an ATM to get some cash for the next few days. The signs at the airport were in Japanese, of course, and spelled out in English, but I still could not read them. Thank God for symbols, which lead me to the nearest ATM and the train that I needed to take from the airport to the city. At the ATM, I took out about $300, which would get me through the first week, I hoped.

The train station was packed, everyone talking and moving a million miles an hour. This was what I kind of expected Japan would be like, just hard to describe until you're right in the middle of it. My train came, and I managed to fight the crowd and found a standing room spot in the middle. There I was with two backpacks, which was everything I owned right now, and I was hanging on to a strap from the ceiling so I don't fall over. I was on my way to the city of Tokyo. The thing about this train was that everyone was looking at me—not just in the train car I was riding in, but I also could see people staring at me from the two cars on either side of mine. It was a little unnerving, but all I could do was smile and politely say hello.

TAKE A DECADE

We arrived at the train station, and after a unique travel experience, I was officially here: Tokyo, the capital of Japan and home to about nine million people. This was the population when I was there; now it is closer to fourteen million. The greater metropolitan area around and including Tokyo has a population of thirty-seven million people, making it the most populated area in the world. This place is a mix of ultramodern and very traditional. You have your neon skyscrapers, and nearby are ancient temples and buildings. Everything just seemed so surreal seeing this place for the first time.

From the train station, I had to take a city bus to the place that I had reserved. I'm so glad I had a reservation because there were enough things going on at this time. The information center was very helpful; first, they spoke English and told me which bus to take and when to get off. The ride was about ten minutes, and I just sat there and watched the world around me, knowing that this was now my new environment. This was definitely not like the States or even Europe. The Asian signs that lit up the storefronts, the people walking and riding bikes, the unique cars that were passing us, and the smell of the city were truly amazing. I asked the bus driver if he knew where I was going, and he said he did. His English wasn't the greatest, and my Japanese at this point was *zero*. So when my stop came, he got my attention so I could get off. I was now on the street, and the bus driver pointed in a direction for me to go and said something, but I didn't understand him completely. I had my map and just needed to figure out the streets. That first block with all my gear on my back and a map in my hand was a crazy feeling. I really didn't know a single person on this side of the planet. It was just me and eight million Japanese.

Down the street, make a few turns, and there it was, home sweet home. It was a row house with a small sign outside that said the name of my place, and the address matched. I walked to the door and rang the bell. The door opened, and a Japanese woman in her mid-fifties was standing there in the entire Japanese garment. Her hair was done up in a bun. The dress she wore looked like an authentic Japanese dress, and she also had the makeup on that made her look like something you might see in a movie. She stood there and bowed about ten times. I tried to bow, but with my day pack in front of me, it was a challenge, so I stopped. This was very cool, and man, did I feel underdressed for the occasion. She checked me in and spoke only the words in English that she needed to really know: *money*, *room*, *shower*, and *food*. She said, "You follow me and I show you the room. First, you take shoes off here. No shoes in the house." This was said with authority and tradition.

Up the stairs and my room was at the top of the stairs. It was small but had everything I needed. The bathroom and shower was down the hall, and she gave me the complete tour. This was basically their home. I came to find out it is rather popular in Japan to do this. The first thing I did was use the bathroom; it had been a long ride, and man oh man, did that feel good. My room was small, and everything was on the floor. My bed was a rolled-up mattress. The table was very short and required sitting on the floor to use it. There was one chair and a small place for my bags. This was a traditional Japanese place, and it was very cool.

Now that I had my room and a place to drop off my bags, I needed a few supplies for the night. So I went down the stairs, put my shoes on, and out the door I went to find food and drink. It was getting late, and all I really wanted to do on my first night was look over some information and get a good night's sleep.

There was a convenience store close by, and it was my first real experience in any Japanese store. I walked in and thought to myself, *Do I have to take my shoes off to go into a store?* So I waited a minute and watched someone go in, and they didn't take their shoes off, so I was good to go. I was just inside the door, and all four of the people working said, "Konnichiwa," which means hello, and this made me feel like I was so special. Now it was time for food and drink. The beer was easy—Sapporo, a beer I have had and seemed to be cheap. Now for food, everything was different and unique. You could buy dried squid in a bag, seaweed wraps, meat that I didn't recognize at all, and a lot of "Cup of Soups." Those I knew, and my hostess had told me about a place to get hot water and green tea whenever I needed it at the house. This was my first real meal in Japan, a cup of soup and a few Sapporos. There at the store, they had a rack of tourist information and maps of the area, so I grabbed as many things as I could, and this would be my reading information for the night.

It was back to the room, shoes off at the door, and I had a stack of information to read for the night. The first thing I needed to figure out was the money exchange and transportation. The yen was stronger than the US dollar, about 120:1. So this means that the beers I bought were about $3 each, which isn't bad at all. The room I was staying in was $75 a night, and that was way too much for my budget; however, I had paid for the first two nights before I left the States. Finding something cheaper would be my main priority during the next few days. My plan was to try and spend less than $50 a day for shelter, food, and transportation. According to my information, it was possible; we would see. The other thing I spent time researching that night was the JR line. The JR line is the main system in Japan, which turned out to be a great form of transportation.

So I had a lot to see and a lot to do. Mt Fuji, local food, local women, and whatever else I could see while I was here. My mind was spinning with excitement, and my body was telling me it was time to call it a night. I had a big day ahead, and who knew what would happen over the course of the next month or so? I unrolled my bed, got a few things set up for the night, lay on the floor, and listened to the sounds of the city while I drifted off to sleep.

*****

The first few days were all about getting my bearings and just getting used to my surroundings. I had one more night at this place and had a lead on another place, which looked like more of a hostel. I was currently staying on the northeast side of the city, and my new place wasn't that far from here. It was a very unique city, old in certain aspects and new in other ways. The streets were busy with people, vendors selling things, and the chatter of people talking, which made this the most unique place I had ever been. It was just so cool being a part of this culture and way of life. It was just the beginning of my trip, and I had so much more to see. *Mundy, you are here in Japan. WOW!*

The days were all about exploring and checking out the city. Taking the JR line, you can get just about anywhere you want. However, it turned out to be a little pricey per ride. I was up north, and anywhere I went was like $3 to $6 each way. Traveling was expensive around the city, which was something I learned quickly. The first day was all about the Ginza district, Imperial Palace, the Nikon building, and the famous crosswalk that you see on TV with so many people crossing on a daily basis.

The Ginza area was a place I wanted to see. This was like the most expensive commercial property in the world. This was Tokyo's most famous upscale shopping, dining, and entertainment district. It's like Rodeo Drive and Times Square. It was so busy and so beautiful, the skyscrapers, the decor, the cleanliness, and the beautiful people. I walked down the street with a pair of yellow workout pants and a white tank top with my day pack over my shoulder. Yes, I stood out but nobody said a thing to me. There was the famous Nikon Building with the busiest crosswalk in the world. I actually went up into the Nikon Building and got as high up as I could go and found an empty room to get a photo of the crosswalk from a great view. This crosswalk is so cool to see from a bird's-eye view. When the lights changed for pedestrians to walk across, it looked like a thousand people crossed in a two-minute time frame. Then the light would change, and the sidewalks would accumulate more people, and then the light would change and another thousand people would cross. I stood and watched this for about twenty minutes; I had this boardroom all to myself, and no one came in and told me to leave.

Finding a place to eat was a challenge at first. There were so many different choices—restaurants, outside vendors, and grab-and-go stores. For the first few days, I lived on fried rice and eggrolls, which you could get just about anywhere. These were the things that I really recognized. I knew they were good, and it was something I could point to and order, so basically, it was the easiest thing for me to eat. I stopped one day at a small outdoor restaurant—and I mean small—it had like eight chairs. Places like this lined the streets, just small family-owned businesses that took up about as much room as your average living room. I saw these people eating this soup, and it looked really good. So I took a seat at the table and pointed to the soup that the person next to me was eating. The man grabbed a bowl and filled it with the soup; he also got me a beer to wash everything down. It had chicken, veggies, a nice broth, small pasta, and these small little potatoes. It was so good that I asked for more and asked him to add more of those little potatoes if he could. He looked at me, smiled, and said, "No potatoes, fish eyes" as he pointed to his own eyes.

"Oh my," I said. I had just eaten fish eyes, and they were really good. *Wow*, who would have thought? Now if I knew this ahead of time, I may have gotten something else, but let me tell you, not knowing is sometimes the best information you can have. I later learned in life that you should always try things three times. Yes, three times is the magic number, and I will tell you more about that later.

My first order of business was relocating to a cheaper place. It was a hostel not really far from where I was now. It was much cheaper, only $25 a night, and this was more in my budget. So I took a bus for a short distance and was dropped off right in front. As I approached the door, I was met with a few more people all traveling together who just happened to be going in at the same time. We all walked in, and we were greeted by a white girl from Australia; she was helping the owner out while he was away for a few days. As we walked in, the desk for checking people in was to the left, and across from this was a common area that people could hang out at night. She checked the group in and then helped me out with a room. We headed up the stairs. The group had their own room, and I was in the dorm-style room. The girl getting us checked in was very nice, and cute, and she was very helpful. She took me to my room, and it was an empty room except for six rolled-up mattresses on the floor. I could tell right away there were others staying here by their stuff. The end mattress looked empty, and that is what I chose. She told me it was proper to roll your bed up when not using.

I said, "No problem as long as I don't have to get up real early." She laughed, and right away, we had a connection. The shower in this place was a little different. It was fed from a holding tank on the roof, and very little water was used in showering. They got wet, shut the water off, soaped up, and then rinsed; it was quick and easy. I wasn't going to have my fifteen-minute hot shower here; that was for sure. Also, the shower area was only available a few hours a day, 7:00 a.m.–9:00 a.m. and 4:00 p.m.–6:00 p.m. It was more of a tradition in Japan to shower at certain times, which was fine with me. It may have seemed a little strange, but hell, everything I had encountered in just a few days was strange, and I loved every minute of it.

The place was clean, and I got a good vibe about it. After dropping off my gear in my room, I went down to the common room, and about five people were sitting around, and I said hello. I had already met the Aussie girl, and there was a girl from Borneo, an English couple, and a guy from Denmark. Now there was me from the States. We decided to get some beers and spent a lot of time that evening picking everyone's brain on what to do and how to go about it. It was just good to have a cheaper place to stay with cool people. We had a group, and the Aussie girl had lived there for a while, so she had great advice and helpful tips. I think she liked me a little and she was right now my best friend.

The one great thing that I found the next day was a fast-food sushi place. It was the fastest restaurant I had ever eaten at. You walk in and find a place to sit. Then right in front of you is this massive conveyer belt that is going around the entire place. There are colored plates with all different kinds of sushi. You grab a plate and begin eating. The only thing you have to order is your drink. It did come with green tea, which I found to be served just about everywhere. It was good and good for you, so I did have my green tea, then I had a beer. The sushi was being prepared by several chefs behind the counter. Their hands could not work fast enough to keep up with the demand. This was just fast food at its best. Then each plate is a different color, which costs a different amount. You take your plates to the front; she counts them, and you pay. So quick and it is so damn convenient. This place would be a frequent stop for me over the next week.

I decided to take a short walk around the hostel and see what I could see. I really just wanted to grab something to munch on and have a beer for the room later. I headed out and turned here and then there and really didn't walk far, and things started to not look familiar. I had a church near where I was staying and was using it as a landmark for directions. It was a large church and could be seen from far away. Well, this had already disappeared with so many other buildings blocking my view and I knew I wasn't that far away. Well, to make this a short story, I was lost for about three hours.

It is during these times that you come across great things. I found this street that was all decorated with the Japanese lamps hanging from a wire that went across the street and a shrine that was still active. I knew I was lost and there was nothing I could do, just enjoy the moment and not panic. It was during this little adventure that I came up with the most beautiful things I had ever seen. There was a vending machine that sold beer and sake. Oh my, I had never seen this before. It was right out on the street next to a Pepsi and Coke machine. So I was able to have my first beer out of a vending machine. There is no real rule about walking around with a beer—just don't make a fool of yourself. You would think that having a way to buy alcohol without any supervision would be a problem. But they didn't have a huge problem with underage drinking, and these vending machines stopped working at eleven each night. It was still so cool for a dumb American like me that loved beer. I will tell you that I used these things many times during my stay.

I did finally make it back and had a great story to tell my new friends. The owner of the place had shown up, and he was a younger Japanese guy, who was very nice. He spoke perfect English; he was the first real Japanese person I could have a conversation with. He also told me he had a place for me to stay for as long as I needed it. He had just returned from a trip to Thailand and was telling me all about it. It had been one of those real far-off places to go, and I couldn't imagine going there. It sounded great and cheap, but I was in Japan, and that was all I had expected to see on this trip, and I already noticed my money was going faster than I had expected.

The next morning, I got up super early to check out the famous fish market. It was the famed Tsukiji fish market, which has since moved location to a more modern facility. I guess I was lucky to have seen the original one that had been in operation for over eighty years.

In order to get the full effect, you are supposed to get there early, like 5:00 a.m., when the fishermen start coming in. I wasn't getting up that early but made it out of bed around 7:00 a.m. and took a bus to the spot. This was not just your average fish market; this was like a whole block and then some. It was right on the bay so the boats could unload at the docks, and it was impressive. Imagine this huge warehouse the size of ten football fields full of tanks and holding bins. Some of the tanks used to keep the fish were the size of something you might see at an aquarium for displaying fish. I was able to just walk around and check out the fish. There were rows of 150–300 lb. bluefin tuna, thousands of pounds of smaller fish, tanks filled with sea urchins, bait fish for bigger fish, and 1,000-gallon tanks filled with live octopus. Guys were using chainsaws to cut the bigger fish, and younger kids were wheelbarrowing ice to pack the fish to keep them cold. There were so many people there, mostly local Japanese business owners buying their fresh fish for the day.

I met this one older Japanese guy, middle-aged and spoke a little English, and he owned a restaurant close by and came here every day to buy his fish for sushi. I followed him around for a little bit and watched him negotiate with the sellers. I'm sure they dealt with each other all the time, but it sounded like they were yelling at each other over the price. Maybe they were; I don't know. I just kind of followed him and tried not to get in his way. Before he left, he invited me to his restaurant, which was right around the corner, and I was getting hungry. We walked in together, and I helped him remove the stools from the bar area and let him settle in. I grabbed a barstool for myself and had a seat at the bar, while he opened up his business. I would be his first customer of the day and had the whole place to myself. He asked if I wanted a drink while he got set up, and I said, "Sure, how about a beer and sake?" It was almost nine o'clock, and I had been up for a while, so why not? I checked out the menu, and when he was ready, I gave him my order: unagi, tuna, shrimp, and whatever else he made for me. The guy had just bought this stuff less than an hour ago, and I watched him prepare my meal right in front of me. He placed the small plates of food in front of me, and I grabbed my chopsticks and dug in—best breakfast ever. For a great experience and a great meal, it cost me about $20, which meant I was already over my budget for the day, so for the rest of the day, it would be sightseeing and that would be it. This money thing was annoying but a reality, and I had to pace myself so I could make sure I got a chance to see as much as I can. All I knew so far was I was having fun right now, and that was all that mattered.

After a fantastic meal, I went out and just started walking. I was not really sure where I was going; all I knew was that I could find the JR line and get a ride back from wherever I ended up. I walked away from the water, which was only common sense, and about twenty minutes later, I ended up in a beautiful Japanese garden, the Hama Rikyu Gardens, which is the garden of the Tokugawa Shogunate. Here was the true Japanese way of life that I thought about, small structures with the unique roofs that were something from a fairytale. There were several ponds with geese and tall swans floating so elegantly around the water. There were small bridges that connected beautiful flower gardens with all the unique shrubs and trees that covered the grounds. It was a very serendipitous moment, so relaxing and a great place to spend time in the middle of a major city. This place reminded me of Central Park in NYC. It was a beautiful oasis in the middle of one of the largest cities in the world.

Life had become a little easier for me after about four days in the city. Transportation, food, and what to do and what not to do had become apparent. It was exciting to still be thinking where I was on the planet, and now, I actually felt comfortable in doing anything I wanted.

That night, we had planned on going to Shibuya, which is a center for Japanese fashion and culture and the younger generation's major nightlife district. It was supposed to be party central for the city, and I had to see it. Up until now, I'd seen hundreds of women, some nice and some so not nice; it was all part of it. I just knew I was excited to see this area of the city.

We left the hostel to the JR line and were on our way to Shibuya Station. Two of the guys had been there already. When we came out of the station, it was like Times Square in New York during Halloween and New Year's Eve all combined in one. Talk about sensory overload. People handed out brochures and even had one group of people handing out condoms. The light of the neon was overwhelming, and just the excitement of the area was so uplifting it was amazing. Holy cow, what a cool place. Girls were dressed up in full Japanese garments, there were short skirts everywhere, and people dressed up like runway models in Milan. They had hats, clothes, boats, and sparkles. It would take these people hours to get ready to come out each night. They were decked right out. I was wearing a pair of cargo shorts and T-shirt; I didn't really fit in, but in a place like this, everyone fits in. We found a bar that served drinks, and that was good enough for us. We had a few beers and then walked around, maybe a shot in one place and then on to another place. I felt like a kid in a candy store. Shibuya is also the place that has a landmark intersection in front of the Hachiko Station. It is the large intersection that you see on any material dealing with Japan. When the light turns green, the crosswalk is flooded with people. This happens all day long, every day, 365 days of the year. I had visited one like this in the Ginza area, and this was another one located here in this section of the city.

We all had a great night and realized we must take the next train back or stay here all night. I wasn't ready to spend the entire night but that would come. We made our way back to the hostel, and there were a few people still up, including the Aussie girl. We walked in, and I had a plan that night, and that was to have a smoke. I knew this was not right, but I did bring a little bud with me for the trip. I had heard it was really hard to get weed in Japan, so I put a little bit in my contact case for the trip. Tonight was a good time, and I found out my little Aussie girl was in as well. We made a bowl out of tin foil and left the building to take a quick walk around the block. She was so excited to smoke because it is so hard to find and very illegal. She informed me that even being caught with a tiny amount was a year in jail. We made our walk, and by the time we got back, everyone was sleeping. We walked up the stairs toward the bedrooms, and I just kind of followed her to her private room and never left that night. We had a great night.

She left early that morning for work, and I snuck back into my room for a few more hours of sleep. It was time to come up with a plan about money and make this trip work. When I got up that morning and got ready, I started talking to the owner of the place. He started telling more about Thailand and how cheap it was. He told me that even with the cost of a plane ticket, time spent in Thailand would prolong my trip here. Japan was expensive, and I wasn't doing anything real crazy and expensive, just doing and seeing what I could afford. There was a lot more of Japan I wanted to see like Mount Fuji and maybe Kyoto. So I had a decision to make and did some homework on the computer, and after about an hour of research, I had made my mind up. I was going to Thailand for ten days. This would allow me to stay here longer. And I would get a chance to get another country under my belt, Thailand!

I bought a ticket for the next day, and the plan was set. I had been here for about eight days now and was excited that I was getting to another unexpected place. My last day was more sightseeing and eating more great sushi. The little fast-food joint with the conveyor belt and plated sushi had become my second home. Last night, we headed down to Akihabara, which is the technology center of Tokyo. This place had a ton of stores all selling technology, from phones to toilets. The streets were lined with business, and it was very busy with a lot of people. Just checking the latest and newest things out there as far as technology was a sight to see. If you were a gamer or tech junkie, this would be your Graceland.

For me, it was an early night, which meant midnight. I did get to spend another night with my little Aussie friend. She and I did the walk around the block and past our homemade bowl and then back to her room. She actually offered me $25 for a few seeds that were in my weed. She said she could grow a plant. I told her, "Honey, you have definitely earned a few lousy seeds by now," and I gave her the little bit of weed I had left. I just have to say one thing about this girl: We had the best "quiet" sex I had ever had. You see, it was a very old building, and you could hear people walking around, and two people having sex would definitely be heard. Oh well, shit happened and we had fun.

So here was an update. I'd been in Japan for about eight days. I'd seen so much so far; the Ginza district, Shimbuia, the fish market,

Japanese gardens, and so much more. It was great here, and loving everything, I would just run out of money if I stayed here until my return flight on Dec 4. Let me tell you, there is so much more that I will do and I'm not leaving until I get to Mt Fuji.

Before my next adventure, I called my parents and spoke with my mom. I told her where I was going just to keep her informed. She was not as excited as I was about this adventure. It's hard to imagine how my poor mother felt getting these phone calls. If you're a mom reading this book, then you can understand what my mom did for me. It was just nothing but love and support from my number one fan. Love you, Mom. I also contacted a few of my buddies back home and informed them of where I was going, and they were excited for me. I was just pulling a Mundy and doing what I wanted.

I was very excited about this and a little nervous of course. I was just getting comfortable with my surroundings, and now I was changing them again. I really didn't know a lot about where I was going except it was warmer and cheaper. I said goodbye to my new friends, and out the door I went with all my gear to the airport. I took a quick bus to the train station to the airport, and I knew how to do it. Now it had only been a little over a week, and yet I just felt comfortable here. At least I had the transportation and food/drink thing down to a science, and really, what more do you need?

This was my first flight ever where I was the only white person on board. It was 90 percent Japanese and 9.99 percent other Asians, and then that 1 percent, yep, that was me. It was going to be a six-hour flight. I had a middle seat, which basically sucks ass, and nobody spoke English. It was crazy to listen to the announcements on the plan and not have a single clue what they were saying. So basically, if we went down, I was frigging screwed because I didn't know where the exits were, and I didn't know how to put on my life vest. *Oh, Lord, don't take me now; I don't have a fighting chance. Ha ha ha...* I did not know anyone at this time in my life that had been to Thailand. It wasn't a tourist destination for Americans at this point in life. The world has since opened up, and Thailand is now a major destination for travelers.

TAKE A DECADE

The plane landed at Bangkok International Airport, and it was already dark out. I had a plan, and that was to make my way to Khaosan Road. There were several cheap places to stay in that area. The one I was looking at was on a street just next to Khaosan Road. I found an ATM at the airport and took out some money, 500,000 baht. I could have taken a million but didn't want to be greedy. As of now, I was not sure of the currency exchange, so this should be enough.

After getting my bags, I found a transportation help desk, and believe it or not, they had an area for cabs going to Khaosan Road. Perfect. When I found the spot outside the airport to catch a cab and when I approached the area, I noticed a couple standing there with backpacks on. I asked them if they were going in the same direction I was, and they were, I recommended we share a cab, and they were all for it. It cost us each like 7,000 baht, which was like US $3, not bad. The cab pulled up, and we told him where we wanted to go. He helped us with our bags in the back of his car, and then we got in; I sat up front and they had the back. When I sat down, the driver made a joke about not having to work tonight. He said, "You drive, ha ha." It was then I realized that I was sitting in the driver's seat. They had the opposite thing that we have. They drove from the right side of the car and drove on the left side of the road. It was so weird to sit in a car on the left side and not drive. It was a first for me, and I just sat back and feared for my life as we made it through the city. Their driving is much different, much more offensive than ours.

Khaosan Road is so unique; this is a world-famous backpacker's ghetto. It is a short street about ¾ of a mile but the heart of this city. It was filled with people selling everything from food to DVDs. The smell of food being prepared filled the air with different aromas, none that I recognized at all. The music, which was a lot of trance music, was blaring all over from shop to shop. The streets were filled with people, and yes, everyone was looking at me. This place was like nothing I had ever seen before. It was a quick walk down the first time because I was a little on the nervous side and wanted to get rid of my backpacks. You are really vulnerable when carrying your gear. It's harder to move, and you definitely can't run very far. I didn't feel threatened at all; it's just that this street was very different. How many streets have you seen a pig's head for sale, which is covered in flies, and someone making food right next to it? At the end of the street, I made a left, and the street I needed was the next one.

The place that I had chosen was right around the corner and seemed okay. I had my own room with a bed, dresser, and a ceiling fan. That was about it, nothing fancy at all. The furniture and bed were probably twenty years old, and it was cheap. I received fresh sheets from the desk and a key for my room. It was warm here, and I'd already worked up a sweat. It was much warmer than Tokyo. The shower was outside across the yard, just a small room with a few places to clean up, basic plumbing to say the very least. It was a pipe with an on/off valve for the water—no hot water, but with the temperature, you really didn't need hot water.

Once I got situated and had a place to store my gear, I was out to see more of this street. It was late, and all I wanted was something to eat and a beer. I was going to grab some information if possible and wait for the sun to come up before I explored too far. You see, this was a place where someone could disappear real quick and nobody would know. I had only seen a few white people but definitely no Americans.

That night, I was asked to buy everything from clothes, paintings, fake ID, chocolate-covered grasshoppers, knock-off DVDs, and yes, women. All I wanted was a few beers and something to eat. While walking down the street, it was easy to find a beer; the local Singha beer was my choice. A beer cost me like $0.60, and that was a great thing. It made me very happy to know that things were cheaper here. Now for food, this was not easy to find. There were a ton of people selling food. I just had no idea what it was. I passed this one guy cooking what looked like fried rice. He made each portion separately in this big wok right on the street. It was a little oil then an egg, a cup or so of rice, and a few green onions. This looked good, and that is what I ate that first night. The cost was about $0.15 for a portion that filled me up just fine. It was served with a plastic fork and what looked like a container you would get a hot dog served in. It was cheap and fresh, which was all I needed at this point.

Tomorrow would be a new day. There was so much to see, and I had ten days here, so let's hope it was worth coming here.

My first day in Bangkok and I was excited about what I might come across. I left my room and headed out with a day pack and my camcorder. So far, I'd gotten some great footage of the parts of Japan that I had seen and would now get some footage of Khaosan Road. I was a little hesitant to take my camcorder out at night, so today would be the first. As I walked up the street, I bought a pastry and water for breakfast, just something quick off the street. Then this gentleman approached and asked if I wanted to see Bangkok and some of the Buddhas that Bangkok was famous for. He spoke okay English, and we were able to communicate. At this point, I was up for anything, and except for the person running my hostel, it was the first real conversation I had with anyone. So he became my new best friend. He told me this: "I take you to three Buddhas, Grand Palace Wat Arun, Wat Pho, and a floating market. It will take about four hours, and you see the city." It was going to cost me about $10 to have a private guide show me around the city, some of the major sites, and I got to ride in a *tuk tuk*. This was an easy choice. "Hell yes, sounds good and sounds like a great way to spend half of the day." We loaded up, and I went through the streets of Bangkok in a *tuk tuk*, which is a motorized three-wheel vehicle with a comfortable seat and a roof over you to block the sun. It was an open-air experience and a great way to see the city. What a trip being where I was right now. I just hoped for a good day and that I didn't end up dead somewhere in this city.

We started at the Grand Palace, which is where the king and queen of Thailand hold all their special functions. It was a *palace*, and that was for sure. Large pillars held up the red-tiled roof with the white walls all around. The arches made up what were outdoor walkways. The landscaping alone was picture-perfect. They spent a lot of time caring for this place. It had a remarkable design and larger-than-life feel to it. It wasn't a castle but more of a very ritzy hotel, except this building was for one family and one family only. Large portraits hung outside the palace with the picture of the king and queen. This place was basically our White House or Parliament; it was impressive, and my personal guide gave me plenty of time to do whatever I want. He was very knowledgeable of what we were seeing and answered any questions I had.

After that, we headed to see my first Buddha. It was the Emerald Buddha, which is considered the "palladium" of the Kingdom of Thailand. The word *palladium* means "an image or object of great importance that the city or nation depends upon for safety or protection." It was impressive to see this Buddha in a yoga position; it was made of jade (a green stone), and his clothes were made out of gold. This was the protector of a great nation, and it was only twenty-six inches tall. It was in the temple of the Emerald Buddha right in Bangkok. We then went to see one of the most impressive things I have ever seen: the Reclining Buddha. It is at Wat Pho temple, which is not far. We parked and as I followed the crowd toward the temple, I could see monks walking around and praying all over the place. The large thin steeples that towered out of all the roofs were very cool to see. These temples were no joke; they were used on a daily basis for education and prayer. It was very much a holy place just like the other temples we had been to. I walked up the stairs and noticed that people were removing their shoes before they entered. I'm glad I noticed this before I just walked in.

With shoes off, I walked in and was blown away by the size of this Buddha. The relining Buddha was 140 feet long, 45 feet tall, and the Buddha's feet were fifteen feet long. It was gold-plated and decorated in a mother-of-pearl illustration of a Buddha. The Buddha was lying on its side with his head up and feet pointed out. Holy cow, this was one of the coolest things I'd ever seen; it was right up there with the Roman Colosseum and Eiffel Tower. After spending about twenty minutes just staring and walking around the Reclining Buddha, there was so much more to see. Rows of golden Buddha's sitting in a lotus position lined the entire wall. The chapels on the property contained close to four hundred Buddha images. I only saw a portion that day. I walked up these stairs, and inside this chapel, there were monks praying and performing some sort of religious thing. There were people sitting inside on the floor watching what was going on. So I removed my shoes and found a place to sit down.

I was on my butt with arms behind me and legs pointed out with my feet crossed. I was comfortable and just relaxing. Well, I had been sitting there for about two minutes, and then a monk dressed in the brown robe with a white rope around his waist pointed at my legs and said something in Thai. I really didn't understand but felt real uncomfortable and just stood up and walked out. Was it because I was white, or was I doing something wrong?

Well, when I got back to my guide, I told him what happened, and he explained what I did wrong. He said, "You were sitting on your butt with your feet pointed toward the Buddha, right?" He explained that feet are the lowest and dirtiest place on your body; it is very rude to point these toward any Buddha, which is why you always see people kneeling on their legs while worshiping a Buddha. The monk was actually just trying to correct me, but I couldn't understand.

The next stop was the golden Buddha, which for me had the coolest story. It was located in the temple of Wat Traimit, Bangkok, Thailand, with a weight of 12,125 lbs. and was about 10 feet tall. So this Buddha had been covered in stucco and glass for almost two hundred years. In 1955, the Buddha was going to be relocated, and when they strapped it up to move it, some of the straps broke due to the weight, and it fell to the ground. What happened next is part of history. Some of the plaster and painted glass had broken from the base, and what was revealed is now considered priceless. It was a Buddha made out of solid gold. It was actually nine parts that fit together, and when they were excavating the Buddha, they found a key that was used to disassemble it to move it properly. The way this was made and the design to create this was so frigging many years ago, like 2,500 years ago. It was just a very cool thing to see with your own eyes.

The next stop for my great day so far was the floating market. This place was on the water, and those long boats sold just about everything you could want. All I could say by this time was that I was glad I'm not driving. It was nerve-racking enough just being the passenger. Anyway, we made it, and I was given some time just to walk around and check out the sites. Okay, this place seemed very dirty to me right away. First of all, the water that all the boats were on was a dark-brown color with garbage floating in the water that you could see. There had to be at least one hundred boats that I could see when I first approached the banks. They were mostly open-bow boats with a canopy of some sort covering a portion of the boat. There was a smell of fuel, stale water, and garbage in the air. Yet to be able to see this was incredible. It may not be the cleanest area, but it was one of the most unique places I had seen. I did buy some pastries from an older lady operating one of the boats and a bag of freshly cut fruit from another boat. I had to get something just to say that I did buy something from the floating market in Bangkok. This was one of those things that I had pictured seeing on TV and being like, *Wow, that would be a cool place to see*, and here I was seeing it for real.

The tour was almost over; I had spent at least four hours with this guy and had seen a lot. What a cool deal to be able to travel around Bangkok for half the day by *tuk tuk*. This was what I wanted to see, some of the bigger sites and things that I had never seen before. I still couldn't believe I was actually here in Bangkok, Thailand.

On our way back to Khaosan Road, my driver stopped at this jewelry store and asked me to come in. I was thinking to myself, *The last place I want is to see is the inside of a jewelry store, maybe the inside of a bar, but not a jewelry store*. He walked in and pretty much insisted I follow him, so in I went. There were three people working, all dressed in suits and dresses. They were very proper and spoke great English. I was greeted like I was royalty and had made this appointment. The guy, who was in his late twenties, started showing me watches, rings, and raw stones like I had asked to be there. I just kept saying, "Yes, that is nice and looks expensive." He then asked if I wanted to make money while being here in Thailand. I knew this was going to get interesting real quick. The guy told me if I bought any precious metals, gold, silver, or precious gems like rubies or sapphires, you could pay a fraction of the cost compared to what they are worth in the United States. Now for the catch: You can't actually take them with you. The deal was you buy them today, and they would ship them to your address back in the States. You could spend $100 and make $1,000 real easily.

Okay, sure, this sounded great if it were only true. This was the part of the tour that I had not signed up for and wasn't expecting. My driver and guide was there the whole entire time and knew there was only one way to get out of this, and that was to play along. So I agreed to try this and decided on a small bar of gold. He was going to mail this to me, and I could sell it for so much more than what I would pay for it. Now I did not want this, and I did not believe for one second that this would get shipped to the United States for me. However, I had to play along to get out of this situation. I agreed and handed him a credit card. The problem was my credit card would not go through. I had given them an old credit card that had expired, and I knew it would not work. They tried about ten times, and finally, I said, "Hey, guys, thanks for the opportunity, but it doesn't look like it is going to happen for me, oh well." That is when I walked up to my driver and said it was time to go. He shook his head, and we left the building. He would have received money if I had purchased something, I'm sure of it, but not my money. Sorry, buddy. It was just a big-ass scam from the beginning, and I soon found out later that they took your money and mailed you a fake stone or watch worth about as much as you paid for it. Nothing was real, and it was all just a way to scam tourists. My driver dropped me off at the corner of my street, and I thanked him and gave him a $5 tip for the day.

The guy that ran my hostel told me that today was a holiday and things would be closed. Tonight was going to be a special night of celebration and it was to "thank the rain gods'" for a healthy harvest. He told me the streets would be packed with people, music, and it would be a very big deal for the locals. I had no clue, but after my little nap and a quick shower, I was back out on the streets. This time, I brought my camcorder.

The streets were on fire with people. Everyone was running around laughing and having a blast. The music was loud, and the Thai people were dressed in more authentic clothes with bright colors. The thing to do was to buy these small floating bamboo candles, light them, and then walk down to the river, place it in the water, say a prayer, and that was that. When I placed mine in the water, there must have been two thousand of these floating by where I was standing. The whole country gave some sort of thanks and had a celebration for this event.

As I was wandering around watching people, I had my camcorder going and was capturing parts of this huge event. I walked by this girl and guy, thinking they were just a young couple; they were both white, so that excited me. There really weren't a lot of white people around. As I approached them, I pointed my camcorder at them and asked if they were enjoying the festivities. She spoke first and said they were having a blast. Her accent was very strong, and I asked her if she was German, and yes, she was. The guy then spoke, and he had a British accent. They were both full of smiles and were happy to talk for a while. They were a really cool couple, and they said they were on their way to get a drink and asked if I wanted to join them. I said, "Well, I'll have to ask all my other friends if it's okay to take off for a while." They both laughed, and I now had someone to hang out with. The German girl, her name was Connie, was 5'4" with short dark hair, a pretty face, and a stunning body. I was attracted to her right from the beginning. The guy from England, James, who was 5'7" and 160 lbs. with blond hair, looked very prim and proper. He had that British accent that I enjoy listening to so much. He was not from London and made that clear, he grew up north of the city, which meant he followed different British football teams than the city people as he described it.

We found a café outside and grabbed a table. Beers were ordered, and we started talking about everything. We had a great conversation and drank a lot of beers. It was about an hour into the conversation that I asked where they met and how long they had been together. Turns out they met two days before where they were both staying. Things just got a little better for me knowing she was single, but I didn't want to upset James. For now, it was just nice to have met a few people that I could hang out with.

I was not sure what time it was, but we decided to leave and go back to their place. I was game for anything, and their place was only a few streets away from where I was staying. James, out of nowhere, asked me if I smoked weed, and I told him yes. He said he knew where to get some if we wanted. I was feeling no pain at that time, and it was still dark out, so we all agreed to leave and find some of the good stuff. We followed him to this really sketchy building. It was an outdoor/indoor bar that looked like a place I really should not be going to. It was dark inside; everyone was looking at us with a look of "What the fuck are you doing here?" We found a small table in the back and sat down. This really nasty-looking woman approached and asked what we wanted. James ordered three beers and asked if so-and-so was here. The beers came, and I just couldn't stop thinking about how people could just disappear in life and never be found. This was a place where this could happen. We laughed about the situation and enjoyed our short time there. It took this guy about five minutes to show up; James made the deal, and we quickly finished our beers. It was time to get the hell out of this place. No need to look danger in the eye any longer than necessary.

We reached their place, which was not as nice as mine. This doesn't mean much, just my place felt more central. They had two separate rooms, and we went to James's room, and he rolled up a big, fat joint. As we smoked, they told me they were leaving tomorrow morning for an island off the coast of Thailand. This was something that I wanted to do and now had someone to go with. We discussed this over a smoke and beer, and within about thirty minutes, I had made my decision and I was going with them. How cool would it be to hang out on a tropical island for five days or so? Connie and James were my new best friends, and we had a plan. After an hour or so, it was time for me to stumble back to my place and get ready for the next day.

Now this next part is for certain eyes only, and it was something that happened on the way back that has made for a great story. While walking home, I was approached by this person. *She* was about 5'2" and weighed about 100 lbs. *She* was a cute little Thai girl that was going to show me a good time. *She* was very upfront and told me she would take good care of me and walked me toward this alleyway. I followed like a drunken idiot and thought that everything was all good. Well, we stopped in this alleyway, and *she* started to feel me up. Of course, at this time, I was having a hard time just standing, let alone doing anything. As we stood there, I kept trying to grab her and feel her up a little. Well, this *girl* was like Bruce Lee and avoided me touching her at all cost. It took about two minutes, and I grabbed hold of her boobs, and guess what, they weren't boobs at all. She—I mean *he*—was wearing a bra with balloons or something in there. At about the same time, I could feel her reaching in my pockets trying to pickpocket me. It took about three seconds to realize what was happening, and I freaked out. I grabbed *him* by his face and threw *him* down on the ground. I pointed my finger at him and said, "Not only are you a dude, you're a thief, you piece of shit." Now it was time to get the hell out of here before my little friend started to scream or something else. After this little experience, it didn't take me long to walk home as I kept looking over my shoulder for someone following me. It was a relief when I walked in my door and used a chair to secure the door so no one could get in. That was a close one in many different fashions.

The next day, actually more like early afternoon because I was not feeling very good, we met up at their place and booked our tickets for the island of Koh Pha-Ngan. My next adventure was going to be a tropical island that had a world-famous full-moon party every month. We knew that the full moon was last night, but so much would still be going on, and it would be well worth the trip. We had bought the cheapest way to get to this place. It was going to be an overnight bus that would take close to twelve hours to get to the port then a two-hour ferry ride to the island and then a thirty-minute taxi ride to where we wanted to go, and that was Hat Rin Beach. This was the center of this famous party, and even though we were getting there a day late, it still should be fun.

That afternoon, we tried to take in a few more sights. We left each other for a few hours before our departure, and this gave me time to get a few things done. I had been in Thailand for a short time and had already bought a bunch of stuff. Everything here was just so cheap, and I wanted it all. I bought something I still have and have never once used. It is a bong made out of bamboo with an old man's face carved on the front. It was just one of those things I had to have, and for $3, how can you go wrong? I didn't want to carry everything like I had in Europe, so I found a post office and mailed a box home.

Around five or so, I met up with Connie and James at the bus station. We knew we were in for a long night in order to get to the island. It was going to be a twelve-hour bus ride, then a ferry to the island, and then we were not sure. It would be something we would take care of once we were there. The bus left Bangkok, and we were on our way. James sat right behind Connie and me. We had something to drink and a few snacks for the trip. We would be stopping along the way to eat and stretch our legs.

The next twelve hours on this bus can be summed up in just one word: *long*. The roads were not the greatest, filled with potholes and a lot of traffic. Cars, buses, trucks, and a ton of motorcycles passed by us as the night went by. We did stop about every four to five hours, always at a place where you could buy food and get something to drink. Just to stand up and walk around was a blessing to the legs. We had fun along the way, and the three of us really enjoyed each other's company. We met another guy, who was sitting next to James, so we started thinking we could find a place for all four of us and maybe save some money. We napped, and Connie and I had some small talk along the way. She was one of those people who really didn't share a lot of herself and her story. She was from Germany and needed some time away from her life. She had ended a relationship but didn't talk much about it. We were probably about halfway there when we kissed for the first time. This made the trip go by a little faster. At least I had something else to do than just stare out of the window at the dark jungle.

We arrived at the port, and now we had to catch a three-hour ferry ride to the island. It was at least daylight by now, and I loved being on a boat, so this part was fun. We found a spot for the four of us to relax and enjoyed a few beers on our three-hour boat tour. The water was so blue, the air was warm, the sun was shining, and it was a beautiful day.

We arrived at the southern port of the island, and we had our sights set for staying near Haad Rin. This was the place to be, and it was the place to party all night long. So at the port, we caught a ride/taxi to the other side of the island. This was not your usual yellow cab; nope, this was a pickup truck with a bench seat on each side that fit about eight people. It was not the most comfortable way of getting around, but it was cheap, and it was all we needed. All I knew was that I was now on a tropical Thailand island, and it was beautiful. Palm trees were everywhere, the white-sand beaches could be seen from the truck, and the place just looked so relaxing.

We were dropped off at a small building near the center of town. There were people waiting to sell you accommodations, and James found a lady that had a bungalow for rent that was right on the beach. It would sleep four and had its own bathroom and was only going to cost us $4 each a night. What a deal, so we followed her down the beach to be our place, and it was perfect. It was just down the beach from where all the bars and restaurants were located and was literally right on the beach. It was a wooded building about ten feet by twenty feet with two full beds and a bathroom/shower in the next room. Now our bathroom was a toilet without a toilet seat, and the shower was a piece of PVC pipe that came out of the wall. It was all very simple, and for us, it was perfect. The lady who rented our place—we called her Mamasan—was an older lady who was very pleasant and helpful. We paid her for the night, and before she left, she told us, "Anything you need while you're here, come and see me—laundry, food, entertainment, beer, smoke, and transport—you come and see me."

As soon as she left, we all sat back, and James and I both looked at each other and said, "Did she say smoke?" We dropped our gear on the beds. Connie and I had decided we would share a bed, which got me excited. I then told the guys, "I'm going to find our Mamasan and just see what she was talking about when she said something about *smoke*."

They were all happy I was willing to ask this question, and I left. She was in the next building cooking, and I asked her politely what she meant about "smoke," and she laughed at me and said, "You want to buy good Thai bud?"

"Yes, I do, and thank you very much." I told her that I had heard it was very much taboo and very illegal.

She said, "Don't worry, it's all good here on the island. Just smoke in your place, not on the beach, and you'll be okay." That was all I needed to hear, and she sold me a bag of weed for $10, and we were ready to have a good time. Back to the room, and I was the hero for the day. We enjoyed our little gift, and all I wanted to do was jump in the water. We all had the same idea; we got changed and walked out of our bungalow. It was like watching a movie, but we all lined up and walked into the sea holding hands—well, I guess it was just Connie and me that held hands. The water was lukewarm, crystal clear, and about as good as it gets. We played around in the water for a good hour and decided it was time to check out the town. We went back, cleaned up, and changed, and now, it was time to check out the town.

Okay, here I was on an island in the Gulf of Thailand on Sunrise Beach in Haad Rin. This was a small town on the southern tip of Ko Pag Yon. This place had been a backpackers' destination since the eighties with its full moon party every month. Now we knew that last night was the actual full moon, but we heard the party lasted for at least three days. So tonight should be an interesting evening.

This place was small and so amazing. The town was centered on Chicken Corner, a crossroads for anything you would need. Restaurants, gift shops, bars, open-air rooms, just like I said, anything you needed was right here. You could grab a beer and walk around the streets. The place was busy; there were a lot of people here from all over the world. It was just amazing watching people enjoy the moment. Right from the beginning of getting out of the truck, I knew this place was going to be a *happy* place—just filled with really good energy and everyone was having fun.

The restaurants were all open-air. It seemed like you always had a view of the clear blue water; that was the main reason any of us were even here. It was a frigging paradise. Most of the places to eat—a lot of them were pizza places—had this cool thing: Eat a meal and watch a movie at the same time. The places had tables and chairs, but also had couches, beanbag chairs, and some actually had hammocks. Next to the menu that was hung outside of each place, they also had their movie schedule for the day. It was a good idea, but I just didn't see myself sitting during the day watching a movie. I wanted to explore this island and check out the sights.

It was around two, and we decided to eat. We found a place and had a great cheap meal: rice, chicken, veggies, and a beer for like $4. I then bought a pack of cigarettes for $1.50 and a tall boy for $0.60 and went down to the beach again to sit and relax. The four of us just sat there enjoying our day. It was so surreal to be sitting on this beach in this part of the world. I can honestly say I never thought this would happen to me.

As the day started to turn to night, you could feel the energy in the air getting stronger, and the music was getting louder. We could hear trance music and see the light of the bars that are right on the beach. There was the sound of the waves hitting the shore, the sound of good music, and the beach was filling up with people. Life was good, and it was only going to get better.

The bar we walked into was right on the beach; the front was completely opened with the view of the sea right there. This bar was like a huge round tent with bamboo supports and a thatched ceiling.

We sat down and ordered a beer. The bartender served our drinks and then asked if we wanted a "tea." We were not sure what he was talking about, so James asked and came to find out mushrooms were legal here and he could make us a magic mushroom tea.

Our bartender made us each a tea, which was in a coffee cup with warm water, lemon, honey, and mushrooms. The cost of this drink was $5 and well worth it. We all said a little something and proceeded to enjoy our drink. The mushrooms had softened a little but still tasted like shit, oh well. We finished our drinks, and we were ready for a great evening. It was so much fun to have a few people that I had just met be part of a night I'll never forget.

The night was great, full of laughter and smiles the entire evening. We partied on the beach all night long going from the beach to the bar and back to the beach. For the most part, I hung out near the water. We just walked up and down, back and forth. I met this girl from Israel and ended up making out with her in the water with our clothes on. It was just one of those nights. We started around dusk, and it was now close to 2:00 a.m. The party was still going. This would be one party I would never forget.

It was around 5:00 a.m. when I made it back to my bungalow. The other three had left earlier, and I was the last one to come home. We were exhausted from traveling all day and then partying all night. It had been a full day; that was for sure. Connie and I shared a bed; nothing happened, just rested my hand between her boobs and went to sleep with a smile on my face.

My first morning on a tropical island in Thailand, I got out of bed, walked out the door, made a quick left, walked about twenty feet to the sea, got about waist deep, and dove in. The water was warm and so refreshing. Wow, what a night. Sex, drugs, and rock 'n' roll—well, no sex, but I did fool around with two different girls—ate mushrooms, and listened to some damn good trance music all night long. Hung out with my new friends and had a wonderful night. Had a good morning swim, which helped out with the hangover a little bit, and headed back to our bungalow. James was searching for something as soon as I walked in. He had misplaced a 500,000 baht bill, worth about $25. Not a lot of money but enough for a full day on this island. He looked all over and searched his bags. After a short time, he concluded it was gone. He had either dropped it on the beach last night or gotten robbed somehow.

We walked into town and did a little shopping. Connie bought a really nice top and a new sarong. I bought a tapestry that looked really cool. The three of us just walked around and enjoyed the open-air shops. Then we ate. It was then that I noticed Connie always getting the cheapest thing on the menu, the same thing every meal so far, and that was rice with veggies, no meat, and it cost about $1.25. She just spent money on clothes, the room, and a few beers throughout the day but so little on food. Oh well, it was her deal not mine. It did interest me, though.

That day, I rented a dirt bike and rode around the island, the forest on one side and the beautiful Gulf of Thailand on the other. To me it was like all the Vietnam movies I'd seen with the palm trees, dense woods, and beautiful sea. The roads were narrow but accessible. I passed buses, cars, donkeys, and mopeds that were built for two but had five people on them. I had it for two days, and it cost me about $8. I refueled it before I returned it, and it was from an old-fashioned pump. You see the fuel in the top of the glass container, and then it was siphoned to the tank. The cost was $0.65. This was why this place is so cool, tropical, warm, and laid-back; it was a party town and very cheap.

So that night, we did about the same as the night before, dinner and then the party. It was another night of a full-moon party on a beautiful beach. There were not as many people as the previous night, but still the beach was full. Around midnight, I remember sitting on the beach with my camcorder and recording an interview with myself. It was at the time that I decided I was going to spend the next five years of my life traveling as much as I could. I was thirty-one years old, and I decided right there on that beach on Koh Pang Yan that I was going to keep traveling. Where I didn't know and how I didn't know, but it was what I was going to do. It was my life, and I was going to live it the way I wanted.

The next morning, we all got up around the same time. By now, Connie and I kissed and slept in the same bed, but that was about it. It was more like the three of us were just one couple and worked well together. It was this morning that I went to check my finances and realized I was now missing a 500,000 baht note. This did not sit well with me at all. I looked everywhere, and they helped look, and just as James had lost money the day before, it was now my turn. Well, you can't cry over spilt milk, so all you can do is just move on, and after I smoked a joint, I was all good again and ready to eat. I just hate losing money, and I'm always smart about where I keep it; something just wasn't right.

Again, Connie bought clothes and ate the cheapest meal. It seemed like she had no money and then had money. She spent it quickly and then was broke again. Well, it was another day on this tropical island. If you have ever watched the movie *The Beach* with Leonardo DiCaprio, it's a lot like that kind of paradise—beautiful beaches, warm air, sea breeze, and amazing scenery. One thing that we noticed on day two was that for about two hours every day, it rained—not just a little trickle but a downpour. It was in the tropics, and we were in the rainy season. Now remember me saying that I could not see myself sitting on a couch watching a movie while I was here. Well, after two nights and two days of having a *great* time, we needed a break, and we did actually enjoy a couple of movies. I watched *The Beach* for the very first time while I was there. It was like watching the *Titanic* while on a boat. It was just so surreal watching a movie about a beach in Thailand, and I was on the same island that this movie originated from. It was mostly filmed on another island, but the story started on this island. I think we had three to four days that this was what we did around 2:00 p.m. to 4:00 p.m. during the rain.

Between the people, landscape, cost, and overall beauty, this was the most incredible place I had ever been. True paradise. It was, however, my last night when I realized what was happening to our money: Connie had been supporting her trip by stealing money from others. James had left some money lying around, and I went out that morning for a quick swim, and when I returned, some of it was missing. I wasn't going to call her out but would inform James at some point.

It was my final morning of six days of a great time, and now, it was back to Japan for more adventure. It was actually a sad moment saying goodbye to my two new friends. Even though Connie stole from me, it was sad to say goodbye. I gave both of them a big hug, wished them well, and said goodbye. It was going to be a long day, and my body was hurting by then and needed a little break.

This was my travel day, and it was a long one. We were up at 7:00 a.m. and in the back of a truck by 7:30 a.m. It was a half-hour ride to the port and then a three-hour ferry ride to the mainland of Thailand. Then I was lucky enough to get the last seat on the bus, which was by the bathroom and the middle seat, basically the worst possible seat on a bus. It was a twelve-hour bus ride from hell, hot and sticky, and I was so tired by then but had nothing to lean on to sleep. I would put my pack on my lap and lean my head on my pack, but this was only good for a short time. We stopped along the way just like we did coming down, and this gave me time to stretch and get something to eat. After twelve hours of a long, exhausting bus ride we were back in Bangkok. I then got on another bus that took me to the airport. I arrived about two hours early, and this gave me time to eat something and find my gate. Then I had a three-hour flight back to Tokyo, Japan, which finally gave me a chance to sleep, and I think I slept most of the way. After arriving at the airport, I then had a thirty-minute train ride into the city then another bus to my new place to stay. So let's see—I went from a truck to ferry to bus to bus to plane to train and to another bus! This whole travel day took me about twenty hours, and all I really wanted at this point was a shower and a bed.

I did choose another hostel to stay in when I got back to Japan, and it did feel good to be back in Japan. I had a great time in Thailand and had so much fun; it just seemed like I was back to business and ready to continue what I started. So yes, I did choose to stay at a new place. I liked the last place and will miss my little Aussie girl, but I wanted to have my own room and not have to sleep on the floor with five other guys. I found a place not far from the other place, just a little nicer. I walked in the door, and there was a Japanese guy about forty years old sitting behind a window. I waited for him to get off the phone, and I then noticed just to my right four people sitting in a common area. They had been talking, but when I walked in carrying my bags, they stopped and took a moment to check me out.

The guy asked my name. I told him and said I had called earlier from the airport. He had my reservation but told me he only had room for me for one night. He may have a room opening up tomorrow; he just wouldn't know until morning. Oh well, one night was good for me right now. I got all checked in, and he came out from the office to show me around. I walked by the four sitting at the table, three guys and one girl. One guy was German, about twenty-six; one guy was Australian, about fifty; one guy was from Iran, about thirty-five; and the girl was from Italy, and she was about twenty-eight. They made the comment about how we didn't know who the president was at the time.

I walked down the hall. There were rooms on both sides, very small. My room was at the end of the hall across from bathrooms that were closed until morning. That sucked, but it was the custom. Oh well. My room was the size of a large jail cell. I could almost touch the sides and had enough room for a roll-out bed, a small fridge, a fourteen-inch TV, and one chair. That was it, but it was all mine, and I didn't have to share anything or worry about things going missing.

I dropped off my stuff, and as I walked out of my room, I got to the four people sitting there and told the group that I was going to get a beer and send out a quick email. They told me they were going nowhere and they would be here when I got back. I found a store close by and bought some food and drinks; an internet café was also close, and I sent out a message to James. I came to find out he had caught on to her little thing and they had gone their separate ways. I hoped for the best for Connie, but that's not a way to travel.

When I got back, the four of them were still there, and I finally sat down and got to know them. The German was a grad student, the Aussie was a pot farmer, the Iranian guy was exiled from his country, and the Italian girl was on a long-term vacation if she could find a job. The five of us hit it off right away. We joked back and forth, and we enjoyed listening to each other's stories. We spent about two hours talking and getting to know them, and they all seemed really cool. The Iranian had actually broken out of prison; the reason he was sent to jail was because he disagreed with the government. He left the country and told us he would never be able to return unless the government changed. The Aussie was older and grew pot illegally and would sell his product and travel somewhere each year. The Italian girl had actually smuggled cocaine up her ass and sold it to the Israeli that she had met here in Tokyo. Her plan was to find a job and stay for as long as she could. They were all as different as it gets, and all had a crazy story to tell. After about an hour talking with them, I instantly liked them, and once again, I had a group of friends to hang out with.

During this time, I took in more of the city and culture and made a few plans for the next part of my trip. A few of us went out one night and went to the Americano Bar, which is a place that white people go, I guess. It was so cool to walk down the street with three other guys, a German, an assize, and a guy from Iran. We were friends now, and it was like we had known each other for years. I love traveling; you can meet people so easily and become friends so quickly. You could tell this bar we went to was a place to pick up

Japanese women if you wanted. For the most part by now, it was more fun to hang out with my new friends and not worry about the women. Not that I didn't want to, it was just a night for a few guys to hang out and just enjoy a night out on the town. We had a few beers and went to another place then to another place and then to another. It was about midnight when we realized we had missed the last train back to our side of the city. We could have taken a cab, but it would cost $120 for a forty-five-minute ride. This was out of all our budgets, so we realized at this point, it was going to be a long night. It was back to the Americano for a cheap beer, and we waited until we had to leave. That happened around 3:00 a.m. when they closed, and at this time, we were back on the streets. It sounds so tragic, but we had a lot of fun just walking the streets and loving the scenery of all the girls walking around. We were like four high school boys talking about each girl that walked by. By this time, we all had a nice buzz, and sleep deprivation was setting in, so we were all a little loopy by this time.

Five o'clock arrived, and we were at the train station ready to go home. We were back to our side of the city by 6:00 a.m. and back to our home shortly after that. It was a long night, and all I did that day was sleep, wake up and eat, and then go back to sleep. The next day was going to be busy; I was finally making my way to Mt. Fuji.

This had been the one thing that I really wanted to do while I was in Japan. It was about sixty miles from Tokyo and cost around $75 one way. This was pricey for my budget, but I had to see this mountain.

The next morning, I was up and packed and ready for my next adventure. The guys and Silvia, the Italian girl, were still going to be here when I got back. They all had another week before moving on, so I would see them when I returned. The train ride was only about two hours and a good view of the countryside along the way. As of now, it had only been the city that I had seen. So when we got out of the city limits, it was nice to see farmland and green rolling hills.

The plan was to find a room, whether it was my own place or a hostel, then get information on getting to the mountain. Then I may try and get to Kyoto for a few days. I had been told by several people that hitchhiking was a good form of transportation around Japan and a whole lot cheaper. That was my plan right now for the next two to four days, and we would see if it worked out.

The town of Fujinomiya was where I stayed the first night. It is the main starting point for trips to Mt. Fuji, and it was just a small little town on the edge of a natural wonder as far as I'm concerned. It was on the train to this town that I was able to see this amazing mountain for the first time. Mt. Fuji is a snow-capped volcanic mountain 12,389 feet tall. It is a major symbol for Japan; it represents a physical, cultural, and spiritual way for Japanese people. The mountain cannot be missed as it is the only large land mass in the area. Even from the train, I could see that it was green for a portion of the mountain, and then the snow started about three fourths from the bottom. It is truly just one of those things that you have to see with your own two eyes.

When I reached the train station, I found a place to stay, which was only about a ten-minute walk. It was a little on the expensive side, $65 a night, yet the cheapest place I could find near the station. It was more of a hotel room, but when I opened the window of my room, there it was again. How cool is it to have Mt. Fuji as your natural landscape right out your window. This hotel was also a stop to pick up people to take them up to the mountain, so I would not have to go any further than outside to catch a ride. The lady who ran and owned the place told me it would take forty-five minutes to an hour to get to the base of the mountain. The weather wasn't tropical like Thailand; it was more like New York. On average, it was forty-five to fifty degrees, so I had been wearing as much as I could. I did have pants, long-sleeved shirts, and one semi-warm jacket. I wasn't cold but had to keep layers on to stay warm during the day. I found a place to eat and grabbed a few beers and something to munch on in my room. The town was small, and there was not a lot to do except stare at this mountain.

The next morning, around 10:00 a.m., I checked out of my room. The bus picked me up at my hotel, and we stopped to pick up a few more people close to where I was staying. It was a twenty-passenger van, and its main destination on a daily basis was Mt. Fuji.

I was hoping that I would be able to keep my big pack in a locker or something when I got there, so I would not have to hike up the mountain with everything I owned; we would see.

It was an hour's ride through lush green countryside. I sat back and enjoyed the landscape and historical communities along the way. How often have you been on a bus and had the opportunity to see baboons running across the street in front of you? They were like chickens running wild around the streets, though a baboon has teeth and can be very aggressive if not deadly. They hunt in packs and have been known to harm humans. I had the comfort of a bus and was able to just watch them cross the streets in front of us without any danger. The ride was beautiful, and the mountain kept getting bigger and bigger. The snowcap ring that was around the top of the mountain started to get a little more real, and at that point, I wondered just how far up I would be able to hike.

The bus took me up to base camp 5, which is the farthest you can drive; this was good. The parking lot was almost full, with cars and buses, and I checked out the main area to see if they had lockers to store my gear; unfortunately, they did not, and that meant carrying everything I had up the mountain. Oh well, what can you do but start climbing? It had to be around noon when I started the hike. You could see the whole entire mountain, and let me tell you, no photo will compare to seeing this with your own two eyes. It's breathtaking, and I'm so excited that I'm actually here.

Mt. Fuji is an active volcano; it has not erupted since 1707 to 1708 and is 12,389 feet tall. It is one of Japan's three holy mountains, and it is by far one of the most recognizable mountains in the world. From what I had been told, I could do this in about five to six hours. Now the difference here was that I was getting a very late start, and I really don't have the proper gear. I had a pair of jeans with an outer pair of workout pants. I had three shirts on and a windbreaker, and I was wearing my hiking shoes that I had worn for the entire trip. The big issue was that I had all my bags in tow, which was an additional fifty pounds at least. So I really wasn't fully prepared to do this hike, but I was going to get up as far as possible.

TAKE A DECADE

Just shortly up the mountain, about a mile or so, I started noticing people coming down. They had done it correctly and started earlier. Most of the people were Japanese, but I did see a few others that were definitely tourists, just like me. The trail was well marked; it was a very open and exposed area. It was a gradual incline almost from the beginning of the trail and not really hard. I was probably an hour or so going up and still passing people coming down. I could turn around and see a good portion of the trail, and so far, it didn't look like anyone was coming up behind me at this time. I keep climbing and climbing and climbing. Taking a break from now and then to have a drink of water and admire the scenery. I'm now on Mt Fuji, not just looking at it but actually standing on the side of it.

About another hour, I reached the snow line, and it did start to get a little colder. I hiked about another thirty minutes through the snow, and the air was getting thin and my packs were starting to get heavy. I stopped at a point and still did not see anyone behind me, and by this time, which was around three or so, I started to question how far up this mountain I could go. What a shame to be so close and not reach the summit.

So I sat there for about ten minutes and decided that the safe thing to do is to "pull the plug." By this time, I figured I was about 75 percent of the way up Mount Fuji, which was more than anyone else I knew had achieved. So at that point, I started the slow walk back down.

I had hiked for about four hours going uphill and would take probably three hours to get back down. This would give me time to get some photos and enjoy this moment as much as I could. So I hustled to get down the mountain and never saw another person. I got back to the base station and parking lot a little after 5:00 p.m. Right away, I realized something was different when I got back to the parking lot. I noticed that all the cars and buses were gone; the parking lot was frigging *empty*. So at this point, I just wanted to get information, and I started reading some of the signs on the doors and buildings. I realized this place closed at 4:00 p.m. and would remain closed until April 1. This was the last day this upper station would be open. It was the last day to hike to Mt. Fuji from this position. This was all well and good, but why the hell didn't somebody tell me this in the beginning?

This really sucked; I was the only person in this area. I was all alone and stranded on Mt. Fuji, and it was going to be dark in less than two hours. Well, I stood there for about five minutes, looking around and hoping to see someone, anyone. It was going to take me forever to walk back to the town. It had taken us a good hour or so to get here. It will take me four hours to walk back and it will be dark by then. The walk didn't bother me, it was the fact that we had seen so many baboons coming up the mountain and I would have to walk right through their territory. I was wondering how fast and far I could run with fifty pounds on my back while being chased down by a pack of hungry baboons. But I had no other choice and would just have to take my chances.

I walked about an hour and was actually thinking that maybe I should just find a place in the woods to camp for the night. I had a sleeping bag, so I should be able to stay warm, but then I thought of what was out there in the jungles of Japan. Well, at about just that time when things were starting to get a little scary, I was saved. A small bus pulled up and offered me a ride. "Hallelujah!" was all I could say to myself. "I'm saved."

The bus driver was Japanese and spoke no English; he just pointed his finger toward the town and then told me, "I take you." That was all I needed to hear, and I got on the bus. The bus was filled with middle- to late-aged Japanese people. They had probably been on a tour and were heading back to town from somewhere. They all tried to speak to me, which was very challenging because I spoke very little Japanese and they spoke zero English. They were so nice; they gave me food and water and just kept smiling and nodding at me.

They dropped me off on a corner of the street, and they all waved and smiled as they drove away. I felt like I was saying goodbye to my family. "Arigato, arigato." This was such a lucky thing to have happened to me. I seriously could have walked off that mountain and gotten attacked by a pack of baboons and no one would have ever seen me again. Well, I was now safe in town and still had about an hour of daylight.

TAKE A DECADE

When I was staying at my first hostel, the guy had told me that it was rather easy to hitchhike around the country. I had told him about maybe getting to Kyoto, but the fare was really expensive, like $200 for a bus ride, and he had mentioned hitchhiking. I've done it before and it always worked out, just never in a foreign country. It would be a first for me, and at this point, after practically walking off Mount Fuji, I was up for anything. The plan was to find a piece of cardboard and have someone write "Kyoto" in Japanese script then walk up to the highway and hope for the best. I really didn't want to spend another $65 to stay here when I could get to Kyoto and find something a lot cheaper.

About a half mile in town, I found a small store where I could get some supplies for the trip. I first went out behind it to see if they had any cardboard near their trash cans, and they did. So I walked into the store carrying a piece of cardboard and went right up to the cashier. He didn't speak English at all, and this was going to be a challenge. I explained and showed him on a map what I wanted to do and that I needed him to write the word "Kyoto" on this piece of cardboard. The Japanese people were just so polite and tried so hard to help you out. This was definitely a challenge. Lucky for me a guy standing behind me kind of knew what I wanted and between the three of us we figured it out. The clerk wrote on my cardboard, and the guy behind me offered to give me a ride to a good place to catch a ride, which was about twenty minutes away.

I grabbed a few beers and a small bottle of sake, along with some snacks and my cardboard sign. I was ready. I accepted a ride from this perfect stranger and was on my way. He spoke a little English but not enough to carry on a conversation. I realized that the further you get out of the city, the less bilingual the people are. He did, however, really try hard to make me feel comfortable and was so helpful.

My new friend dropped me off on the side of the highway that went toward Kyoto and wished me luck. I thanked him and waved goodbye. I found a spot to stand and used my big backpack as a place to lean the cardboard sign up against so I could keep my hands in my pockets and stay warm. I also was extremely thirsty and needed my hands to drink a beer and eat something. I figured I better get a beer or two into myself before I got a ride; this will ease the nerves a little. It was not going to take long to catch a ride. Any minute now, someone would pull over and give me a lift. That is what I thought. Well, the first half hour went by and nobody stopped, then another thirty minutes went by and still no ride. It was now dark out and getting colder. This really sucked, and it was about that time I wondered what was really written on this sign. Who knew what the guy wrote, but all I knew was nobody was stopping.

After two and a half hours of waiting for a ride, it was now time to come up with a plan B. Maybe Kyoto was not going to happen. It was now close to 10:00 p.m., and the traffic was a lot less than it was when I first started. I really didn't want to spend $65 for a few hours to sleep at the hotel I had stayed at the night before. I know that the train would leave for Tokyo at six in the morning, and I may just have to head back to Tokyo and try something else.

So with my tail between my legs and backpack on my back, I walked off the highway back to town. I was going to find a place to be safe and wait the night out if I could. I wasn't going to get a room because I really could not afford to spend $65 for a few hours. As I walked around the town for an hour or so, I walked by this park and noticed that there were people staying there. They looked like homeless people with the shopping carts and makeshift tents. I thought to myself, *If they are here, it is probably a safe area, and as long as I keep my distance, this could work*. I walked around the outside of the park, keeping a distance from the people, trying not to be noticed by anyone. It was dark, so as long as I kept a distance, they would not see me at all. Well, I found an empty park bench that was a little way away from the others. I sat down for a second, and man oh man, did that feel good. I had been walking or standing all damn day long, had just spent 2.5 hours standing next to a highway, and oh yeah, climbed up Mt. Fuji. Basically, I was beat by this point and just needed to stop for the night.

This park bench was going to be home for the night, and I was happy to have it. I put on another layer of clothes, laid my sleeping bag out on the bench, tied my bags to the bench and to myself, drank a bottle of sake, and it didn't take long to actually fall asleep. My new home was rather comfortable, and so far, no one had noticed me and life was good. The only time I was woken that night was when a group of motorcycles went by, and after I got my heart back to a normal beat, I went right back to sleep. Everyone should try this at some point in your life, sleep on a park bench with a group of homeless people close by. It makes for a great story.

The sun came up, and it was time to move on. The greatest thing about sleeping on a park bench is you don't have to check out—nope, not at all, just get up and go. I walked back to the train station and was on the first train back to Tokyo and back to the same hostel by ten o'clock that morning, and all I really wanted to do was sleep. It had been a long few days, and today was going to be a down day, catching up on sleep and figuring out what to do with my last remaining days in Japan.

My groups of friends were still there, and we all got caught up with what we had been doing. Silvia had gotten a job as a hostess at this club and found a place to stay. The guys were staying for a while, basically until their money ran out and then back home. We sat around most of the day and talked about life and what was on our plans for the rest of our lives. This actually gave me an idea that came up during this conversation, and that was to head north for a few days and check out the shrines of Japan.

The shrines of Japan are located north of the city and they are structures that were made for all the emperors that ruled Japan back in the day. It was a quiet place that had a small town and also had natural hot springs that were said to be beautiful. That was all I needed to hear, and the next day, I was on my way.

For my last adventure while traveling around Japan and now Thailand, I was going north a few hours to a small town called Nikko. It was home to one of Japan's most decorated shrines, Toshogu, and the mausoleum of Tokugawa Leyasu, the founder of the Tokugawa shogunate. I really didn't know anything about these people; it would just be cool to see some very unique Japanese buildings. It would also feel so good to just sit in a hot spring. My body could use a little pampering.

The cost to do a round trip was about the same as one way to Kyoto, and accommodations were around $20 a night. This place was not on my radar at all but sounded like a good place to spend a few days.

On the train, I did have a little scare as I almost got left on a car that was going to be disconnected from the train, and once again, nobody told me. Luckily, the conductor woke me up and made me sit on the first car of the train. You see, each stop we made, the train got smaller and smaller. This was not really a huge tourist destination, so not as big of a train was needed to get there. The trip was beautiful; the landscape was green and plush in the beginning, and then as we got closer to Nikko, the trees turned to an autumn look. The reds and the greens mixed so well together to show off a beautiful place.

The town was small, and it wasn't hard to find a place to sleep. It was the very basic shared shower but my own room. It was all I needed and close to everything. This was a national park, and I'm sure during the summer months, it is very busy. At this time of the year, it was perfect, a slower pace and not as many people.

This was historical Japan at its finest and a great thing for me to see. The first day was all about the shrines, walking around and watching the monks conduct their daily routines. It seemed like each place had some kind of ceremony going on constantly. This is what monks do, and that is pray all day long. They eat very little, talk only when needed, and definitely don't drink beer.

How to describe what the shrines looked like is difficult. They were large open-air structures with high ceilings, gold-plated statues, Oriental design, with amazing colors. Each building represented someone or something different; however it was, they were all so special. There was one building that when you stood in the center and hit a set of sticks together, the whole building would echo. Take one step in either direction and it would not work. It was this kind of time and energy that was put into the creation of these shrines. I did buy a pair of those sticks outside from a local person. They are called echo sticks. Another thing about one of the shrines that I visited that day was that this shrine started the saying "Don't speak, don't see, don't hear." It is that thing we have all seen where you have three monkeys, one with their hand over their month, one over his eyes, and one over their ears. I have seen this bunch of times over my life and seen the pictures of this saying. Now I was actually standing in the shrine that created this famous saying. I did buy a small wall hanging with the three monkeys and the saying; I had to have something to represent this moment. I still have both the echo sticks and the wall hanging to this date.

After my time walking, it was time for a soak in a hot spring, which was well worth it. You enter at a gate and pay your fee $5 for an hour. Then I walked up a wooden deck, and on the other side of this hedge row, I could see the hot spring. It wasn't huge but big enough that you were not right on top of others. As I approached the area to get a towel, I noticed maybe twenty people in the water, all Japanese and all enjoying a nice nip in the spring. Oh course, they were all looking at me, but by this point, I had gotten used to being stared at, and I just wanted to relax. Down the small ladder and I was in some very toasty warm water. It was only about five feet deep, and the bottom was actually hard and not mucky, so it was nice to walk around. I found a quiet place and enjoyed an hour relaxing in this thermal hot spring. Oh, baby, did this feel good and just what I needed. While sitting there, I had this memory of a *National Geographic* with a baboon sitting in a hot spring in Japan and wondered if this was the same one.

That night, I found a place to eat and have a few beers. Then I went back to my room for a good night's sleep. The next day was more exploring around here, another trip to the hot springs, and then the last train to Tokyo. I was down to my last few days of this trip and then back to reality for a while.

The last night in Japan I spent with Silvia, my Italian friend. She was renting a room at a house and invited me to stay with her. We really didn't do a lot together but had some good talks at the hostel. She had come here for a while and wasn't really into doing the touristy things. Anyways, it was a place to stay, and she actually had to work, so I had the place to myself to have a few drinks and get my stuff packed for the journey home.

The next morning, we had a big hug and that was it, time to go home. To the bus, to the train, to the airport, it was going to be a long day of traveling. It was sad to leave such a great country, but I was ready to see my friends and family and get ready for the next adventure even though I had no idea what it was going to be. To everyone that I met here in this wonderful country and helped me along the way, I want to thank you for all your support. To the people of Japan, all I can say is don't change at all; you're great just the way you are.

When I arrived at customs, I wanted to get a little footage on my camcorder about arriving back home. The sign that read "Welcome to the United States of America" in red, white, and blue was something I wanted to get on camera. So I broke out my camcorder and was taking footage, and just then, about five guys surrounded me, and they took my camcorder. "Hey, what the fuck" was all I could say. "Give that back. There is nothing on there you want." They kept me there for about ten minutes and rewound my tape and kept playing it to see what was recorded. I honestly thought they were going to keep my camera. I found out it is illegal and very stupid to record information at a security checkpoint while entering the USA. They were kind of dicks at first, and then one guy explained what I had done. They did erase anything that could be used in helping someone smuggle things into the States. Any footage of that area could help someone plot a way to get by security or do something stupid. It made sense, and after they explained it to me and I apologized, they did return my camcorder to me. Welcome back to the United States. It was good to be home!

6
CHAPTER

Life Is Different

The first few days were all about sleeping and seeing my friends. Of course, the first person I contacted when I got back was my mom, and I could tell she was glad I was back, and now, she could get a good night's sleep. Her only son backpacking through Japan and Thailand by himself definitely had her worried.

By now, my money situation had gotten pretty slim, and it was time to make some more. I knew that at this point in my life, I didn't want the nine-to-five shirt-and-tie business. I just wanted to find something to make easy money and not have to put a lot of time and energy into. Before I started Vanguard, I had spent about five years in the restaurant business and made good money.

I think it was Murph who first mentioned going back to waiting tables, and I really didn't want to but knew I could make money quickly. By that time, I had about enough money for one more month and would then be *broke again*, so I needed to act fast. Graydon had mentioned a place that he went to one night, and it was costly but very good. It was Ruth's Chris Steak House, a high-end place to get a good steak. That is about all I knew about the place, but it was worth a shot.

Ruth's Chris Steak House is in the heart of Scottsdale, Arizona, which is one of the wealthier places of the valley for sure with nice homes and nice cars. It had been a while since I had worked in a restaurant and really didn't think they would want to hire me, but the interview at least would be a good experience. Well, lo and behold, the manager hired me right then and there, and I started the very next day. This was fantastic and it took a lot of pressure off me quickly. It was right before Christmas and the New Year, so they needed help, and I needed a job.

I was trained and on my own within about five days and was making $150 to $200 a night. We had to work from four to ten each night. We got a free meal before every shift, so my dinner was taken care of each night I worked. It was a classy place with professional people working with me. For two people to have a nice meal, it was around $120 for everything. So with high checks came higher tips, and it was perfect. I was making some money to stay on top of my bills.

At this point in my life, it was only me and two cats to take care of, so life was simple. I could see my friends when I had time, and really, it was just about banking a few bucks for the future. So when an opportunity arose, I could easily say yes to just about everything I wanted to do.

One of my best friends that I met during this time was Julio. He was one of the bartenders and had been there for a while. He was a light-skinned Mexican who had gained his citizenship in the United States when he was eighteen years old. He was a hardworking guy and had done so much to help himself and his family who still lived in Mexico. He owned two houses and had a small tile business on the side, which I helped him out with a few times. His family had a cattle ranch in Mexico and asked me if I would be interested in going with him for a few days and check out their ranch. This was what I was all about at this time—opportunities to see different parts of the world. Why the hell not? I'm all about checking out a cattle ranch in Mexico.

The plan was to cross into Nogales and head south. The ranch was located near Hermosillo, Mexico, which was about four hours south of the border. Now I had been to several border towns in Mexico: Tijuana, Nogales, and Juarez; this, however, would be the furthest I had ever been from the boarder by car. I had been to Puerto Vallarta in Mexico but went there by plane and never left the resort, so this place would be much more of a euthenics experience.

TAKE A DECADE

We arrived at the closest town near his ranch and stopped at a few of his family's houses to say hello. I watched Julio slip a $100 bill in each of his family's pockets. This is the kind of person he was, very kind and generous, like he told me when I mentioned it to him. "A $100 goes a long way for these people who really didn't have that much." They were his family, and he would do what he could to help them out.

The town was an old Mexican establishment. Mostly single-story buildings of clay and brick. There were no neon signs or billboards advertising for the stores; it was a poor area and it showed. For me, it was a taste of how my southern border brother grew up.

We stopped at a butcher shop. There were no real signs out front saying it was a place to get meat; you basically just had to know this. We grabbed some meat, which was not wrapped in fancy packaging or anything, just you pick out the meat you want, and they wrap it in white paper and hand it to you. Then we drove about a mile to get beer. The beer is all sold in single cans, not in a case or twelve-pack, so we had a bag and just filled it up. It was good old-fashioned Tecta, a local Mexican beer. Now that place did not have ice, so we drove another mile to the place to get ice; again, we loaded up a black trash bag with what we needed, and off we went. With some basic supplies, food, beer, and a few bottles of tequila, we were off to the ranch.

The ranch was about thirty minutes out of this small town and in the middle of nowhere. We approached the gate and proceeded down this dirt road. The whole ranch was like ten thousand acres but butted up to just desert and national land, which was owned by the government. As we drove down the main road, we noticed military vehicles on his family's land. There were about three Humvees and about six soldiers. As we approached them, I asked Julio what was going on, and he told me, "His family lets them use their property as a center point to patrol for illegal activities like drug smuggling or human trafficking." By letting them use their land, they were left alone, and they knew their land was well protected. He said they were usually there three to four days a week all year long.

As we got close, Julio drove his truck up along the side of the Federales and started talking. We got out of the truck, and they were all very professional and didn't speak English, so I had no idea what they were talking about. They motioned for me to follow them, and around the corner on one of their trucks, they had this kitten. At least that is what I thought it was at first. They looked at me and smiled and asked if I wanted to hold it. Julio was translating, and he did not know what it was either. We both got closer, and he said, "Holy shit, that is not a kitten at all—it is a baby bobcat." It was so damn cute, but it was still a wild animal. They had found it during one of their hikes in the desert and were taking it to an animal doctor when they got back. They were feeding it raw chicken and water. Well, I could not be this close to something like that and not try and hold it. Julio grabbed it first, and it almost bit his finger off; it actually drew blood, and we all laughed. I was able to handle it very carefully and get a quick picture of it before it bit me. This little "kitten" was so strong even at this young age. It was very cool and something that not a lot of people get to handle in their life. We thanked the soldiers and proceeded to the ranch.

The ranch consisted of a small single-story house, an average side barn, a stable area, and a few other small buildings for storage. It had no electricity but did have running water in the kitchen and it had a bathroom. This was just what I needed, a rustic Spanish-speaking environment in the middle of Mexico. His older uncle lived and worked there all year round along with a few of his younger cousins. His uncle was exactly what you would consider a Mexican rancher to look like: skinny, weathered face, rough hands, and wearing cowboy boots and of course a cowboy hat. The younger guys all looked the same part: western shirts, cowboy boots, and very tan. They lived in the sun, and you could tell by looking at them. Julio looked as white as I did next to these guys. Now the one problem was none of them spoke English, and I knew just a little Spanish. It worked out okay, just did a lot of listing in the beginning. We stored our gear in the house, which we found out didn't have any glass on the windows, so what was outside could easily get in the inside of the house. Oh well, all was good, and this was something I had never been part of before and excited to check things out.

TAKE A DECADE

After a few beers, we took a little ride on the horses before it got dark. My horse was named Gringo for the Gringo, they all got a good laugh out of that. It had been a while since I had ridden a horse, so I was a little nervous at first. I did not want to make a jackass out of myself. Luckily, Gringo and I got along very well. He was a young horse with a lot of energy, and that is what they told me before I saddled up. So when I got on him, I pulled back a bit and let him know who was in charge. Well, he knew who was in charge, and it sure the hell wasn't me that is for sure.

We spent about an hour just walking along with the horse, and I was getting used to this real quickly. We would walk then trot and then toward the end of our first ride we were running full bore down this old dried-up creek bed. It was so much fun, and I really felt like a true cowboy. Tomorrow will be the true test; I just didn't know it yet.

Back to the ranch, get the horses situated, and get the fire started outside to cook the carina asana. We sat there like we had been there for weeks. It was me and four to five Mexicans just enjoying a few beers and waiting for the steak to cook. Julio was really good about translating for all of us, and I asked a lot of questions, so he was busy. It was a fun evening, drinking beer in a can and eating the meat right off the grill. There were no side dishes, just the meat—well, we did have tequila if that counts as a side dish and that bottle was passed around until it was empty.

The next morning, I woke up and made my way to the kitchen. When I walked in the kitchen, I saw something I had never seen in a house before. There was a horse that had his head in the window and was licking something of the counter. So I walked up slowly, petted the side of his face, and said, "Good morning, beautiful."

The plan for the day was to saddle up the horses, check out the ranch, and see how the livestock was doing. We left after breakfast, which was eggs and toast, probably around 9:00 a.m. or so. We were looking for a certain steer that had an issue they wanted to take care of. It was not like they could just go out into the pasture and get it; we had to find it first. We all rode our horses side by side, and it was so cool to be riding a horse in Mexico with a bunch of true cowboys. Julio reached into his bag, and busted out a bottle of good

107

tequila. He opened the bottle and passed it around as we just slowly maneuvered through the desert. We were riding horses through the Mexican Sonoran Desert, with the sun on our backs and the hot air all around us, drinking tequila right from the bottle. It was a great day, and one that I will never forget.

About five hours into our trip, we found the steer they were looking for. I could tell right away what was wrong with it; his horns were growing toward his eyes, and it was something they had to tend to, or they could lose a two-thousand-pound steer. If the horns continued to grow, they would blind the steer, and he would starve. They had to cut them back, and that was the mission of the day. So for the next hour, we all rode our horses and kept the steer moving in the direction of the ranch. I felt like *City Slickers* from the movie herding a steer to its home. They kept him moving, and I kept him from escaping from my side, which was exciting to say the least. My horse didn't speak English either and didn't always do what I wanted, but we managed to do our part. After about a six-hour ride, a bottle of tequila almost empty, and a steer in tow, we made it back to the ranch. The next step was getting this two-thousand-pound steer into the stables so the guys could take care of it. We got it into an area; his uncle used a rope and lassoed the back of his legs, and another cowboy did the same to the front. They were very gentle with him, and they both backed up and the steer's legs came out from underneath him, and he fell to the ground. At this point, I was sitting on the fence watching the whole process and just like that my world changed. I wasn't just going to be that spectator that watched from a distance and took a picture or two. I heard Julio yell at me to grab a saw, which was just a small hack saw that was right near me. He then told me to cut the horns with the saw. I was like, *Are you freaking serious?* He had a big smile on his face, so without hesitation, I grabbed the saw and walked out toward this massive beast. The steer was actually a lot calmer than I was at this point; it was just lying on the ground with its legs stretched out. So I did what they asked me to do. I literally had to sit on top of this two-thousand-pound beast, grab one of its horns, and about six inches down, they told me to start cutting. I grabbed the horn and started to cut it with this small hack saw.

Well, I was able to get both horns cut in less than two minutes, and then they let the steer up. I grabbed both pieces of the horn and ran to the side and climbed up and over the fence as quickly as I could. I don't think I breathed at all during that moment. Holy cow, I can't believe I just got to do this. They all laughed at me and said I did a good job for a gringo. We celebrated with a shot or two of tequila, and the night was just getting started. What a cool experience, and I still have those two pieces of horn to this day.

The next day was spent relaxing and enjoying some down time. His uncle never got out of bed once that day due to the amount of tequila we had drank. It was a few beer days but a lot of water and food. That night after we had eaten and actually started to feel better, Julio took me to meet another family member, and I really wished we had met him sooner. This guy grew pot for a living, and we had the chance to check out his little farm. Of course this was not legal and not on his property, so it was all good. The guy had plants taller than me and plenty of them. This was his way of making a living, and I had to give him credit. Luckily for me, we did get to sample some of his hard work, which was very nice of him. I liked this guy, and we had a good time that night.

The next morning, we got up and said our goodbyes. It was back in the truck, and we made our way back to the States. We laughed and talked the whole way home. It was a truly fun experience to hang out at a Mexican dude ranch. It did more than I had expected to do, which was always a good thing. Thanks to my friend Julio, I now had another good story to tell.

7

CHAPTER

Life Continues

It was back to work and back to the normal routine for now. Work was going well, and I really liked it. There were good people, and it was a good place for me at this time, flexible hours and the money was good. I spent time with my friends, and life was simple. It was about a month after getting back from Mexico. Jason, Graydon, and a few others were out for the night, and Jason asked us all if we would be interested in taking a cruise at the end of May. His cousin was getting married, and the more people they signed up for the cruise, the cheaper it was going to cost. Graydon and I were like "Hell, yeah" right from the beginning. It would be a blast and something I had never done before. We would fly from Phoenix to Puerto Rico and get on the ship from here. Then from Puerto Rico, we would be going to St. Thomas, St. Lucia, Cerisel, and Aruba. I had never been to any of these places, and I loved the fact we would be living on a boat for a week.

The date came, and we met at Jason's place before we left for the airport. I was leaving the States for the third time in less than a year, not bad for a beginning world traveler. We flew from Phoenix to Houston then to Puerto Rico. The flight was a blast, the first time we had all flown together, and we made the most out of it. The beers started coming and really didn't stop for a week.

TAKE A DECADE

We arrived at the ship about an hour before departure, which gave us time to get everything taken care of. Now almost everyone has seen a picture or something about a cruise ship on TV, but to be on one is another story. First of all, just standing on the dock and looking at this massive floating structure was amazing. Then to go aboard and see the interior, the staircases, the chandeliers, the colors, and the rest of the décor was breathtaking. We made our way to our rooms with a huge smile on our faces and got checked into our rooms. I roomed with one of Jason's cousins that I had never met, and Jason and Graydon shared a room just down the hall.

Of course by now, we all had a beer in our hands and a big smile on all our faces. We laughed and wandered around the ship for the next few hours. The buffet was open, and we filled our faces with some good, tasty food. On a cruise ship, if you ever were to go hungry, then something is very wrong with you; the food never stops.

The first night on board was the best time ever. Everyone was laughing, dancing, drinking, and meeting other people. We spent a while on the top deck and then made our way to the club. This club had everything that a normal club would have. Music, dance floor, unique lighting, a big bar. The place was packed the first night, and the three of us met every girl on that boat that very first night. The night was filled with dancing, laughing, eating, and drinking. At 4:00 a.m., we found out that we could not drink anymore, they actually have to close the bars down for two hours every day, so between 4:00 a.m. and 6:00 a.m., you couldn't get alcohol. To be honest with you, by this time, none of us needed any more. It was time to call it a night, and the next day was going to be a day at sea, so there was plenty of time to party.

We all slept in and made our way to the pool around noon; it was time for some food and a little bit of sun. Just sitting on the deck watching people, watching the games they were playing, and of course the girls on board. It was also time to check out the casino, which was open and ready to go. My goal was to spend less than five hundred for this trip, and that included the two hundred in cash that I had on me. So two hundred in cash and then the rest will go on my credit card. That was the plan, but plans don't always work out so well. All I knew was that I was going to have fun.

That night was very similar to our first night except Graydon and I decided to "check out the boat." We were explorers and wanted to see the "whole ship," so that night, we went through doors that said "staff only" and checked out the behind the scenes. We would get caught, and someone would ask us to leave, and we would just go and find another place. We spent the whole night checking this boat out, and at about 3:00 a.m., I wanted to climb the highest point of the ship, which was the radar tour. You know that tower where the thing spins around slowly. Graydon didn't think it was a good idea, but before he could say anything, I was on my way up. I slowly climbed up the ladder, and when I got to the radar part of it, I timed it perfectly and made my way up past that area. It was another six feet to the top, and within five minutes of climbing, I was sitting on the rung of the ladder, and from my vantage point I could see forever. I was literally two feet taller than any other part of the ship. Like I said, the view was spectacular, but it didn't last long. I sat there for maybe a minute, and at that point, I noticed about five security officers coming from all locations headed right toward me. I decided to climb back down and was met with five guys who really wanted to throw me overboard. "What the hell are you thinking?" the head guy said, and all I could do was explain that I was just a stupid kid and having fun.

"Please don't kick me off the boat. You will not hear another thing from me the whole entire trip." Basically, I had about thirty seconds to sell myself to them or I was going to the brig and maybe even escorted off the boat at the next island. Luckily, they had a heart and gave me a good tongue lashing and let me go. I found Graydon hiding out in the hallway on my way to my room, and we just burst out laughing. "I can't believe you just did that, Mundy," Graydon said.

"It was very stupid, but a lot of fun and something I've done and will never have to do again."

The next few days, we explored St. Thomas and St. Lucia. Most of our time was on the beach and walking around the main touristy areas, checking out the areas and getting a feel for what the island life could be like if we lived here. Both of the islands are a lot of fun and a lot to do, we saw a small portion of each, but that was all we needed.

We had dinner every night then a show of some sort then to the casino then to the club. The third night, Graydon and I ended up sleeping out on the deck. We found a few chairs on the Topless Deck and passed out. The next morning, I woke up to a lady lying beside me not wearing her top, and I had no idea who she was, but this was one hell of a good way to wake up.

Our next island was Curacao, and we really didn't spend a lot of time there. Maybe three hours and it was back to the ship. We took a nap and got ready for another night of debauchery. We spent a good portion of the night hanging out with our little group of friends and actually had the earliest night to bed for the whole entire trip. We were going to Aruba the next day and had planned on actually seeing the island via four wheelers, so we wanted to be well rested.

Aruba was our longest port stay. We arrived at 8:00 a.m. and would not be leaving until ten that night, so we actually had all day. We started with our four-wheelers, which was Graydon, Mike, Michelle, Jason, our waitress, and then me. We had five machines and spent five hours riding these things all over the island, down the street, on the beach, and over the sand dunes. We would stop at local bars, have a drink or stop on the beach, and jump in the ocean. It was the best day of the trip as far as seeing different things. Around 2:00 p.m., we headed back to the ship and had our dinner and got ready for a night out on the town. We went to Carlos and Charlie's club, which is something everyone should do if they have a chance. The place was a blast, and every hour on the hour, he would inform all cruise ship people to drink more because the ship would be sailing— three hours left, two hours left, 1 hour left, then thirty minutes, and then fifteen minutes. It was a great experience and a lot of fun. There must have been at least three hundred people in that bar that were on our ship, so we all walked back together, hooting and hollering. The bar just got us primed up for the night, and we spent the rest of the night at the club or up on top deck drinking and dancing. I think it was around 5:00 a.m. when I called it a night; the next day was our last day at sea, and it didn't matter what time we got up.

Our last day was all about chilling by the pool and relaxing a little. It had been a crazy, busy week filled with a lot of drinking, laughing, dancing, and exploring. It was time to just kick back a little and have a great last day. Our bodies needed a little R&R, and we still wanted to have fun one more last night. So after we had our dinner and got ready for the evening, our last night on the ship was going to be great. Almost everyone was ready to party that night because for most of the day, everyone had relaxed and enjoyed the same thing we all did, and that was sun, pool, and a nap.

We started the night out in the casino, and by now, I had lost $150. We then spent most our time on the top deck, which is where the party was that night. As it got later, the crowd decreased, and by 3:00 a.m., there were just a small handful of us left. Now our ship had a water slide, and I thought it would be fun to run down the slide. The water had been shut off, but the slide itself was still there. So at about 3:30 a.m., I jumped over the rope and climbed a small ladder. With my hands on each side of the slide, I began to run down the slide, twisting and turning just like I would if I had been lying down in the water. What I did not realize is that there was a concert barrier at the end, and when my head hit this, I knocked myself out for a split second. I could feel the blood running down my face and thought to myself, *Oh shit, this really sucks*. I made my way to the nearest bathroom and looked in the mirror. I had busted up my eye, lip, and nose pretty good. Nothing that needed stitches but this little mistake would make me suffer for a while.

The next morning, we had to depart the boat, which meant sitting in the theater area waiting our turn to get off the boat. It was at this time that my face had swollen up, and it looked like I had gotten the shit kicked out of me that night. Most people had a good laugh when I told them what I had done, and boy oh boy, was I paying for it now. Just the sun on my face hurt, and waiting for our taxi back to the airport was painful and very uncomfortable. It turned a long day into a long, painful day.

8
CHAPTER

The World Changed

We made it back from our cruise, and unfortunately, I was not able to go right back to work. I contacted the manager of the restaurant and told him about my little accident and that due to the look of my face, I really wasn't in a position to wait tables. Who would want to order food from someone whose face looks like they fell off a motorcycle? He completely understood, and it would be about a week before I felt ready to get back to my job. I hated to lose the money, but you have to do what you have to do.

After I healed and made it back to work, life got back to the norm quickly. Working and spending time with my friends was all I did for the next three months. I had no real plans on going anywhere. It was all about making some money and just paying my bills and trying to get a little cash in the bank. That is when life throws a curveball and everything changes, which is exactly what happened to me.

I was back to work, and during my shift around six o'clock, the manager came to me and told me I had a phone call. This was at a time before everyone had cell phones, so if you needed to call someone, you called their home number or business number. I reached the phone and was expecting one of my friends to call about something going on that night; they knew I was working, so it had to be important.

I answered the phone, and it was my sister calling from New York. She said, "You have to come home. Dad is in the state hospital. He left the house after Mom, and he got into a fight, and Mom found what looked to be a suicide note." My mom had called the state police, and they found him on a side road with pills, alcohol, and his pistol. Nothing had happened yet. They felt they reached him in time, but things were not good." It was all I needed to hear and went right to my manager and told him what was going on. "I have to leave and don't know when I'll be back." They all reassured me that my job would be waiting for me when I got back, and just like that, I left the restaurant.

After contacting a few friends and getting a few things taken care of, I was on a red-eye flight that night and back in New York by early morning. My mom and brother-in-law picked me up at the airport and filled me in on what had been going on. He was not a happy person, and had been taking a lot of prescription pills. Now this had been an issue for most of my life. It was not the first time something had happened to him because of pills or alcohol.

First things first, my dad had always been a good man, a provider, home every night by five for dinner, and someone whom I had always looked up to. He is one of the smartest people I know. The problem really started many years ago when he accidentally cut off three of his fingers with a saw. This all happened in the early seventies, and pain pills were relatively new and no one really understood the side effects and the addiction that came from these things. He became addicted and never really could fight the battle. My dad is a good man, hardworking and the head of our house. It was just for whatever reason he never really could quit.

They kept him in the state hospital for a few days and then released him with the intention of going to rehab. It was at this time that both my sister and I were old enough to help more when we were younger. Judy was very upset with him, and she actually told me that she wished he had succeeded. She was living near them and could feel how this was tearing my mom apart. It was hard for me because I had not been home and was more concerned with him just getting better.

At this point, my dad was a funeral director and had a big passion for antiques. My father loved to read and was one of the first people in our area to sell antiques on Ebay. He was a very proud person, and this took a lot from him that nobody really can imagine. We stuck together during this time, and I tried to help out as much as I could. After a few weeks with him back to himself, it was time for me to get back to my life and back to work. Time would tell what would happen, and Judy and Scott were close by for my mom and dad. My sister just wanted my mom to be safe and happy as I did. Struggles with addiction affect so many people and their families, but the bottom line is you have to want to get help with your addiction, and at this time, it was up to my father to make the choice.

My mom and dad both took me to the airport, and I gave them a big hug. I told them to take care of each other and that I loved them both very much. At that point, everything seemed okay, and all we could do was pray that it was over. This event did hurt my dad in a very sensitive way. He was humiliated and had lost something because of this event. I liked to say all was good, but unfortunately, I don't think he ever forgive us for doing what we thought we had to do. Even though my parents stayed together, their relationship was never the same. There is so much more about this month that we went through, but for now it is all I want to say.

I spent most of August and the first week of September back home, and when I arrived back in Phoenix, I contacted the manager and said I was ready to come back. They informed me it would be a week or so before they could get me back on the schedule, and that was okay with me. My parents had helped with a few bills and gave me some money to help out before I got back on my feet. This week off gave me a chance to keep in contact with my parents and sister. It was a week to myself to absorb all that had happened.

It was Tuesday morning, and I had fallen asleep on my couch with the TV still on. The phone rang, and it was my mother. She said, "Can you believe what just happened?" It was then that I turned my attention to the TV and realized the United States had been attacked. It was September 11, 2001, and everyone's life had just changed. How 9/11 affected me was that the restaurant that I was planning on going back to work had put out a hiring freeze. Unfortunately, they were not able to get me back on the schedule and didn't know when things would return to normal. All I knew was I had to find something and could not wait too long.

Three weeks went by and rent was due. I had to find something soon or I would be living on the streets. My friend Greg got me an interview at the place he was working called Bleachers, a small sports bar not far from where I lived.

I started working at Bleachers as an assistant manager and bartender, and soon after I started, my paychecks started to bounce. The place was not in good financial standing. About two months into working, I was behind the bar, and two guys walked in and told me they had just bought the place. They told me when the last table was done eating that I was to lock the doors and that would be it for Bleachers. Just like that, everyone who worked there was out of a job, including myself, at least for that night. They were going to shut the place down and completely remodel. Within a few days, I had an interview with the new manager, and I was offered a position as his assistant. So at least I had something, not what I wanted but sometimes it is all about just trying to live. I can tell you this, and just living is no way to live.

It took about a month to get all set up, and we were back in business. I had a great front of the house staff and a full-stocked bar, which was all part of my responsibility. I was able to hire my friend Mary, who had become a good friend and who was also cute. The place looked great, and at first, it was a lot of fun. We had the grand opening, and the place was doing well, and for the most part, everything was going pretty good. Now fast-forward a month, and the job was taking a toll on me. I was working six days a week from about 4:00 p.m. to 2:00 a.m. The only time I saw the sun was on my way to work. The only time I saw my friends was when they came into the bar. It became my life, and I was not digging it that much. That night, I decided that I didn't want to do this anymore. The next day, I put my two weeks in, and they were actually very supportive and understood my decision.

TAKE A DECADE

    What about Mary? Why did her name come up and no one else? Well, I'll tell you we had talked about getting away and driving cross country. She had never done this before, and I thought we could have a great time. About this same time, she had just sold her house, and I told her she could stay with me until she found something else.

    We had set the date, and it was a plan. Drive from Phoenix to Key West, Florida and then back. We were going to go through New Orleans then stay with my friends that lived in Panama Beach Florida then to Key West and back up through Orlando, go to Disney World, and then back. It was going to be about a two-week trip. We spent the last two weeks of my job planning the trip and getting excited to get out and do something.

    My last day of work had come, and I was ready for a vacation. For the past six months after 9/11, all I had done was work, and while working at a bar, there was a lot of drinking and I needed a break. The night before I left, I had spent a few hours with Murph talking about life and giving him the breakdown of our trip. It was always good to talk to my friend, sit out on his deck, have a few beers, and shoot the shit. He did ask me what I was going to do when I got back, and at that point, I had no idea, just wanted to do something fun.

CHAPTER 9

Cross-Country

Mary and I left for our cross-country trip. We drove for about twelve hours, and we stayed our first night in Houston, Texas. Then we proceeded to New Orleans for the next three nights. This was going to be a first for both of us. I had never been there before but had heard great things about this town. We arrived and found a place to stay close to the French quarter, which is the place to be. We checked in and made our way to the famous Bourbon Street, the narrow street filled with bars, restaurants, and famous for the amazing scenery. We didn't plan this out, but we actually arrived on St. Patrick's Day, which is the second biggest party of the year. We were sitting at a table right on the street having something to eat and this huge parade started. It was amazing, people throwing beads and candy all over the street. If you don't know about the beads, guys, get these and offer them to the girls; all they have to do is show you their boobs. Very simple, and I wanted as many of those beads as I could get. Mary and I had a good meal and then started to drink pretty heavily for the next five hours. We were walking up and down the street with a thousand other people having a blast. I was giving girls beads, and they were doing what they were supposed to do. *This place was crazy.*

The next day, I spent time just wandering around this beautiful place by myself for a few hours. The sounds and smells of the French quarter were so unique and for me a special opportunity. There was a "spicy smell" in the air from the food and a "jazzy" sound in the air from the music. Outdoor musicians were playing everywhere along with street performers and other entertainers. That afternoon, I just wandered around and did get a chance to gamble on an old paddle boat that was docked permanently as a casino. I think I won about $75, which really helped me out. Mary and I met up later and continued to walk around and check out some of the stores. It was great hanging out with her. It was just when we got drunk, things changed. We loved all the Voodoo shops. New Orleans is below sea level, so they have to bury their dead in tombs above ground, and just the trees and building gave this place an eerie sense of the whole voodoo thing. We both loved it and took it all in as much as we could.

That night, we were meeting a few of my friends from Phoenix. Scott and Rica now lived in Panama, Florida, and we were going to stay with them in a few days. They had decided to meet us, and I loved hanging out with them. So that night, the four of us walked around the town and spent another night on Bourbon Street admiring the scenery.

We left around 11:00 a.m., normal checkout time, and drove the whole day through Louisiana, Alabama, and then Florida. The drive was spectacular, changing drivers about every four to five hours. We went through swamps, along the coast, and by beautiful beaches. It took most of the day to get to their place, but it was well worth the drive.

In Panama Beach, Florida, we had lunch at an outdoor bar/café, and then all I really wanted to do was lie on the beach. It had been a long three days of partying, and I needed some rest. Well, unfortunately, I fell asleep and got sunburned on the back of my legs. It made for a rough day the next day because all we had to do that day was sit in the car making our way toward Miami. It got dark around 9:00 p.m., and we still had a long way to go, but we decided to just drive until we got there and then get a room and relax a night before making our way south. It was at least 1:00 a.m. when we entered the highway called "Alligator Avenue." This was a road that went right through the everglades and was a great drive. I'm so glad we did this at night because the traffic was light, and we stopped a few times and got out of our car just to get a feel for the area. The light that came off the swamp was unreal. It was the methane gas that created a glow that was kind of spooky but cool to see.

After driving all night long, we made it to Miami in the morning. We had a choice, find a place and stay one night or keep driving and head right to Key West. We made a decision, and that was to keep driving.

If you have not been on this drive, then you are missing something. The road from Miami to Key West is spectacular. It is definitely an iconic road in the United States. It's one road that goes from island to island with water on both sides most of the time. It is famous for the seven-mile bridge, Key Largo, and a ton of souvenir shops.

It took us around three hours, and by now, we wanted out of the car. We were starting to get under each other's skin and needed a drink. The first order of business was finding a campground and stopping at a store for food and drinks. Both were relatively easy to find, and we found the best camping area ever. It's the southernmost campsite on the mainland. It was right on the ocean.

Now it was time to check out the town. We had a map and pretty much we wanted to find the main area, which was around Duvall Street. It was about a half-hour ride, and unfortunately, the sky was clouding up on us. It never rained in Key West, so they say, but that day it rained. We parked the car, and for the next six hours, we walked the streets while it rained on and off the entire time. Duval Street was about 1.5 miles long and loaded with restaurants, bars, and shops. It was a very cool place to hang out. Within a few hours, we had drank enough and walked the strip. It was also pouring rain, and unfortunately, the streets were quiet, so we decided to just head back to our camp and spent the rest of the night at our campsite.

We made it back, and the rain had stopped, but everything was wet, so we just went into the tent and that was when the night changed. We hung out and talked for a while, and someone said something, and Mary and I started yelling at each other. For some reason, for whatever was said, we got into it pretty hard. "You're a bitch, you're a dick, you're a druggie, and you're single." For about an hour, we fought and yelled at each other and then Mary left. She grabbed her bag and purse and said goodbye; she was leaving. "Good," I said, and she jumped in the car and was gone. It was quiet again, and my heart was pounding. I sat by the water and had a few more beers, and at some point in the night, I made it back to my tent and fell asleep, half in my tent and half out of my tent. What a night.

The next morning, around nine, I was woken up by someone kicking me in the side. He was not kicking me hard, just enough to get my attention. At first, I thought it was Mary, but when I opened my eyes and looked up, it was a guy. He said, "Wake up, you have to leave the premises." I wiped my face, stood up, and most definitely looked like hell.

He said, "You caused a disturbance here last night, and you have to leave right now."

I explained the situation. "We had a fight, and you can see that she is gone. No more problems, I promise you won't hear a word from me."

He took a step closer to me and said, "You have one hour to leave this place or I will call the cops" and then turned and walked away.

This really sucks! How am I going to carry all this stuff out of here? I have a tent, a stove, a bag of clothes, a sleeping bag, and a few things of Mary's. This absolutely blows, and what am I going to do? That bitch was all I could think of at that time. Well, I took my tent down and walked over to this guy camping out close by and gave him my tent and stove. *Here you go, buddy, a nice tent and a free stove. Hope you have a better day than I'm having.* Then I walked around and gave everything away that I physically couldn't carry; all her stuff went first. Then I picked up my bags and walked out of the campsite. I made sure to flip the caretaker off while I walked out. "Fuck you, buddy, you piece of shit" was the last thing I said and walked out to the road.

Now what was I going to do? At that point, my cell phone was almost dead, and I really didn't have anyone to call. I was stranded at the southernmost campsite and all alone. My plan was to get a ride to the main road, head north to the first town, and get a Greyhound bus back to Phoenix or even to Scott and Rica's in Panama City. I got a ride to the main road and was dropped off near an intersection. I then started to hitchhike from there to get a ride north. It only took about fifteen minutes, and these two guys picked me up and gave me a ride to the nearest bus station. Once inside, I found an outlet and charged my phone. I just sat there for about fifteen minutes and laughed at my situation. What a mess. Well, at about that time, my phone rang, and it was Mary. "Where are you?" she said, and I told her the whole story. She had gone back to the campsite and was told to leave. So after I told her about my fun adventure, she told me she was on her way. She pulled up about thirty minutes later and got out and gave me a big hug and said she was sorry. I too apologized and we made up after talking for a short time. Life was good again, and we said enough of Key West and headed toward Miami. She did ask about her case full of CDs, and I told her that I could not carry it, sorry. That was all that was said about that night.

    We made it to Miami and found a place to sleep for the night, and I enjoyed a hot shower.

    The next day, we left Miami and headed toward Disney World. This was going to be the last fun thing we did, and then it was going to be straight back to Phoenix. The good thing about Disney was that Mary had a friend who worked there and had tickets for us to get in.

    We had a fun day, walked around, rode a few rides, had something to eat, and just watched everything going on around us. This place is overwhelming for an adult; I could not imagine what a child must think. It really is a special place, and I hope you all have a chance to go at some point. You're never too old for Mickey Mouse; that is for sure.

    Morning came, and the car was packed. We left Orlando, and for the first time this trip, we were heading west; our final destination was Phoenix, Arizona. We did not stop to sleep, just for fuel and food. We switched drivers about every five hours and drove straight through. It took a long time, and all we could do was watch the sun rise and then set, rise again and almost set again before we made it back. It was so good to be home, and when we pulled into the parking lot, we looked at each other, had a big hug, and told each other we did it, two weeks cross-country and we got to see a lot of new things. All in all, it was a fun trip, and we were both safe.

We were back home, and it felt great. Rent was due, and I did ask Mary to pay her portion; this was on the first of the month. Three days later, we got into another argument, and I asked her to move out. I told her we had a great trip, but for some reason, we just couldn't live together. She agreed and moved out the very next day. It was the last time I ever saw Mary. I do hope she has had a good life, but I really didn't miss her. Oh well, life will go on.

10
CHAPTER

What Is Next

After my cross-country trip with Mary, it was back to reality, and reality said I had to get a job. I had quit the restaurant before I left and really didn't have anything planned. Rent had been paid for April, and that had taken a good share of the money that I had left, so I had to find something quickly.

*****

I remember this day like it was yesterday. It was midafternoon, and I grabbed a beer out of the fridge. I grabbed the Yellow Pages, which at this time in our lives was something we all used. If you needed to find something, this was your source. I really didn't want to go back to the restaurant business, I just didn't want to work nights anymore. So I sat down and started flipping through the pages, A to B to C, nothing yet. I reached the "H" section, and at the top of the page was "Hot Air Balloon." Now that would be fun, and I had been up in a hot-air balloon before and had a blast. This would be a cool job.

*****

There were three companies that provided this service. So I called the first two and asked what they had available, and without

TAKE A DECADE

any experience, they could not help me out. The third company was the biggest, and I spoke with the manager and explained my situation. She asked if I could meet her tomorrow, and we set up an appointment. The next day, I drove to the office, which was about thirty minutes away and met the manager. She was very nice, and we had a quick but good meeting. She liked me and asked if I could be here tomorrow morning at five. They did the sunrise balloon ride, so the hours were very early. I went from working nights to working early mornings right then and there.

Our day would start at 5:00 a.m., and all the captains would decide on where they were going to launch from that day. They had certain places that all the trucks could get into and set up the balloons. Once the decision had been made, we loaded up into trucks, usually three to four people per balloon. Once we arrived at the site, we would take about thirty minutes to set up the balloon. Get the basket ready, hook up the burners, unroll the balloon, attach everything together, and then fire up the burners to inflate the balloon. One of the best things was to hold on to the crown line, which is a line from the top of the balloon to the bottom, and when the balloon starts to rise, you just slide across the ground as it pulls you with it—just a fun thing for us; it was like water skiing on land.

Now it was the fun part, driving through the desert, while on the radio with the captain, doing our best to follow them as best we could. After an hour or so, it was time to find a place to land. The captains had a bird's eye view of the area, and they would tell us to make a turn, maybe through a ditch or through some trees. Most of these places had no roads, so we had to make our own to get to the landing area. The trucks were Ford 450 diesel machines that could go almost anywhere. It was so much fun driving through the desert chasing our balloon. Once the landing area had been determined, we had to be right there when the balloon touched down. Grab the lines and try and lay the balloon down as quickly as possible so the wind would not take it for ride. Once the balloon was secured and down flat, the passengers would get out, and we would have a breakfast set up for them with champagne to celebrate. The captain would thank them and tell them about the tradition and open up the bottle of champagne.

Unfortunately, the money wasn't the greatest, and financially, I was struggling. It was around the middle of the month, and Murph called, and we talked for a while, and he recommended that I move in with him and Kari and try and get a head start. I accepted right away and was so thankful to have such a great friend. I didn't know how long I would live with them, but right now, I needed a little help, and they were gracious enough to let me stay with them. I also knew I needed to find something else to help pay the bills. Working the hot-air balloon was a lot of fun, but there were still a lot of hours in the day for me to be doing something else. Near where Murph and Kari lived was an Embassy Suites Hotel. It was not really what I wanted, but the location was great, and they were hiring. I had an interview, and as always, they fell in love with me and offered me a job. I was back to waiting tables and bartending a little on the side.

The biggest thing that happened during this time was I met a new person and she would change my life. Her name was Tiffany, and she worked at Embassy Suites with me. Now it was not a physical attraction with this girl. However, she was a great person to talk to. After just a few days, she told me what she really did and that was work at Yosemite National Park in northern California. She was from New Orleans but living in Phoenix because this was where her boyfriend is from. She has been working at Yosemite for seven years during the summer and then found something during the winter to keep her busy.

After just a few weeks working together, she said to me, "You would love working at Yosemite and would fit right in." It wasn't the first time she had said it to me, but after a few times, I started to think more about it. That night, I talked with Murph and told him I might give it a shot. Why not go to Yosemite National Park for a season? The season started around the end of May to sometime in September. It would be for five or six months, and it would be nice to get away and try something different. The money was not the greatest, but it would be more than what I was making right now, and it would be just one job.

That was it, and within just a few days, I had applied and received my application. At this point, I had already called my mom to let her know what I was up to now. As always, I started the conversation out with "I have a wonderful opportunity to do something different."

She would always come back with "Where are you going now?"

"Mom, I am heading to Yosemite National Park in Northern California." As always, she was supportive and, of course, concerned. I was leaving again, and who knew what could come of this trip?

I figured that I would be gone for maybe six months. When I returned, I would have money in the bank and at this point be able to get my own place. I loved living with Murph and Kari, but it would be nice to have my own space. A few days before I left, I was able to see a bunch of people, Jason, Graydon, and all my other friends. I told them that I would be back in five or six months and life will go back to normal. At least this is what I thought would happen, and man oh man, if I only knew where this was going to take me.

This was going to be a place I had never been before. I had seen thousands of photos of Yosemite and always hoped I would get to see the park. It is crazy how life works, and during this beautiful drive through California, on my way to the Yosemite, it was so surreal that I was going to be working there. It was another adventure, another journey, and another opportunity to see this amazing world.

11
CHAPTER

Yosemite

The entrance to the park, the way I came in, which is from the west, is by far the best way to enter the park. Once I had entered the forest, I came to this long tunnel that cut right through the mountain. When I reached the end and entered the park, I was completely blown away with what I was seeing. There on my left was a huge pasture filled with a ton of wildflowers, but what really got my attention was the huge mountain of El Cap; that was something to see with our own two eyes. It's a spectacular sight, and to think that people actually climb that vertical face. I was in awe of what I'm seeing and finally pulled over just to get a better look at this amazingly beautiful place.

Yosemite National Park is 1,200 square miles filled with deep valleys, gorgeous meadows, giant sequoias, and spectacular waterfalls. Yosemite was first protected in 1864, and today, it is still very much a place for outdoor people to see things that can only be seen here. You can camp, hike, rock climb, enjoy waterfalls, and see wildlife. I'd been there less than a half hour and I was already in love and knew that I made the right choice in coming here.

After marveling at the scenery, it was time to find the HR department and get checked in. The buildings were all wooden with chimneys made out of stone. There would be a group of buildings then a path that would connect the next small group of buildings.

The entire place had this camping/outdoor feel to it right away. Yosemite Valley is the main hub for everything. It is here where most people spend their time while visiting the park. The valley has a few small stores and a huge hotel with a restaurant. The place was busy. People were there to visit, and others like me were getting ready to work for the season. I found a place to park and followed signs to the office area. Just then, guess who walked around the corner? Tiffany and her friend Tara. "Well, hello," she said, "you made it."

"Yes, I did." And I gave her a big hug. I told her, "This place is remarkable, and I'm so excited to be here." She thanked me for coming and told me she had just come from the HR office and there was a position available at the high camps where she was working. The thing was I had a job here; I just didn't know what it might be. They waited to meet people face to face to see what position would meet their expectations. Tiffany had told me that my first year, I would probably have to work in the valley, which was fine, no problem at all; it was just very crowded. The employees were part of a union or something, and positions were filled by seniority, which was fine for me; I would have to start at the bottom.

Thousands of people come to Yosemite every year, and it takes a lot of employees to take care of everyone. The staff has certain camping areas with five hundred people plus staying in one area. We would be living in big canvas-style tents that could sleep three to four people, shared bathrooms and showers. If this was what I would have to do to work here, live with five hundred other people, then that was what I will do. It would just be very busy all the time and never really have any space for myself.

Tiffany had told me about a position that had not been filled at Tuolumne Meadows. It was a night shift job, which was from 9:00 p.m., to 5:00 a.m.; the position meant cleaning the kitchen/restaurant every night and basically keeping an eye on the camp at night. One of the requirements for this job was a bear encounter course that I would have to take. This would be a cool place to work, only working and living with thirty-five to forty people, two people in a tent, and a chance to see and do more in the park. It was the hours that really sucked, working all night long while everyone was sleeping.

Well, to be honest, I wasn't sure but went with what Tiffany and Tara told me. "It's a good job and will get you out of the valley your first year." So after talking with them, I made up my mind; I was going to work at one of the high camps with Tiff and Tara.

I did have to stay in the valley for a few days. We had to get classes done and pick up our clothes, fill out paperwork, and all that fun stuff for a new job. It was still a lot of fun and meeting a lot of people. Tiffany and Tara had left, and they gave me direction, and I told them I'd see them in a few days. All I really had to do was take a few one-hour classes in the park, and I had my "bear awareness class" as well.

Anyway, the first night was just sitting around drinking beers, which came from the small store, a five-minute walk from our camp, and getting to know people. I was sitting talking to this guy, and these two girls walked by. Robert, who was a piece of work—a nice guy, just a little rough around the edges—shouted out to the two girls to come over. I was thinking right then and there, *Robert, you don't have a chance with these girls, but I'm happy they are coming over*. As they approached, I realized they were both not Americans but from somewhere else. Both girls had darker complexions, and they both looked Spanish, Mexican, or something. Well, this was the first time I met Ximana, pronounced "he-ma-na," and she was from Bogate, Columbia. Actually, I came to find out there were many people working here this year from overseas. These two girls happened to be from South America.

They walked up and started to talk with Robert; he introduced me as his friend. He did most of the talking, and all I could do was stare at Ximana; she was very attractive and spoke English. Her friend was also very cute but did not speak English as well. We talked for about five minutes, and they had to leave. Robert looked over at me and said, "I'm going to get her," and I thought to myself, *Buddy, you don't have a chance in hell to get a girl like that*. She was about 5'6", about 125 lbs. with dark skin and long black hair, and I knew as soon as I saw her that I was definitely attracted to her.

So the next day was all about HR stuff, getting a few classes that I had to take, getting all my uniforms and clothes that I might need, and hanging out at Curry Village, which is the name of the employee area of Yosemite National Park.

It was midafternoon, and I was getting bored, so I decided to walk over to the pool area and maybe lie out for a few hours and get some sun. It wasn't really hot that day but warm enough. I approached the pool area, and the first person that I saw lying there was Ximana. I walked up to her and said, "Hello, how are you today?"

She looked up and with a big smile said, "I'm good, how are you?" Well, I told her I was much better now and asked if I could join her. She said yes with a big smile, and the ice had been broken. She and I sat there for about an hour talking and laughing about everything we had been through so far, while being employees here at this wonderful park. Her English was good enough for us to carry on a great conversation. At certain times, she would have to take a minute to say what she wanted to say in English, but it always came out correct. We had connected, and unfortunately, she had to go to work. I asked her right then what time she got off, and she told me around 8:00 p.m. She was working in a kitchen making sandwiches and small things for the bar area.

"You're off at 8:00 p.m., so maybe when you're done, we can do something—go for a walk, drink a bottle of wine, or something." She agreed, and it was all set up.

The next several hours were all about planning my night. I had to find a nice spot to walk to that was not too far yet kind of private, buy a bottle of wine, get a hold of a blanket, and find two glasses. I felt like a sixteen-year-old getting ready for my first date. Actually, that was the easy part; the hard part was waiting for time to go by till I could see her again. Time did go by, and a little after 8:00 p.m., I saw her walk up to me. She asked if she could take a quick shower, to which of course I said we had plenty of time. It took her about twenty minutes, and she was ready.

Now I have to say I did feel like a stud when she walked up to me. I was sitting at a picnic table with four other guys, including Robert, who was a really cool guy and jealous but happy for me, and about five to six other people just standing around. She walked up looking beautiful and told me she was ready. I stood up like I was ten feet tall, grabbed her hand, threw the backpack over my shoulder, and away we went. This would give everyone something to talk about now.

Earlier, I had found a spot not far from camp, down a small hill, right near a creek, and about as secluded as you could get with a thousand people nearby. It was perfect for us; we laid out the blanket, opened the wine, and right then and there began a wonderful relationship. At this point, it was just the first night. We talked and laughed and got closer and closer as the sun set. By the time it was dark, we were about as close as two people could get. We had the perfect spot, so clothes became an option, and about two hours into our evening, we were naked. That was our first of many nights together.

The next day was my last in the valley and then up to the high camps. So Ximana and I did have one more night together, and it was wonderful, a complete night, and I really liked this place. I had been here less than three nights, seen so much, met a beautiful girl, and yes, I *really liked* this place.

The last thing I had to do was another bear safety course. The class had about twenty people, and I met two girls that were going to be working near me, so I offered them a ride, and they both accepted. We hit it off, and after that last class, which ended early, I told them to meet me at a certain point and we would leave. This gave me a chance to grab a few things and see Ximana before I left. The high camp was about an hour away. So it was not really far, but without a car, it was the other side of the planet. Would I see her again or not? I really didn't know at that point.

My two new friends were in my car, and we were off to see more of the park and get to our destinations.

Tuolumne Meadows is one of the largest high-elevated meadows in the Sierra Mountains, 8,600 feet above sea level. This meadow has been explored and studied by past pioneers and present visitors and scientists. It truly is a special place with the Tuolumne River slowly passing through the granite mountain range. It was early spring, and the wildflowers and grasses were coming alive, giving it a picture-perfect moment, which is just what I did—stopped the car, got out, and took a "picture-perfect photo."

We arrived at the camp, which was going to be home for me for the next five months at least. As I pulled in, I noticed the white canvas tents along the right side of the parking lot. Then straight in front was a building that was a wooded structure the size of a small house. Then to the left were more white MASH-style tents set up near a few smaller buildings. I parked the car and started to walk toward the building, and out from one of the closest tents appeared my friend Tiffany. "Welcome home. Glad you're finally here," said Tiffany, and we met each other for a big hug and proper greetings.

The two girls went off to find their boss, and I asked Tiffany, "What do I need to do? Check in with someone or wait till they find me."

What to do? I was so excited I couldn't help myself. She said, "Move into your tent, and I'll show you around." It sounded like a plan, and I went and found my new home.

It was a white canvas tent with a wooden door, room for two big beds on either side, two small shelving units, and a wood-burning stove. The only place on the entire property that had electricity was the main lodge, so there was no power in any of the tents. Not for the employees or the guests, this was all part of staying at one of the high camps. For me it was perfect, and I could not believe I was actually here.

Tiff and her friend Tara, who had both worked here for the past eight years, spent the next few hours walking me around and introducing me to people and showing me the camp. Just outside of my tent, there were several sections of a tree that were arranged together for a hangout area for everyone. So my first night, we sat around drinking Sierra Nevadas and getting to know each other.

I had three days before I had to start work, which gave me time to get to know this place a little bit. There was a store about a mile away. It was a quick car ride or a great walk, which is usually how I would go there. All we had to do was walk out of my tent, go to the creek, turn right, walk along a beautiful creek with a few swimming holes and waterfalls, then walk across a beautiful meadow, through a tree line, and the store was right there; it took about fifteen to twenty minutes door to door. This was also where our showers were located. The showers at our camp were for guests only. The main lodge consisted of a wooden structure that was the kitchen, the coolers, the employee lounge for eating, and that was it. Then attached to the main building was a huge industrial tent setup for the main check-in area and for the restaurant that was there for the quest. So you walked in the back and you were in the kitchen area then turned left for the lounge or straight ahead to a set of swinging doors that led into the restaurant area, a setting for fifty people. It was very rustic, but we were eight thousand feet high, and what did you expect? The guests come here for hiking, rock climbing, and a moderate camping experience. They lived in a tent without power with only a wood-burning stove to keep you warm. It is truly an amazing outdoor adventure.

My last day, before I had to start work, I wondered what Ximana was doing. I really had nothing to do, so I decided to drive an hour back to the valley and see if I could find her. It was also another reason to make this amazing drive again. I got to the Curry Village and went to her tent. She was not there, so I decided to check out where she was working, and they said she left a half hour ago. Okay, maybe she was back at her tent by now. Well, I ended up running into her on the way back and asked if she wanted to come up to my camp for the night. She said yes right away, and we were off to her tent so she could grab a few things. Within fifteen minutes, we were on our way back to my camp. It turned out we both had the same days off Wednesday and Thursday, which worked out great for us in the future.

That night, I had the room to myself, and I introduced Ximana to everyone that I had met the past few days, which was 85 percent of the staff. It was a great night for both of us. It was just the beginning of the season, and I had been very lucky to meet someone. It was going to work out great because we still would have our separate lives and see each other a few days a week. The next day, we hung out for most of the day, and then I took her home. I had to report for work that night at 9:00 p.m., which was so weird, and I really didn't know if I was going to like it or not. Oh well, we would see.

With Ximana back safely, I was back to camp a few hours before I had to start, and I was a little nervous. What had I signed up for, and what exactly was I going to be doing? Well, the time came, and off to work I went. I walked to the lodge, which was like thirty seconds away, up the steps and into the back door, and went right to the

TAKE A DECADE

kitchen manager, Tammy. She was six feet tall with black hair, a bigger woman and kind of intimidating at first. She and her wife, Jennel, had been the main chefs at this camp for twelve years or so; both of them were two of the nicest people you could ever meet. They both spent about an hour with me going over everything. They showed me around the kitchen and gave me instructions on how to clean the grill properly, which was the heart of the kitchen. The first part of my shift would be mostly cleaning—kitchen, floors, break room, floors in the restaurant area—and getting all the garbage out into a bear-safe container. Then it was more just keeping an eye on things when everyone else was sleeping, except the nighttime auditor, which happened to be Tara and Tiffany. For the most part, I just walked around and made sure no bears got into anything. The last part of the night was sitting by the fire and waiting for time to go by. The job was going to be easy, and it would have advantages that I didn't know about yet.

My roommate showed up the next day, and he was awesome. His name was Regan, which was his last name but the only name he used. He was a seasonal vet here at Tuolumne meadows; it was his eighth year there, and he was going to be in charge of the waitstaff. Anyway, he was from Buffalo, New York, which gave us an instant bond, me being from upstate New York as well. He was easy to talk to, and we hit it off right away. We had a great relationship all summer; unfortunately, we really didn't get a chance to do much outside the camp together because of different days off, but we still had fun. Reagan was one of many that made for a great experience overall.

So I'm going to take you through a typical day for me after living here for a few weeks, starting with my job. Nine p.m. was the start of work. The waitstaff, which was about ten to twelve people, were just finishing up their last tables, and usually by 9:15 p.m., the chefs were done, and they were ready to leave. The kitchen staff made up eight to ten more people that work there, and usually by 9:30 p.m., they were all gone. The first thing I would do was clean the grill, which would take a half hour. After the grill was done, I wiped down all services then swept and mopped the kitchen and restaurant area. It usually took me less than three hours to clean everything. Then I took the trash out and sprayed off the mats that went on the kitchen floors; this was all done outside, and the air always felt so good. Once the floors dried, the mats went back down, and with a little bit of extra cleaning I tried to do each night, my job was done by 1:00 a.m. It took me about four hours each night to do what they asked me to do, and I tried to do something a little extra each night.

The rest of the night, I was sipping on wine while talking with Tara. We would sit by the woodstove in the lodge and talk about life. I would walk around the camp a few times a night just checking on things, but really, it was just something to do. At least three nights a week, I would leave early, and Tara would clock me out when she did, at 5:00 a.m. The job was easy, and because I did a great job, the kitchen manager, Tammy, pretty much told me to enjoy a good meal every night and just clean up after yourself. So usually, around 1:00 or 2:00 a.m., I would make something to eat. Steak, fish, chicken, it was all there in a huge walk-in cooler. My favorite was trout and a small steak, which I had at least three nights a week. The restaurant had a wine keg on tap, so we were able to drink wine most of the night. It was all about a few hours in the beginning; bust your ass, and the rest of the night, I could do whatever I wanted.

I was in bed by 5:00 a.m., before the sun came up, and usually awake by 11:00 a.m.

I would get up and get cleaned up, grab something for breakfast and then out to explore the park. It was either hiking from the camp or a quick drive somewhere to check things out. We could drive to a lake and walk around, climb a mountain, rock-climb, and hang out at the other camp, walking to the store a few times a day, or spend the day just swimming at our close swimming hole near the camp. There was something to do and someone to do something with every day. I would be gone until 5:00 or 6:00 p.m. then back to camp. Around seven or so, I would take a quick nap and get ready for the night. Then it was back to work, and I started my day all over.

The days went by fast at first. There was just so much to do, and it took me a month or so before I started to just relax and just enjoy the day. One thing I loved to do was work on my rock-climbing skills, and there was a huge traverse, which is a rock-climbing term for a boulder that has a horizontal route that you can practice on. This was about a ten-minute walk in the woods, a huge boulder, 1,000 tons easily, and I would spend time trying to climb from one side to the next without falling, and if I did fall it was only two feet, so no one got hurt. I started this at the beginning of the season and could hardly do three moves before falling, and by the time I left, I had been able to go from one side to the next without falling. I was so proud the first time I did this; too bad I was there by myself. Oh well, I did it.

Ximana would come up usually on Wednesday morning; she found a bus that could bring her up and bring her back down for like two dollars a trip. It was a park bus and worked out great. She preferred coming to see me because it was quieter than the valley, and we always found something to do for the night or just a day trip. It was great because she would always get there early and walk into my tent, get undressed, and climb in bed with me. Wednesday mornings were my favorite.

Hot Springs

There were so many cool things that I was able to do while staying in Yosemite National Park. One day I was off, about eight people were going to the hot springs and asked if I wanted to go. *Absolutely.* So we loaded up in a few cars, and off we went, and it was already dark by that time, so it was going to be a long night. We drove about thirty minutes on dirt roads and through meadows; we came to the end of the road and all got out. It was a ten-minute walk, and we reached a natural hot spring. It was big enough for at least ten people and we all got naked and climbed in. We sat there in that natural "hot tub" under the stars for at least two hours, drinking beer and laughing about how crazy good our life was going. It was a beautiful night to be sitting in warm water, looking up at the stars and having nothing but good people around me.

Rock Climbing

The first time I tried climbing with a bunch of people, I failed and could not do it. I needed to figure this out because this was the thing to do around here. So I practiced on my traverse and started going with a few people around the camp. After a few small climbs, I was feeling much more confident and was ready for something bigger. One of the guys asked if I wanted to go with him and do a multipitch climb. "Sure," I said, and away we went. Now most rock climbing that I had done was me climbing up and someone on the ground making sure I was okay; they were called the belayer. Anyway, this multipitch climb was so different. We both started at the bottom, and he climbed up about 200 feet, then from there, he belayed me up to where he was located. Then while I was hooked into the rock with a carabiner, I lay back up at least two hundred feet and guided him up the next level. While I was assisting him on getting to the next level, my legs were just shaking. Trying not to look down was impossible, and all I saw was big rocks. If this line broke, I was dead for sure. Well, he reached his next level, and it was my turn to follow him. It was so challenging and scary that it took all the fun out of it. Before I reached him, I had fallen twice, and each time I slipped from the rock, my heart lost several beats. But we reached our goal of four hundred feet, and now, it was time to get back down. He went first, and I tried so hard not to screw up. We basically rappelled down the cliff, first to the first level and then to the bottom. I had never been so happy to see flat land. It was at this moment that I admitted to myself that was I was not a big fan of heights. I don't mind climbing a mountain when my feet are firmly on the ground, but to be dangling from a rope four hundred feet above rocks on a vertical cliff is something that I can say I've done.

Gas Station

This was not just your average gas station. This place was a bar, concert venue, place to get great food, and a place that people migrated to from all over the mountain. People came from the high camps and nearby Mammoth, which was a mountain town in the Sierra Mountains. It was a very cool place to visit. Our camp, which was at the top of the mountain, gave us an interesting drive down the mountain each and every time. We were at eight thousand feet plus and had to get to the bottom of the mountain, so the Tiago Pass was a fast road down with cliffs on one side and a sheer drop-off on the other side. No matter how many times I did this drive, it was always exciting. What if I lost my brakes? I'm a dead man for sure. Now going up the mountain was a different story, slow and steady was all you could do.

Friday nights, the gas station had live music and the place would be packed. Grab a burger or something else to eat, and they had the best mango margaritas you have ever had. Now, you could still get gas at this place, but the owners had made it so much more. Good food and good drinks and you could sit outside on a picnic table and enjoy the mountains around you. Mono Lake, which was a saltwater lake, was right nearby. There were amazing views of the valley, and did I mention they actually had a trapeze stage setup, so once in a while you would be able to watch them practice swinging through the air? The whole place and vibe was amazing.

Hot Springs Camping/Giant Redwood Trees

This was an epic weekend for Ximana and me. She arrived on a Wednesday morning as usual, and we left Tuolumne to adventure out a little bit. We found a small campground that had individual hot springs at each campsite. My friends at camp had told me about this, and I was like, "What?"

"Yes, they have about ten sites, and each site has a hot spring pool or tub to relax in." I told Ximana about this and she was all in. The plan was to camp out and see the giant trees. I'll be honest; I really didn't know that these mammoth trees were here in Yosemite. I felt a little stupid but was quite excited to see them now that I knew they were close by. So anyway, we camped out at a small campsite, and we had our private hot spring tub. So there were about ten sites, and they were spaced far enough apart that you had privacy. We got the tent set up and dinner prepared, so it was just the two of us, so why not get naked and enjoy one of Mother Nature's best gifts, an outdoor natural hot spring? It was a great experience and a great night. We sat in the tub for hours and watched the sun go down and the stars brighten the sky. We had our fire going, a little chicken and beans for dinner cooking on the stove, cold beers, a beautiful woman, and surrounded by nature. This was one of my best weekends with her and such a cool thing to experience.

So the next day, we packed up and headed to see the big trees. That was all she could say—"big trees"—and this was something she really wanted to see while she was here. Ximana would be returning to Bogota, Colombia, at the end of the season and wasn't leaving until she saw them. Well, we drove a while and entered the place where we could park our car and walk around inside the park where the grove was located. So we walked, and we started to see these "trees." They were so much more than just a tree. Holy cow, let me tell you something: These things were prehistoric-looking. They looked like they were not real, but they were as real as it gets. These trees were called giant sequoia or "giant redwood" or just simply "big tree" as Ximana called them. They were the most massive trees in the world. They grew to an average height of 165 to 280 feet tall with an average trunk diameter of 20 to 26 feet. The oldest was 3,200 to 3266 years old, and the general grant tree had the greatest diameter of any tree at 28.9 feet. So just take a second and picture this: The average 6-foot-tall man had a wingspan of about six feet, so to get around this tree, it would take five grown men to get around this tree. It was one of the places and things that you could only get a true feel of how big these suckers are if you stood next to one. It was a great experience, and we had a blast all day, just walking around marveling at these trees and taking in the whole day. Her quest was over, and she could now relax about seeing the one thing she really wanted to see. Again, it was a great weekend all around, hot springs camping, and giant redwoods with a beautiful person and sex under the stars.

12

CHAPTER

New Friends

Well, at this point, in my life things were going great. After several months of being part of such a close-knit community, actually enjoying my job and the flexibility, and the adventures that surrounded us; it was definitely the people that you met along the way that made the difference. This is when I got to meet my friend Julian.

It was midafternoon, and most people were out and about working or just taking care of business, but that day, the camp was quiet. I walked out of my tent and was heading up to the lodge when someone yelled, "Hey, do you know where Tiffany is staying?" I turned around and saw this guy younger than me, about 5'7", about 160 lbs., and had short blond hair. He walked up and shook my hand, and he had those eyes of a tiger, kind of yellow with a hint of blue.

I said, "Yes, she is probably at the front counter working till three or so." He said okay and was off to find her. I can honestly say when I first met Julian, there was something that rubbed me the wrong way. He seemed cocky and had this attitude about himself that I didn't like. Julian had worked up here many years ago and was just passing through the area and wanted to stop and see Tiffany and Tara, whom he had known for years.

Well, Julian ended up staying at the camp for longer than expected, sleeping in Tiffany and Tara's tent, and everyone was helping him out with food and drinks. Julian arrived with no money in his pocket, just a bag of clothes and that was it. He became the center of attention in the camp real quick and didn't even work there. Now the rule is that you can have a guest for three to four days and then they have to leave the park for a while. Well, Julian had the ability to avoid the one person that oversaw this aspect of our camp, the head security guy. It was his job to enforce the rules around the camp and keep everyone safe. He became Julian's nemesis, and the game was on. He would catch Julian from time to time, and it was always the same story. He would say, "I just got back today. I was gone for seven days."

The guy would look at Julian and say, "Dude, I saw you yesterday. It is time to go." He would leave for a few days at a time but always return. The day that Julian and I connected was about three weeks into his little game, and the guy busted him for being at the camp, and I came out and told the guy he was my guest this week, and that was all there was to it. It was that day that Julian and I started our friendship, and I started to help him out with whatever he needed. I would bring him food, beer, whatever. Julian was a very smart person—high IQ, great chess player, entertainer, and unfortunately his own worst enemy. He liked to party and had paid the price of being homeless and never really knowing what was next. He didn't have a great childhood. He was born in Florida to both parents who were drug dealers, ran away from home, and lived with his aunt in South Carolina, and he pretty much had just been traveling around the world with not a lot to his name. Most people could not live like Julian had, but for him, it was just a way of life.

It was around the first of September that things started to sink in a little, and that was when the season was coming to an end. At this point, we had all started to plan for the huge end of the year party. Normally, they said that by the third week of September, the tents started to come down, and it was all based on the weather. As of Sept 1, it was starting to get a little cooler during the day and the fires were going in everyone's tents.

The end-of-the-year party was set, and the theme this year was "under the big top." It was about a week or so before the party, and a few of us went shopping and bought a few things. This was a dress-up party, so everyone had to come in a costume. We walked around this store in Mammoth, and I found the perfect thing. I was going to be the ring toss guy. I bought the rings, a bunch of small stuffed animals, and a loud shirt for less than $20. My costume was set.

In the meantime, the thought of what I was going to do in a week when this is all over was on my mind. I could get a job in the valley and live here all winter. My other choice was going back to Arizona, and I knew I could stay with Murph and Kari for a while. I really didn't want to go back just yet; I wanted something more. I asked Julian what he was going to do when this was all over for the season. He was pretty much living in my tent by then, and we had started to really bond. He said that he had just talked with a friend of his in Alaska, and he just bought a boat and got a permit to fish for shrimp in South East Alaska.

I looked at him and said, "You are going to Alaska and work on a shrimping boat? You have got to see if he needs any help."

We talked about the operation, and honestly, that night, I was excited for this chance. It was a long shot if this guy even needed more help, but by then, Julian knew what kind of person I was and that I would work my ass off. So the next day, I was up and out doing something; it was just a few days before the party, and we were all planning and getting things set up. I saw Julian headed my way, and I stopped and waited for him to catch up. He walked up to me and said, "Guess what? You are going to Alaska." I screamed. He said he had called John, who was the captain, and he told Julian that he did need help and would be happy to give me a shot.

It was another phone call to my parents. My mother answered, and I told her I have a wonderful opportunity to do something a little different. I proceeded to tell her that I was going to Alaska for the winter and work on a shrimping boat with two other guys. She said, "Okay, this is a surprise, and what can I say? Have fun and be careful and make sure you call as much as you can." She knew as much as I did about what was going to happen; all I knew was I was excited.

The next day, we made arrangements to get from Yosemite to Ketchikan, Alaska. I came to find out a couple of the other guys were heading north to Seattle. We could catch a ride with them to Seattle and then fly from there. The captain had paid for our tickets to get there. I made enough to live and have a good time. Unfortunately, I had very little saved, maybe $200, and that was it.

13
CHAPTER

So it took just under twenty-four hours for my life to completely change and all for the better. I was going to Alaska, and we knew how we were getting there. Everything was set. Now all we had to do was have a great end of the year party and spend a few more days with Ximana.

"Under the big top" was the theme, and it was a blast. I went as the ring toss guy, I had three rubber rings with a pole to throw them on and stuffed animals around my waist on a belt for the prizes. That night we had clowns, the bearded lady, the power lifter guy, and so much more. It was all held in the restaurant area, which had plenty of room. We went through at least three kegs, a bunch of wine, and who knew how much liquor. There were probably seventy-five people from our camp and nearby camps. This was the party of the year, and if you were close, you were there. Ximana came up from the valley and we had fun. The one cool place was the pillow tent. That day, as part of the beginning breakdown, they took all the pillows from all the tents and put them in one tent. It was called the Pillow Tent and the place to go and maybe get in trouble. It was a dark tent filled with pillows at least halfway up, and certain people liked to get a little freaky in there. I think Julian spent half the night in this tent. He had sex with Tara and maybe someone else, who knew?

The night started around 6:00 p.m., and unfortunately for me, I was still up at 6:00 a.m. cleaning everything up.

We did sleep most of the day, and late afternoon, I drove her back. We got to her camp, and we hung out for about an hour. Earlier that week, I had bought her a picture frame and had a photo of the two of us in it. She had gotten me a small gift as well, and we exchanged them and did a little bit of crying. There were no promises going into this relationship from the beginning, and I wasn't sure what the future would hold. We talked that night about coming back next year and maybe going to Bogotá, Columbia, to see her. I was headed for Alaska, and who knew what could happen after that? We would see. I gave her one more kiss and one more hug. I turned and walked away with tears in my eyes. She too was crying, and we both said it was the best summer of our lives. Even though at that time I thought for sure I would see her again and spend more time together, it was actually the last time we saw each other.

Back at camp, it was all about preparing for the next day. Now one thing that I had to do was figure out what to do with my car. Tiffany had agreed to drive it back to Phoenix, and her boyfriend might be interested in buying it. So with my car going back to Phoenix, I was able to put a few things in the trunk and at that point just had my backpack and one other bag. All I needed was some warm clothes and personal stuff.

The morning had come, and it was time to leave. I can honestly say we had a great send-off. There were maybe ten people left, including Tiffany and Tara, and they were all there to see us off. The last thing I did before I left that place was give Tiffany a big hug and thank her so much for what she had done for me. It was then that four guys that we had just met this year arrived in an old car packed to the ceiling. We honked our horn, waving to all our friends, pulled out, and waved goodbye to Tuolumne Meadows and Yosemite National Park.

We had three days to get to Seattle, Washington, to catch our flight. We reached the Oregon border, and I was now in a new state, and we needed to find a place to stay. Well, there were four guys who had little money and were willing to suck it up a little and not get a room. Instead, we drove until it was dark and then found a turnoff on a dirt road, found a small spot where we could park, and just laid out sleeping bags next to the car under the stars. We had driven most of the day, and it was good to just be able to stretch out a little.

We all slept for about five hours, and that was about it; time to fly and get back on the road. Our next goal was to get to Frank's sister's house in Portland, and we could crash there one night, and then the next day, he would get us to Seattle. It was a long few days with a lot of driving, but the scenery around the northwest was spectacular. I would love to spend more time here in the future. This trip was all about getting to Alaska.

On the third day after leaving Yosemite, Julian and I had made it to the airport in Seattle. Julian was going back to a place he felt comfortable, and I was checking out something new. The time at the airport was fun. We had a beer, and I just kept using my ATM card to buy things. I was trying to keep track in my head, but after fuel, food, casino, and beer, my account had to be getting low. Oh well, as soon as we got to Alaska, Julian said that John would maybe float us a few bucks until we start making some, so I wasn't really worried.

Well, it was once again that I was leaving a great experience for hopefully another one. The past few years had been so good to me: Europe, Japan, Thailand, Mexico, Caribbean, a cross-country trip, and Yosemite. Now in just a few hours, I'd be landing in a whole different world. I couldn't wait to see what happened next.

CHAPTER 14

Alaska

Julian and I had a great flight that took less than three hours. All we did was talk about our future. It wasn't all about the money we could make but more like the opportunities and what we might see while we are out on the boat. He had lived here before, and it sounded like he knew what was going on, but we would see. He did give me a lowdown on John, the captain. He told me he could be rough around the edges, actually a bit of a dick at times yet a nice guy, and it should all be good. All I knew was that I was headed to Alaska to work on a shrimp boat. Forrest Gump would be so proud of me.

As we got close, the landscaping from the window of the plane started to change. Now I had just spent six months in the mountains, but the mountains that I could see looked more real and much more rugged. This land was God's country, and Alaska was the final frontier.

We touched down at the airport and departed the plane; the next thing was catching a ferry to the mainland. You see, this airport at Ketchikan was on an island, and you had to take a boat to the main part of town. This gave us time to get our bags, and we had about twenty minutes before the next ferry. *Let's have a beer and celebrate the arrival to Alaska and a brand-new adventure.* I ordered the beers, and Julian and I enjoyed a cold one. Our plan was to get to the mainland, hitchhike to where the boat was stored, and spend the night on the boat. It was the last week in September, so nights were starting to get cold; we had our sleeping bags and hopefully a heat source on the boat. We would see, but first things first, we would enjoy our first beer in Alaska.

Time came to leave, and I went to go pay and guess what, my card was declined. I got the big *Declined* and was like, *Oh, shit*. I called the bank, and I was overdrawn by $28. This meant we had no money. We went through all our bags right there at the bar and searched for change and whatever we could come up with. We ended up with just enough for the two beers, no tip, but she completely understood and was very nice about our little dilemma, and we had the $4 for the ferry. That was it and I was broke. I had no money, not even a penny. Between the two of us, we landed in Alaska penniless. What a great way to start this adventure out.

We catch the ferry and walk up to the main road leading out of town. The town of Ketchikan is very cool. It was a main destination for cruise ships during the summer, so they have a lot of souvenirs shops, bars, restaurants, and cool things to do. Unfortunately, all of the above cost money. So it wasn't about exploring town at this point. It was getting to the boat and seeing what was onboard for us to survive for a few days. We got to the road, and within a few minutes, a guy pulled up and offered us a ride. We jumped in the back of his pickup truck and had a nice airy ride out of town. We left the main area near town and passed a huge boat junkyard filled with old boats and a few homes that looked a little rundown. It seemed that the area we were in was a poorer area, but let me tell you the landscape surrounding Ketchikan was picture-perfect. I said to Julian as we rode in the back of the truck, "Holy shit, dude, we are in frigging Alaska, unbelievable."

Julian knew where the boat was stored, and it was about three miles from town. The guy stopped; we grabbed our gear and thanked him for the ride. Julian and I walked into this boatyard, filled with boats out of the water on barrels and some being worked on and some that were just falling apart. There were a few sailboats, mostly power boats of some sort, and from what I was seeing, they all needed work.

Julian grabbed my arm and pointed toward this boat and said, "That is ours right there, the Winning Hand." It was about sixty-eight feet long and twenty-five feet wide; it had the wheelhouse up front that was close to the bow, a cabin area behind it, and then mostly the deck. It was held up by about twenty barrels and looked rough. This boat did not look like it could float. It had been out of the water for a year getting a rebuilt engine and had not been cleaned since it came out of the water. *Holy shit*, was what I first thought. *I'm going to spend a month out to sea on this thing?* This would be my first boat job ever, and I really didn't know a lot about boats. I'd never been shrimping before, that was for sure, and I just hoped I didn't get seasick, which had definitely been on my mind. Maybe this was a great boat, and I just didn't know. All I knew was that my first impressions of the Winning Hand were not the greatest.

We walked to the boat, and there was a ladder going up to the back deck. With the boat out of the water, it is at least a fifteen-foot climb to get to the deck, and the mast was standing at least one hundred feet above the ground. We climbed the stairs, and I was now on the back deck. It made up for a large portion of the boat, and Julian explained that we would have about one hundred shrimp pots stacked on here at some point. We then walked into the cabin area. First, there was a small mudroom about 4' × 4', which is a place to hang all your outdoor gear, so the stinky scent of fish could stay outside. Then we went through the next door, which led into the cabin. The head or toilet was to our right, which was just a toilet and sink, no shower. The captain bunk was to the left, a small room with a twin bed and desk, nothing fancy, but it was separate. The table, which would seat four people, was on the left, and a small galley was on the right. The galley had a two-burner cook stove, which was heated by the boat somehow, a small sink with running water, a few cupboards with dishes, and a small refrigerator. Just past the table was the bow of the boat and that had four very small bunk beds in which four people would really have a tough time; two people was really max. Now just before you reached the bunks, there was a hole in the ceiling that led to the wheelhouse. It was about twelve feet long and five feet wide. I was not huge but had the captain's chair and what looked like decent instruments in the wheelhouse. The boat was not huge but would be okay for the three of us. Unfortunately, the boat was a complete mess and needed a cleaning before we could actually live here. There were cobwebs all over and trash lying around; it smelled like it had been closed up for ten years. The whole place needed a quick cleaning, and that is what we did. We had nothing else to do and no money to do anything, so we got to work.

By the time we had made it to the boat and got things cleaned up a little, we then needed food. Inside the cupboards were a few cans of food and a bag of stale bag chips. One can was cream corn, and the other can was stewed tomatoes. It was not exactly what I expected to have as my first meal in Alaska, but hey, when you're hungry, anything is good. We opened both cans, washed out a bowl the best we could, dumped both cans together, used a fork, and mixed it all up together then used the stale chips as spoons and sat at the table and ate our first meal together in Alaska.

There wasn't anything at all to do that night, and it had already been dark for a few hours, so we called it a night. Now I had one of the bunk beds up front, and let me tell you they were small. The length was good; it was about 7.5 feet long. The width of the beds, however, were only about 20 inches wide. When I first got into my bunk, the ceiling was like right there about as much room as in a damn coffin. I tried to roll over on my stomach and realized that I couldn't; it was not wide enough to roll over, so I had to climb out of my bunk and go in on my stomach. This was by far the narrowest bunk bed I had ever had to sleep on. I lay there for about ten minutes and just thought to myself, *Wow, this is different and another first for me. What have I got myself into?*

We slept in, and around noon, we made our way back to the airport to meet John. We didn't have any wheels, so we hitchhiked. We figured from there, we would get some supplies and hopefully some food. It had been a little over two days since we had anything real to eat, so the belly was rumbling.

John's plane was on time, and Julian noticed him walking toward us. He was about 6'1", 200 lbs., bald, and he had this little Hitler-looking mustache going on. He walked up to us and didn't even really stop. He just said, "Let's go, the truck is right over here." He looked at me but didn't say a single word to me. He walked really fast, and we made it to the truck in a minute flat. The truck was a beaten up, old, and rusty truck that was used as a boat dock truck. The truck and the boat looked a lot alike. All I knew was that you couldn't drown in a beat-up truck, but you most surely could in a beat-up boat. We got in the truck. I was sitting in the back. It was a four-door, so I was not in the bed of the truck but in the back seat. Just as John sat down in the driver's seat, he reached down the front of his pants and pulled out an ounce of weed and set it on the seat next to him. Julian then had a chance to finally introduced us and he reached over the seat and shook my hand. "Hi, I'm John," was all he said. First impressions are indicative, and at this time, all I could think was it could be a very long month.

Julian and John caught up, and we had a bit of small talk during our ride back to the boat. I was glad that in the first few minutes of their conversation, Julian informed John that we were both broke. John's response was "Me too." He said he had spent everything he had on this boat, but we knew he had credit, so we were not going to starve. Instead of getting supplies and maybe something to eat, we headed back to the boat, and pretty much, at that moment we started working. John gave us an overview of what we needed to do in basically three days. That was when the boat was scheduled to go back in the water. John's explanation of what he wanted us to do was very vague. I really had no clue what he wanted; I just hoped Julian did.

We worked primarily on cleaning the boat for the first day, inside and out. The entire boat needed a good scrubbing, so that was where we started. John left and spent a good portion of that day running around and picking up supplies. He did bring back food, and that was all we really needed. It was sandwiches and chips, and boy, did it taste good—nothing fancy but rejuvenated me for sure. John was also a smoker, so we had him grab a few packs of cigarettes for each of us. The deal was he would get what we needed for personal supplies like smokes and dip, then at the end of the trip, we would pay him back for things like this.

TAKE A DECADE

Midafternoon, we had a delivery, and it was a generator to run the blast freezer for the shrimp. It was a big generator, 6' × 4' × 4', and weighed a lot. We hosted it with the small crane that was on the boat and secured it next to the entrance to the freezer. It took up space on the back deck, but we needed something to make sure the shrimp stayed cold.

With the boat cleaned and the generator hooked up, it was time to work on lines, which basically took the next two days to complete. We had to measure out our main lines—they were five hundred feet long—then tie a tagline from the main line for the shrimp pots about every fifty feet. We were going to have 120 shrimp pots on the boat when we left. This was the number of pots we could have according to his permit for shrimping. So this meant we had to string 120 lines into several main lines, and it was just very tedious work, and the last day we worked on lines, it rained the entire day, so this made for a cold and wet day. Julian and I did most of the lines, and John worked on the engines and other things on the boat. We would all be working, and John would start swearing, climb down the ladder, jump in the truck, and take off for a while; he really had no patience at all. It only took about a day or so to get used to John. Luckily, we both smoked weed, and that was our common bond. He asked if I could roll a joint, and I proved my worth right there and then. John did have a sense of humor and liked to laugh. Julian and John would bust on each other throughout the day, and for the most part, we were having fun.

It was at the end of our third day, and the time had come to get this boat in the water. We were all just hoping it would not sink in the harbor. We laughed about this, but I could tell John was actually nervous. In a way, this would be the maiden voyage of an old boat that had been worked on and a new engine put into it; we were all just crossing our fingers it works.

The machine used to move the boat from the barrels to the water looked like a huge sling with giant bands around it. This thing came up along the side, and these straps were placed under and around the boat, then it lifted the boat evenly and slowly, maneuvering it toward the water, then slowly eased it into the water and the straps are removed. Holy cow, the boat was actually floating, and John had fired up the engines. It ran, sounded great, and did I mention it was floating?

We spent a few hours getting everything on the boat. We found a place for everything and made sure it was strapped down and stored away. John did buy a few basic supplies, food and drinks for the trip. He also made sure he had plenty of cigarettes and me a few cans of dip, very nice of him. The truck was parked in the parking lot, and it was time to take off. John was at the helm with the windows open, I was at the bow, and Julian was at the stern. I got the signal from John to release the bow line, and then I ran back to the stern and jumped on board. Julian got the signal to release the stern line, and he too got on board. We looked at each other, and with a big smile on our faces we both said, "This is it. We are on our way."

We were leaving Ketchikan to head north toward Sitka, Alaska. This was where John was from and where the rest of our gear was located. It would take most of the day to get there, and this would give us a little sea time to make sure things were running right. We spent most of the time in the wheelhouse with John, just talking and learning more about what we would be doing. We did engine checks and got to know the boat a little bit more. It was going to be a twelve-hour trip, and so far, so good. That day, I cooked our first meal, which was breakfast stuff, eggs, bacon, and toast. Nothing fancy but gave me a chance to get a feel for the galley and what we had to cook with. Breakfast became my meal to prepare each day, and I actually loved this time, alone and inside.

As we made our way up the coast, I went outside several times and just stood on the back deck and looked all around. The shore line was filled with dense green forest, mountains in the background, and the dark ocean all around us. The seas were not bad that first day, two- to four-foot swells and very little wind. We had a ton of seagulls flying all around us, and the smell of the salty ocean air was so good. It was sixty degrees that day. This was just one of those days that it was good to be me. I still couldn't believe that I was off the coast of Alaska on a shrimp boat, and this would be my home for the next month or so. *Wow.*

We had a great first run with the boat. Everything went smoothly, and the best part of this trip was I didn't get seasick, which was definitely something I was worried about. I had been on boats plenty of times, just not on the open ocean.

We arrived in Sitka and got the boat refueled first and then found an opening on the dock. John left for a few hours to take care of some business and returned with a truck full of food. His parents had bought all our groceries for the trip, around $1,000 worth. This would be what we had to survive on for a month while we were out to sea. We had everything from eggs to hamburger helpers, meats and cheeses, to Red Bulls and water. Every cupboard, refrigerator, storage place, nook, and cranny was filled with something. We had a good supply of food and drinks, but we would not be taking anything alcoholic on this trip. Alcohol and boats don't always mix well.

Next, we loaded all the shrimp pots and bait that we could get. The shrimp pots were round, about four feet in diameter and two feet wide. They could be rolled by one person but were a little heavy and awkward for one person to lift them. We rolled them down the dock and stacked them six high. So we had twenty stacks about twelve feet high on the back deck, and that took up all of the back deck except for about three feet at the end to work from. Each stack had to be secured, and all the stacks had to be tied together. This would prevent them from falling into the ocean. After all the pots were stacked and locked down, we left the dock to go get our bait. It was close by, just a harbor south of where we were. It was a fishing cannery, and they sold us the heads from all the fish that they had processed. Even the head of a fish is worth something to someone here in Alaska. They were mostly codfish and a few salmon heads, and this was a messy and stinky job. They shoveled the heads into fifty-five-gallon plastic barrels, and we then lowered them down into the blast freezer. We left two on deck so they would be ready to go in just a few days, and the other ten buckets would stay frozen until we needed them. It was then time to clean the boat one more time before we left. Fish guts and blood had made our boat look like a horror movie scene.

It was Sept 30, and it was Julian's birthday. We could not start fishing until October 1, so our plan was to spend a few hours in town, have a meal and a few beers, then head out tonight and spend the night getting to our fishing grounds. That way, we could actually set our gear that morning on the first and start making some money. We found a bar, and John ate with us and then left. He told the bartender only two drinks each for us and that was it. He didn't want us drunk on our first night. We managed to have more than two, but it was all good. So after our last meal, drinks, and a few final supplies, John picked us up at the bar, and we made our way to the boat.

It was time to throw the bowline, cast off the stern line, and head out into the North Pacific Ocean. We were all excited, laughing and joking around. The temperature was in the high fifties, so all I was wearing was a pair of jeans, a T-shirt, and a ball cap on my head. But we all knew the weather would change at some point during this trip. We were prepared for the worst and had plenty of warm clothes. We had gone to a thrift shop and bought a bunch of clothes for us to wear.

One thing we had not done before leaving was practice getting into our "life suits" in case the boat went down. These were required by the coast guard to be on board, and we had to know how to get into them quickly in case we got boarded by the coast guard. They required that all boats out of Alaska had these survival suits and be able to get them on in a certain amount of time, like forty-five seconds. So we spent about thirty minutes practicing and timing each other to see who could do it the fastest. John was the quickest, but we all got it under forty-five seconds and were ready to go. We also had a few weapons on board in case we ran into any trouble. John told me this after we left. He said he had actually been shot at before and things can get crazy out here at times. Thanks, John, for easing my mind. Not only did I have to worry about the freezing ocean around us, but I also got to worry about people shooting at us—yeah, this was so reassuring. *What the fuck have I got myself into?*

That night, I spent a lot of time just out on the back deck. The sky was filled with bright stars and a nice ocean breeze, and the moonlight lit up the water around us. I climbed up into the crow's nest, which is the highest point on the boat. It is a metal rung ladder that goes straight up about twenty-five feet above the deck. If you want a view of our surroundings, then this is the place to see everything. You can see bow to stern, portside to starboard side, and all the water around you. The boat works its way through the waves, and up in the crow's nest is where you can feel the boat swaying more than any other part of the boat. If you get seasick, this is the last place you would want to be. For me, I felt like the king of the world up there, and the view was spectacular.

We made something to eat and spent time checking the boat out and joking around. I did get some sleep, still just trying to get used to having such a narrow bunk to sleep in, but I did enjoy the swaying of the boat on the ocean. I felt like a baby in a crib being rocked to sleep. The whole cabin area was heated from a diesel-burning stove that heated the cabin and the same stove we used for cooking. It was always nice and warm inside no matter how cold it was outside. So that night, I was warm and did manage to get a few hours of good sleep.

We were all up before the sun came up and watched a beautiful sunrise over the ocean and land. We decided to make breakfast now because we were getting close to getting started. I made bacon and eggs with toast. John always ate right at the helm, and he was always served first. It's a rule on boats—captain gets served first—and the other rule on boats is to keep the captain happy no matter what happens.

With our bellies full and the sun up, it was time to get this show started. Julian and I went down and got all suited up: boots, orange rain pants, gloves, and a hat. The weather still wasn't that cold, but we would be getting wet, and that would make us cold. We headed out to the bait container and started hooking up bait. It was this big safety pin that went through the eyes and would be hooked to the top of the pot. We baited up about fifty or so and then made our way to the back of the boat. Again, with all the gear on board, we had about three feet of room to actually work. The ocean was right there and looked really cold, and I did not want to fall in and die on day one, so I made sure to watch my step. We didn't have our sea legs yet, so both Julian and I stumbled around that first day until we got used to it.

John had one of those can noise makers where you pull the trigger and a loud, annoying sound happens; well, we also had one. From where we were working, we could not see the wheelhouse at all, so it was all based on sound. When we heard the sound of his go off, we knew it was time to start fishing. We threw the first buoy into the water and watched as it floated behind the boat. Julian and I then started to hook a bait and a plastic container filled with dog food, which was also used as bait. We secured both these items in each shrimp pot, closed and tied the door, then hooked it to the line and let it fall into the ocean. We put about ten pots per line about fifty feet apart with a float on each end. The shrimp pots would soak for twenty-four hours at about four hundred feet deep. We set all the 120 pots in the same area, probably over the course of 10 miles or so. We weren't positive there would be shrimp, but we were going to give it a shot.

Just getting the gear into the water took about five hours. Once the deck was clear of everything, we now had time to get ready to process everything the next day. We had more buckets, all used for different things. We made our processing place more comfortable and got the freezer ready to store the shrimp. It was all just trial and error at this point. We got things set up for how we thought things would go, but that was something that could change real quickly. By the time the sun went down, we found a place that we could anchor up for the night. As long as the fishing was good in the area, we could use this bay to return to each night.

We were ready to eat and call it a night. John had made dinner, which became his thing to do for all of us each night. That night, we had steak and potatoes, which was the best meal of the trip. We had a lot of food, but we had brought more quick and easy things to make. The first night was special, so we had a good meal. After we ate, we shared a big, fat joint and talked about what to expect tomorrow. John gave us a rundown of what to do, but by the time we smoked the joint, I had forgotten everything we had talked about—just kidding. I remembered the part about not falling into the ocean and getting tangled up in a line and sinking four hundred feet to the bottom. Tomorrow was really going to be day one of a lot of work. Tomorrow, I would become a true professional shrimper.

It was 6:00 a.m., and we heard the engine turn on. It was time to start what was going to be one of many long days on this boat. Most days were the same; we got where we had a schedule or pattern in doing things however you might call it. A typical day on an Alaskan shrimping boat went like this: On deck and dressed by 6:30 a.m. Start hauling gear, which was the hardest part of the day. John got close to the floating buoy, and we would throw a line with a big hook on the end called a gaff. The gaff is used to catch the line that the shrimp pots are connected to; start pulling it in until you get the main line. Grab the main line and wrap it around the hydraulic hoist and push a button. This would bring the whole entire string from the ocean floor. When the first pot was visible and within reach, we would grab it and pull it on board. Now there was only about a two-foot railing around the boat, so we had to work very close to the water, and we didn't have much to secure ourselves to when we were working the rail. Once the shrimp pot was on the deck, we opened it up and dumped the shrimp into a bucket and then dumped the bucket into a holding tank under the deck. The shrimp pot would be stacked on the back deck until the string had gone through. If the fishing was good, we would rebait, circle back, and offload. If the fishing wasn't that good or we had to move, then we would stack all of them on the deck. The fishing was good in the area, so we stayed in the same spot for a while.

Going through the gear would take from 6:30 a.m. to 3:00 p.m. We would stop around 10:00 a.m., and I would go inside and make breakfast—eggs, bacon, toast, pancakes, whatever we had. We would stop for about a half hour and then be back at it. Once all the gear had been gone through was when the fun part really started. Now we had to process everything we had caught that day. We started by draining the holding tank of water, and then one of us would climb down into the holding tank, which was about five feet deep, fifteen feet long, and five feet wide and full of shrimp. We would take a five-gallon bucket and scoop up as many as you could get, hand the bucket up to the next guy, and fill a bunch of buckets with shrimp. Then we would fill the tank back up with water so the shrimp wouldn't die. Julian and I would then stand for hours and hours, taking the heads off the shrimp and sorting them by sizes. We each had big buckets next to us, one for jumbo, large, and medium. We threw the small ones back into the ocean so they could get bigger.

Now it would be around 8:00 p.m., and we would stop for dinner and a quick break then back to sort and weigh all the shrimp. We had small three-pound boxes and filled each with a certain amount of shrimp. So jumbo shrimp would fill a three-pound box with maybe fifteen to eighteen shrimp, whereas it might take thirty to thirty-five mediums to fill the box. That was how shrimp are sold, all by the amount it took to fill a three-pound box. It would take a few hours to sort everything, and then it was time for the worst job on the boat, and that was climbing down into the blast freezer, which was on average –25 degrees. It was a blast freezer, so it had to be really cold to freeze the shrimp quickly to keep them fresh. One guy would hand down the boxes, and the other guy would stack the boxes on shelves. Once all this was done, it was time to clean the boat with a little bleach and scrub the deck, processing tables, buckets, and anything else we used that day. It was usually anywhere from 10:00 to 11:00 p.m. when we finally went in for the night. We would smoke a joint, have a snack, and total up our day's catch. On the days we were fishing, we averaged 500 lbs. a day, and that was completely processed. Right from the ocean to the box and by taking the heads off each shrimp, the value of our catch increased. One thing about shrimp was that they did have a needle-like nose, and they actually gave off a poison. Now it was nothing that was going to kill you, but let me tell you my hands were so sore that first week. They actually swelled up, and it was hard to make a fist. It was something we all dealt with until our hands hardened up and we got used to it. I can say this and tell you right now, working on a boat in the North Pacific Ocean was hard-ass work, and it is no joke, the danger that is all around you every minute of the day. Life on a shrimping boat was so unique compared to anything I had ever done in my life.

We worked hard every day, and each day was the same yet different. You never knew what was in the next pot or what might be attached to the next pot. One thing that was always cool and happened several times a day was we would pull a pot out of the water and attached to it would be an octopus. Now the reason we would catch so many octopus was that they fed on shrimp. It was one of their main staples, and I guess octopus like shrimp as much as humans do. There were days when we would catch five to ten per day. You could usually tell when pulling in the line; it was a little heavier. The pot would surface, and there it would be, all draped over the pot, trying to suck those little guys out. One guy would grab the pot, and the other would peel the octopus off. We would then cut the head off the octopus and throw it in our bait containers. The tentacles—well, let me tell you this—are delicious. Each night, after we got done going through all our gear, we would take a quick break and have a snack, take the tentacles, and thinly slice them and eat them raw. This was a sushi special and the freshest octopus you could ever have. They were like a chicken with their heads cut off. Take the head off the octopus, and the tentacles would still move around the deck of the boat. The biggest one we caught was over six feet long. They gave us something else to eat, bait for the next pot, and excitement each time we caught one.

We fished every day on this boat except for a few Mondays when we decided to do something a little different. Instead of catching shrimp, we went sea cucumber hunting. Now these things look like big slugs that lay on the bottom of the ocean. The way we caught these things was by scuba diving for them. They were usually found in about thirty to fifty feet of water. John would dive down and fill baskets with these things. Julian and I would haul the baskets up, dump them into another bucket on board, and then poke each one of them with a knife. This would let the water out and make them more valuable. Now these sea cucumbers are a delicacy in Japan. There are four thin slices of meat in each one and served as a meal in Asia. We tried them on board, and I had also had them in Japan—not bad, a little bland for me, but hey, it was food, and food meant money for us.

About three weeks into our trip, we started to run low on food. Most of the good things were gone, and we were down to the basics.

We took a few hours one morning and went out to a little deeper water and set a few long lines. They were not exactly legal, but if used for food and not resold, we would be okay. We took a buoy and attached about fifty hooks on it, used some of the octopus tentacles as bait, and let it out slowly behind the boat. We set out about three of these long lines and let them soak for twenty-four hours. We spent the rest of the day going through gear and doing what we do day after day.

I do have to mention one thing real quick, and that is the weather. We had been out for about three weeks, and the temperature had dropped. By now, things had gone from comfortable to damn cold. We had added layers each day and made a wind break for our processing area to keep us from freezing every night. It was a boat, so we did get wet every day. Either we stepped into one of the holding tanks and took water up over our boot and a wave would come in and drench us, or it would rain. One way or another, we got wet, and that was just part of it. Not only did we get wet and cold, but also, almost every day, there was some blood involved. Most of the time, it was our hands from a hook or a line. We had a joke and that was whoever bled first had to go into the hole first. Anyway, it was near the end of October, and winter was right around the corner, and things got cold. It is hard to work with two jackets, three layers of pants, gloves, a hat, and boots while working on a boat. We did what we had to do to survive.

Anyways, after a twenty-four-hour soak, it was time to see what else we could eat. I was sick of pasta and wanted something else. We found the buoy, and I threw the gaff and got the line. John came down from the bridge and maneuvered the boat from the deck, which had a drive station near the action. We got the line hooked into the hydraulics and started bringing the lineup. The first ten hooks were empty, and then we noticed the color of a fish. It was about a forty-pound halibut, and this was what we wanted. Halibut is a great-tasting fish and huge around here in the Alaskan waters. We kept going, and after about ten hooks more, we caught a small shark. It was like two feet long, so we took the hook out, snapped a few pictures, and threw it back in the ocean. With only a few more hooks to go, we really wanted something else. One halibut would not feed the three of us for a week, so we needed one more. Well, be careful of what you ask for, and with only a few more hooks to go in our lines, we got the big one. It was about a 130 lb. halibut that put up a huge fight on the surface, and we got very lucky to land this thing. Most halibut fisherman have some kind of gun on board to shoot these things before they hit the deck, so John used his shotgun with a slug and was able to shoot it before we lost it. So hey, with just a few lines and octopus tentacles, we were able to catch enough fish that day to survive the next week or so on the boat. That night, we had fresh halibut with rice, and it was so tasty. It was something that didn't come out of a box and was actually good for you.

Last week on board, we ate halibut for almost every meal. It tasted so good the first few days, but by day seven, it was all I could do just to eat it. When you're hungry, anything tastes good, but when you have to eat the same thing for one whole week, it can be a challenge. Halibut and eggs, halibut and rice, halibut and pasta, baked halibut, fried halibut, and well, you get my point.

It was about halfway through our trip John wanted to stop by a few friends' house that was near where we were fishing. Their names were John and Kevin, and they lived on a float house and ran an oyster farm. It was dark when we got there, so I really didn't get a good look at the place. They had a small wooden house that was built on a big raft. These places are common in Alaska because people can live on the ocean and not pay property taxes. It is a very hard way of life because you are so far from anything. So we stopped by one night and smoked with the guys, and they told Julian that when we got done shrimping and wanted a job, we could stay with them. At this point, I had no idea what I would do after this month was over but appreciated the invite. It was just good to talk with two other people for a few hours before we headed back to our routine.

The last week on the boat was the hardest for several reasons. The weather was the biggest challenge, and it started to get real cold. Temperatures by now were just above freezing, and each day, we would have to spray the deck down to get rid of the ice. The winds had picked up, and dealing with our gear became harder to control.

The days became longer, and the routine became more of a challenge each day. We still had a job to do, and the season ended on October 30, and we were going to fish every day we could. It was around this last week that John gave me a great compliment. He told me that he was happy I had come up with Julian and that I worked hard, and more importantly, he said, "You listen well. I never have to tell you something twice, and you work hard." I appreciated the compliment and did my best each day to prove my worth.

We were on that boat for thirty days and what a great experience. One thing about this trip was we didn't have a shower. Most people take a shower each day. Well, we went almost a month, and I'm sure we smelled like the sea. We were all in the same boat, so it didn't really bother us. We cleaned up each day, took a sponge bath in the sink, brushed my teeth, and I did laundry once while we were at sea. I took a fifty-five-gallon garbage container and cleaned it out. I then put my clothes in, added some dish soap and cold seawater, used a stick, moved the stuff around as best I could, rinsed everything by hand, and then hung everything in the engine room. It was a little better, but they really didn't come clean. At this point, they were going in the trash at the end of the trip.

We finished the season with at least twenty-five thousand pounds of shrimp. It was a good haul and should give us each somewhere around $3,000 each, which is what we were told. Well, things didn't work out quite as smoothly as they should have because in order to get the money, we had to sell the shrimp first. This was news to me and did not make me very happy. When we first started John had told us that he had some of it already sold and would have no problem getting rid of the rest. Seemed to me John had dropped the ball on his part of the operation. We would do what we could and hopefully find a way to sell our product and get some cash in our pockets. I did have a few bills to pay.

The day came, and we were out of time. By sunset on the thirtieth, we had to have all our gear out of the water and report our last catch. It was a time of joy with the radio turned up, and the fact we made it through this ordeal was impressive. With everything secured, we turned the boat and made a direct course for Sitka.

TAKE A DECADE

We arrived late in the day, and we were so happy to see other people and actually stand on a flat surface that wasn't moving. We got all tied up, and those first few steps on the dock felt so weird. My legs felt like they had cement in them and just didn't work like they should. This was a good case of sea legs, and it was weird. With the boat tied up, John said he would be back in an hour or so. Julian and I cleaned up a little and got our stuff packed up, ready to get off this boat as soon as possible. John returned with a twelve pack for us, a few packs of smokes, and bad news. We had to stay on the boat one more night. John was leaving, but Julian and I had to stay one more night. The thing is we had nowhere to go. John had a small place, and he wasn't about to get us a hotel room. Oh well, what was one more night?

That night, we were tied up to the dock, and at least we could talk with other fishermen. We ended up trading twenty pounds of shrimp for two nice king crabs. We attempted to make a seafood gumbo, but the beer got in our way. We had not drunk for over a month, and the first few beers went down so good and right to our heads. After a few, we decided to walk into town and find a bar and have a few drinks. John had given us a few bucks but nothing close to what we were owed, and ewe made our way to the nearest bar. The bar we chose happened to be hosting a Halloween party, and we had a blast. We spent all the money John had given us, and at some point around 2:00 a.m., we made it back to the boat. The gumbo was burnt and tasted like shit. We ate what we could just to put something in our stomachs and tossed the rest in the ocean—what a waste. We looked back on our stay on this boat, and our first meal was old chips and cream corn/canned tomatoes, and our last meal was burnt gumbo.

John arrived the next day and found a place for us to stay for a few days. It was at his parents' house; they had a guesthouse. It was just what we needed, to finally be off the boat and away from John for a few days. That day, I took my first real shower in over a month. It was the best shower in my life. I was under that water for at least thirty minutes just enjoying hot water running over my body. Also, to just lie in bed was a true treat for us. I could actually turn over in the night without having to get out of bed, and I could sit up without banging my head. Just these two simple things that we take for granted every day was a treat for me.

Julian and I went shopping and bought a few snacks and more beer. We spent the next day lying around and watching movies. It was just what we needed, our first day in almost six weeks that we had nothing to do, just eat, drink, sleep, shower, and watch movies.

John did come by the last day, and he had sold some of the shrimp. He gave us each $1,000 and said when he sold the rest, we would get us more money. It was something and allowed me to pay a few bills and get caught up with that stuff.

At this point, we had decided to take John and Kevin's offer and head down to the Oyster Farm for a month or so. Julian had contacted them, and we asked John to give us a ride back down to where they were located. It would be about a five-hour trip, and John had no problems helping us out.

That night, we went out, had a good meal, and drank a lot of beer. It is just what you do after fishing for a while, get drunk and spend all your money. I didn't spend all my money, just a little because I did want to keep a few bucks in my pocket for the next adventure. Julian, however, was quick to drop a few hundred that night. He didn't care at the least; money didn't mean a lot to my friend. If he had it, he spent it and enjoyed doing so. Julian did not have a single bill to pay; it was just day to day for him, and I always admired him for that.

The next morning, John picked us up, and we fueled up the boat and made our way south toward Ketchikan. John wanted to keep the boat in the same place we had first seen it, so it worked out great for all of us. We got a ride to our next spot; John docked his boat for the winter and flew home. We spent most of the day just hanging out in the wheelhouse, smoking joints, and talking. It was tough because we were leaving a lot of money on the table. John had not sold any more shrimp, and they were being stored near his house in a walk-in freezer. He didn't seem to be in any rush to get on this, and it frustrated me because I wanted the money that we had earned. We had a good trip besides this; it was relaxing, and we just sat back and enjoyed the scenery. The mountains now had snow on them. The clouds were low that day. There were birds flying around the boat, and it would be the last trip on the Winning Hand. She turned out to be one hell of a boat.

CHAPTER 15

Float House

It was midafternoon, the beginning of the second week of November, and winter was right around the corner. We rounded the corner of the bay, which was called Callie Cove, a small bay maybe two football fields deep and about four football fields wide. It was a small bay on the west side of Prince of Wales Island, which was located about fifty-five miles west of Ketchikan, Alaska. This was my first time seeing this place during the day. Built on a raft stood a small two-story cabin, maybe 20' × 40', built with wooden studs and cedar shake boards on the outside. The small house was on a large raft made from huge trees with wooden deck boards covering the entire service. This raft was maybe 60' × 60', and the ocean waters surrounded it. On the same raft, there were two smaller buildings. One looked like it was for firewood, and the other was small, and I had no idea what it was for. Next to the main house, there was another building on its own separate floating structure, a white building that looked like a work building with maybe a room above it for living. In front of this structure, which was called the "scow"—for whatever reason, I don't know, but this is what they called it—was a small boat maybe twenty-two feet long with a cabin area and set up with what looks like fishing equipment. This was my first time seeing this place, and it looked like a lot of fun, and man oh man, we were in the middle of nowhere. We passed a few small homes along the way, but for the most part, this was the first piece of civilization we had seen the entire trip down. This was going to be my home for who knew how long.

As we approached the dock, the door opened, and both John and Kevin came out to say, "Hello, welcome, and glad to have you guys here to help." John and Kevin were fifty-fifty owners of an Oyster Farm. They had permission to live and work in this area, cultivating and growing oysters and other forms of shellfish. Their home was an outdoorsman's dream come true. It was rustic and simple, and this was an opportunity for me to live a very different life in such a beautiful landscape. With the ocean all around us, the small islands in the distance, and the plush green forest at our backs, this was going to be a beautiful place to spend some time. How long? At this point, I had no idea; it was just new and exciting.

The five of us did the tour of the entire float house. In the main house, we walked in, and to our right, there was a small, very dirty kitchen with big enough space for maybe two people. There was a sink full of dirty dishes, counters cluttered with everything, an average-sized stove that had not been cleaned in a long time, and a small refrigerator that looked very seventies-ish, maybe because it was green. Then to the direct left was the woodstove, which was partially surrounded by boots, jackets, and rain pants and then a small living/dining area. There were two couches that looked rough but usable and a four-seat table that was in front of the window facing the forest. A staircase on the right side of the first floor led to the upstairs that had a small bathroom, which we were told at this time did not work and was filled with a bunch of junk. Then the rest of the second floor was divided by a sheet and an old blanket. One side was Kevin's, and the other side was John's. It was absolutely trashed. Clothes, boxes, and just a bunch of junk were all over the place. The whole place wasn't much, and even though it was not the cleanest, it still had this warm and welcoming feel to it. Basically, it was like a hunting lounge on the water.

The one thing about the setup of the float house was there was a lot of deck space in the front of the house. This was the place they did a lot of the work, so it was all used. Behind the main house was a small building for wood, and next to it, the other small building that I didn't know what it was turned out to be their processing area for packaging up the product they sold. It had stainless-steel tables and a sink that took up the entire area. Also, behind the house was a canoe and a really small dingy tied up to the deck. That was it for the main house area.

Next to the main house was the Scow, which was a little larger than the house but set up completely differently. The bottom area was open with a few rooms off the main walkway. This was where the generator and all these tools and fishing equipment were stored. Then we walked around to the side of the building, and there was a staircase outside that led to the second floor. This was, at one point, a nice two-bedroom apartment with a small kitchen, a large living room area with a woodstove, and two small bedrooms off the living room. Okay, I did say *at one point*, this was nice. Well, time had taken its toll on this place, and it was rough. The ceiling was the first thing you noticed because half of it was falling in the kitchen. The woodstove that was just inside the door was all rusted and didn't look that safe. Both bedrooms had a bed and dresser, and that was it. The place was rough, and guess what, this was going to be where Julian and I stayed. No heat and no running water, just a place to sleep at night. Julian gave me the choice of which room. One faced the main house, and the other faced the woods. I chose the view of the woods, which was through a window about 2' × 2' and had plastic on it so you really couldn't see anything anyway. It really didn't matter because the only time in this room would be to sleep.

We dropped off our gear, and all went back to the main house, and John and Kevin both smoked, so we had a bong hit off their new glass bong and had a bit of a welcome to Callie Cove celebration. John didn't hang out long because he had to get his boat taken care of, and he knew that Julian and I were a little pissed about not having more cash. We made sure we both looked at him, and he said, "I will sell the shrimp and get you guys cash soon, I promise." We said our goodbyes, and I made sure to thank John for a great experience. A month of my life spent on a shrimping boat. Thank you!

TAKE A DECADE

    We helped John take off, and it was now just the four of us. They were excited to have some help with the oysters. There was always a lot to do living this way and running a "farm." They were making an investment in us to help out and maybe make their business better. This was great for both of us. I was getting another adventure and they were getting good help. The payment was not much—$10 an hour while we were working with the oysters, and room and board was included. There was a lot of other work that would need to be done like maintaining the float house, wood, and cleaning up that we would not get paid for; this was more for the room and board. This was all good for Julian and me; we would hang out here for a month or so and then see what happened.

    We had been there about an hour when John informed us that John, Kevin, and Julian were going to Juneau by boat to pick up supplies. I can guarantee you my nerves all stood up at the same time because that meant that I was going to be here by myself on the first night. Yes, I had a moment of panic when he said this. He soon followed up with the fact that a friend of theirs, Mike, was coming over for the night to help out. John said with a smile on his face, "Mundy, I'm not going to leave you out here by yourself—that would be rough. No worries, buddy, we got you." This guy Mike and his two other brothers lived on a float house about five miles away, which I guess was your closest neighbor. They helped out the guys, and the guys helped them out. About this time, he could be seen making his way into the cove.

    Mike pulled up with his small boat, and at first glance, I would have rather stayed here by myself. He was about 6' tall, 250 lbs., with long greasy hair with a red cap on, big golden-rimmed glasses, a scruffy beard, and he was missing several teeth. I looked at Julian, and he started to laugh. "Mundy, you will be fine" and gave me that grin of his and laughed. It took about five minutes with John and Mike talking about what to do and went over a few things. Mike and I talked, and at this point, it didn't take long for my nerves to disappear and put my mind at ease. It was going to be safe, and I would be fine. He just looked like a serial killer, but actually, he was a tough Alaskan who had spent his entire life surviving and living off the land.

Mike and I had a good time. We first loaded up in his boat and headed out on the ocean to check out some crab pots that John and Kevin had set. He gave Mike permission to see if anything was there, which was a big thing for someone to give up their spot, but Mike was helping them out and they were helping him out. We pulled up to the first one, and Mike got so excited. We pulled three large Dungeness crabs out of the first pot. These guys were at least 14 inches wide. They were amazing, but watching Mike smile and laugh like a little schoolgirl with half his teeth missing and not giving a flying fuck, now that made my day. We made our way back to the float house and he got the water boiling and the butter melting. This gave us time to have a drink and just sit and shoot the shit like old friends. He was an interesting person and for him, I was an interesting person, so we had a great time just swapping stories and enjoying the delicious crab.

That night, I slept in Kevin's bed and Mike in John's. I didn't want to do anything with our future rooms until Julian got back. Also, the main house was heated, and at that point in the season, it was getting cold at night. My first night at Callie Cove was very memorable, and with everything that had happened in the past twenty-four hours, it did take a long time to fall asleep, and that night, I slept like a baby.

The next day, I was up around 8:00 a.m., and I could hear Mike doing something downstairs. I made my way down, and he had been up for a while and ready to go for the day. He asked me if I had done any trapping, and the answer was no. He said, "Get yourself ready and let's go set a trap for a wolf." Did he say *wolf*? Yes, he did. Holy shit, what a way to start off this adventure. Of course to most people in the lower 48, trapping is a horrible thing, but here it was a way of life, and a wolf hide could put $500 in someone's pocket.

So I grabbed a bowl for cereal and that was when I noticed that there was no water in the sink. Mike took me outside and showed me the only fresh water that was available. It was a hose that ran from land, through the ocean, and up on the deck. It had an on and off value, and that was the only freshwater going to the float house. So anytime you needed fresh water for cleaning, cooking, brushing your teeth, or anything, you had to go out on the deck and use the hose. Well, I cleaned a bowl, had some cereal, brushed my teeth, and I was ready for the day.

We loaded up in Mike's boat and headed out. We headed upstream from the house, and I just sat back and enjoyed the amazing scenery. Lush forest, island after island, the ocean, and the crisp feel of the air against my face, it was such an amazing place to be at during this time of year.

We traveled maybe twenty minutes and Mike found his spot. We approached the shore slowly, and I was able to jump off and get the boat tied off. We walked maybe one-eighth of a mile back through the dense forest, which was actually a challenge. The ground was overgrown with stumps, branches, and a lot of moss. He found a good spot and tied the deer carcass he brought as bait around a tree and placed a large trap, which was tied to a tree, underneath the bait. He said, "I'll let this set for a few days and hope for the best." All I knew was that I was a professional trapper now and I really hoped we got something. We made our way back to the boat, and we grabbed a few logs to put in the fire when we got back. For about two hours, we just drove around on the boat, and Mike pointed out as many things as he could. This was my backyard now, and it was so cool just looking at everything from the forest to the ocean around us; my head was on a swivel that day.

By the time we had made it back, which was now late afternoon, the guys had returned, and I was happy to see my friend. Julian and I had been side by side for like three months now, and it was good to have him back. The guys had bought some food and parts to work on the float house. They had also come back with some party favorites: booze, smoke, and some of that white stuff. They were all excited and ready to get some work done around the house.

Mike left, and I told him thank you for a great first night experience. We would see plenty of him in the future, and I looked forward to it. That night, Julian and John picked on each other; Kevin and I just laughed at their stupidity. We talked and laughed until it was time to call it a night. Julian and I did make some time to clean our new accommodations, just enough for that night. Tomorrow, we would go through everything and make it the best we could. We also were going to start working the next day going through the oyster nets and getting our feet wet in this industry.

By the second week of November, it was getting dark by 6:00 p.m. and light around 7:30 p.m. So daylight was a factor, and we knew that it was only going to get darker earlier each day. It was around 8:00 a.m. that I got up, and Julian heard me, so he got up as well. We walked over to the house, and John and Kevin were both up and ready.

It was time to punch the clock and start work. First was getting the proper attire, and that was at least two layers of normal clothes then fishing rubber overalls, green muck boots, and a hat and gloves. It's like we had to add twenty pounds of clothing just to stay warm and dry. We loaded up in another boat they had. This one was about eighteen feet long and six feet wide with a flat hull bottom that was great for the area due to the extreme tides. The boat was made out of aluminum and was powered by two 225 cc outboard motors. It had a center console area, but besides a small windshield in front of the wheel, it was completely open.

The four of us loaded up and left the dock, heading straight out to where they kept the nets. When we left the float house, there was land almost all around in the form of small islands with waterways all around each island. This is what southeast Alaska is made up of, and that is a ton of small islands, and most all of them are uninhabited. However, just beyond a few islands was nothing but open ocean. We would see that in the future. It was nice having parts of land around us to keep the wind and seas more accessible for our needs. It took only about ten minutes and we were in the channel between islands, and we could tell the water was moving quicker and definitely deeper. This is where they had their nets anchored.

We pulled up, and all I could see was a bunch of logs tied together, forming an area maybe twenty feet by seventy-five feet. They approached slowly; Kevin jumped off on a bigger log and tied the boat to a stake that was hammered into the log. He was just balancing and standing on a log out in the middle of the ocean with very cold water underneath him. At that point, we all made our way out on a log, and with the best balance ever, we did everything not to fall in. The guys proceeded to explain the whole situation. Under these logs were nets tied to these spikes. You could see the spikes with something hanging from them. The nets needed to be pulled up and taken back to the float house. John got down on his knees and grabbed a line and started to pull up. Kevin grabbed the other side, and they pulled up a blue net that was 6 feet tall and 2.5 feet in diameter. It was covered in seaweed and ocean slime. It was difficult to see what was inside, but by the way they were struggling, it looked heavy and very awkward to completely get it out of the water. Once out of the water, it was all they could do to get it into the boat without falling in.

Julian and I got right to business and grabbed hold of one and proceeded to get it out of the water. They were very heavy and again balancing logs and trying everything not to fall in. The worst thing that could happen was to actually drop the net. It had happened to them, and they were not happy. You dropped a net and there went $250 for the cost of the net and then the entire product that the net could produce—it was like throwing away $2,000. After they explained it that way, we were very careful. Basically, the rule was to fall in the water before you lost a net. We got the message loud and clear, and we were very careful. We got about six of them and put them in our boat. John said, "the plan is to start right here and go through all of these in order over the next month." There had to be at least three hundred or so nets, which was fine with me. I was making money.

We made our way back to the float house and began processing the oysters. We took the nets out of the boat and laid them on the deck. Kevin grabbed this gas-powered high-pressure pump. He placed one hose into the ocean and turned it on, and the other end on land was shooting water out at a high pressure. He then started spraying each of them, and you can start to see what is inside. Once they are cleaned of all seaweed and slime, I could see how these nets were designed. Again, they were six feet tall and had shelves in them about every foot or so. There was one side of the net that was tied up with a bright-orange color line that went the entire length of the net. John untied one end and pulled this line out so the whole side opened up. He then grabbed the net and turned it upside down, and all the oysters fell out on the deck. We opened all six of them, and we had a good-sized pile of oysters of all different sizes. There were more oysters in one sitting than I had ever seen before. Then they grabbed a table made of wood with metal mesh covering the bottom. The table was the perfect height to work from, and they then used a snow shovel and placed a pile of the oysters on the table. We went through and separated any of the oysters that were big enough to sell. Basically, anything four inches or better was good to go. Anything smaller would be put back into the nets and taken back to soak longer. So the four of us spent the next four to five hours going through all the oysters.

Now I love oysters, and yes, we did get to eat our share. They had a bottle of red hot sauce on the table, and any of them that were broke were fair game. I had at least a dozen my first day and would have many, many more. Once the big ones were sorted, they went into smaller bags and put back in the water, hung off cleats on the float house. These would be sent out later to a big seafood processing plant near Anchorage. We then placed the small ones back in the nets, sewed the nets back together, which does take time because you can't have any large holes or they will get washed away, and then took them back to the logs and rehung them to grow larger. Then we went back to the float house and sprayed the entire deck off all the slime and guts that the oyster nets had left behind.

We had started around 9:00 a.m., and by 3:00 p.m., we had gone through six nets. Now that they had more help, we figured we could go through more each day. So this was a basic day of working on an oyster farm, about six to seven hours, and that was about the amount of daylight we would have during most of the winter. Each day was different for the amount we got, but I would say that at least fifteen to twenty dozen a day. Then it was time for a smokey smokey break and get something to eat. Almost right away, Julian had taken the role as chef, so he started cooking, and we all warmed up and had a drink.

As the darkness approached, it was time to get the generator fired up. This was for a few small lights and maybe a little TV—yes, we did have a TV, which was satellite and very limited. There were maybe five channels with only one primetime channel, so each night, we did get to watch something for a few hours. The generator had a battery back that it charged, so we would run the gas generator for a while and then rely on a short period for light with the charge. For the most part, we entertained ourselves, joking and busting on each other, and we played a lot of cards.

By the time it was pitch black, I loved walking outside and just staring at my surroundings. The ocean in front of us, the islands in the distance, the forest behind us, but it was always the sky that got the most attention. With no lights for miles away, the sky was as bright and magical as you could imagine. The air was getting crisp, and the smell of the ocean around me was *un*real.

Now for a little sidenote. I have mentioned several times that there was no running water inside the house. That means no toilet, right? Well, you are correct. To take a leak was easy. That was done just by standing close to the edge and peeing in the ocean. Now for the number 2 business, and that was not as easy. You actually had to use a small canoe that was tied up on the backside of the house, paddle to shore, get out, and find a spot. I've had to do this in all sorts of weather, and it was never once fun, not once. It was cold and wet every time I had to go. I got on a system with my body and made the trip once a day during light hours, and it just became part of my day. It was always a good idea to bring a weapon with you just in case. Hey, it was just part of this incredible world we were living in.

That night, Julian and I spent an hour or so cleaning our house. With about five garbage bags, we pulled all the hanging inculcation and garbage that was in our space. We planned on doing so much, but to be honest, it was never going to look good again. It was a place to sleep, and that was about it. For most of my stay here, I slept in my sleeping bag with a blanket over that, long johns, a long-sleeved shirt, and a hat on to keep my head warm. Almost every night I could see my breath at night, and almost every morning, I could see my breath when I woke up. It was just the way it was, and we just got used to it.

On my third day at the float house, we spent the morning going through another six nets, which again produced maybe ten dozen or so oysters. The day went quicker because Julian and I had an idea of what was going on. Then by early afternoon, we got set up to go get wood for a few days. I asked, "Why not get a bunch of wood for like a week or so?" and Kevin responded by telling me that with that much wood on the float house in the area that they kept it, it could weigh that section of the float house down too much and literally sink the whole operation.

We loaded up in the boat, John, Kevin, Julian, me, and our trusty dog, Joy, who had definitely got a lot of attention from both Julian and me. Chainsaws, fuel, axe, and one rifle became something we took almost anytime leaving the float house. We were off to find wood, but if a deer had stuck his head out, we would also have dinner.

We headed downstream and just slowly drove the boat close to shore. They were looking for a dead tree that was close to the water. The closer we could get the boat to the tree would mean less struggles getting the wood to the boat. After about thirty minutes, we found one. It was visible from the water, and John found a place close by to dock the boat. We all got out carrying something. I chose the ax, and my thought was that I now had a weapon as well as equipment, and that made me feel safer. We got to the tree, and John dropped it as best he could. He cut the branches and started to block it up. The three of us started rolling the rounds down to the boat and with everything we had lifted them into the boat. The boat of course could only handle so much weight, so the one tree filled it up. It took about an hour or so to process the tree and load up the boat. Then it was a slow ride back to the float house. This would become a very routine operation that just had to be done, and I think it was one of my favorite things to do. It was a pain in the ass getting the wood to the boat, but we always got to see something—maybe it was a sea lion, sea otter, eagle, or just a new bay.

The nights were fun. We partied, ate, and always set up a game plan for the next day. Julian was always a good part of the entertainment, busting John's balls and him giving it right back. There was not a day that went by that we all didn't have a good laugh over something that had happened earlier that day. It was just four guys living a completely bachelor life. All of us were single except for John, who did have a girlfriend we would meet later.

I was in for a big treat the next day. After, we spent a few hours and went through several oyster nets. Today, we were going to town—well, we were going to get fuel and a few supplies; I didn't know if this was actually a town or what. We loaded up in the boat with about five empty fuel cans that were used for the boat and generator. We headed toward civilization. I was excited to see other people and maybe get a can of dip. Yes, I was still chewing tobacco and drinking when we could, but it is not like we could just run down to our local convenience store and get whatever we wanted. Things were harder to find and of course more expensive.

It was about a thirty-minute boat trip, and I could finally see a dock for boats, and just up on land, I could see several trucks just sitting there. We pulled up to the dock and secured the boat. One of the trucks was actually John and Kevin's. It was an old beat-up Chevy that didn't look like much, but it ran, and that was all that mattered. Julian and I jumped in the back with the fuel cans, and we made our way up the pothole-filled road for about two miles and there it was, Naukati. The town of Naukati Bay is a very small town with a population of about 113 people. It had a small store, which was where we could get fuel and a few supplies. It had a small boat garage, a single-room school, and maybe twenty or so other buildings that were houses for the people that lived there. This was the closest place to get basic items. They had beer/liquor, cigarettes, milk, bread, canned foods, and they did have chewing tobacco, *yeah*. With this place being so remote, things were not cheap. It was $10 for one can of dip and $45 for a big bottle of Jack Daniel's. Oh well, whatever the cost, we were going to get what we needed. The guys introduced us to whoever we came in contact with, and everyone was super nice and very accommodating. We spent about an hour just hanging out and getting everything we needed. John informed me that there was a bigger store, which was in Craig, about an hour and half to two hours away. They usually made that trip only a few times a month, and at that point, they would stock up on everything they could afford. While we were there, I called home and had a great talk with my mom, letting her know how her son was living now and that it was all going great. Of course she was worried, and that is why I love my mom so much.

Back to the boat and on our way back to Callie Cove. Time was a factor, and this was a good time to inform everyone that everything we ever did relied on one thing, and that was the tide. Alaska has some of the most extreme tides anywhere. They can make or break just about anyone and anything. Boats have been sunk or stranded on the shore. People have been lost and died just because of bad timing with the extreme tides. On our way here, we had to go through this narrow area. On low tide, the boat would probably scrape the bottom of the boat, which was not a good thing at all. So timing was everything wherever we went. We had a little yellow tide book on our table, and that became one of the first things I looked at each morning.

Back home, all the fuel had been distributed. The generator was ready to go, and all the fuel tanks for the boats were full. It was dark, and it was time to enjoy some of our hard-earned money, and the bottle was passed around, no glasses needed. Julian made up some pasta that night, and we enjoyed a good warm meal and a few drinks. That night, we played some cards, and by god we finished that bottle before we all called it a night.

It had been almost a week, and today was Tuesday, which meant we had to get the oysters ready to be picked up. That morning, we took all the oysters we had taken so far and took them out to the processing house. We put together these boxes that were wax-lined with plastic bag containers and sorted out all the oysters, filling each box with a single layer of oysters and securing them for the next step. This took us two to three hours to do, and as usual, we laughed and joked around while we were doing this.

It was probably around 1:00 p.m., and I could hear a plane or something, and Kevin spoke up. "He is here."

"Who is here?" I said, and Kevin said, "The float plane to pick up the product." I thought someone would be coming by boat, but I was wrong. The plane landed right in the cove and slowly made its way to the float house. He approached, and we helped him secure his plane. The plane could hold four passengers or up to so many pounds in weight. It was a single prop plane, and it looked to be in great shape. We then proceeded to carry the boxes to the plane. We had about twenty boxes with at least five dozen or so in each and a few other boxes with clams that they had gotten before we got there. We then untied the plane and gave him a push. He fired up the engine and flew away with all our hard work for that week. This would become a normal Tuesday, the day the plane came and took whatever we had to sell to a big fish processing plant in Anchorage.

It was that night that John and Kevin asked us if we wanted to try to make a little extra cash, and I was all about it. At this point in my life, I didn't have much money at all, and I knew at some point, I would need to have money to leave someday. Of course, we were still waiting for John to sell the shrimp and give us our money, but we had not heard anything yet. I asked, "What do you have in mind?" They asked if we wanted to go and dig for clams. I had never done this before, and it sounded like fun, so why the hell not?

The deal was that we would take the boat and head to a beach that they had rights to dig on and get bottleneck clams. Just to let you know, it was dark by now, and this was the best time to get them because of the low tide. It happened at different times, so once again, the tide dictated what we could do. With five-gallon buckets, small hand-digging tools, a bunch of large onion bags, flashlights/head lamps, and a gun, we got all bundled up and headed back out on the water. It was a twenty-minute boat ride, and let me tell you, life is so much different at night on the water. The sky is amazing, but there is that eerie feeling of what you can't see at night. The water is darker and colder-looking. The forest is really nonexistent because you can't really see anything, just make out the shore, and that is about it.

Kevin gave us a quick lesson on what to do. You wanted to look for places on the beach where you could see tiny air holes, and that is where the clams had buried themselves during the low tide.

They were usually down about six to eight inches, and you took your digging tool and made your way down until you reached them. Sounded easy enough, and I was ready to get started. With my head lamp, bucket, and digging tool, I went to town. We all stayed rather close but not right on top of each other. I did have to ask a question and that was "Are there bears around here, or have they all gone dormant for the year?"

John said, "They should be mostly settled in for the winter," but with a chuckle, he was like "You never know." Then he grabbed the gun and said, "This is why we brought this."

Then of course, Julian said, "All I know is that I can outrun John, and that is all that matters."

We were there for about two hours, and we had gotten enough for one night. Besides being extremely cold, the tide had started to make its way back up, so thank God it was time to go home. I did, however, manage to fill two buckets. John and Kevin had filled four each, and Julian had filled around three, which was not a bad first time out. The financial reward for all of this was $10 per bucket. Now this didn't seem like much, but the way I looked at it, this money could be my spending money, and I could just bank everything else. They liked to go out and do this three to four days a week and I figured doing this and getting three to four buckets a night could pay for my dip and alcohol for the week. It actually was fun, but the elements around us made it a very miserable experience as well.

With us arriving here in November, we did have Thanksgiving to look forward to, and Julian was set on having a big dinner. He was the chef, so it was up to him to get things ready. The guys had made a trip to the store a few days before Thanksgiving and picked up some of the supplies. That was the first day. It was just Julian and me alone for the day, and we had a great day. They had brought us some oyster nets to go through, and I'm pretty sure I did most of them alone. Julian liked to sleep in and then take time to do nothing for periods. I knew him well and loved him for who he was, not always the most motivated but always good for a laugh. It seemed that I was more interested in actually making some money, while he was just happy living. There was nothing at all wrong with that; I just knew that it would take money to get home at some point, and I just liked to work. What can I say?

Now this next part may seem a little disgusting, but it is the way things work here. I've mentioned a few times how we didn't have running water, and if you had to take a shit, you had to paddle to shore and do your business. Well, I had been on the float house for about three weeks and still had not had a shower. Yes, for most people, going three weeks without a shower is just not normal, but when you live in the bush, it is a way of life. The float house had a shower; it just did not have a water source. So that night we cleaned out the shower, which was about the size of a small RV shower, just big enough for one person. The trick to this shower was we had to haul water from the freshwater source, up the stairs, dump into a holding tank, turn the generator on, and then hook up the small hot water heater. The heater was an efficiency unit that could heat small amounts of water. The deal was two five-gallon buckets per person. So the four of us all hauled our ten gallons, dumped into the holding tank, and waited about an hour for things to warm up. As I was the green horn, they graciously let me go first. We each had about a three-minute shower with lukewarm water and let me tell you it felt great.

November 25 had come, and it was a holiday. No work, just eat, drink, and party. We had the four of us, the three brothers and Otto. This guy Otto was what you'd think of when you think of a burly dude, hardcore, a loud laugh that could be heard a mile away, long black hair with a black beard, a gold miner, a survivalist, and a really cool person. He always wore Carhart pants and jacket and just had that "I'll do whatever the *fuck* I want." The first time I met him, I was actually a little nervous. He seemed like the kind of guy that would just punch you in the face for looking at him wrong. He was rugged but really turned out to be a gentle giant. He lived by himself on a float house about ten miles away going the other direction.

It was a Thanksgiving Day that I will never forget. Julian had the turkey in and the mashed potatoes were ready to go on the stove when we were ready. Kevin and I spent about an hour, and we went out and checked our few crab pots and shrimp pots that we had set a few days earlier. There were about six beautiful Dungeness crabs and at least 2 lbs. of decent-sized shrimp that came out of that hour's worth of work. When we got back, John, Don, Mike, Dale, Otto, and Julian were out on the deck processing oysters, clams, and mussels. They were having a blast, and when we returned with an epic catch, we became superstars. "Holy shit, that is awesome," Julian said with a bottle of Jack in his hand. The beers were flowing, and the party favors were making everyone feel about as good as you can.

So about two hours after prepping and partying, it was time to eat. I remember and still have the picture of that Thanksgiving meal. Turkey and mashed potatoes were about the only normal thing that you would have for dinner. We had a little different menu, all from the sea and all fresh that day: Dungeness crab, oysters, mussels, shrimp, and bottleneck clams. What a feast for being in the middle of nowhere. We ate, we laughed, we drank, and we enjoyed a great day with some good people.

What did you get when you mixed eight guys partying like rock stars who lived on a float house out in the middle of nowhere, trouble in the lower 48, but out here, who cared because there was *no law*? Have you ever tried to jump on a floating log in the ocean? Have you ever shot beer cans out of the sky? Have you ever shot a fully automatic weapon at absolutely nothing? Have you ever loaded up a boat with eight fucked-up people to do a midnight boat ride? Well, my friends, welcome to an unforgettable Alaskan Thanksgiving.

16

CHAPTER

After a few days of having fun, it did take us a day to feel normal again. Life went on as usual, oysters, wood, food, and a few projects. One of our first rewarding projects was to plumb in our fresh water to the float house. It sounds better than it actually was, but we did find a way to actually get running water to the sink in the kitchen. It was amazing to have water come out of the sink faucet. We no longer had to wash our dishes, brush our teeth, and clean up at the end of the day from a hose out on the deck. We were now civilized people. Well, kind of, we still did not have a shower or a toilet, but for where we were at, this was a plus.

As the days went by, so did our daylight. We had to start working harder with our days getting shorter. By mid-December, we had about six hours to do our work. At around 8:30 p.m., it was light enough to see, and by 3:30 to 4:00 p.m., it was dark. We had to go through the nets, which were our bread and butter, and we had to get wood because that was our heat. Those two things were done during day, and everything else was done after dark.

I had made a plan finally, and it was to leave a few days before Christmas and fly back to New York and spend the holidays with my family and then back to Arizona. I really had no idea what was going to happen, but I had spent a few months up here and figured it was time to head south. The guys were cool with me leaving, and it was going to be hard leaving Julian—he was my best friend and I would miss him—but I wanted to see my family, especially my mom. It had been a few years since I was able to get home for Christmas, and this year it was time. My plan was set, and I purchased tickets. I still had a few weeks, and we made the most of it.

So John and Kevin had already planned on leaving a few days before I left, so they could see their families and be back to help Julian out with everything after I left. It was sad to say goodbye to them because it had been such a great time, and every day was a new experience. They settled up with me for the hours I had worked and headed out on the Carla Babe, home for the holidays. The money paid for my ferry ride, flights, and enough for Christmas presents when I got back to Potsdam. It was all I could ask for, and I was very happy to have had this privilege to live and work in such a unique atmosphere. We were still waiting for our money from John for shrimping and this really started to bug me. It was tough to get hold of him, and he basically was ignoring us, and that pissed me off more, but there was not a lot I could do about it. If I got the money, great, and if I didn't, there would be more to make in the future. At least I had enough to get home and see my family.

Julian and I had the place to ourselves for my last two nights, and we did what we wanted. We fired the shotgun at anything that would move, drank most of the day, and started to think what we could do next. We went fishing, explored more areas, and drank and ate everything in the house. We didn't work at all, just had fun. The day before I was to leave, we were out on the boat, and the engine quit on us in the middle of the ocean. This was just a small ten-foot skiff with an old engine. We managed to get it back to the dock, but my nerves were shot about this time knowing we had to leave by 6:00 a.m. to get me to the ferry on time. We took the motor off the boat and brought it inside. Julian was not a mechanic but smart enough to troubleshoot a problem. He was a very smart guy, just never really applied himself in any one area. So that night, we tore the damn thing apart, changed our plugs, drained any fluids, and hoped for the best. I did take a shower that night before heading home and just kept thinking, *Is this boat going to get me to the ferry? Let's hope so.* If not, it would be a tough phone call to tell my mom I wasn't going to make it. That night was a long and restless night.

We both got up. It was still pitch black out, and I carried that damn motor back to the boat and put it on. *Please work...please work,* and it did turn over. With my bags packed, I threw them in the boat, and we headed out in the dark with me holding a flashlight in front of us so we could see where the hell we were going. Normally, we could get to the dock in thirty minutes; this boat was much slower and took about fifty minutes. We made it this far, but we still had an hour and a half drive to get to the ferry on the south side of the island. That too was slow going because of the roads and weather. Time was ticking, and I was chewing on my fingernails the whole way. Well, we did make it with about three minutes to spare. It didn't take us long to say our goodbyes. I just hugged him and told him I loved him and would call when I got home.

The ferry left, and I watched Julian drive off. Was our time together done, or would we see each other again? I truly hoped so because he was a good person and always up for an adventure and a good party. We had spent the last five months together, and man oh man, we had a great time—Yosemite to a shrimping boat and then to the float house. He was one of the best friends I had, and I always knew he would do anything for me because I think I was one of the best friends he ever had. The two-hour trip from the island to the mainland was sad for me, but I was excited to see my family in Potsdam and then back to Arizona to see my friends there, especially Murph.

The ferry ride was smooth, and I actually got an hour of sleep. Today is going to be a long day, up at 5:00 a.m., the whole boat motor thing, fifty-minute ride in the dark, two-hour ferry ride to Ketchikan, Alaska, a five-minute ferry ride to the airport, and then a flight to the east coast with a layover. It was an all-day adventure, something like eighteen hours of travel even with a three-hour time change.

17
CHAPTER

My parents picked me up at the airport, and we had a great ride home. It was good to see both my mom and dad. Everything seemed to be going good for both of them. My dad was busy being a funeral director and antique dealer. My mom was babysitting several kids at my sister's house, including her newest grandchild, whom she absolutely adored. My sister Judy had three children, Michael, Samantha, and Scotlyn. The two girls were with her second husband, Scott, who was a UPS driver and a good father. Judy started working with disabled children after she received her master's degree at Potsdam State. She was perfect for this job and had done this for most of her adult life. It was a tough job, and she, of course, excelled at her job. My nieces were both still young, and Christmas was a huge deal in our house. It was my mom's favorite holiday, and it was a great time to be home.

The holidays were great—good food, plenty to drink, and always a good talk or two with my dad. He loved the fact I was seeing the world. He did understand that I wanted to travel and see the world; this was something he had always wanted to do. My dad had spent time in Germany while in the Air Force and traveled around a little. He just always wanted to see more but never had the chance after getting married and having kids. All in all, it was great to spend a week with my family during the holidays.

After the first of the year, I headed back to Arizona. Murph and Kari told me to stay with them until I got my feet on the ground.

I just kind of hung out for a few days, had the chance to see everyone, and had fun just being low-key and relaxed. The financial aspect of my life wasn't that good, so something had to be done. I decided to get in touch with Julian just to see how everything was going. I left a message, and about four hours later, he called me back. "What's up, Mundy? Good to hear your voice," he said, and it was good to hear his voice. We chatted for a while about what they were doing and how everyone was doing. He said, "You know, you could always come back here. We need help." I thought about it for about a day and called him back. I told him I would love to head back to the float house; there was something about living so carefree that I just needed more time to do it. That night, when Murph got home, I told him what I was going to do, and he just laughed and said, "Have fun, and you always have a place to stay when you get back." The plan was set, and I was going back to Alaska.

Julian and I were in contact several times that week. The plan was he and Kevin were going to meet me in Seattle for a few days, have some fun, and then head back. John and Kevin had agreed to pay for my flight from Seattle if I could get there. There was a small problem, and I did not have a lot of money. If I flew there, that would take about everything I had. The other choice was by Greyhound, which would take longer but was definitely cheaper.

Murph took me to the bus station, gave me a big hug, and I was on my way to Seattle by bus. Looking back on this, I should have traveled by plane. It would have been a lot faster. The bus ride from Phoenix to Las Angeles was about nine hours, and I was the only white person on the bus. Everyone else was Mexican, but I had no problem with that after traveling as much as I had over the past few years. We had about an hour or so in Las Angeles, switched buses, and we headed north to Seattle. Now this trip, which covered about 1,200 miles, took about twenty-eight hours. All I knew was that when I got to the bus station, I'd meet up with those guys and we would probably enjoy the party favors that I had hiding in one of my bags.

We arrived at the terminal, and I was off the bus as quickly as I could. I looked around for Julian. I had sent him my itinerary by email, so he knew when I would be getting there and where the bus stop was located. I walked inside and searched the entire bus terminal—well, guess what, no Julian and Kevin. So I had to find a pay phone and call up to Alaska, hoping to talk with John to see where the guys were staying. I left a message, and rather quickly, I got a phone call back. I was expecting to hear John's voice to tell me where they were, but lo and behold, it was Julian. Now how could Julian be answering a phone call in Alaska if he was supposed to be here in Seattle? "Sorry, Mundy, we didn't make it—no money and Kevin decided he didn't want to go."

"Well, this information might have been helpful two days ago," I told him, but what could he do? Kevin just didn't want to leave, so Julian was stuck.

Julian told me there would be a plane ticket ready for me at the airport tomorrow. He told me to hang tight and he would see me soon. Okay, now I had to find a really cheap place to stay for one night. I have about $50 to my name, and that was it; really, that was all I had to my name. Thankfully, there was a hostel not too far from here, and the cost was $25 a night for a bed. I've stayed in hostels all over the world but never in the States.

Seattle is a beautiful city with a ton of stuff to do if you have money, and I had none. So without money some people might do nothing except sit around and feel sorry for them. Not me, I walked around the city as much as I could, sightseeing, everything I could see without spending a dime. The Space Needle, Pikes market, and the downtown area were what I could walk to and not have to spend anything. All I needed was a cheap meal and a place to sleep. Tomorrow, I would take a public bus to the airport, get on a plane, and be back at the float house by tomorrow night. I thought it was going to be that easy. Boy, was I mistaken.

I got to the airport and head to Alaskan Air to get my ticket. I waited in line, and when I was next in line, I went up with my driver's license and said, "My name is Stephen Mundy, and I have a flight reserved for today."

She checked her computer and said, "I'm sorry, sir, there is no ticket with this name reserved for today."

Julian! I love that guy, but sometimes his thinking and planning don't always match up. So I found a pay phone and called the store.

"Hi, this is Mundy. I need to get in touch with anyone at Cali Cove as soon as possible. Here is my contact number, which is a pay phone in the airport." I left the message and figured it would take a while for anyone to get back to me, so I found a bathroom and a hot dog stand, $3.50 for a dog and chips. I went back to my seat and stared at the phone and ate my lunch/dinner. I did have to ask several people not to use that phone because I was expecting a call any minute. Well, three hours went by, and the phone rang. I jumped up and grabbed the phone.

"Sorry, Mundy, I'm so sorry we just booked your flight, and the quickest is tomorrow afternoon—it's the only one we could get." He apologized, but it was Julian, and I should have known. Well, it looked like I was staying here for the night. It was not the ideal place, but it would not cost me anything as long as I didn't get kicked out. It was already getting dark by the time I had gotten this information, and it looked like it was going to be a long night here at "Hotel Seattle Airport." For about the next hour, I walked around with my bags, which were my backpack and daypack, checking out the airport and searching for the ultimate place to sleep for the night. I had a small blanket that I kept from the bus ride. I laid the blanket out on the ground and used my bags as a pillow. Sounded like a great way to spend the night, on a hard-ass floor in an airport.

After scanning the entire terminal, I found a place that was being used by others who were staying the night. It was a walkway between two sections of the terminal. It looked as good as any place, so I found a spot, laid out my blanket, and used my bags as a pillow. My stomach was growling, but I could not afford to eat again that day. I tied my bags to my legs just in case someone tried to grab and run with them. That is something I did not need to happen to me at this point. The place seemed safe, and all I could do was prepare the best I could. It was an okay night. I would sleep for thirty minutes, and something would wake me up. I'd sleep for a while, and an announcement would go off and I would wake up. It wasn't my ideal situation but just something that will make a fun story to tell someday. Guess what? That someday has arrived, and there you have it.

The next morning, it was early because the airport was busy. I woke up, packed up all my stuff, and headed to the bathroom. I cleaned up as best as I could and then back to where I was sleeping to hang out for a few more hours before I could get my ticket. I did find a place to at least watch a little TV, which was nice. If only I had more money, I could sell the cocaine in my bag, but with my luck, it would be to an undercover cop, and I just did not need that to happen. So I waited until noon to get something to eat, another hot dog and chips. This time, I put everything I could on that hot dog—onions, cheese, mustard, and even relish. I hate relish, but it was filling, and I wasn't sure when my next meal would be. I needed at least $2 to get on the ferry in Ketchikan. My flight and ferry to the island had been paid for, so I now had about $12 to my name, and that gave me maybe one more meal.

After lunch, I waited in line again with my fingers crossed that hopefully this time, when I handed the lady my driver's license, there was a plane ticket waiting for me, and luckily for me, there was one. My flight was in about three hours, so I went back to my spot for a nap, and I now felt like a normal person again, not some poor schmuck that just hangs out at airports. I was now a passenger and had every right to be there.

The time came to board, and I was so happy to be getting on a plane; almost two days at this airport was enough for me. The flight to Ketchikan took about two hours, and I was so glad to see the mountains, and it kind of felt like I was home again. Off the plane to the ferry boat and after a five-minute ride, I was now on the mainland of Ketchikan. Now all I had to do was walk about a half mile to the ferry boat and be on my way. It was going to feel good just to sit back, enjoy the scenery, and finally relax a little. I got to the ticket counter and gave her my name. "Yes, Stephen. We have your reservation. Unfortunately, the last ferry for the day left about thirty minutes ago."

My jaw dropped and all I could say was "Figured this would happen, it has been one of those days, actually four days now." I took my ticket and found out that the first ferry would leave at seven tomorrow morning. Then I contacted the store and left another message for the guys: "Ferry left, have to stay here tonight, leave at 7:000 a.m., please, please, please pick me up around 9:00 a.m." That was it, and now what would I do?

Well, I was in Alaska, it was January, and it was cold out, probably just hovering around 32 degrees. There was no place to stay inside at the ferry station; it was just a booth. No money, no credit cards, no travel checks, no way to get any money, it was going to be a long night. Now I had been here several times; the first time was when Julian and I had first arrived. I remembered there was a boatyard just outside of town; it was a salvage boatyard with a lot of beat-up boats that would never see the ocean again. My thought was that if I could find a boat with a cabin, I could break in and at least get out of the weather, so I threw my pack on and headed for a walk. It was about a mile outside of town, and by now, it was almost dark, so I had the night to my advantage. Nobody would see me, and I could sneak in, find a boat, and call it home for the evening.

As I approached the yard, I did a really good scan of the area and at this point had seen nobody walking around. It looked deserted and just might work. I walked into the yard and spotted an orange lifeboat that would have been used on a cruise ship or something. It was enclosed and looked like a good spot. I got close to the boat, which was up on fifty-five-gallon barrels, did a real good look to see if anyone was watching, and threw my pack up into the boat. I then grabbed the edge of the opening and hoisted myself up into the boat. It was covered. There were benches to sit, and except for about six inches of water on the deck, it was dry and out of the weather. It was not the Ritz-Carlton or even a Motel 6, but it was going to have to work. I laid my sleeping bag out on a bench, secured my other gear, and called it a night. Now I've slept in some crazy places over the course of my travels, but this was definitely toward the top of uniqueness. Believe it or not, I did get some sleep probably because I was exhausted and hungry.

The next morning, as soon as the sun made its way above the horizon, I poked my head out the window, looked around, threw my bags out the door, and jumped out myself. I made my way back to the ferry boat, and at 7:00 a.m. on the dot, we headed out to sea, and all I could do was laugh to myself and take a big sigh of relief that I was finally on my way.

Julian was there to meet me, and we had a good laugh and talked for the two-hour truck ride back to Naukati. We parked the truck, and it was good to see the old boat back in action. Another thirty-minute boat ride, and I was finally at the float house. John and Kevin were both happy to see me, and when I told them my whole ordeal, we got a big laugh, and then we all indulged in my little gift that I brought back. That night we had a few beers, a line or four, and I had the best night's sleep in my cold room that I had ever had. What a trip and just to recap: Leave Phoenix for a day and a half bus ride, one night at a hostel, then almost two days at an airport, then a flight to Alaska, a night in an abandoned boat, a two-hour ferry ride, a two-hour truck ride, and then a thirty-minute boat ride to get to my destination. For anyone who has had a crazy travel adventure, I hope you enjoyed this one.

So it was back to work as usual. I could tell that in just a few days that the oysters were starting to get fewer and fewer. We had gone through so many of the nets before I had left that we only had maybe twenty-five or so to go through, and then we would start all over again with the first ones we went through two months ago. It only took me a few days to realize that the guys really didn't need me, but I was glad to be back and it was good to be hanging out with Julian. He always was up to something, and you just never knew what was going to come out of his mouth. He made me laugh but could definitely get under your skin if you didn't know him like I did.

At least a few days a week, we would try and do something different: either go fishing, find a different spot to get wood, go for a hike somewhere, spend a day hunting, or just cruise around in the boat. One day, we were out taking a boat ride, all five of us, and we noticed this huge log in the water. We were far away but could see something floating. Our first thought was a new log to hang more oyster nets from. We could tie it up to the boat and drag it back. We had the whole plan figured out even before we knew what it was. Well, that log was not a log at all; it was a humpback whale resting on the surface. As we got close, the whale dove down, showing off its gigantic tail, and we all were in just a state of *awe*. Wow, that was the closest I had ever been to a whale. The whale dove deep, and we thought it was gone; well, guess what—it wasn't. The humpback whale came up and out of the water like a missile, and it was a spectacular sight to see. However, the whale came back down into the water and almost tipped us over. We all got a good soaking, and when we realized we were not going to tip over, we all let out a cheer.

Another time we were out and about in the surrounding playground that we called our backyard, I saw something else that I will never forget. It was late afternoon, and we had been fishing for a while, and Kevin pointed out a tree in the far distance. "Guys, look at that tree. It is pure white," he said, and we all started naming trees that it could be. Again, we were way off. As we slowly approached, it we noticed that it was kind of moving, yet there was no wind and all the other trees around it were not moving at all. We got closer, and we all realized it was a tree, but the tree was completely overtaken by bald eagles. Yes, the national bird, a predator, survivor, and highly protected. I've seen a bald eagle or two in my life. They are a beautiful bird, and everyone knows what they look like. This, however, was once in a lifetime to see hundreds of them completely taking over this entire tree that was at least sixty tall. We stopped the boat and just slowly floated by and watched them interact with each other.

The bald eagles that we saw that day were spectacular, but we thought it was a sign. That night, we had a huge snow storm. Now it was Alaska, and it did snow here. We had several other days where it snowed, but living on the ocean, it does help keep the air a little warmer, not today. That night, we must have gotten two feet of snow easily. Most of the time, you could just sit back inside next to your warm fire and have a warm drink. Not for us, we had to shovel and shovel and shovel for about three days straight. You see, when you're living on a big raft on the ocean, there is only so much weight it can hold before it starts to sink. The snow was that heavy wet snow, and you could see how quickly the raft started to slowly get closer to the water. For about seventy-two hours, we spent morning, noon, and the middle of the night shoveling off the raft. Two guys would work at it for a few hours and then switch up with someone else. That was all we could do to save ourselves from sinking in the ocean. It looked beautiful, but man oh man, was it a sketchy few days for us. Again, the bald eagles, did they know there was a storm brewing, and did all meet up to discuss their plan of action? I think so.

To some people, this next story will seem cruel and unethical, but once again, this is the wild, Alaska the final frontier. Their friend, who was an Inuit Alaskan who lived in a small village north of Juneau, came to visit us for a few days. His village was more in the mountains and definitely more secluded than most people live. He was darker skinned and looked like what I would call an Eskimo.

His mission was to shoot a few sea otters for their pelts and other portions of it. He was allowed to shoot five sea otters a year. There was a season only for the native Alaskans to shoot sea otters, and for anyone else, it was illegal. A sea otter is anywhere from three to five feet long and can weigh fifty to one hundred pounds. They are the largest member of the weasel family and have an extremely thick coat. This is what makes them very valuable for Inuit who can hunt them. The pelts can be used for so much: shoes, gloves, hats, and so much more. Each pelt can bring them about $1,000 cash, which can go for fuel, food, and additional clothing.

Our guest had spent about three days out trying to get one. It wasn't that he could not find them; just getting one was difficult because he was on a boat, the waves were a challenge to navigate, and a sea otter's head were all you really get a shot at, and it was about the size of a beer can. He came back after the third day, and we could tell he was frustrated. Kevin spoke up and said he would go out tomorrow and see if he could get one. Well, I spoke up and said, "I'll go with you." The plan was set; tomorrow, after our work, we will give it a shot, knowing it was completely illegal to hunt these animals as a white man.

After we had our stuff done, Kevin and I set out to help this guy out. We headed about thirty minutes to another part of the island, another new place that I had never been to. As we got closer, Kevin pulled out his gun. It looked like a small machine gun. He said, "This is an M-13 fully automatic weapon. The gun is legal but not for hunting."

TAKE A DECADE

"So we are going to use it to hunt, right?"

"Well, yes, legal or not, it doesn't really matter. We are not exactly in your town pond doing this. This is the middle of nowhere, and hopefully, the law is far away."

Kevin let me go first, so I stood on the bow of the boat, and we moved really slowly with the boat waiting for one of them to pop their heads up. Kevin spotted one. "There you go, Mundy. That is one." Within a split second, it was gone. At least now I knew what to look for. About two minutes later, I saw one. I aimed at my target and pulled the trigger. *Bam bam bam bam...* I emptied the whole cartridge in a split second. Holy shit, that was awesome. You could see the bullets hitting the water in a pattern as I moved. It was the coolest gun I had ever shot, and I felt like a madman with it in my hands. I did, however, miss the sea otter completely even with a fully automatic gun.

It did take a few minutes to reload, and there was the cost of the shells and it wasn't like there were a lot of sporting goods stores nearby, so we had to hunt smart. He said to only shoot one bullet at a time. If you missed, you might get another shot before they went under. I was at least on my second clip before I actually was able to get one. Kevin and I high-fived and started to scream. Yes, we got one.

"Good shot, Mundy," he said, and I felt pretty good. We got to the otter, and it was not quite dead, so we had to put it out of its misery. Kevin and I spent three to four hours. We went through about seventy-five shells, and we ended up getting three for our friend.

We pulled up to the dock, and everyone came out. They all smiled when they saw what we had gotten. Our Inuit friend was so pleased and so thankful for the time we spent doing this for him and his family. He thanked us for days for what we had accomplished. I'm not a fan of taking anything for just pleasure. There had to be a reason to take any animal from this world. The Indians did it, the white man did it, and for me, it was the right thing to do for this person.

It was the beginning of March, and Julian came into my room one night and said that he was thinking about leaving. As of now, we still had not received our money from John. We had talked to him a few times, and it was always the same thing. "I'm working on it," he would say, but we knew he really didn't care. John did not need the money and couldn't really care less. Julian and I were tired of it, and Julian had the plan to go back and try and sell the shrimp himself. I hated to think of him not being here, but he had to do what he wanted to do, and he was getting tired of the float house life. The plan was that John, Mia, Kevin, and Julian were going to leave, take Julian to Sitka, where the shrimp were at, and they were going to visit family and get supplies in Juneau. That meant that I would be alone on the float house for the first time ever.

It was sad saying goodbye to Julian. Was our time together up, or would we get another opportunity to do something else? We didn't know. He told me that he would send money ASAP, which would be great, and he would keep in touch. They pulled away from the float house, and all I could do was wave goodbye. In about three minutes, the boat had disappeared, and they were gone.

That night was so quiet, almost too quiet. I'm not a person that gets scared, but my mind can wander around and get the best of me. Every noise you hear is so much more intense when you are living alone hundreds of miles away from civilization. It was fun, though, I took the boat out for a ride, went through a few nets, chopped wood, and had a swig of my bottle of Jack Daniel's that they had bought me for staying behind.

The next day, I spent cleaning up the entire float house. Everything from the dishes to the woodshed was cleaned and everything organized that day. It gave me something to do, and it looked nice. Hopefully, the guys would notice and see that I was productive while they were gone. It went quickly, and after the second day, it started to feel nice being alone. I thought to myself, could I live out here alone for a given period and survive? Who knows? Maybe someday I will have that chance, but so far, my life has been spent with others around me, and that has been wonderful.

It was day three around 2:00 p.m., and I started to hear an engine in the distance. They were back without Julian but with supplies. It was good to see them, and all three of them said how nice the place looked as soon as they walked on the deck. We offloaded the boat and talked about getting Julian set up and their time at home. It was definitely different without Julian. Even that first night, things just weren't the same.

The next few weeks were all about the same. We had gone through all the nets by now, and the oysters were growing, just not as quickly. So much had been done in the past few months that work was really slowing down. The guys informed me that even though there was not a lot going on right now that I could stay here for as long as I wanted. We would always find something to do. With the potential to make money starting to slow down, I did start to think about what was next. My plan was to return to Yosemite around the end of May when that season started up. That would mean staying here for another 2.5 months. The one big thing that probably got to me the most was the weather. It had started to rain at the beginning of March, and it rained almost every day. It was southeast Alaska, and this was just something that happened this time of year. It just made doing things a little more challenging, and it seemed you were always wet somewhere or everywhere. Constantly drying off, just to go back out and get wet again. Working on the deck, getting wood, going to town to get fuel, you name it and it was a wet situation.

After about three weeks of this, I got a call from Julian. He had sold the shrimp and had $1,200 for me. I was ecstatic over this, and it made my day. Finally, we had the money from the shrimp. It wasn't exactly what we had thought it would be, but at this time, it was close enough. Julian mailed it to me, and I got it about five days later. I asked him what he was going to do, and he said, "I'm thinking about heading to Maui, Hawaii, for a while to get out of this weather. Do you want to meet me?" He had lived there as well for a time, and he knew a few people. We talked for about twenty minutes on the phone and thought about it for about five minutes and decided, why the hell not? I could go to Maui for a month or so and then head to Yosemite. Wow, just like that, and we had a plan and I was excited. We would meet up in Hawaii and keep this adventure going. I knew my time with Julian was not up yet. We had fun together, and both had the desire to seek out new things.

That night, I informed Kevin and John of my plans. I figured I would leave around the first of April. They were happy for me and understood why I wanted to leave. I started searching flights and was taking my time to find the right one. Julian and I were communicating the best we could. The day before I was going to book my flight, about two weeks out, Julian called and said, "I can't go to Maui." He told me that he had been out that night, got his hands on some cocaine, and had gotten arrested for possession. They arrested him but let him go until his court date. They kept his passport, which was his only form of ID. Julian had not had a driver's license since he was nineteen. He lost it in South Carolina and never got it back. So he was stuck in Alaska for who knows how long. "I'm so sorry, Mundy, but you should still go, it is a great place" is all he could say. That night, I did some thinking and really wanted a change.

The next day, we went into town to get fuel and a few supplies. This gave me time to call home and let them know what I was planning. My mom answered; it was always good to hear her voice. I said to her, "Mom, I'm leaving Alaska and have an opportunity to check something else out." She asked in a very low tone, "Where are you going now?"

"Mom, I'm going to Hawaii for a month or so and enjoy some nice warm weather."

"Hawaii," she said.

"What are you going to do in Hawaii?"

"I have no idea but will figure it out when I get there." She wasn't surprised because by now she had received calls like this before. She happy for me, but as a mother she was always worried that I would be okay.

John had mentioned taking the ferry from Ketchikan to Washington. It would take around three days to get there by boat. Time was on my side, I had no one to see or nowhere to really get to, and so this would work out great. That day, I set up my itinerary for the trip. They would pay for what they could with their credit cards, which would pay me for my hours worked. This was the plan: We would leave on Tuesday with the float plane that picked up our product. He would fly me to Ketchikan then spend one night in a hotel in Ketchikan. Once in Ketchikan, I would get on the ferry for Bellingham, Washington, then I would take a train to Seattle, spend two nights there in a hotel, and then fly to Maui. I had time and wanted to be pampered a little bit. I wanted to spend a few nights at a hotel or something that had running water, heat, TV, and a hot shower. After the weather and the life I'd been living for the past year, a few days of R&R was well deserved.

It had been about 4.5 months, minus two weeks at Christmas that I had been living out here, and it was a true adventure. Those last days also gave me time to express how grateful I was to Kevin and John for giving me this amazing opportunity to live a life that I could have only imagined would ever happen for me. I was truly sad to say goodbye.

Tuesday came, and my bags were packed. I spent the morning joking around with the guys and helped get the oysters ready for shipment. Around 2:00 p.m., I could hear the plane approaching and it was a bittersweet moment, sad to be leaving, but on the other hand, excited to be leaving. I was going to be spending the night in a hotel, and that was just so exciting for me. The simple things are sometimes the biggest things. The plane landed, we loaded up the product and I gave everyone a big hug and said my goodbyes.

The float plane took off, and I asked the pilot if we could fly over the float house. He said, "No problem at all, we are going that way anyway." We took off, and I was able to see from a bald eagle's view of where I had spent a great 4.5 months of my life. Again, it was a bittersweet moment to see the whole operation, the three buildings, the boats, and my three friends standing on the raft waving good-bye. It was a tearful moment to see it disappear as we flew over the mountains. Goodbye, Callie Cove. Thank you for such an incredible adventure. This whole experience taught me a lot about the world and about myself.

We landed in Ketchikan, and by now, I knew this airport very well. I headed out the door with what was remaining of my gear. I left a lot of my clothes behind because they were either all beat up or just not needed where I was going. Stephen Mundy was actually headed to Hawaii for a month of true R&R. So I really just had my backpack filled with a few clothes and my basic stuff that I had been using for the past year.

Ketchikan is not a huge place; it is a port for cruise ships during the season and known for their totem poles that are everywhere. It is a cool Alaskan town, and I had seen almost everything I wanted to see. All I really wanted was to get to my room. It was right in the heart of town and close to everything. I checked in, dropped my stuff off, and went to get a few supplies for the evening, a six-pack of beer and something to eat. I also needed to grab stuff for the three-day ferry ride, which I was looking forward to. For this trip, I bought snacks, beef jerky, and a bottle of bourbon. They would have food and drinks on the boat, but I knew I needed to watch my money as best I could. At this point, almost everything had been paid for by John and Kevin, but once I touched down in Hawaii, it was up to me. At this point, I had about $1,200 to my name, and that had to last until I found a way to make more. Hopefully, it would not be hard. We would see.

The next morning, I was up and ready and feeling like shit. I had finished my six-pack and had a few pulls from the bourbon. All I had to do was get to the boat and sit back and relax. The ferry boat was not far from town; it was a short walk and there it was. It was a large boat big enough to hold passengers, trucks, cars, and other equipment. I made my way to the main gate; my ticket was paid for, which was like $120 for the three days. I made my way to the top deck, which would be my home for the next few nights. They had lounge chairs on the top deck that you could sleep on. This was the cheapest way to take this ferry ride to Bellingham. The "open-air experience" is what they called it. It was $40 a night, compared to an actual room that cost more like $125 a night. I was a budget traveler, and this was perfect. There were about twenty-five lounge chairs that were under an awning that had those outdoor heaters. The whole deck was completely open, which made for a great view. We were toward the back of the boat, so it would make for a great view of the landscaping as we made our way down the west coast of Alaska and Canada.

As I picked a chair, others were doing the same. Mostly younger people like me were looking for a cheaper way to get to the next destination. We all were starting to talk back and forth. Where are you from, and where are you going? Everyone just got comfortable as the boat left the dock. It was going to be very nice to be on a boat and not have to work. Just kick back and enjoy the ride.

After we were on our way, I did spend an hour or so just walking around. Checked out every deck that I could get to and found the main things, food and bathroom. It was perfect, and as we headed down the coast, it was absolutely breathtaking. The white-capped mountains, the rugged coast line, personal boats, and the surrounding ocean was what I had for a visual, and let me tell you, it was perfect. I hated to close my eyes because I did not want to miss anything.

Several of us had been smart and brought aboard something to "drink," and we all shared. That first night, maybe ten or so people just sat around talking story and enjoying a drink or two. It was again so relaxing to be on a boat, enjoying the scenery that one could expect traveling down the west coast of Canada. Islands everywhere with their own little secrets, small communities that lived along the sea coast, the Forever Mountains in the distance, and a view of sea life from now and again. We passed along Banks Island, Princess Royal Island, and Vancouver Island during this three-day trip. Life was good.

The next day was very similar, staring off in the distance, watching the wake of the boat from the back, and taking a nap or two. It felt great not to have to work for my survival for a few days. Who knew what to expect in the very near future, but today was a day where all that mattered was I didn't have to do a single thing except enjoy life. How often can you really just sit back and enjoy that little thing we call life?

The ferry pulled into the harbor of Bellingham, Washington, which is located on the northern part of the state, just south of Vancouver, Canada. This would be the first main city south of the border. It would be from here that I would take a train to Seattle, which would take about three hours. The train, which was Amtrak, was a rather cheap form of transportation—$20 for a one-way ride and I always love traveling by train. Met a few people on the train and had some small talk. Nothing major, just sat back and enjoyed a conversation with another person that I would never see again in my life, but for now, we were friends.

Took another train to get closer to my hotel, which was close to the airport. This was something I booked on the float house and just wanted something cheap and a quick ride to the airport the next day. Got off the train and decided to walk to the hotel. I really needed to stretch my legs and had nothing else to do. It took an hour or so, but it was good to get some exercise. I was also able to pass a store to get some supplies for the room: Beer, chips, and chocolate were all I really needed because that night, I was going to eat like a king. Yes, that night I had planned on ordering a pizza, which is not something I had done for almost a full year. There was no pizza delivery in Yosemite and definitely none in Alaska. This was something I had planned on for a week and couldn't wait to sit on my bed, watch a movie, drink beer, and enjoy a delivered pizza right to my room.

The next two nights were spent eating whatever I wanted as long as it was delivered and in the hot tub, which was two doors down from my room. Life was good, and I enjoyed every minute of being pampered. Life was about to change for me, and I had no idea. Tomorrow, I was flying to Hawaii and I had no idea what to expect.

That night, my last night of nothing to really worry about, was spent calling home and talking with my parents, talking with Murph, and contacting Graydon, whom I had not talked with for a few months. I had spoken with Murph a few times during my stay but not Graydon. Graydon was always a positive and supportive person. As always, he said to me, "Mundy, you are living life, like it was meant to be lived, good luck, keep in touch, and I love you, my friend." My life has been filled with great people, and he is definitely one of them.

The next morning I was up early, had called for a cab, and was ready to go. When I got to the airport, boy oh boy did I have a flashback; I knew this airport inside and out. It was my home for almost two nights when I was heading back to the float house. There is where I slept, my hot dog stand, my drinking fountain, and most of all was the phone that I watched for hours while waiting for Julian to call. I'm so glad I don't have to live here like that again. I had just two hours before I left and time for a beer. I had spent all those hours watching people drink, while all I could do was order one hot dog a day and drink from a water fountain. I felt like the king of the world, a real high-class person. That might have been one of the best beers I ever drank.

The moment had come, and my flight was called. Holy shit, I was on my way to Hawaii, a place I never really thought I would ever get to. I had seen many pictures and TV shows about Hawaii, but really not in a million years did I think that I would be able to spend a month there. It would be about a five-hour flight before we got there. It would be around 3:00 p.m. when I landed, so this would give me a chance to get my bearings before it got dark. This is what I told myself as the plane took off. Was I a bit nervous? Yes, I cannot lie. *Hope this works out for you, Stephen Mundy*, was all I thought about for the next five hours. *Hawaii, here I come!*

18
CHAPTER

Hawaii, Year 1

It was April 6, 2013 when I arrived in paradise. After a year of living a little on the extreme side, it was time to just simply relax and enjoy the nice weather. Hawaii was the fiftieth state located about 2,500 miles off the west coast and in the middle of the Pacific Ocean. To be truly honest, it was not a place that I really had on my radar to go at this point in my life. When Julian mentioned it and talked about how awesome it was, I figured for a month it would be a lot of fun. I just couldn't believe he was not going to be joining me.

We landed at the Kahului Airport (OGG) around 3:00 p.m., and it was sunny and about 75 degrees. I could not wait to just hold my head up to the sun and feel the heat on my face. It had been a while since I'd seen or felt the brightness and heat from the sun. We departed the plane, and I was instantly outside. As soon as you leave the gate, the hallways are all outside. This was an open-air airport, which was something different than any other airport I had been to. I could feel the warmth of the air as soon as I was out of the gate. I proceeded to the baggage claim area and was amazed that this place really had no doors or walls for this part of the airport as well. I waited to get my bags and started to look for an information center or something with housing opportunities. All I hoped for was a cheap hostel with a bed and shower; this was all I really needed. It was about this time that I did get a little nervous. I was alone out here. I knew absolutely no one. I had a little bit of money but not much, and except for making my way to a place called Lahaina, I was clueless to my surroundings. Oh well, there was not much I can do now except figure things out and make things happen.

At the center of the baggage claim area, I noticed the information center. After getting my bags I headed over to see what they had to offer. As I was approaching the area, I noticed a guy doing the same thing. As I got there, he had walked over to the phones and was making a call. This guy stood out because he had a backpack on and just looked like a traveler. The information center was nothing more than a rack of brochures for everything you could do on the island. My focus was a place to sleep.

There were only a few options for hostels, so I called the first one that seemed to be the closest one to the airport. It said right on the brochure it was less than three miles from the airport. This would be perfect for the night, so I called the number and they did have space. "Thank you, I'll see you soon" was all I said. I walked out of the baggage claim area, again not having to open a door or anything; I just walked out. After checking things out, I looked around for that guy with the backpack, and he was gone. The taxi looked like the best bet. I found one and told him where I wanted to go. My bags were loaded, and I was off to see what my future held.

Once we left the airport, we traveled a short distance. I saw a few stores, a gas station, and a few palm trees. Then we hit the industrial area, through a few side streets, and then we had reached my destination. The cost was $25 for a six-minute ride. Wow, that hurt. My money situation at the point of landing on this island was about $800; that is all I had to my name. This was it, and I had no job or any way in the near future to make any money, so every dime counted.

I opened the door to the hostel, and the guy whom I saw at the airport was just checking in. I introduced myself, and he hung out while I got checked in for the night. I told the guy two nights just in case I needed an additional day to get acclimated. The guy's name was James, and he was from England, visiting for a week to surf and learn more about hydroplaning, which is a new form of surfing. My first real question to him was "How did you get here?"

"They came and picked me up. All I did was ask for a ride and they were at the airport in two minutes. How did you get here?" he asked in his British accent. I told him I had spent $25 for a cab; I just didn't think to ask that one simple question about pickups. I noted this one for next time.

James and I hit it off, and we went to get a few beers and something to eat. He had one week and wanted to see as much as he could. I was there indefinitely at this point. I wanted to see the island but also wanted to find a job and a place to stay for a month or so. We talked that night and decided to rent a car, which was from a rental company, for the week. We could see the island; this would get me to where I wanted to go, but it also gave us a place to sleep for a week. This was perfect for both of us. We will not have to spend money on a room, just split the cost of the car and gas for a week. It would not cost more than $100 each.

The next day, we picked up the car and both wanted to see a beach, sit in the sand, and jump in the Pacific Ocean. The closest beach was in Paia, which the guy at the hostel said was a cool little town with a lot of hippies and down-to-earth people. This was perfect, and when he said hippies, I figured someone would have a joint or two to sell. I wanted to enjoy a little Maui wowie as soon as possible. Paia was ten minutes away. I parked the car near the beach and asked the second person I saw if he had any bud, and guess what? He did. This was about as lucky as I could get, literally the second person and he said yes. I bought a dime bag from him, and we headed to the beach.

The beach was beautiful but a little on the windy side. We sat and had a beer, smoked a joint, and spent the next few hours with a map trying to figure out what to do. Our first spot would be the southern side of the island, and then around day 4 or so, we would make our way north to the town of Lahaina, Hawaii. The plan was set, and we sat there enjoying the sun, the heat, and the beautiful palm trees that surrounded the entire beach.

James and I checked out of the hostel on day three and headed toward the town of Kihei, which was on the southern side of the island. It was on what the locals called the leeward side of the island, which meant less wind and better beaches. Maui was divided by two mountain ranges. You had the mountain range to the south; that was where the highest point of Maui is located. This place is called Haleakala State park, which was something to see, and we will get to this later. The northern range is the Iao Valley state park, and this is located on the northern portion of the island.

The first day with the car was great. We made our way to Kihei and found a place to park close to the beach. When you first get here, it is so hard not to stare at the ocean; the blue color is just amazing. There were people everywhere walking around, playing on the beach, and enjoying their lives. The women walking around in their bikinis and sarongs were more than my poor little heart could take. It had been a while since I had even seen a good-looking girl, and now they were everywhere. Sensory overload was what was happening. It would be tough just talking to a girl right now, but it wouldn't be long before I gave it a shot. For now, I was just soaking up this amazing place and talking it all in. I've seen hundreds of pictures of Hawaii, but let me tell you, to see and hear the beautiful blue ocean crashing on the beach and the surrounding landscape is breathtaking.

James met up with a guy whom he had heard of on Kihei beach. He ran a surf shop and had done the hydroplaning that James wanted to try. He was a local guy, maybe in his forties, and was born and raised on Maui. He was a very cool person and actually loaned us a few boards to go out and try surfing. We paddled out and had a blast for a few hours surfing—well, trying to surf.

Later that afternoon, we found a grocery store and loaded up on supplies, a cheap cooler, bread, cold meat, peanut butter, a case of water, and a case of the good stuff. We were set for the next few days. Restaurants were not an option for either of us, and this would be much cheaper. That night, we found a beach with a few parked cars and just hung out on the beach. I had made the choice to sleep on the beach. We had room in the car, but I had a sleeping bag and thought that sleeping under the stars would be great. After a few beers that night, I left James the car and walked down the beach. I found a quiet spot where I could not see anyone and laid out my bag on a small patch of grass near the sand. *What a view*, was all I could say to myself. With the soft breeze of the ocean and the gentle sounds of the ocean hitting the land, it was all I needed to fall asleep.

For the next few days, it was the same thing: Drive to a different direction and check out the beaches and scenery. Stop and walk around for a bit, make a sandwich, drink a beer, and just stare out into the ocean. We also found a thrift shop, and I was able to find a few pairs of shorts and a few T-shirts. Some of my other stuff went right into the trash. Of course, I needed something for my feet, and it was like day two that I was turned on to Locals, which was the basic footwear for the local people. They were black thong-style shoes that were sold in every store on the island. One very cool thing was a sign that I saw walking into a store. "No shoes, no shirt, no problem"… and this was the way it was here. You could walk into any business with or without shoes and a shirt. You had to love the way of life that people lived out here.

It was day five, and James only had a few more days, so we made our way to Lahaina to see where I would try and get established. The drive up the coast was remarkable, the ocean on one side and the mountains on the other. The blue ocean with the waves breaking on the shore was just so cool to see. The boats that were out to sea looked like a lot of fun, and hopefully, that would be me soon. I missed being on the ocean, the movement, the air, and the view.

We entered the town of Lahaina, and I fell in love. Shops, restaurants, bars, and other entertaining things were on one side, and the ocean was right there on the other side. We drove through the whole town and just admired everything there was to see; the girls were everywhere and they looked all so good. James decided he wanted to get a place for his last few nights. Nothing really expensive but just something with a bed and shower was all we needed. He was willing to pay for it, and I was grateful to have this opportunity. We had spent the last four nights, me sleeping on the beach and him in the car. We had used the outdoor showers to keep clean, but he wanted something a little nicer the last few days. This would give me a chance to start looking for a place to stay.

That night we spent just walking around and checking out the area. I walked down to the small harbor and hoped that I could get on one of these boats doing something. Lahaina was going to be my home for a while.

I found a local paper and started to make a few calls. I left a few messages and really didn't get anywhere my first day, except I did find a hostel, which was good news, because that would be my next step once James left. There was this one place that had a room available and was right here in town. It was in my price range, $600 a month. At this point, I had about $650 left and no job. After leaving about three messages, it was on the fourth call that she finally picked up. "Hello, would it be okay to stop by and check out the place?"

She said, "Sure, come over whenever. I'm here now."

The girl answered the door, and she was on a crutch for a leg injury, which is another story. She had an English accent, and she too was from England. I told her I had spent the last six months in Alaska, and that was all it took. She too had spent time there and had worked on a crab boat for a while and then came here just like me. We talked for about fifteen minutes and checked out the place. I was honest about not having a job and just trying to get started. She told me that I was a little older than most people living in the house, but she liked me and told me that I could have the room. The only problem was the room wouldn't be available for three more days. The person was moving out at the end of the week, and I could have it then if I wanted. It was perfect, right in the middle of everything, close to the ocean, and I could afford it. I would be moving in on the fifteenth of the month, so she told me all I needed to pay was half the rent and a security deposit. This could have ended the entire deal. I had $300 bucks but didn't have an extra $600 for the deposit. She could tell right away that this was a problem and spoke up and said, "Just pay the $300, and when you get a job, you can get me the security deposit later." I actually gave her a hug, thanked her so much, and handed her $300. I told her that I would see her Friday the fifteenth and thanked her. Her name was Debra, and we became good friends. Debra had also told me about the hostel that was just three doors down and walked out to the road and pointed to it. This was awesome, so I walked down to the hostel and asked about availability. They had plenty, and I told them that I would be back tomorrow. What a relief. Things were looking good, and I was very happy. I still had a few bucks in my pocket and had a place to move into soon.

That night, we hit a few bars. I drank the cheapest thing I could, and James and I talked about our crazy week. I thanked him for being in the right place at the right time and would be sad to see him leave. He was my friend, my only friend, and he would be leaving tomorrow. I was back to being on my own, which was a little nerve wracking, but I had met him and would meet others.

We checked out of our room around noon. James and I said our goodbyes and he dropped me off at the hostel. This was my home for the next three nights before I could move into my room. I checked in, and this guy JR helped get me situated, finding a bed and showing me around. After I got situated, I walked down the street, grabbed a beer, and headed out to the beach. I just could not get enough of sitting on the warm sand staring at everything new. Wow, I still couldn't believe I was actually here and couldn't wait to talk to my parents about my first week in paradise.

During my stay at the hostel, I spent a lot of this time just checking things out, walking around, and getting a feel for what I could do for work. It was also time to kind of relax and enjoy Maui. I had a place to move into, and that was a big thing to get accomplished. This took pressure off me and allowed me to get an idea of what I could do while I was here. There were a ton of restaurants, activities around the island, and the opportunities around the harbor.

The day had come to move into my new place and I was so excited. Just to have a place to live, my own room, shared kitchen and bathroom, close to everything, and a step in the right direction. Debra met me when I first arrived, and she showed me around a little bit more. It was a five-bedroom house with three bathrooms. The house was a single-wall "cane house," which was used way back in the day for people who worked in the sugarcane fields. You walked in, and this was a good-sized living room with a few couches and a TV. To the left was a small hallway that led to three of the bedrooms and two bathrooms. The kitchen, which was very good size, was at the far end of the house, and it had a bedroom/bathroom located off it. I had the room that was off the living room, and it was perfect. It had a bed, dresser, and a small closet. It took me all of five minutes to unpack the few things I had, and my room was set up. I did ask Debra for the keys to the place, and she kind of laughed and said there are none. We don't lock the front door, and I don't have a key for your room. Things were very safe around here and we just didn't lock anything. This was great in a way because I did not ever have to carry a key around to get in and out. This was just one less thing to have to worry about.

That day, I was introduced to two other roommates. Allen, who had the room at the back of the house, was a caretaker for a big house on the island. He was friendly and welcomed me to the house. Allen was 5'8", a thin guy with brown hair and a rather quiet person who just kind of kept to himself. He did love to play pool and cards, which is something we both enjoyed doing, and we spent many nights playing poker. My next roommate was Danielle, and she was a cute blonde around twenty years old. My first thought of Danielle was she was a party animal and most definitely someone's girlfriend. I came to find out she was not a partying person; she was more of a homebody, who worked and was always trying to do the right thing. We became good friends, and from the first few days being around her, I always just thought of her as a younger sister and loved to pick on her. One other guy lived there, JD, but had not met him yet.

My first few days with a roof over my head were spent looking for work. I had applied at a few restaurants and had actually gotten hired on the spot at Bubba Gump's. It was a job, and the fact that I had worked on a shrimping boat was kind of a cool thing; it was just not really what I wanted. I did not want to spend my short time here waiting tables; I wanted to do something that would be more exciting and unique if possible. But hey, with only a few bucks in my pocket, I was appreciative to get anything.

So with having a job, which would start in a few days, I headed back to the house. It was day three, and I was just walking out of my room and I finally got to meet JD. He was a good-looking guy 5'9", 160 lbs. with short brown hair. We made eye contact, and he walked over and introduced himself. We had a few words to say like "Welcome to the island, and welcome to the house."

He then asked one question that changed everything: "So, Steve, where are you from?" I told him that I had just spent six months in Alaska but was originally from upstate New York.

He said, "I'm from Rochester, New York, so I know upstate, what town are you from?" I told him that I grew up in Potsdam, New York, and he was like I know Potsdam. My buddies and I would go up there and hang out for the weekend and party at the bars. He listed off all the bars that I had also been to, and we had a connection.

He said, "What are you doing for work?"

"Well, I just got hired at Bubba Gump but would prefer something on the water working on a boat or something."

He asked what I was doing right then, and I told him absolutely nothing. He asked me to follow him to where he worked and he could at least introduce me to the manager of the company he was working for. So I left with him, and we walked and talked like we had known each other for a long time. He was a Steelers fan, and I was a Dolphins fan, which was the only thing we disagreed on.

JD introduced me to Karla, the office manager of Island Marine Activities. This company did dinner cruises, whale watch, snorkel trips, and excursions to other islands and they were always hiring. Karla, JD, and I talked for about ten minutes; let her know what I had done in the past. Waited tables, worked on boats, and everything else that I could tell her in a short period. She said right there and then, "You're hired, and can you start tomorrow?"

"We need help on the dinner cruise, and I think you will fit in perfectly. Meet here tomorrow at 2:00 p.m., and Joe the first mate will show and tell you what to do. JD and I left, and I was so appreciative for him doing this, and we went and had a beer together. This would be one of many beers that I would drink with JD. This is what I wanted to do, work on a boat. I would be waiting on tables but in a completely different fashion, and this was very cool with me.

Life had begun for me here on the beautiful island of Maui. I had a place to live and had landed a job that would pay the bills and hopefully be a fun place to work. That night, JD invited me to go to a going-away party for this girl, Carmen, who was moving away. The party was at her house, and it was packed. Beautiful girls walking around everywhere, and everyone was either drunk or getting drunk. He introduced me as another upstate New Yorker and a new employee of Island Marine. It was a great night. It was so amazing to have so many people just say hi and welcome me to the island.

Another person I met that night was Larry, who also worked for the same company. Larry was 5'7" with blondish hair, and he looked like he was in good shape. He and I hit it off right away, and between him and JD; they filled me in on who was available and who was not. JD had a girlfriend, but Larry was single. Larry had been on the island for about nine months and worked on the snorkel and dinner cruise boat. He was a funny guy who loved to mess around with people and was everyone's friend.

My first day of work, I was excited, nervous, but looking forward to getting started. It does not matter what job you have; that first day is always tough because you don't know anything, and I always feel useless and in the way of getting things done. That day, I met Joe at the office, and he gave me a quick briefing. We left the office, walked down to the harbor, and got in this beat-up truck. Then we drove across town, which only takes about five minutes, and we entered what looked like an industrial area. This is where they had a kitchen and warehouse for all their food. The dinner cruise served a meal, which was prime rib, chicken, or veggie meal served with potatoes and a vegetable. We started to load the truck with warmers filled with food, plates, silverware, linens, and everything else they used. Then we drove back to the harbor, and there were about six people waiting for us, mostly girls, and they were all beautiful. Carmen, Christy, and Larry were among them, and these were people that I had met the night before. We waited about ten minutes for the *Maui Princess* to pull in and disembark the people that had just come back from Molokai. Once the boat was empty, we loaded everything from the truck onto the boat, including the staff, and then left the harbor. Once we left the harbor, we made our way just outside the harbor to a mooring ball used to secure the *Maui Princess*.

This was my first look at the island from the ocean, and it was spectacular. I realized why so many movies and photos have come from this place; it was an amazing sight. The mountains in the center of the island looked rugged and untouched; everything was so green and fresh-looking. From the boat, I could see more of what Lahaina looked like, and it was the best-looking harbor town I had ever seen.

The *Maui Princess* was a 120' × 40' boat with three levels. The bottom level was used for storage and supplies; the second level was the main cabin area that had the benches to sit on for the ferry ride. It also had the galley, which was used for cooking and serving of the meals. The helm of the boat was in the front of the boat and had everything needed to maneuver the boat. The *Maui Princess* was equipped with four large diesel engines and could get up and go if needed. The top level was set up with tables that were used for the dinner cruise. It was completely open, and what a great place to have a meal, floating down the coast of Maui and enjoying a prime rib dinner. Just being on the boat was fantastic, and I was getting paid to do this. Life was good.

That first day, everyone helped out, and I did whatever Joe wanted me to do. First, we had to break down the benches and put up tables in the middle level then get the food to the gallery to keep from getting cold and ready to serve. White tablecloths were put on all the tables on the top deck, garbage cans ready to go, drinks ready for the guests, and everything else needed to make this experience great for all the 150 guests that would be on boat that evening. Once all the big stuff was done, we all sat around and polished silverware and got some of the smaller things ready.

I was sitting at a table with three girls, all just wearing a bikini tops and shorts, and we were talking, and Miles, who was a beautiful Asian girl from California, asked me if I wanted a drink. I said sure, and the girls all kind of laughed. Well, she returned with four cans of sprite, which was not my favorite, but it would work. Miles handed me a can, and I said thanks and took a drink. *Oh no, this is not just Sprite*, I said with a smile on my face.

And she said, "It is a work drink, and just keep it on the low low and don't let the captain know." My lips were sealed, and the four of us enjoyed a nice cocktail while polishing silverware. This job was the best, working with beautiful girls and getting to have a drink or two throughout the night.

With everything ready to go, we left the mooring and headed out to sea. Another boat in the company called the *Lahaian Princess* brought out the guest for the dinner cruise, and we did an at-sea transfer, just getting both boats side by side and they had a gangplank that connected them, and the passengers made their way from one boat to another. The guests were given a drink and made their way to the top deck to find their seat. Then Joe made an announcement about what to expect and introduced all of us to our guests. Then it was time to start bringing up the meal and more drinks. The cruise was an open bar, which was set up on the top deck so the guests did not have to go far. Meals were served and the guests mingled; we had live music on the middle level where they could dance and drink. Dessert was served there as well, and everyone had a blast. The crew spent time cleaning plates and getting rid of the garbage and that kind of stuff. That day, I just followed a few people around and helped out with whatever I could. I did spend much of that night cleaning plates and taking care of the dirty dishes. It was a job, and I didn't mind at all. After the three-hour cruise was done the *Lahaian Princess* came back, and we offloaded the guests back onto the shuttle boat. It was then time to strip down to our shorts and T-shirts and start cleaning. However, before we started cleaning, we had the option to eat what was left over from that night. I dug right in and had a piece of prime rib and potatoes, and at that time, we were allowed to have a drink. This one drink the captain knew about; the others she did not. Oh well.

Once we were completely done, it was time to party. That night and many nights after this, we all met up at the Blue Lagoon and enjoyed a cold beer and a shot or two. This was how the day went, and after just a few days of doing this, I had it down to a science and really, honestly looked forward to going to work.

That first paycheck came in, and I was super happy to have some money in my pocket. It had been a rough few weeks not having a lot of money. By the time I got my first check, I was down to my last $20.

It was time to buy food and clothes. It felt good, so I went shopping and got some supplies for the week ahead. I also went to a couple of thrift stores and picked up a few pairs of shorts and more T-shirts. This was all anyone really wore and all I needed. I did get a few pairs of "slippers" to have just in case. Slippers are what the locals call flip-flops. They are the state shoe and about all you really need to wear.

Now with a little money in my pocket and I knew rent would be covered, it was time to really go out, and that is what I did. Tuesday night was the night to hang out at Moose's, which was one of the main bars in town. They had a DJ and great drink specials that night. It was also the place that all the local hotels in the area send their single women to have a *good time*. Now this might be a bad thing, but it is what it is. I did meet a girl that night, and I found it easy to talk with anyone who was not living here, just visiting. The tourists loved to meet local people that lived and worked on this island. They were here for a week, and then they would leave. That night, I did get drunk, met a girl, and took her back to my place. The rest is history, and to be completely honest, I didn't remember her name.

It was about my second or third week, and it was the first of May. My plan had been from the beginning to stay for a month or so and then make my way back to Yosemite for a second season. I did love working there and would have the opportunity to move up in the ranks and make more money. But I was having a great time in Maui. I met a lot of cool people and was making pretty good money. Between my hourly wage and tips, I was making $800 a week, and this was more than what I was making in Yosemite. Plus, I would have to save for airfare and transportation back to Yosemite, and that would cost $1,200–$1,500 by the time I got a plane ticket and then a bus to the valley. What to do, what to do? I took a few days, talked with a few people, weighed out my options, and by the first week of May, I made my mind up and decided to stay on Maui and enjoy more of this life. There seemed to be so much that I had not seen or experienced, and this opportunity might not be there again, so I decided to spend at least a year here and see what happened. I did get in touch with Tiffany and let her know that I wasn't coming back. She understood but would miss not having me around.

TAKE A DECADE

It had been almost a month on the boat, and I was starting to do the first mate gig a few days a week. It was a little more money and easier work, but I still did everything to make things happen. It was that day that another new guy started; he was not going to be working for the dinner cruise but more maintenance for the boats. His name was Joel, and he instantly fit in with our little group. Joel was from Southern California and had gone to school in Arizona to diesel mechanic school. The fact he had lived in Phoenix gave us a common bond right away. He was living just north of Lahaian in a one-bedroom place and just like me a month ago moved here not really knowing anyone. Joel and I became friends that day, and still to this day, I am in contact with this guy. Joel was six feet tall, 220 lbs., laid-back, good-looking, and loved to fish. He could fix just about anything and helped a lot of people out with their vehicles. Just a great person, and like I said, he fit right into our little group perfectly.

Joel and I started to do a little fishing after we were done with work. We got permission from the Atlantis Sub company to fish off their boat that was used to work on the sub. It was located just outside the channel where the boats came and went out of Lahaina Harbor. It was called the *Red Rhino,* and everyone knew this boat. It had a generator that was always on. It had lights that shone on the water and a good little fishing place. We would always have company of some sort and a few beers. There was always a fish or two that would be caught, sometimes even a small shark. It was something fun to do, and someone always caught a fish.

It was around the end of May when I had the pleasure of driving the "Road to Hana." This was one of the most beautiful drives in the world and has been published in many articles as a ride to remember. It was with my roommate John, who wanted to be a cop, who was a lot of fun to hang out with. He was an easygoing guy who liked to have fun. John and I had met a few girls from the bar, and they were going to go the next day; they invited us and we were in.

Now the road to Hana is 52 miles from Kahului to a small town called Hana. It has 59 bridges and over 620 curves. Even though it is only 52 miles, it takes 2.5–3 hours to drive. It is spectacular because it goes through a tropical rainforest. You have the forest on one side and then parts of the ocean on the other. If you ever visit Hawaii, this is a must-do and will take you a full day to complete. Hana, like I said, is a small little town with one or two stores and one gas station. It is a remote place on the island with a lot of history. Hana is one of the wettest places on the planet, and on the other side of the island, which is Lahaina, is one of the driest places on the planet. So you go from one extreme to the next.

We made the drive and stopped along the way for photos and just to check things out. There were several food trucks and one cool spot to stop a few miles before town. This was the place to get a real coconut opened with a machete and drink it from a straw. It was a must stop because the food here was better than anything you would get in town.

Hana has several things to see. It is hard to enjoy all the spots in one day, but they were only going to be here once and wanted to see as much as possible. This was perfect because I knew I could come back at any time. First stop was the Black Beach, which is just like it sounds, a beach with black sand. Just a small portion of the island had a lot of very dark stone and lava that created this unique place. The seas were so crystal clear that day, and we walked out in the ocean as far as we could and could see forever under the water. After that and a cold drink, we went to Red Sand Beach. Yes, the sand there is more of a red color than your normal brown sand. This beach was a short walk but well worth it. I could have stayed there all day long, not just because it was a nude beach but because it was beautiful. Okay, I lied; it was because it was a nude beach. The scenery was actually very nice.

Then we went through the town and to the Seven Sacred Pools, which was amazing. This is the place you can hang out for a while and swim from one pool to the next. Each pool is separated by a waterfall, so you can actually get to about the third pool okay; beyond that, it gets a little sketchy. We just played around, got some sun, and spent a good portion of our day there. Another must-see if you go to Maui. This is a snapshot of a great experience, and the beauty of the rainforest, beaches, and the ocean views are tough to put in words. It really is something you have to see with your own two eyes. It was a

TAKE A DECADE

great day for the girls, and John and I had a blast. They left the next day and we never saw them again. Thanks, girls, for a great few days.

After about four months on the island, I had a group of friends that were priceless: JD, Joel, Larry, Eric, and there were Kathy, Cathie, Jamie, Miles and many more. It didn't matter what was going on; I would see a majority of these people every day. If it wasn't at work, then it was on the beach or at the bar or party. We had become a family away from our families, and it was a happy time. Larry and Jamie, who had gotten together, became two of my best friends. Jamie was a beautiful blonde with larger boobs, who was so much fun to hang out with. She loved life and loved Larry. Just to have a group of people to do things with was exciting. Somebody was always planning something or had an idea for the next day. Let's go surfing, head to another beach, go snorkeling, play volleyball, etc., etc. It was like we had every day off, yet we all worked. It was a great time in my life. It was freedom like I had never had before.

I went to the island of Lanai for the first time with some people I worked with. Kristen, Tim, and Carry had made the plans one night, and the date was set. Lanai is one of the smaller islands in the chain; it is, however, the only privately owned island. This island was owned by the Dole Pineapple Corporation, but in 1961, another company bought a large share of the island and built a luxury hotel and golf course. Just a little tidbit for you: This is the island that Bill Gates got married on. This was a place for people who lived on Maui to "get away," and the best part was you could camp out on the beach.

The four of us met up that morning with tents, sleeping bags, food, and beer. It was recommended that you bring everything you need because the store closes early and is a pain to get to. To get to Lanai, all you had to do was take a thirty-minute ferry ride, which left right from the harbor, to the small harbor on Lanai. During these thirty minutes, we all sat on the bow of the boat and drank beers and laughed and joked around. Kristen was twenty years old, Tim was twenty-six, and Carry was twenty-four, so I was the old guy, but age just didn't matter here. You are as old as you feel, and I still feel young.

Once we hit shore, we walked a short distance to the camping area and got all our stuff set up. The plan was to rent a jeep for a day just to check out more of the island. So after we got situated, we walked up to the hotel, which was a five-star resort. This place was amazing, and at $750 a night, it better be. If it was good enough for Bill Gates, then it was good enough for Stephen Mundy. The lobby of this place was hard to describe, contemporized with an upscale beach scene. You just have to see it, sorry. We went through and asked about renting a jeep. The hotel staff gave us directions. He said, "We have a free shuttle to town for our guests. Are you staying here, sir?"

I said, "Well, yes, I am, thank you very much." We jumped on the shuttle, and away to town we went, which was five minutes away and not much of a town at all. There were very few businesses; mostly it was just houses for people that worked at the resort. There were about 3,500 people that lived on this island, so it was not busy at all. Majority of the residents either worked at the resort or golf course.

We walked down the street and reached the home of the person who rented jeeps. I approached the guy who was working on another vehicle and asked if we could rent a jeep. He looked at us and said, "Sure, you can take that blue one, and it is $50 a day." He walked over to the jeep, and the keys were in it. All he said was "Don't take it on the beach because you will get stuck."

I told him "No problem" and was ready to sign the paperwork.

He looked at me and said, "This is a small island, no paperwork needed. Have fun." I asked if we needed to bring it back filled, and he said, "You can if you want, but you don't have to."

"Do we bring it back here at the end of the day?"

He asked if we were camping, and we said yes. He said, "Just leave it down there, and I'll get it tomorrow." Okay, that was easy, and we loaded up and we were on our way. I've rented cars before and driver's license, insurance, cost, and fuel were always a part of renting a vehicle. Here, it is easier than your ABC.

We were off and spent the day exploring the island. There was shipwreck beach, which is where a cargo ship went aground during

TAKE A DECADE

WWII and was still there. There were tons of pineapple fields to see, and we drove through a large portion of the island that was volcanic rock, which was not really good for anything but cool to see. As we drove around that day, we would stop at a small beach, run and jump into the ocean and swim around for a while then go back to the jeep for another beach. The day went by fast, but I could honestly say I saw a majority of the island.

We drove back to the beach and made a small fire to cook our dinner. By now, it was dark and we had just begun. We were told that you could go up to the pool and use it as long as you didn't get caught. Well, we had to try, and I went first. I made my way up and grabbed a dirty towel that was used around the pool and walked right up to it and jumped in. The water was so warm, and it felt great. After they had seen my success, the other three joined me, and we spent at least two hours swimming in this gorgeous pool and enjoying the hot tub as well. The four of us swam around and drank beers and mixed drinks until I could not see straight. By this time, it was after midnight, and I was spent. Between the sun, swimming, exploring, eating, and drinking, I had enough and made my way to the tent on the beach. Nighty night!

The next morning, we all felt like shit and packed up our gear and made our way back to the ferry. Another thirty minutes back to Maui and a seven-minute walk home, and it was back to bed for me. I had a really good time and needed just a few more hours of sleep. What another great thing to cross off my list.

My job was going well; I was making money and having fun every night. It was like four months after working the dinner cruise and being the first mate that JD asked if I would be interested in helping him out with the Molokai's boat. This was an activity where tourists could spend time on another neighboring island of Maui.

Molokai is a very unique island. It is home to about 6,500 people and is best known for its leprosy colony, which is located on the Kalaupapa Peninsula. This area is on the northern part of the island, which is very difficult to get to, surrounded by high cliffs and rough waters. The only way to get there is either by hiking down the cliffs, or you can take a mule ride to the bottom of this place. This is where eight thousand people were sent over the course of a century. There are still a few people that have lived their whole life here never to see anything else. It is a small number, probably less than ten people who are in their eighties and nineties that still live there with nurses and staff. Father Damien was a leader and a savior to help these people out at the beginning of the century. He too died of leprosy many years later but not without a fight. The island is known to have only one stoplight, and the majority of the residents grow crops and fish, and live off the land.

When JD asked, I honestly wasn't too excited to change my routine. Working on this boat meant getting up early, like 5:00 a.m. early, and spending the day on the island. It would mean having my nights off, which was the time to have fun. He wanted to get off this boat and start working on the snorkel boat, which was one of the funniest and easiest boats the company had. He had been doing the Molokai run for a while and was getting burnt out. JD had done so much for me that it was the least I could do for him. So at the end of that week, I would start training on that boat and see what it would be like. The one thing was the money was better. I would be getting a raise, and that worked for me.

The first morning I had to get up at 5:00 a.m., it just sucked, and there is no other way to describe it. This was the time I was usually going to bed, and times had changed. It might do me good to get on a better schedule, but the one I was on right now was a lot of fun. Anyway, my first day on the boat, I had two of my friends JD and Larry. These two guys would teach me the ropes and see what I could do. The captain of the Molokai run was Captain Allen, and he was a true captain. You did not call him Allen—it was *Captain Allen*—and he had worked most of his life on boats and had seen so much. He was mid-sixties with gray hair and a gray beard, and he had salt in his veins.

We would meet at the dock at 5:30 a.m., fire up the dinghy, and take it out to the *Maui Princess* that was mourning out of the harbor. The boat would be dead silent until we checked the engines and the rest of the boat and then fired it up. Our job was to help with the lines, get a small breakfast prepared for the passengers, and then get the boat safely into the harbor. The only place this boat could go in the harbor was the north side of the fuel dock. It was straight back and then straight out when we left. This was dangerous because of the swell, wind, and tide, and we had to get it tied up quickly. Dealing with four-inch lines is no joke; if one of those lines snapped, it could easily take your head off in a split second.

We would then check the passengers on board not to exceed our limit of 150 passengers. Then it was time to leave. The first few times I did this trip, it was so cool seeing another portion of the island from the ocean, and it felt great each day to have that smell of ocean air. It took about two hours to make the trip, and with this, we had to cross the Kalohi Channel, which is one of the most dangerous channels in the world. It is located between the three islands, Maui, Lanai, and Molokai. Today was an average day, four- to five-foot swells with a mild wind. As we got underway, Captain Allen called me up to the bridge for a talk. He wanted to get to know me a little and see if this was something I could do. I told him about my past, and we swapped stories for a while. Today, he said, "The seas are good, but this can get very scary out here," and he needed to know if I could handle it. I assured him that I would listen and take his guidance and told him that I was a fast learner and was ready to give it a shot. Captain Allen turned out to be one of the best people I ever worked for, a straight shooter and a very smart person.

After my talk with the captain, I headed back to see JD and asked, "Where is Larry?"

He laughed and said he was below deck, not feeling so good. "Larry gets a little seasick on this trip."

I just laughed and said, "Why does he do it?"

"It's Larry, and he loves the island and the challenge of getting here." This was true of this guy. Larry loved to be pushed as hard as he could go, and I looked forward to doing a lot of adventures with him.

We got to the harbor of Molokai, and it is just a huge concrete dock two hundred feet long and thirty feet wide. We backed up to the dock; one person had to jump off with a line, and the other guy threw the other two lines. This is a little dangerous because if you fall, you're going to get smashed between the dock and the boat. Get the boat tied up and then offload our passengers; get the excursion group together and introduce them to their guide. Then it was just us, and the fun began. Well, I mean fun like cleaning the boat, checking the engines, and doing side projects every day. Some jobs were better than others, but most of the time, you would rather be doing something else.

We had one job that had to be done every month, and that was greasing the rudders. This meant that one person would have to dive under the boat and loosen a fitting to allow the grease to completely fill the unit. I had been on the boat for maybe a month, still part time, still working the dinner cruise boat as well. Captain Allen asked if I had ever scuba dived before, and without really thinking, I said, "Yes, not a lot, but I have done it." Well, I had signed myself up for something unique. He helped get my tank and everything set up. He told me where to go and what to do when I got under the boat. So I made my way to the swim platform and eased into the water. Like I said, I had really never done this, just watched John in Alaska dive for sea cucumbers. John had given me a real quick overview: the BCD, tank, pressure, ranges, and so on. This was by no means enough training to actually do this in these waters. But I said to myself, *What better way to learn than just jump right in?* And that is what I did.

As I was floating on the surface, looking up at him, getting my bearings, and building up some nerve, I slowly released the air and began to sink. Now this pier or dock whatever you want to call it was held up by huge four-foot-thick, thirty-foot-long concrete pillars underneath. This made for a great place for fish to hide and feed, and it was pitch black underneath the pier. As I sank, I could see a definite line in the water from light to dark. Under the boat was still very light and with good visibility. The bottom, which was about thirty feet down, was not really visible, but I could see the sandy, murky bottom. I was told to not drop the wrench because I would not find it. The bottom was a foot of muck from all the boats turning it up over the years. It was so eerie that I almost pulled the plug and was going to tell him I wasn't ready, but the diving part was okay. I was only down maybe 10 feet under the 120 foot boat, and this part was

TAKE A DECADE

going okay. It was the fact that I thought any second, a tiger shark was going to swim out of this black hole and eat me. Yes, I thought for sure my time was coming to an end, and I thought to myself, *We have to do this once a month, fuck.* Well, I kept my big boy pants on and did the job. I loosened the bolt and watched for the grease to start leaking out, then I used the wrench and banged on the hull to let them know inside that it was complete. Then all I had to do was tighten the bolt and swim back. That was the worst because my back was to the pier and I just waited to feel the teeth and jaws of a huge-ass shark eating me right then and there. Well, folks, sorry to disappoint you on a shark story, but I did not get eaten and made my way up and out of the water in record time.

The time had come that I would be taking over JD's spot full time, which was okay. This job did have different hours but more money, and I was learning a lot more about boats. For me to leave the dinner cruise, they had to hire someone, and this is the time to introduce Shawn. He was 6'3", 190 lbs., with blond hair and born and raised on Maui. He was a local, but he did not look like one. Shawn had his arms all tattooed up and looked like a surfer/skateboarder. We became friends immediately, and his house became a big party place, which was used many a night. Shawn and Jamie were married, had a child, and were both under twenty-five years old. They met, got pregnant, got married, and were doing great. He was a good choice to replace me as I was to replace JD. I still filled in once in a while but mostly just ran the Molokai run.

By now, I had bought transportation, which was a two-wheel beach cruiser. It only had one speed, and that was slow; I was never really in a hurry. It was a great way to get around because everything was so close. Most people that I knew only had a bike, moped, or maybe a beater car.

The whole summer was super busy, and things were going great. I was making money, and by now, I was only six months here and I had a savings account with almost five thousand. It was unbelievable to think that I arrived on this island with $800, no job, no house, and no friends just six months ago. Now I had everything I had hoped for except a girl. Don't get me wrong; I was having *fun* but kind of wanted something more. A lot of my friends had someone, and a lot of my friends didn't, so it was easy any way I went.

One night, I was filling in for Shawn, and a new girl had started. Her name was Ronnie. Her real name was Veronica, but she went by Ronnie. To be honest, the first time we met, I did not think anything of it, and she was just another good-looking girl working the boat. She was 5'6" with dark skin, curly hair that went to her shoulders, and a nice body. A few days later, she came down to the Blue Lagoon and joined a group of us having drinks. She was very spunky and had the attitude of "I don't care what people think."

She told us she was here for a few months and then going to Oahu to go to school for physical therapy. She had played rugby in college and had actually made the US women's team but got hurt and quit.

So a few weeks had passed, and I had run into her a few times around town. She was staying at the same hostel I was at for a week and now lived right across the street from where I was living, at the Spinnaker Apartments, which was a great place to go at night because they had a hot tub. Then one night, we ran into each other at a bar and really started to talk. She was a middle child with an older sister and a younger brother. Mom was from the Dominican Republic, and her father was a white man who taught English as a second language on the island. Her parents fell in love and got married and then moved to New Jersey, which is where she grew up. Her parents had separated in the past five years, and her dad lived in Vermont and her mom in New Jersey. The thing about her was she had traveled a lot just like me, and that night, we told each other travel stories and talked about future plans until the bar closed. We went back to her house, and as soon as I shut the door, she started to kiss me, and I kissed her right back. That was our first night together and the start of something new.

The one thing that we talked about in the first conversation was her going to school, and I wanted to travel somewhere else and was thinking about Africa. This was a place that I had always wanted to go. I wanted to see the Big Five animals and the Nile and spend some time in South Africa. The research that I had done for a potential trip was very little, and I still had a lot of questions. A trip like this would take more things to consider than my trip to Europe and Japan. Vaccinations were required, and having more money would help. I figured to spend a few months there and see what I wanted to see would cost approximately $10,000.

Things were good. I had a girlfriend but still did whatever I wanted with my friends. My friends were her friends now, so it was just a big group of people having fun and enjoying each other's company. We did have a great time and spent many nights together. Ronnie was Latino and could be very feisty sometimes, especially when she was drinking. She was always up to doing anything fun and challenging, which was what we were all there for.

This gives me an idea to talk about one of the best and scariest hikes I have ever done. It was called the Commando Hike, and it was a blast. We must have had ten to twelve people that went on this the first time I did, Larry, Shawn, JD, Joel, Ronnie, Kristen, Tim, Chris, Carmen, Kathy, and myself. It is located off the road to Hana, so we loaded up in several vehicles and made our way to the other side of the island.

This was not a trail that I could ever give direction to; you had to go with someone that knew the trail. We found the spot to stop; it was Larry and Shawn who had done this before, and they took the lead. The trail started by walking through a cow pasture for a half mile, then you came to a lava tube, which was amazing. It was a tunnel that was formed out of hot lava back in the day. It had water running through it, which you had to walk and swim through, all the while navigating rocks and ledges that you had to climb up. The lava tube was probably the length of a football field, so it was really dark in there when you get to the middle. All you could see at that time was a small window of light at one end and another window of light at the end. Going through this, you got wet and dirty from crawling up rocks and ledges to make it to the end. It was a blast just being able to experience this lava tube, which took a while to get everyone through.

Once you were out of this, it is a short walk to the first of 3 jumps. The first jump was off an old hanging bridge that looked like it would collapse if you walked on it, but we watched Larry then Shawn walk out and jump. The first jump was maybe twenty feet into fresh crystal-clear water, which was a little on the cold side for all of us because we were used to the seventy-degree ocean water. It felt so refreshing, and we were now in the rainforest, which was amazing. The trees hung over the water, large rocks were scattered everywhere, and it really felt like the jungle. We came to a small beach that had a fifty-foot waterfall splashing into it, and we all swam there for a while, jumping off rocks and climbing into the falls. Then we had to hike on land for a short distance until we got to the second jump.

Now Larry had told everyone in the beginning that there is a big jump, but it was easy, and you had to do it to get down. There was no other way down except to jump. We reached the spot, and I took one look over the side and was like, *Holy shit, you were not kidding*. The jump was around sixty to seventy feet, which was by far the highest thing I had ever jumped off. The top was grassy and gave you a good running start, but we all looked over the side, and we laughed and said, "Who is first?"

Larry spoke up and said, "I'll show you guys it is safe and I'll go first." He stood back from the edge, and with a short running start, he was gone. "Ahhhhhh" was all we could hear, and we all looked over as he hit the water. He disappeared under the dark surface to finally pop up with his hands raised out of the water yelling, "That was awesome."

Sure, easy for you to say. You're down there, and we are all still up here. I heard a few of the girls say, "Fuck that. There is no way I'm jumping." Then Shawn went, and I was next.

All I knew was that I couldn't look over the edge because I'll never do it, so I backed up, took a deep breath, and just *did it*. It felt like I was falling forever. It actually took my breath away a little because I held my breath from the time I left the cliff. When you hit the water, you definitely know it because of the slapping you hear and feel when entering the water from that height. I will say this and will not lie; it stung for a while once I came to the surface. All I could say was "Son of a bitch, that smarted a little" but was so glad to have done it. I stared up at the group and yelled, "I did it. Who is next?

And be careful on your landing." I swam to the side of the pool and watched my friends do the same terrifying thing that I had just done. One by one, you could see the terror in their face as they fell seventy feet to a cold, dark body of water. We all loved it and knew we had a great story to tell everyone else.

The third jump was another short walk away, which went through the forest, and it was so beautiful seeing the lush green tropical rainforest scenery. The last jump wasn't as high, but it had its problems, and that was you had to clear a few rocks. For this one, you needed a good jump, or you would end up hitting the rocks, and basically, you would just die, simple as that. Again, Larry led, and we watched him run and jump and miss the rocks—oh, good. We were one for one on this jump. I went after Shawn, and this jump did not hurt as much, but when I hit the water and not the huge boulders, I felt much better. I'm alive and not a mangled mess, thank God. One by one, we all jumped and all had our stories to tell. After that, we walked back around the same pasture we had started from and made our way back to the vehicles. This was the best hike I had ever done with some of the coolest things to see and do. I told myself, *I did it once and never again.* I thought this would be the case, but after time goes by, you forget about the fear you felt and do it again and again and again.

This led me to the next thing I was able to do while in Hawaii, and that was get PADI certified for scuba diving. It was something I had always wanted to do, and a good friend, Chris, who has been mentioned in the last story, was a scuba instructor.

Chris had agreed to help me out, and my friend Shawn's wife, Jamie, decided she wanted to as well. This gave me a dive partner for the test, and we received our books and started studying. Most people ended up having to do pool dives and then one open-water dive. Here in Hawaii, it was all open water. Jamie and I did the course, did our necessary dives, and took the test with Chris at the Blue Lagoon. What could be better than to take an exam at a bar with your friends? We both passed with flying colors and now could rent gear and dive anywhere in the world.

We did a lot of shore dives because this is where you could see more than out deep. We had a few areas like Maula Harbor that was one of my favorites. Easy to get in and there was an old pier that had been destroyed during a storm, and it had a ton of concrete, rebar, and rocks that made for a great habitat for marine life. I saw just about everything you could see from small fish like "Nemo" to eels and sharks.

One time, I was diving, and I was down about twenty-five feet, and it was a beautiful sunny day. I was focusing on the bottom when all of a sudden, the area around me got very dark. The sun that was shining down on me was now being blocked by something big. I thought to myself the same thing you're thinking right now: *shark*. This was it; I was going to get eaten by a shark on this beautiful day. It took me all the nerve I had to slowly roll over and see this thing that would soon eat me. I slowly rolled over and was pleasantly surprised to find this giant sea turtle hovering right above me. This turtle was at least five feet long and three feet wide. It had to have been a hundred years old and weighed close to five hundred pounds. It was massive and probably one of the coolest things you can see while diving. I spent ten minutes swimming with this guy as close as one foot apart at times but never touched it. The turtles are endangered, and it is a common rule not to touch them. We as humans have diseases that can harm the turtles. This was amazing to see and experience while diving off the coast.

Another dive I did with Larry was a night dive, which became my favorite time to go diving. With the light in the water, you see a different world. Everything looks brighter, and the marine life looks so much different at night. We decided to dive just outside of the channel, which I had not done yet. It is a little deeper water, and there is the tide and waves crashing against the rocks, which makes it a little more dangerous. Larry and his buddy, who was a local, took me to the end of the rocks that form the channel going into the harbor. Larry yelled for me to jump in, and that was just what I did. Just then, a wave caught me and threw me up against the rocks. That sucked because I cut my foot and was banged up a little. I got back up, and he was just laughing as hard as he could.

"You should have seen yourself. You jumped in, and within a split second, you were back on the rocks." Glad he found that funny.

TAKE A DECADE

All I knew was that I had cut my foot, and it was bleeding. This probably should have ended our dive, but I was not giving up. This time, I made them go first, and then I went in, making sure to time the waves a little bit better. As soon as I got in the water, I could feel the stinging of the saltwater on my cut. I didn't care and kept going. I did, however, make sure that I had either one of them on each side. So if a shark came in, it would have to go through one of them first before it got to me. We spent about twenty minutes, went through a tank, and saw a ton of fish. This time, it was the moray eels that really stood out. They were about the ugliest, nastiest, yet beautiful things in the ocean. We were anywhere from six inches to one foot away from them. They just hung out in clumps of coral with their mouths full of teeth waiting for something small to swim by. A diver is not small, so unless you stick your finger near them, you're safe. Even though I was bleeding the whole time, we did not see any sharks that night, which was probably a good thing.

Okay, it was time for a time out for me to just relax. There were a hundred stories I wanted to tell and talk about everyone that I had met and now considered good friends. I want to tell you everything day by day, moment by moment, but it would take a lifetime. Don't worry; I'm not even close to being done, but I do have to move on.

It was around the middle of October that I started to think more about what I was going to do. Ronnie and I were having fun, and together, we would talk about our futures. She was starting school the first of January, and I had made up my mind that I would stay on Maui until March or April, which would give me a whole year here in Paradise. It would give me time to make more money and get everything situated to travel to Africa.

Work went on as usual, and as the end of the month got closer, more and more people were talking about the biggest holiday here in Lahaina. It was Halloween, and I guess this place turned into quite the party. Many people I had met had been here for Halloween, and they easily said it was the biggest party on the island and the place would get crazy.

Living at 795 Wainee was about as good as it gets. Our house was a two-minute walk to Front Street where everything would be happening. They said it was the Mardi Gras of the Pacific and the biggest party of any island. Everyone was talking about what they were going to wear, and I still had no idea. It wasn't until a few days before that night an idea came to mind. I was going to go as a "weird doctor that gave *free* breast exams." It was perfect, and it was time to get my costume ready.

We had the spot to be, so a bunch of people got dressed at our place, and the party got started. Ronnie and I had hung out all day helping each other with our costumes but agreed to hang out with our friends. We would see each other, but I hung with the guys and she with the girls. They were going as sexy cheerleaders, and they looked good.

My costume was great. I had a silver wig, a white doctor coat, a set of crazy teeth, a pair of black eyeglasses, and a sign that read "Free Breast Exam." I did the part very well that night and got a lot of compliments. Larry went as a kissing booth, JD was a devil, Joel was Evil Knievel, Eric was a green leprechaun, and that was just the beginning. We left the house with beers in our hand and headed to Front Street. The place was already packed, and when we reached the street, I honestly felt like this was Mardi Gras. The streets were filled with thousands of people. Girls were walking around half-naked, and some had just painted their boobs with different colors—just about any costume you could think of and then some. There were four guys dressed like Mt Rushmore; one group went around as a "club" with ropes and bouncers and everything. It was amazing and loads of fun. We drank all night long, going into bars, getting a drink, and then walking up and down the street, which was only one-half mile long, so it was packed. Cops were everywhere but letting everyone have fun. I did not see one altercation that entire night.

All I did was walk around, get drunk, and ask girls if they wanted a free breast exam. I had this voice and movement that made it fun, and believe it or not, I had twenty-two girls allow me to give them a free exam. That means I got to touch forty-four boobs that night—well, actually forty-six with Ronnie earlier—and the best thing was that no dude knocked me out for touching their women. Ha ha. I lasted until about four and then went home, and a bunch of us kept parting. My one cute new roommate said something about the hot tub across the street. "Say no more. Follow me," I said, and we had some fun for about an hour. She took her clothes off, and I took mine off. What's wrong with two friends sitting in a hot tub together naked at 4:00 a.m.? My answer to that is "Absolutely nothing." We didn't have sex but had fun, and we can leave it at that.

As the sun started to rise, it was time for bed. Everyone was safely back home and most definitely sleeping. The next day, which I slept through, actually went by way too quickly. Ronnie came over when she got up, and we ate and went right back to sleep. We never asked each other about our nights, and I know we both had a blast.

October 31 was Halloween, November 1 was recovery day, and November 2 was my birthday. It was a tough few days for my liver, but we stuck together and made our way through it. That day, I had to work and was going to work on the dinner cruise boat as well, so it was going to be a long day, but these were good money days for me, $300–$400 for working a double, and I needed to save as much as I could. The plan was to meet up with a few friends and Ronnie after work at the Blue Lagoon, have a few beers and a shot, and call it a night. Larry had called and told me he would meet me at the harbor at around ten. He was there when I got off the boat. I could have easily walked across the street to the Blue Lagoon, but he said this was easier for an old man.

We pulled out, and he drove right by the bar, passed a great parking place and everything. I said, "Dude, where are we going? They are inside waiting for me."

He said, "Relax. I just have to make one stop first." If I had known this, I would have just walked over. I was thirsty and told Ronnie and Joel 10:00 p.m. We started to drive further out of town, and he then pulled down toward Babe Beach, which was a popular little beach in Lahaina. Many parties had been held on this beach. I looked at Larry and was actually getting a little pissed. He just looked at me and started to laugh; he loved to annoy me if he could. We had the brotherly bond that allowed us to fuck with each other when we could.

He pulled the car over near the entrance of the beach and said, "Get out, let's go."

We walked down to the beach, and I was not happy at this time until I turned the corner and noticed about fifteen to twenty people, everyone that I knew, and they all said, "Surprise, *Mundy*, happy birthday!"

Ronnie walked up and gave me a hug and kiss, and Larry just stood there laughing. "Wow, you were getting pissed at me, weren't you?"

"Yes, I was, you asshole." And I gave him a big hug. Wow, this was completely unexpected and so surprising. My friends had done something that meant so much to me they would never know.

My roommate Debra was there, and she said something so kind. "You know, this island has accepted you when your friends do something like this for you." I was humbled and so happy to have friends that would do something like this for me. So here we went again, another thing to celebrate. They had a keg of beer and snacks, and we hung out on the beach until 2:00 a.m. drinking, laughing, and having just another great day.

The past week had been crazy. Our household had gotten a little bit bigger as well. With Halloween came some other people. Debra's husband, Cory, had arrived a few days earlier, not so much for Halloween but to see her. They had met in Alaska, which is where he lived most of the time, but was going to stay here for a while. He was a very nice guy and a good person to have around. So there were now two in their room. Then Danielle had her boyfriend move in, Jeff, who was JD's cousin. Jeff had visited JD before I got to the island, and he and Danielle had hit it off. Jeff was 5'9", around 170 lbs., with blond hair and in love with his new girlfriend. Jeff and I hit it off right away, and I always loved his honesty. Jeff and I would later work together, but for now, he was another roommate. Allen and Crissy had become close, more than friends, but I would never consider them boyfriend and girlfriend. So when I first moved in the house, we had five roommates, and now we had almost doubled.

795 Wainee Street had given birth, and the dynamics had changed—all for the good, I may add. It was shortly after the first of November that Ronnie had moved in with me. First, she was there all the time. Second, she was leaving in a month or so, and third, we

were having a lot of fun together. It worked out great, and we were just one big happy family. We helped each other when we could, had some meals together, and just had fun.

Most of the end of November and December was spent working, hanging out with friends, and making money. When I get an idea in my head, I really try hard to stick to it. I wanted to go to Africa, and this was going to happen. I just needed to actually do more for this type of trip. Life just gets in the way sometimes, and you get into routines that are hard to break. For example, on my days off, it was relaxing on the beach, doing a hike, and celebrating something on the island. For a trip to Africa, it needed more attention, and I promised myself that right after the first of the year, I would get started.

As the holidays approached, I made the decision that I would not be going home. There was a lot going on with work, it was a busy time, and my goal was to save money. Ronnie and I did want to do something fun and different and decided to go somewhere and spend a few days in a different place. We decided to go to the big island, which neither of us had been to yet, spend a few days around Christmas, and get to say that we were on that island. We found flights for under $100. We booked a room at a place in Kona; that was very reasonable and in the center of the town. It wasn't much, but it gave us a chance to do something different. This would also be the first time we went away together.

For those few days, we slept late, ate when we were hungry, and fooled around a lot. Kona was different from Lahaina, and it was bigger and spread out more. We walked where we wanted to explore and did spend time on the beach. The beaches on Kona were rockier and not as sandy as on Maui. This was because this island was the newest of all the islands and still had an active volcano on it, which had erupted recently. With this said, this island was actually still growing, and at some point, it would move away from the volcanic vein that was creating it, and the volcanic rock would slowly break apart and start to form more of a sandy landscape around the coast. But before you quote me, you should check with your local geologist about what really would happen. Anyway, it was a few days of R&R for me and time away from everything else. It was a great Christmas for both of us, and that morning, we had our little gift exchange, drank a bottle of champagne, called our families from the resort, and then made our way back to reality. We enjoyed our time together, and I wondered if we would ever be able to do anything like this again. Our time together was coming to an end. She would be leaving the second week of January for school.

Things change for a reason, and hopefully for all of you, change has been good. This next part was just the opposite, and for some, it would never be the same. New Year's Eve was here, and it really wasn't a huge deal or a big celebration as I had hoped for. After Halloween, nothing would ever really compare, and most people had said that New Year's Eve was rather quiet. They did have fireworks on a barge out in front of Lahaina, but the excitement wasn't like Halloween, which was fine with me because I had to work the next morning, which would mean I would get maybe two to three hours of sleep.

That night, a few of us had gone to Front Street, watched the fireworks, and then went home. Ronnie and I were in bed actually fooling around, and her phone rang. We stopped what we were doing, and it was her sister, Tanya, calling from New Jersey. We both figured she was just calling to wish her sister a happy New Year, but it was like 5:00 a.m. East Coast. Ronnie answered the phone, and her expression on her face turned for the worse real quickly. She asked a few questions, talked for maybe two minutes, and the last thing she said was "I'm on my way."

Ronnie looked at me and started to cry. She told me her younger brother had fallen down a flight of stairs at a party, landed on the back of his head, and was now at the hospital unresponsive. She jumped out of bed, got dressed, grabbed her purse, and said, "I have to get to the airport."

I said, "Wait until tomorrow. Let's get more information and go from there."

She looked at me, and with tears in her eyes, she said, "No, I'm going now." Debra and Cory were up and heard something going on. They came to the door, and I told them what was up, and they agreed to take her to the airport. I did not want to go because I had to work in a few hours. She was not happy about me not going and, I could tell, very disappointed in me. Ronnie left with just her clothes on her back, her purse, and I gave her $800 cash, which was all I had available at 1:00 a.m. Ronnie was gone within ten minutes of hanging up the phone.

Ronnie made it back to New Jersey and met up with her family at the hospital. Danny had fallen down a flight of stairs. He was *not* drunk. It was just a fluke accident, but he had sustained a severe head injury. He was unconscious when she arrived, and the family had met with some of the best in the business for brain injuries. They waited and hoped for three days to get some sort of response from him, but nothing changed. It was on the third day that she called me and told me that they had decided to pull the plug and let Danny go. He was a good-looking mature guy, and he died at the age of twenty-two. As you could imagine, she was upset. She and her entire family had to go through something that you would not wish on your worst enemy. She cried almost every day on the phone, and all I could do was listen and give her hope. I look back, and that fact that I didn't want her to go was a big mistake on my part.

It was different without having her around, and I did miss her. I would joke with her that at least I was getting some sleep, which would usually make her laugh. So much had changed for her, and what was she going to do? Was she going to go back to school, or would she stay there? It was all up in the air.

Ronnie had been gone for a few weeks, and I did miss her. I was just lying in bed, and it seemed just like the night I woke up in Arizona and had the idea to backpack around Europe. A plan had popped into my head, so I thought about it for about a day and then called Ronnie. I asked how everyone was doing and just wanted to feel her out before I mentioned everything. She seemed to be having a decent day, and they had done something that her brother had liked to do, which made her happy. I said to her, "You got a minute? I want to run something by you and see what you think." I told her, "Instead of you starting school in a few weeks and me going to Africa, what would you think about taking six months and traveling around South America?" I had done a little research and you didn't have to get any shots, it was rather cheap, and we could leave in a month. South America had always been on my list of places to go. To see the Amazon Jungle would be a major accomplishment. It was just that I had spent time thinking and planning for Africa that South America would be another time in my life. The time, however, was now, and we could do this. By the first of the year, I had close to $8K in my bank account. I would have another month to work and could be close to $10K before we left. It would be enough money for us to get started.

Ronnie was quiet on the other end and I could tell her wheels were spinning. She said, "Let me think about this. This is a lot right now."

I told her to take her time. "No worries, one way or the other."

She called me back that next day, and I could tell she was in. "Yes, I will go, and it sounds like a great idea," she said. Her only major concern was money, and that she didn't have. Fortunately for her, she had lost her job and would be able to collect unemployment. I had money to get us started with the plane tickets and the first part of the trip.

Ronnie arrived back in Hawaii around the third week of January. She moved right back in with me, and the planning began. It was so good to see her, but the healing of her brother's loss had just begun. There were several really bad moments between us, and it had to do with her grieving and me not sleeping. Like I said, we had a few really tough moments that could have ruined everything.

After this trip, I pictured myself back in Arizona. For the past year, I had been paying for a storage unit with a bunch of my stuff. It just seemed to be the logical plan, and that would be to return there and start all over again. At this point, I was open to anything but trying to keep some sort of plan.

It was around the first of February, and we had found airline tickets and had made a plan of attack for this trip. Our date for departure was February 20, which only gave us a few weeks. The tickets we found were from Los Angeles to Lima, Peru, and the cost of a one-way ticket was $385 each. We only had to get a ticket to Los Angeles, where there was a company that had standby tickets for

TAKE A DECADE

$99. The plan was to fly to Los Angeles and stay with her friend for a few days. Ronnie had never been to Las Vegas before, and we decided to throw that into our itinerary. We would rent a car, drive to Vegas for a few days, then fly out from Los Angeles.

The weeks leading up to our departure were filled with parties and seeing as many people as we could. Besides working, I tried to hang out with my friends because I honestly didn't know if I would ever see them again, and that was sad. Joel and I played some golf; we went fishing a few times and played poker with our little group, which was always good for me, ha ha. It was a time for a little reflection in my life. I had left Arizona for Yosemite, and that turned into time in Alaska and then a year in Hawaii. It just never seemed real that I had done so much and was getting ready for the biggest trip of my life.

A few days before we left, some of our friends had a little going-away party for us, which meant so much to me. It showed that I had found and surrounded myself with some of the greatest people I would ever have the privilege to know. It would not be the same not seeing JD, Joel, Larry, my roommates, and all my other friends on a daily basis. It was just time to seek out something new and keep this ball rolling that had started over a year ago. There were a lot of hugs and well wishes for both of us, and of course, a few tears were shed that night.

The day before we left, I boxed up a few things and stored them in our tool shed in the backyard. I told Debra that I would get in touch with her when I got settled and she could mail them to me, which was okay with her. Our bags were packed, and we were ready to go, taxi cab waiting outside the door. It was time to leave. "I'm leaving on a jet plane and don't know when I will be back again, so kiss me and say goodbye…" And you know the rest of that great song. It was just so fitting for our departure that I sang it all the way to the airport.

This was it; I was leaving a place that I had only thought I would stay for a few months. It turned out to be a great year! For me it was a "year without a key." I mean that for this entire year, I never once had a key, no car, no house, no work key at all. For me, this was the best year of my life, and I was sad to be leaving but excited for whatever would happen next. Stephen Mundy was now going to South America for a six-month backpacking trip that would take us to who knows where!

19

CHAPTER

South America

It was time to start this amazing journey. We left Hawaii, and we were up and away. As we left the ground, it was weird leaving this place. So much had happened in a year, and I wondered if I would ever return. Hawaii was a special place in my heart for the people I had meet and the things that I had done. Would I ever return, or was that it for this place, and who knew what would be next?

Ronnie's friend picked us up at the airport, and we spent the first night with her. We actually had the opportunity to do something fun that first night, and that was going to the Oscars. Well, we didn't actually get to go the Oscars, but we did go down and stand on benches across the red carpet area and watch the celebrities arrive in their limos. It was a fun first night and a great way to start our trip.

The next day, we rented a car, and we drove to Las Vegas. I had been there about ten times, but she had never been before, and it was close. I was always up for a Vegas trip, and seeing there was "no gambling" in Hawaii, not even a scratch-off ticket, it would be fun to try my luck. We left the city, and let me tell you, it felt so good just to drive a car. It had been over a year since I had driven more than two miles at any given time. This was an open road, and the drive through the desert was amazing. To be able to see forever the cacti, the open land, and the vastness of the desert made for a great day.

We had our windows down and talked and laughed the whole way, which was about a six-hour drive.

We made it to Vegas just before dark and found a room at the Tropicana, which had mirrors all over the place. I guess it was big back in the seventies when it was built, and we actually enjoyed them ourselves. Then it was out to the strip for the whole experience of this amazing town. Las Vegas is all about the lights, the people, the sounds, and the ability to walk from one casino to the next with a drink in your hand. You have got to love free drinks even though nothing is really free especially if you're gambling, which I was. I ordered a couple of drinks, and while I was waiting, I thought it would be a good idea to bet $100 on black at the roulette table. Well, it hit red, and those free drinks just cost me $100. Ooh, well, it was part of it, and I always knew my limit.

This would be a good time to let you know about my money situation. I left Hawaii with about $9,500, and she had about $100. This was all I had and would be the only money I would get until I started to work again, and who knew when that would be? Ronnie had checks that would start being deposited into her account in two weeks. I had no problem helping her out in the beginning, and this was something we both knew, and I told her not to worry at all—it would all work out. We spent a good portion of the night just walking around and enjoying the sights. I did spend a few hundred on a new camera, which is something I really needed. It was a digital camera and would be perfect for this trip.

We got back to her friend's house, and it was time to get our bags packed for the last time. We both had our big bag with most of our clothes and personal items in it. We then both had our day packs that had some basic things for the plane ride and most of our important docs. This was not the first time for either of us, so we knew how to pack. Keep enough stuff in your carry-on bag to survive for a few days in case they lose your check-in bag. I've learned to keep money in both bags, have copies of important documents like passport and driver's license in both bags, and a change of clothes just in case.

The day had come, and it was up and away for us. Our flight was on time, and we ended up scoring a great seat all to ourselves with room to spare. The flight was only about two-thirds filled, so we had plenty of room. You just have to love international flights not only for the free booze and food but for the opportunity to go to a foreign country. Oh, who am I kidding; it is all about the free booze and food. Our life was great, and Ronnie and I were already having a great time. We laughed at each other. We laughed at the situations around us, and we laughed at the fact we had no idea what we were getting ourselves into. We were both explorers of the world and ready for whatever might happen.

Peru

We arrived in Lima around 4:00 p.m.; it was good that it was still light out. At the airport, we went through our first border crossing and were asked all the usual questions: "How long are you staying?" "Where did you come from?" "Bringing anything with you?" and the checking of our bags. It was all good, and I got my first stamp from South America in my passport.

We found a tourist station at the airport, and they were able to find us a place to stay. It was about a twenty-minute bus trip and about a fifteen-minute walk to get to our first hostel for this journey. We had a plan, and away we went.

Lima, Peru, which is the capital of Peru, is on the very dry, arid side of the Pacific Ocean. It is a very busy and not really a pretty city. Lima has a lot of the industrial areas, a ton of people, and we knew that there really isn't a lot to see in Lima, and this was just our starting point. We did take in the scenery on the bus, and it was very obvious we were not in the States anymore. Things looked different right away. We were now in a South American city, and it was so cool.

We found our place without any trouble, and the young guy who checked us in spoke English. This allowed me to do all the talking, which worked for both of us. Nine out of ten times, it would be me who would ask questions or start the conversation. Here in a Spanish-speaking world, Ronnie would probably have to do most of the talking, so if I could speak, I spoke. Anyway, we got checked in to our room, which was huge, like twenty by twenty feet with a small bed right in the middle. It did have its own bathroom, which was nice, and it was cheap, about $8 for the night. We walked around and picked up a few things for the room, beer and snacks. This was the time to figure out our exchange rate, and this was done by buying a few beers. We figured that $100 is equal to about 360 Peruvian dollars (PD). It cost us like five Peruvian dollars for six beers, which meant that a beer was like ¢30. We found a place close by to have a meal, which was chicken and rice and was filling and cost like $3. With the money thing figured out, it was time to plan our first adventure.

Before we had left Hawaii, I had bought the book *Lonely Planet Guide to South America*, which is a great traveling guide. We had made the plan to head north of Lima to a place called Mancora. It was a quiet little town that was known for surfing and beaches. I know we just left Hawaii, but to be able to surf in a foreign country would be great, so that was our first plan. We found the bus schedule and could leave tomorrow and head to Mancora. I was ready to leave Lima as soon as we checked into our room. It was kind of funny, but I was a little worried Ronnie would take off day one on me. When we checked into the place, I noticed nothing but guys there, and even walking around, there were a lot of dudes. Now I couldn't care less, but it seemed that all dudes we saw that first few hours were good-looking guys. Not just good-looking like me but really good-looking. I was thinking, *This is great. Where are the women?* Well, I was pleasantly surprised and happy to hear that the reason all these guys were here was that they were having a casting call for male models at the time. There was a big convention going on, and every dude who thought he was the shit had an opportunity to show them their stuff. Our hostel manager said he would be glad when it was all over; it was a lot of male testosterone in one place. I would be glad when I looked good for Ronnie again, so I was ready to leave.

We were at the bus station around noon. It was nice we didn't have to get up at the crack of dawn. We paid for our trip, about $22, and it would be about an eighteen-hour trip. This was going to be a long day, so we bought some supplies, food and drink (beer), and we were ready for a long trip. The bus was on time, and it was a double-decker bus, and we were able to get the best seats in the house. We had the two seats right above the driver; it was perfect. We were told that there was a bathroom, which wasn't bad, and that we would stop several times to get food and stretch our legs. The bus also would be playing movies during the trip, and most of them would be in English. It was very nice and a great start to our journey.

We left Lima, and it was great to see the countryside. The landscape was that of an arid area. We were close to the ocean, and you could see sand dunes and not a lot of greenery until we got further away. We spent the first four hours having a few drinks, talking, and watching the world go by. We were about six hours into our trip, and we stopped at a road stand that had food and drinks. The road stand was just a few small wooden buildings that looked kind of rough, not really clean-looking, and run by true Peruvian people. It was cool to see, and we did get something to eat and drink, chicken and rice with a beer.

Our next stop, which was about six hours later, was the end of the fancy double-decker bus, so we had to transfer to a regular bus, which was your basic greyhound bus, and continued on our way. By this time, we were getting tired, and it had been dark for a while now, so time to get some sleep. We both had our eye patches, neck rest, and earplugs. We stored our bags under the seat and got some sleep. We must have been asleep for a while because when we woke up, we were only about thirty minutes away, and it was daylight again.

We got to the bus station, and there were many locals there asking if we needed a place to stay. It took about three minutes to ask a few questions. Ronnie spoke Spanish too. At this point, we wanted a surf place, our own bathroom, and closeness to town. The guy, who had it all, took us to our place, and it was perfect. It was a wooden building with a view of the beach, not fancy at all. It had surfboard rentals and was rather cheap, about $10 for a room. So far, things had been rather cheap, which was a good thing.

We dropped off our gear and headed for the ocean. We rented a few boards that day and spent a good three hours surfing and relaxing on the beach. It was just like Hawaii but so different in its own way. We were having such a great day until we went back to the room. We got back, and I wanted to take a few pictures of the area. I looked in my bag where my camera was, and it wasn't there. I checked my big bag. I knew it wasn't in there but looked anyway. I could not find it, so I tore everything apart and soon realized that my camera had been stolen. It had to have happened on the bus because we had the only key to the room. The guy who checked us in told us straight up, "Don't lose the key, it is the only one. No one will be going into your room for anything." So it didn't happen there. The bus was notorious for theft, and we were told this in the beginning. I knew we had our stuff in our day bags under the seat, and that was probably when it happened. The person behind me stole it while we were sleeping. As soon as this sank in, I lost it and got really pissed. I just spent $200 bucks on this camera, and it didn't even last a week. This was very upsetting, and I had what you might call a small tantrum.

Ronnie just sat back and watched, then she started to laugh, which made me even madder. She walked over to me and said, "Listen, there is nothing you can do about it. Now don't let it ruin your trip. We will find another camera, and it will be okay." Well, it did help, but I was still pissed. We decided to go down to the common area and see if anyone was around. It was rather quiet, but they did have a Ping-Pong table, and we decided to play. However, you had to buy a ball, which cost $5 for one. This was a little high because hell, our room only cost $8, and this little white ball was that valuable. Well, it was, and I paid the $5 to play. I served to Ronnie, she hit it back, and then I slammed it back to her, and it went flying. She looked at me through the paddle on the table and walked away.

"You have got to be kidding me. Let's play."

She said, "I'm done. You are miserable, and I don't want to play anymore." That was the extent of our Ping-Pong experience, and I was the proud owner of a $5 Ping-Pong ball. Now I was pissed, and we had a nice little argument when we got back, then we had silence for the rest of the night. Silence was good, and it is what we needed. We slept next to each other but didn't say much.

The next day started great, a few apologies and it was water under the bridge. Camera was gone, but we had a nice new Ping-Pong ball. We spent that day walking around town and enjoying the scenery. They had this flea market going on, and we walked around, enjoying a beautiful warm day. That day, we met this guy who was missing part of his lower jaw. My first thought was from chewing tobacco, but we talked to him for a while, and he had lost it to a rare cancer. Very nice guy, smart, and we walked around with him for a few hours, just had something horrible happened to him. It was tough to look at; you could see his tongue and teeth from the side. I felt so bad for him, but he was still living and happy to be alive. We invited him to have dinner with us that night, but he said eating was something he did by himself, and we understood. We said our goodbyes and never saw him again.

Mancora was so relaxing and so much like Hawaii, with the beach, a small boardwalk and cool people. We spent that day walking up and down the beach, and planning our next trip. We both wanted to visit Machu Picchu, which was one huge thing on our list of things to see. We would have to go back to Lima and catch a bus from there, so after a few days of the beach life and surfing, we boarded another bus for the return trip on the 18 to Lima. This time, I made damn sure no one would get into my stuff and steal my ping-pong ball!

The bus ride was the same, and we stopped in the same spots going back. It was just another travel day, but this gave us time to start our books we had brought and start our journals that we had decided to write in along the trip.

Once back in Lima, we went to the tourist booth and got information on the next bus to Machu Picchu. We had planned on getting a room for the night and probably leave the next morning. There was a bus leaving in two hours, which we could take. Now the trip to Cusco, which is where we needed to head, was a twenty-four-hour bus ride. It would be a long-ass trip, which we were told was not the most comfortable, but it was the cheapest way to get there. We talked for a few minutes and decided to take the next bus, which would save us getting a room for the night and get us there a day earlier. The plan was set, and now it was time to find food and drinks for this trip, which was going to be a long one.

The bus left on schedule, and we were now heading to Cusco, which is the main hub before Machu Picchu. The first six hours went by, and we stopped to stretch our legs, grabbed something to eat and drink, and then we were back on the bus. This bus ride took us up and over the Andes Mountain Range, which was a spectacular site to see. There were huge mountains in the distance, and the landscape had turned from the dry beach scene to more jungle and mountains. We watched movies that were playing, had a drink or two, read for a while, and would take a nap whenever we were tired. There was not a lot to do on the bus, so you just relaxed and did what you could. Now the last hours of the bus ride were the worst I had ever encountered. We had made it to the mountains, and it was apparent. The bus was climbing, our ears were popping, and we hit switchbacks going up the mountain. All we did was go side to side in our seat, one right after another. I have never been car sick in my life, but six hours of this and I was on the verge of losing my stomach. It was growling, and I felt myself starting to sweat. If this went on much longer, things would not be good. Luckily, we hit the top, and things started to straighten out a little. We were definitely at a higher altitude, and we could feel it in the air. When we made it to Cusco, I had never been so happy to get off that bus. It was the roughest form of transportation that I had ever been on.

We arrived in Cusco around 4:00 p.m., which gave us time to get our barring before it got dark. Cusco was a city in the Peruvian Andes and once the capital of the Inca Empire. It was an amazing city to see with its archaeological remains and the Spanish colonial architecture that is apparent on every building. Plaza de Armas was the main square for the city, and it was close to where we found a place to stay. We found this place in our *Lonely Planet Guide* and it was perfect. We had our own room with a shower, which we needed by now, and they also had a laundry service. We had been on the road for a week or so and only had so many clothes, so we took full advantage of this service. It was so much for an article of clothes; we gave her everything we needed cleaned, which was maybe twenty items. She would wash, dry, and return to our room; the cost was less than $2. This was a great deal, and we found this service several times throughout our trip.

That night, we did get some info on getting to the ruins. We would have to take a train for three hours to a small town near the sites. It would cost about $25 each for the trip, which was a little bit more than expected, but if you want to get there, the train was your only choice. We wanted to stay in Cusco for a few nights and then head out. We did get our tickets in advance, so we were guaranteed a seat. This would give us a few days to explore around Cusco and leave on the third day.

The next day, we walked all over, up and down streets and alleyways, and saw so much. The arches, the carved wooden balconies, and all the Inca ruins made this place very cool to see. We did a little barhopping and enjoyed good meals at several outdoor cafes. We lounged around the room a little and spent some time doing our research. As soon as we had made plans for one leg of the trip, we were trying to plan for the one after that. It gave us something to do, and I loved the fact we had so many opportunities.

After a few days of Cusco, we boarded the train to go to Aguas Calientes, which was the town near Machu Picchu. We followed the Urubamba River, went through the sacred valley, and had these amazing canyon walls all around us at times. The train itself was not very comfortable, and it was one that had seats that faced the people near us. It was four to a bench facing one way and four to a bench facing the other way. Besides looking outside, we stared at some locals for three hours. The seats themselves were made of wood and not great for the back, but it was what it was, and we were on our way to see something amazing.

We arrived at the train station at Aguas Calientes, and the first thing we noticed was that this little town was built on the side of a mountain. From the train station, it is all uphill and not a gradual hill, more like a 45-degree incline. We grabbed our bags and started walking uphill. The first thing we noticed was that almost every place that served food served pizza, and this sounded so good. It wasn't like there were a lot of options for food; literally every place was a pizza place.

We found a hostel to stay at, and we had a small room with a shared bathroom. There were nicer places to stay, but we wanted something simple and cheap. Once we had that taken care of, we wandered up and down the street until our legs were sore. Ronnie gave in, and we found a place to sit and eat and relax for a few hours. We had a good pizza and a few beers, which tasted so good after eating a lot of chicken and rice this past week.

This place was very cool, and we found many places that had a deal. You could watch a movie while sitting on a nice couch, enjoy a few beers, and have a pizza brought right to you. This is what we did that night after it had gotten dark and we had seen what we wanted to see.

We woke up around ten, and we made it to the train station around noon. We had about a thirty-minute ride, and we were at the gates of one of the "new seven wonders of the world." What is Machu Picchu? Well, let me tell you, Machu Picchu is the symbol of the Inca Empire and was built around AD 1450. It was built on a mountain peak about seven thousand feet above sea level in the Andes Mountains. There were around 150 buildings ranging from bath houses to temples and sanctuaries. The compound had one hundred flights of stairs, some of them carved from a single stone. The stones that were used to make this are said to have been rolled up the mountain by nothing more than man power. It is said that no wheels were used in getting these things to where they are now, which is extremely impressive. All the stones are dry-stacked, which meant they did not use mortar to hold the stones together. They were cut to fit each place. It is said this place was either an estate for an emperor or it was used as a secret ceremonial center. It is amazing, but this place went undiscovered for centuries until a Yale professor, Hiram Bingham, discovered it around 1911. A lot of the Inca civilization were destroyed during the Spanish conquest, but because this place was so well hidden, invisible from below, it was not found for a long time. It was truly an archeologist gem and was truly worth seeing.

So those are the facts about this place; now for my opinion. I stepped into the grounds, and the first thing that caught my eye was the mountain peak that hovered over the entire area. This was a spot to see this place, but we just walked in. The entire village was a maze of smaller buildings with just the walls standing. The walls were

TAKE A DECADE

made from stone, but the roofs were made from wooden material and have since deteriorated. The paths between the buildings were a maze in itself, but when you don't really know where you're going, it is always the right way. We walked around, in and out of as many structures as we could. It is hard to describe what it was like witnessing this wonder of the world with my own two eyes. When we made our way up the solo peak that you see in every picture, the view of the ruins was priceless. The fact that this place was constructed when it was and how hard it must have been to do this is mind-boggling.

What a day and a day that I will always remember. We got back to the town and chose another pizza/movie place to have dinner. While we were eating, I told Ronnie that after dinner, I needed to find an ATM and get some money. I had enough to pay for tonight but needed to pay for our room and train ride back. So when the check came, I asked our waiter if he could point me to the closest ATM. He looked at me and said, "No ATMs here." The closest ATM was back in Cusco, and that did me absolutely no good. But I had a hundred-dollar bill in my backpack. I asked the server if he could change a $100 bill, and he said yes. *Well, problem solved*, I thought. I left the restaurant and ran uphill to our room. I grabbed my backpack and found the $100 bill that I had hidden in my bag, ran back down to the place, and gave him the bill to cash us out and we could be on our way.

Well, this is when things changed quickly; he said, "I cannot take this bill because it is damaged." He showed me the bill, and there was a small rip in the note. It was like a 1/16 inch tear in the bill, and he would not take it. I paid the bill with what I had but knew that we didn't have enough to get back. It was either we find someone to exchange this $100 bill or we would have to live here, get a job, and become one with the Incans. So we left and found a bank, went in, and tried to exchange this bill and got the same reply. Not even a bank would take this bill. There had got to be someone and the bank teller told us that we might be able to find someone to take it but would not give us the face value. I'd be damned if I was going to get less than a hundred bucks for this bill. We walked around and found a guy that offered me $75 for the $100; I said no and tried several other people. Well, guess what, after an hour or so of dealing with this, I gave in and took the exchange. It was enough to get us back, and that was all I could do at this point.

Well, we paid our tab for the room and bought our tickets back. We didn't have much left, but we were not going to have to live here for the next year and that was a good thing. We took the train back, and as soon as we got to Cusco, I found an ATM and got some cash. That was a close one, and we learned a good lesson: Make sure where we are going either has a source of money or bring extra.

We spent that night in Cusco and tried a few new places out. Each place was more unique than the last. Everything was so Spanish that it felt like I was in a movie where we were at. That night, we decided we were going to make our way toward Lake Titicaca, which was right on the border between Peru and Bolivia. It would be an eight-hour trip, a $16 trip, and we could leave in the morning. This would get us there before dark and give us time to find a place to stay.

We left the next morning and took a bus to Puno. The scenery was again amazing; the mountains are endless and the hills are very apparent. We traveled all day with a few stops here and there and got to the train station around 4:00 p.m. Potosi is one of the highest elevated cities in the world. It sits next to Lake Titicaca at an elevation of 12,556 feet above sea level. It really didn't faze me until we started to walk around. We found a place to stay that was about a ten-minute walk from the station. Our room was on the third floor. When we walked into our room, we were both gasping for air. Holy shit, it felt like I had just walked twenty miles. The air was thin, and the elevation was affecting us big-time. We relaxed a little and checked out our new home. It was more like a small apartment than a room. We had a bedroom, a bathroom, and a small kitchen filled with cooking stuff. It was then that we decided we would try and cook at home tonight rather than going out. Every meal we have had so far had been out, and it would be nice to cook our own meal.

We got situated and made a plan: Let's leave here once and get everything we need and make this hike only one more time. First stop was a tourist office, and we booked a trip that would be a one-night, two-day trip. We would visit the floating islands, stay on one island with a local family, then the next day visit another island and then back to Puno. It sounded great, and this would give us the full experience. Then we walked around town and got everything we needed to make a romantic dinner. We found most of our supplies from outdoor vendors. One person was selling fresh chicken, another sold us a few veggies, and then we went to a small store to get more of the basics. It was here that I saw an older lady selling something that looked like leaves. I asked her what she was selling, and it was coca leaves. You put them in your cheek and just kept adding leaves as the day went on. This was awesome, and I had just found a replacement for my dip, which had been all gone for several days. I bought a bag of them for ten cents, which would last me a long time. I started right then and there and put a few leaves in my cheek. This was the stuff that cocaine was made from, and it didn't take long for my cheek to get a little numb and I had more energy. This was the natural way to enjoy this and was completely legal and normal for the locals. All I knew was that I liked it and gave me something to do rather than smoke.

We had bought everything we needed for dinner, a bottle of wine, and a few beers. We made the walk back and up to our room, and once again, we were winded once we got to the top. This elevation is something else, let me tell you. We were over twelve thousand feet of elevation, and that was actually the elevation of the first base camp going up Mount Everest. So this was no joke.

We prepared a great meal and had a very romantic dinner. We lit a few candles, made a tablecloth out of a sheet, worked together in preparing a meal, and just had a great evening. Once we went to bed, it was another story. I lay down and was extremely tired and needed a good night's sleep. Once I was close to falling asleep, I would wake up gasping for air. I could not lie flat on the bed and get enough oxygen; it was so weird and a little scary. If I did fall asleep, would I wake up? That was the million-dollar question. This went on for several hours, and every time I would get close to falling asleep, I would wake up gasping for air. Finally, I found a few pillows and fell asleep sitting up, which seemed to work better. It was a long night.

The next morning, we left our place and took a cab to the dock to meet our boat. We would be gone for a few days out on the lake, and this was going to be a great way to see the sights. Lake Titicaca is the highest navigable lake in the world and considered the birthplace of the Inca civilization. We left the port and made our way out into the lake. It is so calm, and the reflections from the landscape just mirrored right off the lake. It was a special place, and I'd only been on it for a short time.

We make our way first to the "floating Islands," which were what they sounded like. We approached this island, and it was definitely made out of something besides dirt and rock. The Uros islands, of which there are about seventy, are man-made islands made with the Totora reed, which is found along the shores of the lake. It was a buoyant reed, and when put together in a mass amount, it can actually make an island.

We docked the boat, and we had the chance to get out and walk around this island. It was about half the size of a football field. It had three structures made out of bamboo and reed and was like walking on a field made of weeds. It was very cool and one of a kind. The Uros had been living this life for centuries. They originally made these islands to use as sneak attacks against their enemies. They soon found out they were slow going and actually a disadvantage. At one point in their history, they had been captured and made into slaves. Things had moved on, and now they were a quiet fishing community.

They had created this boat, which looked like a mix of something from the Vikings and Disney World. It had this creature designed in the front and a big tail thing at the back of the boat. It was so cool, and we got to take a short ride around to see a few other islands. All in all, this was something I had never imagined, and it was so unique to have people living this way.

We left the floating island and made our way to the island called Amantani. It was an island on the Peruvian side of the lake. It has about 3,600 people living on the island divided into about 800 families. The island had two mountain peaks and the hillsides were terraced, which made the land workable for the locals.

We would be staying a night here with a local family and got to experience the island through their eyes. We got to the dock, and we were introduced to our host. She looked Peruvian; she was short, heavyset, and dressed like most Peruvian women. They loved brighter colors, especially red, with a dark long skirt, old shoes, white shirt, and a red scarf that covered her head and shoulders.

She walked us to her home, and it was a mud brick home with wooden doorways and a ceramic tile roof. It looked very Spanish, something that would be seen in most parts of a Spanish-speaking culture. She lived in the room downstairs, which is where we had our meals. Her room consisted of two beds, one for her and one for her son. There was a small kitchen with just the basics and a table for eating. The floors were made out of cheap wood, and for the most part, it was just dirt. Our room was up a set of stairs outside. The door to our room was no more than four feet tall, so I had to bend over just to get in. We had a small bed, a table, and one chair. The room was about 12' × 12', and besides a small mirror on one wall, it was bare. Now the toilet was something special. It was a small building away from the main house, and all it was, was a hole in the ground. It looked like someone had carved a big hole in a rock and dug a hole underneath it. You put one foot on one side and the other foot on the other side and did your business. It was rough to look at, and it was not a clean place at all. For them, it was the norm, and at least they had a place to go.

So we spent the night here and had our meals with our host, which was a lot of good soup, bread, and fish. She made us breakfast, lunch, and dinner. The next day, we had the chance to walk around the island, and all we saw were rock walls dividing the land. Each person or section of the island grew certain crops like wheat, quinoa, potatoes, and other vegetables. Then on certain lands, you would find sheep and cattle roaming the hillsides. The one thing they didn't have was gas-powered equipment. The island was worked and farmed with all hand tools and hard work. It was a good place and very cool to see.

That night, they had a party for all of us, and we met up at a barn dressed in local attire. Ronnie had a Peruvian dress on, and they gave me a pair of pants and shirt made on the island. We danced to local music played by the man of the village and ate and drank local food and drink. It was a lot of fun to have about twenty of us all holding hands and spinning around in a big circle laughing and singing.

It was exciting to stay with a local family on Lake Titicaca. Before we left, I gave her son, who was about six years old, a whistle that I had brought with me. I asked her if he could have it, and she said yes. I handed it to him and showed him the whistle and a compass, and he ran away with it, blowing it at the top of his lungs. His mother was going to hate me in a few days.

The next day, we loaded up in the boat and went to another island on the lake called Taquile. This island had about 2,200 people, and the island was 3.5 miles by 1 mile in size, so it was not a big place. The island was known for its hand-woven textiles and clothing. The hats, scarves, and blankets were some of the best made in Peru. This would be one of the most unique places I had ever visited. We get to the dock, and we were told we had five hours to wander around, check out the town, grab lunch, and just enjoy the day. So Ronnie and I grabbed our day packs and set out to explore.

We walked up the street, and the first thing we saw was a group of men standing around, dressed in typical Peruvian clothes, and they were knitting scarves and hats. There were about five of them, and they were standing in a group, shooting the shit, and knitting. It was just not something I was used to seeing. If it were a group of women, I would not think anything about it, but a group of guys was different. As we walked around the streets, we noticed a lot of this: The guys were knitting and the women were processing the wool. This was normal here, and to be a super stud on this island was to be able to make a living by knitting hats and scarves.

After our tour of the islands, it was back to Puno for one more night. We were going to check out the southern end of the lake, which would be about a three-hour bus ride the next morning. We found a place to stay close to the terminal, and the next morning, we were on our way. We were going to spend a few nights at a place called Copacabana.

TAKE A DECADE

Playa de Copacabana was on the Bolivian side of Lake Titicaca. Just the name itself was the reason to check it out. It was a small beach town located on the coast of harsh and rugged surroundings. There was a rough dirt road to get there, and the landscape was just mountains of jagged rocks. Once we saw the town, we could tell it would be fun to stay for a few days. The entire town was built around the water. There was no place that would not have a good view. We found a great little hostel with our own shower and balcony. The balcony faced the water, and we spent many hours just sitting out there enjoying drinks. The place had this Caribbean feel to it—bright colors, aquatic designs on the walls—and everyone seemed happy.

We spent two nights here, and besides renting dirt bikes one day, it was all about the view from our balcony. So we rented dirt bikes for a few hours one day, and that was an adventure. They gave me this nice 125 cc bike that had power. They gave Ronnie this small moped-looking thing that I was surprised ran. She had never rode a motorbike before, so they gave her something small. Well, we were off, and down the beach we went. The town was surrounded by rugged mountains, so we really could not go that far. We just spent the time up and down the beach and went as far as we could. We got as far away as we could, and her machine stopped running. She was not going that fast, and I didn't think it was getting enough gas, so we switched rides, and once Ronnie got a taste of a nice bike, guess who got to ride the small piece of shit the rest of the time? It was fun anyway, and even with that little bike, it was better than walking.

This place was a great resting spot for a few days. There wasn't a ton to do except enjoy each other and the view. So this would be the end of our first country. The next day, we would enter Bolivia, our second country for who knows what. All I could say was Peru had been a great first step on this journey, and I couldn't wait to see what happens next.

20
CHAPTER

Bolivia

We arrived in La Paz around 5:00 p.m. from Peru. This was our first border crossing, which was an experience. It was a very rustic/rough-looking crossing. There were no fancy buildings, just a brick building with a bunch of armed guards. Peru and Bolivia had their moments from now and again, so the border could be a hotspot. We hit it on a good day, paid our $25 entry fee, got our passports stamped with our second stamp, and we were now in one of South America's poorest countries.

Our experience in this country was amazing; we had the opportunity to do so many unexpected cool things while we were here. First was La Paz, a large capital city in Bolivia, one of two capitals this country has. Our first view of the city was from a mountaintop from our bus. The driver pulled over, and we all got to see was the city from a bird's eye view. It was spread out with a distinct main central area, which is where the larger buildings were, but it looked more residential than anything.

We got into the city and found a place to stay. It had been a long day, so basically, we got a few things to eat and drink and made it an early night. When we were checking into our place, I asked the guy what might be happening over the course of the next few days, and we were in luck that there was a big soccer/football match tomorrow, and he told us where to get tickets. Just like that, our day was planned. We just relaxed a little, read up on this country, had a few beers, and called it an early night.

The next morning, our plan was to go into the city further, score a few tickets, and then head back to the room for a nap and then go back down for the game. Well, that all changed when we got there. The streets were already lined with people partying for the game. We ended up staying down there for the entire day. We were getting a bite to eat, and I asked our server what we could get inside the stadium. She told us that we could buy food and drinks, just no *alcoholic* drinks. She informed us that the crowd got wild, and it was too dangerous to the fans and players if everyone was drunk. She did, however, tell us that we could bring in our own stuff. Here in La Paz you could bring in your own booze. This just didn't happen in the States at all; you couldn't even bring in a mini, let alone a bottle of something.

So after we ate at an outdoor café, our next mission was to find a liquor store before the game started. We walked a few blocks and just continued the hooting and howling with everyone else. We had picked up a few cheap banners, and we also got our faces painted, so we were all in for this event. We found a liquor store just a few blocks away. We went in and chose a bottle of bourbon to enjoy the match. The girl behind the counter asked if we were going into the stadium, and she said, "You can't take this bottle into the stadium."

"Wait a minute, we were just told the complete opposite."

She said, "You can bring in the booze, just not in this bottle," so she grabbed a plastic bag about the size of a gallon bag and proceeded to dump the liquor into the bag. We paid, and she handed me the bag.

We walked down the street; I'm just holding this bag. We walked up to the main gate and went through a security checkpoint. They wanted to see our ticket, went through a metal detector, and also had our bags checked. This was all happening as I held a bag of brown liquid in my hand. They could definitely see it but just didn't care. We found our seats, grabbed a Coke to mix it with, and enjoyed our first drink inside this beautiful stadium. Just some things seem really weird when you can do something in one country but not your own.

The stadium held 75,000 people, and it was packed. The match started, and the chants started. All we heard for the beginning of the game was "*Bo…liv…ve…a, Bolivia.*" If we heard this once, we heard it one thousand times. It was awesome, and we joined in like we were from the country. The match was exciting; it wasn't just a few local teams—it was the best of the best in these two counties. Bolivia did lose 3–1, but we had a hell of a good time.

That night, we did have a bit of an argument, something that has happened before when both of us had too much to drink. We yell, say stupid things, decide to go our separate ways, and then we pass out, and it is all over by the next day. It is something about the two of us, and we can get into it at times, her being Latino and me being a Scorpio. Sometimes they just clash, but for the most part, we get along really well. We tell each other we love each other almost every day.

Our next big adventure was leaving La Paz and going north to a mountain resort. This was a place mentioned in our books and recommended by a few of the locals. Really quick, the resort itself was nice. It was more of a three-star hotel in the States; for the Bolivians, it was a five-star all the way. It wasn't about the resort; it was how we got there. The two ways to get there at this time was we could rent a bike and pedal the forty-three miles, or we could take a small van. We chose the van, and it was an experience. The road we had to travel was considered at this time as "the world's most dangerous road." It was a road that cut through the side of a mountain. The road was forty-three miles and took about three hours to travel on with sheer cliffs on both sides. Going down, we had two-thousand-foot cliffs with rugged mountains to our right, which left us exposed to falling boulders and landslides. To our left, we had a two-thousand-foot drop-off from a road that was only ten feet wide. We approached other vehicles and had to get so close to the edge that we could not see the road from our seats. There were no guardrails, just a sheer drop-off that had taken hundreds of lives. It was a very scary and heart-pounding three hours. With each curve we went around, all we could see were crosses left behind for the ones that didn't make it. This road was closed in 2007 and replaced with a safer route for the locals to get back and forth from the jungle. It is just cool to say that I have been on one road that was so deadly in the past.

After our few days at the "resort," we made it back up the road of death. Again, we survived to tell the story. For our last day in La Paz, we visited the famous "Witches' Market." This place was a trip. It was several blocks of some of the most unique things I had ever seen for sale. The "witch doctors," who were called Yatis, were always wearing a black hat with a coco pouch filled with potions. They tried to sell us so many weird things. We could have bought dried frogs, dried possums, potions for just about anything, herbal medicine (no grass, I asked), and the best was llama fetuses. These were the special items used with a lot of locals to keep bad spirits away from your home. They would bury a llama fetus under their house for good luck. We passed on those. It was a very different place and cool to see.

We left La Paz for a twelve-hour bus ride to our next spot, which was Sucre. This was the other capital of Bolivia that handled the jurisdiction for the country. There wasn't a lot to see here except a big city, but it was on our way to our next spot, which was Potosí, Bolivia. We knew this was going to be a long ride, so we brought extra drinks and food. We always stop during a long trip, but it was good to have our own stuff with us. So we headed out, watching the mountains and the jungle go by us. We watched a few movies and had a few drinks. We were all good until about the last few hours, and our eyelids were getting heavy. We decided to try and catch a few zzz's before we got to Sucre. Well, things got a little crazy from this point on. We actually ended up sleeping right through our stop. When we woke up, we were about thirty minutes from Potosi. We were like, *Oh well, this is where we wanted to get to anyway*, so hey, we just did the whole fifteen-hour trip at once. This was good because we saved money on a place to stay and we might get this leg of the trip for free. We thought we had scored; now for the letdown. We got off the bus, and they started unloading all the bags from below the bus; people walked by us and grabbed their bags and were gone. We waited and waited until all the bags had been taken off the bus. Ours were not there, and I even pulled up the other doors on the bus to check; this pissed the driver off and he yelled at me to get away from his bus. Just this time, Ronnie came over, and he told her that the bags were tagged and taken off at their tagged place. We paid for our bags to get to Sucre, and they took them off. *Our bags were gone.* We ran inside and asked if they could check to see if our bags were three hours away. She said they had no way to contact them; all we could do was go back and check. You had got to be kidding. We had just gotten here, and we now had to pay for another ticket, wait an hour before the next bus left, and hope like hell our bags were still there. We went and had something to eat, and both of us were sick to our stomachs. What are the chances they were still there? It had so much of our stuff, clothes, documents, gifts, and money. We were screwed, but we had no choice but to try and hope for the best.

We left an hour later for the same place we had just been. It was a very quiet ride; we both had the same thing on our minds. Well, we made it to our original destination, and it was already dark out. We went into the main terminal and went right up to the desk. An older lady came over. Ronnie told her what had happened, and she said to us, "Follow me and we will check…in English by the way." She opened this door in the back, and I could see a bunch of bags. We entered the room, and it was the best feeling ever. There they were, both of our bags, sitting right beside each other. I turned to the lady and gave her a big hug. She wasn't expecting this, but I loved this woman right then. She smiled and could tell we had been worried. I gave her the whole story and told us it had happened before. We just got very lucky.

That night, we spent the night in Sucre and were so happy to have our bags. The only good thing about this day was the TV. Yes, they had a small TV in our room, which was a first for us. I started to scroll through the channels, while Ronnie took a shower, and guess what I found, a porn channel. You have got to love those Bolivians. I told Ronnie. She laughed and said, "Take a shower." For all of our misery that day and painstaking worry, we were rewarded with a fun-filled night of hot sex while watching our little TV.

The next day, we both had a good smile on our faces and had a good laugh. This was another thing we hoped we would never do again and learn from our mistakes. We finally got to Potosi about the same time we had originally planned on, this time with all our bags. *Yeah.*

Potosi is another high-elevation city sitting in the southern highlands of Bolivia. The elevation of this city is 13,343 feet above sea level, which makes it one of the highest cities in the world. By now, we had acclimated to the higher altitudes, and the coca leaves were helping me out. The city is well known for its long mining history. There is a working mine south of the city that is known for producing a lot of silver.

Now the one thing about this place was there were no people at the bus stop asking if we needed a place to stay. It had worked like this for most of the trip: Get off the bus and ten people try to sell you a room for the night. Not here, so we had to do some walking, a good mile or so, to find a place. We found one for the next two nights, and it was very basic. It had a bed, table, dresser, and a really small shower. After the room was taken care of, we found a place to eat. While we finished our meal, a middle-aged guy came up to us and asked if we wanted to go down into the silver mines. He told us for $20 each, he would pick us up tomorrow and give us a nice tour of the mines. We agreed and made plans for tomorrow morning around nine. With that set, we just wandered around the streets and saw what we could.

It was a quiet city, not a lot of people walking around. The buildings were all older, paint falling off the exteriors, and even the roads were rough. This was a place on earth where people just didn't have much but were still very happy. We walked around, and coming down the street was a baby alpaca, which is very similar to a llama. Both were very popular around here and were used for many different purposes. They were used for clothing, manual labor, and they did eat them as well. Well, this one was about as cute as it gets. I leaned down, and the damn thing came right over to me. I started to pet it, and it just rubbed up against me. It was so cool to be petting this gorgeous creature. As I was petting it, a little girl about four years old comes out and walks right over to me, the whole time just staring at me. She gets close and grabbed the alpaca around the neck and pulled it toward her. She was telling me that this was hers and she needed to bring him home. Just then, with the little girl and the baby alpaca, Ronnie snapped a photo, and it was one of the best pictures taken on this whole trip. I stood up and thanked her for sharing her pet with me for a short time, and we watched them walk up the hill into a house. Just little things like this make traveling so much fun.

The next day, our guide met us at 9:00 a.m. right out front of our hostel. He told us there were a few others joining us, and we drove around the city for thirty minutes, picking everyone up. There were about six of us all together. No one from the States, mostly Europe, and everyone was cool. We stopped at his main office, and we took care of the money, and he gave us things to wear. We all were given yellow pants and a jacket, boots, and a helmet with a belt attached to it. We loaded back up and drove south to the mines.

The Cerro Rico is a mountain with a peak at 15,827 feet above sea level. The mountain has been mined since the eighteenth century. It is not a place where a lot of people have gotten rich; it is just about the only way around here to earn a living. We pulled up to the mine, and it looked more like a dump. It was sad, but you could see a bunch of people scavenging through the piles of garbage for something to either sell or eat. Our guide told us that busloads of people came here every day to find something they can use. It was a very poor area, and this just showed how poor it really was.

We got all dressed in our gear—pants, jackets, helmets, and then this belt, which I was still not sure what it was for. I would soon find out. As we walked toward the entrance, our guide told us that it was customary to bring the miners gifts while we walked around. He took us to this little wooden shack, and a girl was selling these bags full of gifts for the miners. I just grabbed one and gave her $5. I asked the guide what was in the bag, and he told me a pack of non-filtered coco cigarettes, a bag of raw coca leaves, a detonation switch, a small bag of highly explosive materials, and one stick of dynamite. You had got to be kidding. I opened the bag, and sure enough, everything he said was in there. I had just bought my first stick of dynamite and highly explosive material. This was just cool in its own little way. We could have gotten in the car and gone home; my day had been made. But it just got better.

TAKE A DECADE

We got to the entrance, and to the side of the opening was a statue of what looked like an angel. Our guide told us that in the entrance to every mine was a shrine for the miners. The angle shrine was to ask for help and prosperity while they risked their lives. He also told us that at the bottom of the mines was a devil shrine to ask for safety and the ability to return to their families each night. I said a quick prayer, and we walked into the mine. Our guide came over to each one of us, turned something on our belts, and with a lighter, he lit each one of our headlamps. We had a flame coming out of our heads, and this was a little different. The reason for this was that the miners did not use flashlights and lanterns; they used acetylene gas instead. When they were deep in the mines, they got into small tunnels and very confined spaces. If the light went out, then it was because of a lack of oxygen in the area, and they needed to get out quickly. So they used this gas as a light source and for safety. Again, this just made this better and better.

We walked into a very small tunnel maybe four feet high and the walls were four feet wide, just big enough to get a wheelbarrow into. It took us about ten minutes of walking down when we ran into our first group of miners. These guys all had black faces and were wearing the same thing we were. These guys had a rough and rather short life. The average age for these miners to live was only in the mid-forties. Most of them started in the mines when they were as young as ten years old, and this was their way of life. They each had a section of the mine that they had bought, and they got whatever came out. Like I said earlier, very few ever made it big. The miners were pounding holes into the rock to get a stick of dynamite into the hole to blow that section. He handed me his metal rod and hammer, and I gave it a shot. Holy cow, after just a few minutes, my arms were killing me. This was no joke and not easy. They had to pound a whole twenty inches long to get a stick of dynamite and a detonation switch to blow that wall. We hung out and watched, and I gave them cigarettes and a bag of coca leaves. They all had a big wad in their mouths as well as I did by now.

We proceeded further down, and at one point, we had to lie on our stomachs and wiggle our way through this opening to get to another tunnel. It was not for someone who hated small spaces. As we got down further, we passed a few more groups until we got to a group of guys that were done pounding holes; it was time to blow the wall. Our guide asked if we could stay, and he said, "Sure, just hid behind that wall." I gave them my bag of explosives and detonation switch; I was not ready to give away my dynamite. We all moved out of the way, and the countdown began. "Three, two, one…*blast*…three, two, one…*bang*…three, two, one…*boom*." After the very first explosion, all our headlamps went out. It was pitch black, and all I could taste was dirt. He relit each one of our lamps and told us because of the blast, our lights went out. The tunnel was covered in dust, and it was hard to see the person next to you. This was awesome, and I could not believe we just witnessed an explosion underground so close to the actual blast. This definitely would not happen in the States, way too much liability. After the dust cleared, we kept walking and spent about two hours underground. We reached the end of the mine, saw the "devil shrine," and I finally gave up my dynamite to the last miner we saw. They were all very appreciative of the gifts, and we truly had a one-of-a-kind adventure. Our guide told us that we had gone almost two miles underground and covered just a small portion of what this mine has to offer. We thanked him for a great time, gave him a good tip, and he dropped us off right at our hostel.

    The next day, we just wandered around, just exploring. The streets were a little busier but nothing like it was in La Paz. We did have to make plans for our next adventure. Our guide told us of the salt fields that were on the southern portion of the country and real close to the border of Chile. Our plan was to explore Bolivia and then check out Chile for a week or so. We found a company that did a jeep tour that was a three-day, two-night excursion that gives you a great view of the salt flats and a few extra things. We had to get to the city near the flats, which was called Uyuni. The company that did the tour was well known and one of the best. We got all the info, and the next morning, we jumped on a three-hour bus trip south for $10, hoping we could get there before they left. If not, we would have to wait a few days, and there really wasn't a lot to do in Uyuni.

TAKE A DECADE

Well, we got lucky and arrived an hour before they were leaving. They had room for just two more people, so we got lucky twice in one day. The cost to do this was $75, and that covered the jeep and some food, and they would be able to drop us off at the border, which was excellent. We paid the fee, and we loaded up into two jeeps, twelve including the two drivers, and set out for another very cool and unexpected journey.

After driving for a short time, we entered the Uyuni Salt Flats Preserve. As soon as you were here, you knew where you were. We drove off the road right onto the lake that once was here. As far as we could see, it was nothing but white with the mountains surrounding it. If it had not been 75 degrees, you could have sworn that we were surrounded by a fresh coat of pure white snow. It was incredible to see and to actually be on this place riding in a jeep made the moment even better. We drove straight across the salt flats for a good hour or so until we could see what very well could have been a mirage.

As we got closer, we noticed this island-looking place was exactly what it was, and that it was an island when this place was a lake. It was called Isla Incahuasi, which was a small rocky hill with a bunch of cacti growing on it with a few small little buildings. We arrived and had time to wander around and get some photos. This was a place where you could get a photo with an illusion that certain things were happening. We took a photo of what looked like me holding Ronnie up on my bicep. All we had to do was lower the camera to the focal point, and she stood back a little, and voila, I was holding her up. This place had a trail to the top of the mountain/hill, and from here, we had a 360-degree view of the entire deserted lake. Now this place was unique in a lot of ways. First and foremost, a good portion of the salt that we used for popcorn and corn on the cob came from this place. We were told 90 percent of the table salt used in the world came from here. During the rainy season, this lake got a few inches of water on it, and it turned into one gigantic mirror. So they used this focal point from space to actually calibrate weather satellites. This was a cool stop, and we had a bit to eat and a cold beer here in the middle of the salt flats.

We then kept driving for what seemed like forever. The people in our van were quiet, and after about thirty minutes, we had gotten to know each other with all the small talk, and really just spent the time staring out the window watching this world go by. We got to what seemed like the edge of the lake, and we could see we were approaching a small building. It was a "Salt Hotel'," and it would be home for the night. The place was small and only had about fifteen small rooms. We were lucky to get a private room but had to share the bathrooms. We got there and were greeted by a few people. Now when I say this place is made out of salt, I mean it is all salt except the windows and doors. The walls, the floor, the table, and even under our mattress was all salt. I know this because I licked the walls and the table, and yes, it was salt. We had a buffet-style meal—chicken, fish, rice, fruit, bread, and tea. It was a good meal and filled me up. We walked around that night, and when the sky got dark, the stars erupted in the sky and created a picture-perfect moment. We were standing on six feet of salt with the stars lighting up the sky for one hell of a moment.

The next day, we headed further up the mountain. We had left the smooth ride of the lake behind and started to travel up. This took a big portion of the day, but when we got to where we were going, it was all worth it. The only problem was the temperature had dropped by thirty degrees. Once again, our host showed us to our rooms.

Here we had one big bunk room, and Ronnie and I found our two bunks. We got unpacked a little and added a few layers to keep warm. They took our group on a little walk, which was something to do and warmed us up a little. They took us to a volcano, which was not active but still had the cone-shaped look to it. We all walked around the entire area, and the red rock against a brown stone looked like something from mars.

So after our group meal, a few of us took the directions from one of the workers and walked to Laguna Colorado. This was a shallow salt lake in the middle of the mountains. It was no more than five feet deep at its deepest point. The lake contained borax, which is a component of many detergents and cosmetics and is used as a fire retardant. The contrast with this and the salt made the area around the lake this reddish color. The big thing about this place that was apparent as soon as we approached the lake was the number of flamingos all over the place. Not just a few like you see in the wildlife parks, but I'm talking about thousands of wild flamingos flying around. They would fly for a while and then rest, standing on one leg like usual. It was impressive to see so many and in the complete wild.

On our way back, I noticed a cool shell and picked it up. I handed it to Ronnie and told her she should make a necklace out of this. The reason I bring this up is because I started something that would last the rest of the trip. It was a fun thing for her, and there were a few very boring moments for me—more on this later.

The next day and our last day on the jeep tour, we went further up this mountain. It was crazy how high we were climbing, and thank God for the jeep. Our destination that morning was the Sol de Manana Geyser basin, which was on top of a mountain. The first thing about these geysers is that they brought me to the highest elevation I had ever been, and that was 16,400 feet above sea level. When we got out of the jeep, the temperature had dropped again, and now it was bone-chilling cold. We only had light jackets and a few articles of warm clothes. We got out, and the geysers were going off. This was not just one geyser but more like twenty. It looked like a part of a movie when the whole planet is exploding and the world is coming to an end. It was spectacular to see these geysers letting off steam from molten lava below where we were standing. The steam would reach thirty feet into the air and give off a much-needed warmth. You could only get so close before the steam was actually burning hot. It was unreal, and here in a third-world country, you could get as close as you want, just be careful. Near the geysers were a hot spring and a hot mud pond. First, the mud pond, it was just like it sounds. This one, however, was actually bubbling from the temperatures below the surface. It was eerie to look at, and I could not imagine how hot that thing was. Next was the hot spring, which felt great. It was frigging cold out, and just to take your socks and shoes off and put your feet into warm water was so refreshing. One guy took it all off and jumped in. Not me, I just could not do it; he was a crazy guy.

Once back in the jeep, it was all downhill from there. We spent the next few hours just driving and once again found our way back onto the salt flats. It was an hour's ride from there, and we were at the checkpoint before the border to Chile. We said our goodbyes and gave the driver a $20 tip, which would be like getting a $100 tip in the States. We had a great time, and I will never forget this experience.

21
CHAPTER

Chile

After such an amazing trip with the jeep, we really had no expectations for what would be next. The one sad thing that I had to deal with is that I had to give up my coca leaves. They were legal in Bolivia but illegal in Chile, so I gave my bag to the driver, and he was happy. So after a short bus ride, we were finally at the border. The place was similar to the first crossing. It wasn't a glorified building with statues and booths to drive through. Everyone got out, and everyone went inside. Being American helped I think because they knew we had the means to get home if necessary. Also, we would be spending money, which they liked. We did get charged an exit fee and an entry fee to get out of Bolivia and get into Chile. It was just another way to get $25 from us, and we paid and said nothing. Once over the border, things changed real quickly, and not for the bad. It was maybe a few miles, and we hit a road. Now it may seem small to you, but it was a nice road, well paved like the States and actually had lines in the middle to navigate traffic. We saw big green signs on the side of the road with distance to other places. It was like we had gone from one extreme to the next.

Chile, you see, is one of the richest countries in South America. The country has the Andes Mountains to the east and the Pacific coast to the west. It has a lot of beachfront property along its coast that is in high demand for the locals. Our first destination to start this country was San Pedro de Atacoma, which was the closest city over the border.

We found a cheap place to stay, and it was filled with local Chileans. It seemed fun, and I felt a lot of energy from this place. The locals came here to "sand dune surf," which was just like it sounded. Find a sand dune, and take a modified surfboard and surf/sky down the mountain. It sounded like fun, and Ronnie was all set to try it. For me, it just felt like an accident waiting to happen. First of all, she would have been the one to get hurt, and I would have to carry all the bags from there on out. I did talk her out of it, but she called me a *pussy* even though I told her she would be the one to get hurt, oh well. Instead of doing that, we went to the mall. Now I do sound like a big pussy, don't I? Oh well, at least I had no broken bones.

So yes, we spent the day at the mall, which was well needed, and it felt good to be around something that reminded us of home. The mall had all the big stores and a food court, which is where we ate. Guess what I had for my first meal in this country—McDonald's, and man, did it taste great. There's nothing like a Big Mac and the best thing is the value meals come with a frosty cold beer if you want, and I wanted. After our fantastic meals, we found two stores we were looking for, one for me a tobacco shop that had dip. Now I had to give up my coca leaves. The store we found for Ronnie was a bead shop for making jewelry; I told you that I had started something. She had already made her first necklace out of that shell and was all about making jewelry and selling it along the way. It would give her something to do; it was just the shopping that was so frigging boring. However, I sucked it up and did what she wanted because I love her, and if she is happy, then I can be happy.

After the mall, we made it back and started to talk. How far could we get into Chile being we were on a little bit of a time frame? We were to meet her sister and brother-in-law the first part of May in Salvador, Brazil. We still had a lot of ground to cover, and we talked about a few things that night. First, she had already been to the major city, and things here were more expensive. If we headed south too much, we could miss out on parts of Argentina that we wanted to see. It was a tough decision, but we decided that night to head east toward Argentina and forfeit more time in Chile.

The next morning, we were back on a big bus heading to Argentina. It would be another long trip about eleven hours and $30 later, plus the fee to get into the country. This would be our fourth stamp in our passports, which always made me smile.

CHAPTER 22

Argentina

From San Pedro de Atacama to Salta, Argentina was a long trip but so scenic that it actually went by fast. We started with sand dunes then to more salt flats, open desert that went on forever, and more mountains. It was late afternoon when we arrived, giving us just a short time to find a place to stay.

Salta is a provincial capital in northwest Argentina. It is known for its Spanish colonial architecture and a lot of Andean heritage. The city centers around the Plaza 9 de Julio, which is a square in the city with café-lined streets and two very impressive structures. There is this neoclassical Salta Cathedral and the El Cabildo, which is an eighteenth-century historical museum, once the city town hall. Both structures were amazing and stood out as soon as we got there. We found a place to stay close to everything with the help from our tour guidebook. Now there were not a bunch of things that really interested to stay here long; it was more of a stopover until we could get further south.

It was dinnertime, and we were ready for a good meal and a cold beer. Now we had been told along the way that Argentina was known for their grass-fed beef. We had been living on chicken and fish, a lot of rice, and very little beef. The food was good, but I was so ready for a good steak. We found a place that had an inside setting and was rather nice. By now, I had been picking up some Spanish and doing my own ordering. We placed our order with the server and enjoyed a cold beer. Our meal came soon after, and I was hungry and ready to eat. I cut a piece of the steak and placed it into my month. Wow, this didn't taste at all like what I was expecting. It had a very different flavor. I took another bite, and again, this was not good at all. I told Ronnie that I thought this meat was rotten, and if this is what they thought a good steak was, they were way wrong. The server came over and asked how things were, and I told him the truth: "This meat is not good. I think it may be spoiled or something."

He looked at me with a bit of a smirk and said, "Sir, you didn't order a steak. You ordered *liver*."

What the fuck? I hated liver and would never in my life order it. I told him I wanted a good steak and I would be happy to pay for the liver as well but really wanted a true grass-fed Argentina steak. He said, "No problem, it will just take a few moments." He brought me another beer, and I watched Ronnie eat her fish, which she said was delicious. Ten minutes later, my whole life changed. He set my plate in front of me, and it had a three-inch-thick filet that was the size of my fist. It was served with potatoes, veggies, and a homemade roll. I cut the first bite and placed it into my mouth, and this was pure pleasure. The steak melted in my mouth; it was the best steak I had ever had. The filet was juicy, easy to cut, and cooked perfectly, and I savored each and every bite. There was not a single scrap on my plate when I was done, and when the check came, it made this meal even better. He didn't charge me for my mistake, and the whole meal cost $5. This filet/meal in the States would have been $50–$75.

With our bellies full, we just went back to the room with a few drinks and ready to see how we could get to our next spot, which was Mendoza. We relaxed, talked, and got a good night's sleep. When we woke up the next morning, Ronnie's stomach was not feeling good. She wasn't really sick but did not feel right. So we made the decision to stay one more night and get her feeling better before another long travel day. It was better to feel crappy in a room with a bathroom than to feel crappy and sit on a bus all day.

She needed something to settle her stomach, so she wrote down a few things to get, and I went out to find the pharmacy. The pharmacy was about two blocks away and had everything she needed. I went back and gave her something for her stomach, bought some ginger ale as well, and got her situated for the day.

So with Ronnie all taken care of, I took off and wandered around the streets of Salta for the day—up and down, in and out of shops. I stopped in for a few beers and enjoyed a day to just do whatever I wanted. So far, this trip, we had done everything together, and this was the first time I had the day to myself.

I stayed away most of the day, giving her time to sleep and get better. When I got back, she was up and feeling much better. The stuff she took had worked, and she was now hungry. We decided to go back to the same place as the night before. It was close, and we knew it would be a good meal. We went inside and had the same server. He joked with me and asked if I wanted the *liver* again, ha ha. We both ordered the filet that night, and it was as good as it gets—again.

The next day midafternoon, we boarded the bus to Mendoza. This would be an eighteen-hour trip; it would take most of the night and get us to Mendoza early afternoon. This was not a problem; we were in no hurry. Once again, we stocked up on supplies and sat on a bus for another day. We had become pros on the whole bus thing. We sat where we could see the movie screen, far away from the bathroom, and she always sat on the inside and me on the outside. We also made sure our bags were secured and not easy for anyone to get to them. We had become professional travelers by now.

Mendoza is located right in the middle of the country, and it is the wine capital for Argentina. This was the reason we wanted to check this place out. This city was destroyed by an earthquake in 1861 and rebuilt with very wide streets and wide sidewalks. They did this so if another earthquake hit, the buildings would not destroy each other. The city was rather new for the times, and it felt very modern right from the beginning. Mendoza was a major hub for a lot of outdoor activities: hiking, mountain climbing, rafting, and in the winter months, skiing. I fell in love with this place immediately, and it had a very good vibe to it.

We checked out our book and found a place to stay. It was close to everything, and the guidebook gave it great reviews. Let me tell you, they were right. This may have been one of the best places we stayed during this entire trip. As we approached the building, we could hear noise coming from the patio. They had this indoor/outdoor bar patio place that was the place to be. We checked in, and they only had dorm rooms available; it was four to a room with a shared bathroom. It was no big deal, and we decided to stay for at least three nights. The guy showed us the room, and a young couple was just getting unpacked. We met John and Meg from Indiana, United States. It was the first people in a long time that we had run into from the States. They were in their mid-twenties and a cute couple. The four of us bonded quickly and spent a majority of our time together. That night, we sat out in the bar area with at least thirty people; most seemed to be locals just here for one of the many things to do. There were a lot of travelers there as well going in all different directions. They told us that they had booked a wine tour for the next day when they first checked in. "You guys should come with us," they said, and I walked right to the front desk area and booked the trip. It was leaving around noon and would go to four wineries, a tour of the city, and pickup and drop-off were right here. For $25, it was a done deal.

    The next day, we had a blast with our new friends, did the entire wine tour, and tasted a lot of amazing wines. The wineries were similar to the States, rolling hills with grape vines everywhere. Each winery we drank as much as we could and then sometimes a little bit more. Between the four of us, we all bought a bottle so we could have our own little tasting when we got back to the hostel.

    The bus ride to and from the tour gave us a really good look at the city as well. It was clean, new-aged with green grassy areas, a beautiful fountain that was the center point of the city, and well-dressed people. Besides the one day in Chile, this place seemed to be more up to date with the times. I guess this had a lot to do with it getting destroyed and then rebuilt.

    The four of us enjoyed a nice meal together that evening. We all got steaks, and we all said the same thing, "Unreal." We got back to the hostel and uncorked a few of the bottles. They had mentioned another excursion they wanted to do while they were here and asked if we would be interested. They wanted to go white water rafting, and we could book the excursion right here. So we finished one bottle of wine, and John and I went to check it out. They had room for tomorrow, and the cost would be around $30 each. This was a good deal, and we booked it right then and there. We all cheered for our day we had and again for the day ahead. We sat outside, drinking all four bottles of wine plus a handful of beers. The four of us made our way back to our room, talked, laughed, and finally passed out. The morning would come soon enough, and we needed some rest.

I was not the only one who woke up feeling a little on the shitty side. We were all moving a little slower, but we knew we had a good forty-five-minute ride to get to the place. This would give us time to sober up and get something to eat. I sat for most of the ride with my eyes closed, telling my body to get over it and help me through today. *I promise I will not drink a lot tonight and get a good night's sleep.* It was easy to say that morning, but who knew how the day would go?

We got to our destination, and the river was right there. The water was moving slowly in front of the building, but this is where we ended, not began. There were at least fifty yellow rafts stacked up all over the place, and people just finishing their trip were taking pictures and laughing. Everyone looked like they were having fun. We were put into groups of six with a captain. We had a couple from England join the four of us, and they turned out to be really cool and made for a good group. We were given paddles, life vests, and a yellow helmet. Then we had to help move rafts to the bus to get us up stream. Our guide didn't speak English, but we could easily understand what he was saying. The biggest thing about this guy was that he looked like John Belushi. He could have been a twin or a damn good look-alike if John Belushi were still alive. Anyways, we got all our stuff, loaded up the bus, and headed out for another thirty-minute ride to get to the starting point. By now, I had started to feel better and was getting excited about this opportunity. This was something I had never done before and always wanted to. I guess my first time would be here in Argentina.

We got unloaded and got the rafts close to the edge. We put on our life jackets and helmets, and the captain got us in the boat.

Ronnie and I were in the front of the boat just sitting on our knees facing forward. This was the best spot to be for the ride. We did, however, switch with the others so they too could get the adventure of being in front. So with everyone in the boat, all on our knees with paddles in our hands and huge smiles on all our faces, the captain jumped in, and we were now moving quickly right off the bat. He said one side paddle or everyone to paddle, and we hit our first set of rapids. We went straight up with the first wave and straight down into the water. We were wet from the first wave and absolutely loving it. The rapids were taking us down at a good speed; we were avoiding big rocks and paddling in whatever direction our captain wanted us to. We got out of the first set of rapids, and we all just starting hollering and laughing. That was so frigging cool; we couldn't wait to do it again. We would hit a few slow spots, and this was when all the rafts would have a water fight with each other, which our captain started right from the beginning. These rapids were class 3, which aren't the fastest, but for us, they were all we could handle. We would hit some of these waves or rocks, and we were sure we were going to flip, but we never did. It was a three-hour trip that I wish could have lasted three days. We were soaked, our stomachs hurt from laughing, and when we got back, I felt like a professional white water rafter.

We made it back to our hostel, got ready, and went out for dinner. They were leaving tomorrow, so tonight would be our last night to hang out with our new friends. It had been fun to have someone else to talk and do things with.

The next day, we checked out a few small cafes, did a little barhopping, and enjoyed this modern city. We saw the Plaza Independencies, which was a semicircle fountain with lush green grass surrounding it. We also visited the Mercado Central, which was a crazy indoor market with butchers, produce sellers, and food vendors. We ate here and enjoyed more of the delicious meat they had to offer. This would be a place that I would stay longer if I had the time. We had other plans, and that was to keep moving. Our next spot on the map was Buenos Aires, Argentina. This would be the furthest south we would reach, and from there, we needed to make our way to Salvador, Brazil.

STEPHEN MUNDY

It was sad to leave our hostel because this place was a blast, but who knew what would be next? The only thing we knew was we had another fourteen-hour bus trip ahead of us, and it would be a travel day. Our plan was another night bus, so it was time to get supplies and find another book to read. We were back on a bus, more movies to watch and a good time to catch up on some sleep.

23
CHAPTER

Argentina: Let the party Begin

We reached Buenos Aires just before it got dark the next day. It is crazy to spend so much time on a bus, but it is the best and cheapest way to get around. We had become pros at it by now. We knew where to sit, what drinks to bring, and who sat where. I always had the aisle, and she had the inside. This was so nobody would get her in the night, ha ha!

Buenos Aires is Argentina's big cosmopolitan capital city. The place is huge and not your typical city. It is lined with nineteenth-century buildings with a touch of glamor. We found a place to stay, another hostel, which wasn't far from the bus station. We actually got a ride from the guy who worked there. He was good-looking, had long hair, and spoke English well. Ronnie was happy to have him as our guide. The hostel was large and rather quiet. He showed us our room, which was a room with five bunk beds in it, but for now, we had the place to ourselves. We took the beds at the back of the room and used one for our gear and would sleep in the other one. I don't think we had not slept in the same bed yet; big or small, we slept together. After getting situated we walked out, and a few of the guys were hanging out, talking. They called us over, gave us each a beer, and asked if we wanted to go out with them later to a club. I really didn't want to go, but I lost this one real quick. I was tired and just wanted to get a good night's sleep and check out our things tomorrow; nope, that didn't happen.

We grabbed something to eat at a café close by, came back, and took a quick nap. At 10:00 p.m., I got up, took a much-needed shower, and at around midnight, we left with these guys. I really didn't trust them yet, so I was keeping an eye on things. They seemed nice, but you never know. We got to the club, and it was going off, people dancing everywhere to trance and dance music. It was so loud in there it was hard to hear ourselves think, but after a few drinks, we just fit right in. The guys turned out to be cool, and they were not going to rob us and leave our bodies somewhere for a fisherman to find. When we left, the sun was coming up, and it was blinding. Come out of a crazy hip-hop club, and the sun is the last thing you want to see. Oh well, buttercup, suck it up. We made our way back to the hostel, and we slept the whole day.

When I mean we slept all day, it meant we woke up and it was 5:00 p.m. Luckily for us, they had an all-day breakfast place close to where we were staying. I had eggs, bacon, toast, and coffee at 5:00 p.m. for breakfast and dinner. It hit the spot, and now we needed a nap. Instead of a nap, we found a movie theater that was just down the street and playing all the top movies in the States. So instead of sleeping, we watched a movie, *Monster*, about a serial killer, and it was fantastic. Then we headed back, and the guys at the place asked if we wanted to go out again. We took an hour-long nap, took a shower, and did the same thing that night we had done before except at a different club.

So we had this groundhog thing going for about four days, and it was taking a toll on our bodies. The original deal was to stay here for about four nights and then head north. It would be the furthest south we would get, and it was time to start making our way to Brazil. We had to get productive and take care of a few bits of business. We had to get a yellow fever shot, which ended up taking two days to find the place and then get back to the same place the next day. We also wanted to see something else in the city besides clubs, our breakfast place, and the movie theater. It just meant not partying all night long and getting up earlier. So the sixth day we were there, we made our way to see the famous balcony where Evita was shot with Madonna singing the famous song. It wasn't much but something. We also wanted to get hold of US currency if we could. We had been told that in Venezuela, you could exchange US dollars for more than they were worth. It was a chance, and we would at least have more US currency on us.

We ended up staying here for seven nights, and on the eighth morning, it was time to leave. We had a blast but in a different way. We partied every night at a different club and saw the nightlife of this beautiful city. There was so much more to do here, but for us, it was a great time. We just needed to leave for our liver's sake.

Our goal was to travel north to the border of Argentina and Brazil. There we would get a chance to see a major attraction, the Iguaçu Falls. It would be a long haul to do it in one day, so we found a place to split the trip up a little. We could go to Iberia Provincial Reserve and maybe get a chance to see some wildlife. This worked for both of us, and it would take twelve hours to get there, and we could go at night, which would save us another night here. The plan was set, and we were on a bus late that afternoon.

After another long evening watching the world go by, we reached our next spot, and it was definitely different from the city. The Ibera Provincial Reserve is a protected area in northern Argentina that is a mix of swamps, bogs, stagnant lakes, and lagoons. It was a complete change from the city. We arrived at the bus stop, and it was easy to find a place to stay because there was only one. It was an older home with several small buildings on the property that housed travelers visiting the area. The place included a room and two meals a day, breakfast and dinner. It was a family-style place, which meant we all ate our meal together. There were about twelve of us staying there. We did have our own room, but it was a shared bathroom. Just being able to look around and see nothing but nature was a happy relief for me.

We got situated and walked around the property. At around 5:00 p.m., we had our first meal together, which was a lot of fun. Everyone introduced themselves. We all shared stories about traveling and got some good information from people that had been where we were going. The meal was great: meat, potatoes, veggies, bread, and pudding for dessert.

After our meal, the host of the place took a few of us on a sunset boat ride through the grassy marshes and swamps of the area. There was a lot of wildlife in this place, two types of alligators, caimans, a ton of birds, and the largest rodent in the word, the capybara, which can grow to 4 feet in length and weigh up to 150 lbs. This was one big-ass rat, and I wanted to see one. We were out for a few hours going up and down water channels. The first thing was a caiman about three feet long. These things look just like a baby alligator but are their own species. The guy grabbed one right out of the water, and we all held this creature that was cute but scary at the same time. We saw 4 alligators resting on a beach, and almost toward the end of our trip we finally saw a group of the Capybara. They had a cute face, big bellies, whiskers like a rat, and small little ears. We stayed out on the swamp land until dark and watched the sun set over the green shrubs that filled this large area. It was a good chance to get some fresh air and see some wildlife.

The next day, we wanted to walk into town about thirty minutes away. We left our house, and it was great to have nothing but trees, shrubs, a dirt road, and a gentle breeze on our walk. We reached this row of big trees on each side of the road. The trees created this tunnel effect and looked beautiful. As we got closer, we started to hear something in the trees. As we got closer, we started to see the branches moving. Once we were under the trees, we could see what was making all the noise, and it was a bunch of howler monkeys going crazy. They jumped from branch to branch and howled like nothing I had heard before. These were the first monkeys we have seen, and we just slowly walked along and tried not to piss them off. If you have ever seen a picture of a howler monkey, they have some serious teeth and claws that could make our life miserable. As we walked, they followed us from tree to tree and watched us like a hawk. There must have been at least fifty monkeys in this group of trees, and it was awesome to see these things in the wild. We made it to town safely and in one piece. Now the town consisted of six buildings, all single story and made out of wood, stone, and straw. There was a small store, and we went inside. The shelves were bare except for a few cans of food and a few drinks in the cooler. Luckily for us, they had some beer, which wasn't cold but would work for later. We spent about twenty minutes and had seen the entire town. So we turned around and walked the same dirt road, through the same set of monkeys.

That afternoon, the host of the place wanted to take a group of us on a nature walk. I was all in, and Ronnie was all out. She had seen enough of nature and told me to have a good time. We left the house and walked right out of sight in a matter of minutes. We had this twelve-foot wild straw grass around us in minutes and just kept walking down these paths. The grass would get shorter and we could see the water, then we walked along the banks of the channels until we would disappear in the long grass again. We saw more caiman and four large rats on this trip; we just didn't see any alligators. The reason I bring this one hike up is that I had a photo taken of me, and I've always said it could be a good book cover.

We stayed here for two nights and Ronnie would ask, "Did you get your wildlife fix for the time being?" and I smiled and said it was great. The third day, we left after breakfast for another long bus ride. It would take us about eighteen hours to get from where we were until we reached the falls and the border. We left on a Wednesday and would get there on Thursday. Up until now, I have never mentioned a specific day of the week. As far as we were concerned, they all just blended into one another. This time, it mattered.

This trip was a long one with a few stops but a lot of rough roads and nothing new to see. Our goal was to cross into Brazil on Saturday, make our way to Rio, stay for a day, then make our way north to Salvador and meet up with Ronnie's sister by Wednesday. Once again, the actual day of the week was now an issue. We had a goal.

We arrived in Puerto Iguaçu, which was the closest town to the falls. The weather was not the greatest; it was still raining and everything was soaked. We found a little family-owned hostel that was close to the bus stop and close to a few stores. The falls were about eleven miles away, and after we got settled, we jumped on the first available bus to the falls. It was early afternoon, so we had plenty of time to spend the day there, and with the weather, this was all we could do.

The Iguazu Falls were on the Iguazu River, which bordered both Argentina and Brazil and made up the largest waterfalls in the world. Most of the falls were on the Argentina side, so we were at the right spot to see them. These waterfalls were made up of 275 different drops, with the highest drop being 269 feet. Now I had seen Niagara Falls several times. Niagara Falls only has a drop of 165 feet, which is very impressive. Victoria Falls in Africa has a drop of 328 feet and is just one big falls with a single curtain of water pouring off it. Then there is Angel Falls in Venezuela that is considered the tallest with a drop of 2,648 feet. All these waterfalls were impressive, but we were here and this being the largest was something to see.

We paid our admission fee of a few dollars and started walking down a dirt path toward the top of the falls. As we got closer, we could hear the roar of the water before we could see it. Once we were standing on the bank of this river, we were immediately impressed. The river was really wide, and we could see Brazil from the banks of Argentina. The water was moving so fast, and we could see it disappear over the edge. The mist in the air was as far as we could see, and it was time to get closer. This falls had a walkway that you could walk out onto and be standing right over the water. We had the opportunity to walk out a good one hundred yards near the waterfalls. The walkway was made from steel mesh, so you could see the water right under your feet. We were maybe five feet off the water and completely surrounded by its force. It was the sound of the water rushing under us that really made the experience a little nerve-racking. I was trying to get over how this walkway was even constructed and how many people must have died doing it, though I later found out none. The sound of the falls below us, the rushing of water underneath us, and the glory of actually standing so damn close to it was an adrenaline rush like I had never had before. My heart was pounding just thinking if anything went wrong with this walkway, we were done.

We stayed on the top portion of the falls for about an hour, and then we started to make our way to the bottom. The rock around us was all wet from the rain and the spray, so we took our time. We got about halfway down, and we took a break to see it from another view. Just then, this guy walked by and told us about a high-speed boat that took you into the falls. We both looked at each other and agreed that would be fun. The only problem was the last boat ride was leaving in fifteen minutes. We picked up the pace and made it to the bottom with minutes to spare and got the last two seats on the last boat of the day. We were just two lucky people, I guess.

This was a high-speed boat with twin 225 cc Yamaha engines, and the front of the boat was all comfortable seating with a view forward for everyone to get a good look. The boat held about twenty-five people at a time and one captain. We left the dock, and we were going 40 mph in seconds. This was a high-speed boat heading right toward the bottom of the falls. It didn't take long at all to get close, and he started to slow down. We were at the bottom of "the Devil's Throat," which is where the river came together and formed the biggest falls. We inched closer, and we could now feel the mist from the falls. We looked up, and it was a sight to see, this amount of water flowing over this one spot with the force of one hundred elephants. We got closer, and we were soon all getting wet from the falls, and everyone was hooting and howling like a bunch of little schoolgirls. It was amazing to be under this falls and looking up at its wonder. The captain went in and out of the falls for a good half hour. We checked out as many as he could get to, and it was a lot of fun. In the beginning of the trip, we had a guy sell us on a video of the falls. He told us it would be our video and he would record us on this trip. It was $20, so why not? It would be a good souvenir for us in the future. Well, when we got back to the room, we played it, and it was an advertisement for the high-speed boat ride. We were not in the video at all. Oh well, we still got photos.

We made it back to our hostel, and the rain had stopped for a while, but everything was wet. Our new place was almost like a camp. Our room was inside, but everything else was outside with screened-in porches and a screened-in kitchen. So we found a store, bought food to prepare, and had a relaxing evening with a few drinks. We had to go the next day to get our visas to cross the border. This was one crossing we had to have our visa taken care of before we reached the border. The government building was five miles away, and this would be our main thing to do tomorrow, which was Friday. We got here Thursday and saw the falls, would get our documents Friday, and would leave Saturday.

Friday came, and we got up around 11:00 a.m. It was good to get some sleep and lounge around for an hour before we had to get going. We figured we could get the visas taken care of and then go and get lunch somewhere. We had slept in, and by the time we left, we were both getting hungry. We took a bus into the city and found the place we needed to go. It was around 1:00 p.m., and we had no idea how long this process would take and thought about getting lunch first and then getting the visas. I walked up to the door, and there was an old sign, very dirty and hard to read. It said the hours were from 9:00 a.m.–5:00 p.m. We made the choice to eat first and then take care of business. So we walked down the street and found a basic place with sandwiches and small stuff; it was perfect. We sat there enjoying a good sub and something to drink, and we were happy again. I looked at the time, and it was only 2:15 p.m. We walked back toward the government building, walked up the stairs, and I went to open the door. It was locked, and the light was off. Just then, I looked at the sign on the door, and this time, I looked at it closer and realized the sign said "Open 9:00 a.m.–2:00 p.m., not 9:00 a.m.–5:00 p.m. From where I first saw the sign, it looked like a 5 and not a 2. All I knew was this sucked.

So this is why I mentioned the days of the weeks. We were now stuck here until Monday morning. Our plans had just changed drastically, and we now had nothing to do but wait all weekend for this place to open. This pissed me off so much. Now we had to pay for three more nights here and then travel straight through without getting any time in Rio de Janeiro. This was a mistake that would cost us money and time, both things we hated to mess with.

Well, it was a very boring three days. Not only did it rain the whole weekend, but there was also just not a lot to do. We read, slept, made all our meals, and drank. There was a store close by, so we were at least able to get food and drinks. We did take this weekend to enjoy each other if you know what I mean. I tell you sex is the best thing to do to pass time.

Monday morning could not come soon enough, and we were standing by the door when they unlocked it. The process of getting our visas only took about fifteen minutes. There were more questions than usual, and we did have to pay a $100 visa fee. This was triple any other fees we had to pay up until now, and I asked why so much. The agent told us that the United States charges Brazilian travelers a lot of money as well, which was more than other countries. So if the United States did it to them, they were going to do it to us. It was fair, and we gave them $100 each, showed them our yellow fever shot certification, and were ready to go. This time, instead of a stamp, we got a piece of paper that took up one whole page of our passports. It looked cool, and that was all that mattered.

After getting our visas, we were on the next bus out of here. We had a long way to go, and we had a short time to do it. It was Monday, and we needed to be in Salvador by Wednesday. It wasn't the end of the world if we were a day late, but Ronnie wanted to see her sister and spend as much time with them as possible. They were going to travel with us for about three weeks. The bus arrived, and we were ready to go. We would be covering a lot of ground in the next few days.

24
CHAPTER

Brazil

We crossed the border without any problems; we had our visas, finally. Now all we had to do was sit back and enjoy a very long ride. It was going to take us twenty-four hours to get from the Iguazu Falls border to Rio de Janeiro. We would be stopping along the way, but we had stocked up on food and drinks for the ride.

The ride was long yet enjoyable. When you are on a bus for this amount of time, you just take time for yourself. It does get boring, so I'm like a little kid. I need to have several things to do and just go from one thing to the next: read, sleep, watch movies, bathroom, eat, drink whatever it takes. Ronnie worked on her jewelry, and this kept her occupied for a good portion of the trip. She now had a carrying case for all her stuff. She had bought more materials and tools in Argentina, so she was all set. The only thing was this was another bag to carry, and guess who carried it *a lot*?

Well, twenty-four hours went by, and we are now in the city of Rio de Janeiro. It felt and smelled like a beach city. We got off the bus and took in the warm air and the smell of the ocean. Now we had a day to get to Salvador, so we checked on the bus schedule and times. "Oh my, are you kidding?" is what I said to the agent. She told us that there was a bus leaving for Salvador in one hour, and it would take thirty hours to get there. Holy shit, we had just gotten off a twenty-four-hour trip, and now we had to do a thirty-hour trip.

So there was not really much to say about the next thirty hours except it was a long trip. When we would stop, all I would do is walk around as much as I could just to get the blood flowing. After this trip, both of us were on the delirious side a little. Our sleep schedule was all screwed up. We had just eaten when we were hungry and drank during the trip, but that did require a lot of trips to the bathroom, so we moderated that as well. We finally made it, and it was around 8:00 p.m., so it was dark when we arrived. It was just good to be on solid ground, and we would see everything tomorrow. We looked at each other and said, "We made it."

Tanya had given Ronnie the address, so we actually for the first time on this trip had a place to go to that was all taken care of. It was a half-mile walk, and our legs were stiff at this point, so it was hard to get going, but it felt great to actually walk.

We arrived, and Tanya met us at the door. Tanya was about 5'3", 125 lbs., with a thin build, short dark hair, a dark complexion, and she had a big, beautiful smile. Dillon came over as well, and he was 6'4" with brown hair to his shoulders; he was well built and a good-looking guy. These two had been together for five years and married for three and were getting ready to have kids. This was a good getaway for them as well after losing Danny. We got situated. They showed us our room, had a little small talk, and someone mentioned drinks. It had been a long few days, and a cold beer or three would do us good.

So Dillon and I spoke up and said we would go for a walk and find a liquor store and get drinks. The girls agreed, and we were out the door in a flash. The door had not even closed behind us when Dillon asked if I smoked, which he knew I did because Ronnie had told him. So we left the building, and we had a plan. Dillon had gotten there a while ago and had scoped out the area and found a park that had a lot of Rasta-looking guys hanging out. So our plan was to quick go to this park, ask around, and then get drinks. The park was close and kind of on the way, so when we got there, it was dark except for a few streetlights, and we saw two older black Rasta guys hanging out. We walked up to them, and Dillon asked in Spanish if they had any smoke. They looked at us both, started laughing, and said, "Ya man, we got your smoke," in English. They asked how much, and we just needed a little, so we gave them $20, and they gave us a very nice bag, which would last us a long time.

Just as the deal was going down, we turned around, and the girls were both staring at us with a look of "Are you kidding me?"

I put the bag in my pocket, and the two of us walked over to the girls and said, "What?"

They weren't mad, just worried we would end up in jail or something. They told us, "You don't know how things work around here, and the first day, you try this."

All I said was, "Don't worry. I know what I'm doing." This is the same thing people who are in jail say right before they get arrested. Oh well, we had what we wanted, and it was a done deal.

Now it was the four of us who went to get drinks, and we laughed about our little thing right away. The girls were like, "You two just met and are already in trouble together." Dillon and I bonded that night, and I can say right now that Tanya and Dillon are good people and our time together was enjoyable.

We got back to our rooms, had a few drinks, and started talking about things we could do over the next three weeks. There was a lot to see and a lot to do. We told them about some of our adventures, and it seemed so long ago that we had visited Machu Picchu, which was one of our very first attractions. Time was flying by in one way, but it still seemed like we had a lot of time ahead of us. I'm not sure if I mentioned this or not, but we had to be in Cancun, Mexico, by the first part of August. My buddy Graydon was getting married and I was in the wedding, so we had a time frame, but it was only the first of May right now.

Salvador was known for its Portuguese colonial architecture, African/Brazil culture, and a tropical coastline. The city was large like most cities, but it did have a few specific neighborhoods that we had read about. That first day was all about checking out the sights and getting some exercise. The Pelourinho neighborhood was one of our first places to explore. It had cobbled streets, which are always a cool thing to see, and colorful buildings, a beautiful Spanish church, shops, and bars. The first drink we all had was a famous Brazilian drink called a Caipirinha. It was a very refreshing and a very strong drink made with fresh lime juice, sugar, and cachaca. Now cachaca is the main ingredient just like tequila is to a margarita. It is local liquor that by itself doesn't really taste that great. It has a funky grassy flavor, but mixed with lime juice and sugar, it is delicious. This was our main drink for most of the time. It had a kick to it just like tequila, so we had to be careful.

We were walking somewhere and passed a small park. There were about twenty guys and girls all practicing a form of martial arts and dance. It was called capoeira, which is a form of defense and dance that dates back to the fifteenth century. Capoeira is an element of dance with acrobatics and music. They will dance around doing kicks and moves, place a hand on the ground, and kick up into the air. They are constantly moving to the music, taking turns to enter the circle to practice their moves. It is said that the slaves used this to stay in shape and for defense against hash owners. There is a huge deal to martial arts that can be seen right away, but back then, the slave owners saw it as only a dance and were amused by the techniques. To think that the slaves were practicing to kick their asses right in front of them.

I'm not sure how many different places we stopped for Caipirinha, but we could drink right on the street, the way it should be, and we were feeling great. We did stop and eat and tried a lot of the local dishes, which were all really good. The one thing we did all enjoy was the fresh fruit.

We had made plans for the following day to head out to an island off the coast for Salvador. It would be a thirty-minute ferry ride, and we would stay on a beach for a few days and enjoy the ocean. That night, we got our backs ready and got a good night's sleep because we were getting up early to catch the first ferry.

The sun was up, and the weather was perfect, 75 degrees and a nice breeze. The ferry ride was nice just looking back at the city and the blue ocean all around us. We were excited to play in the water, relax on the beach, and probably have a few drinks. The island was in the distance, and all we could see was white sandy beach.

We got to the dock and started walking toward the main gate. We all had our big backpacks and day packs hanging in the front. I was also carrying Ronnie's jewelry box. We walked up and saw a taxi sign, and about that time, this guy asked us if we wanted a taxi. We agreed it would be nice to get dropped off at our hostel, so the guy motioned for a taxi. At this point, I hadn't even seen a car, so it might take a while. Just then, this short, stocky Brazilian guy came over to us pushing a wheelbarrow. He said, "Your taxi is here."

What the fuck is this? Is he going to push each of us to our hostel? I was confused. We found out then that there were no motorized vehicles on this side of the island, no cars at all. The plan was he would put all our bags in the wheelbarrow and push them to our hostel. So he loaded them all up and tied them down with a rope. The damn wheelbarrow was now as tall as he was. He asked where we were staying, and we told him the second beach. There was the first beach that was good for surfing, and the second beach had the bars and hostels. The son of a gun pushed that wheelbarrow across two beaches and up a small hill. He did stop a few times, and by the time we got to our place, he was dripping in sweat. We gave him $20 for his effort. The cost was only $5, but he had worked his ass off. I actually felt bad, but this was how they made money.

Our rooms were right on the beach, an open-air atmosphere. We had a small balcony, and Tanya and Dillon were right below us. We got situated and made our way out to the beach. We dropped our stuff, and the four of us just walked right into the ocean, and it felt wonderful. It was not cold at all. There was great visibility and nothing but sand under our feet. We talked right then and there and decided to stay here for two nights and three days. We would take the last ferry out on the third day, which would give us plenty of time.

That day, we had a great meal at an outside restaurant, and we all tried something different and shared with each other. We had beers as we sat there talking and laughing for a few hours. We spent time going from the beach back to our rooms and back to the bars. By the time the sun was setting, we were all very happy. The plan was to go back to our rooms, take showers, and get ready to check out the nightlife on this island. They say that this island is known for "the island where the nightlife never ends."

We got ready, and it was around 10:00 p.m. by now. Both Dillon and I had had a chance or two to sneak off and have a little smokey smokey. The girls knew what we were doing, but we thought we were so clever, ha ha. We walked out of the hostel and down the beach. We stopped for a drink to walk with, and we had no real plans, just see what is open and what place is the best. We passed a few clubs/bars, and there were a few people there, nothing crazy, so we might have a drink and go to the next place. Well, it took us about an hour or so just walking along the beach when we heard music coming from a building at the end of the beach. It was on a hill, and as we got closer, we could hear the music and see a few lights. This was the place to be.

It was amazing, completely opened on the sides so the fresh air was blowing in. The DJ was playing Brazilian dance/trance music, and the scenery was extremely nice. The girls and guys were dancing salsa style, and the shaking of the hips was fun to watch. I could help myself, and I was not alone. We got drinks, found a table, and got out on that dance floor to shake our stuff. The lights were flashing around us, the music was great, the dance floor was packed with at least one hundred people, and the drinks were flowing. We stayed there until the early morning; it was like 5:00 a.m. when we left. By this point, we were all feeling pretty good and ready for bed.

Now this next part is tough to write about because it is not who I am, but it happened, and I need to tell you. We get back and I'm beat and ready for bed. It has been a long day and we want to have another fun day tomorrow. So I got naked and got in bed; my head hit the pillow, and I could have been asleep in seconds. Just then, she thought it would be funny to flick my nuts. She did, and I sat up like someone had just dumped cold water on me. She stood there with a drunken grin on her face, and I told her, "Don't ever do that again." I lay back down just trying to ignore her and she did it again. Now, it hurts when a man's nuts get flicked, I don't care who you are. I yelled at her this time and told her to go to bed and leave me alone. I lay back down and she did it a third time. I sat up, and she had this stupid grin on her face, and I grabbed her by the shoulders, and without any thought to it, I slapped her right across the face. Her stupid drunken grin went away real quickly. She started crying immediately and fell to the floor, not from the slap but just to make it worse. "I told you not to do that again, and you did it three times," is all I said. She stood up and told me she was leaving. She grabbed her backpack and packed all her stuff up in about two minutes and told me she was calling the cops. She turned around and walked out of the door.

I stood there and just said to myself, "What the fuck just happened?" We had such a great day and now I was going to get arrested in Brazil at six in the morning for slapping Ronnie. I put some clothes on and decided to smoke a joint that I had. I went out onto the balcony and put my feet up. I lit the joint and told myself if I ended up going to jail, then I was going to go high. I sat there and waited for someone to knock at the door. Thirty minutes went by, and the sun was now coming up, and I just sat there waiting for someone to knock at the door. An hour went by and I was so beat, so I lay down and guess I fell asleep. No one knocked at the door until later that morning. I woke up startled, and it was Ronnie, and the first thing she said was "sorry." She came in, and we had a good talk about what had happened and we were both wrong. We kissed and made up, and that was the last time that has ever happened in my life.

The next afternoon, we all met up on the beach, and they knew what had happened because Ronnie had gone down to their room. No one said anything; it was water under the bridge, and we continued our day like nothing had happened. We were all a little hungover, though, so it was more about food and swimming in the ocean for most of that day.

The last day was all about the beach and ocean. We hung out as long as we could, and our tans were looking pretty good by now. We had a late lunch and took the ferry back to Salvador before it got dark out. We were back in Salvador and decided to stay at a different place that was cheaper and closer to the bus terminal. We called it an early evening because we had an early bus ride the next day.

We left our hostel, which was a place we would return to several times, and walked to the bus terminal. It was going to be a six-hour ride from Salvador to a small town in the jungle called Lençóis. It was also going to be our first road trip together. Ronnie and I had spent a lot of time on a bus getting from place to place; now we had other people to enjoy the experience with.

Lençóis was a former diamond mining town located in the mountains surrounded by forest. This place had waterfalls, caves, and a lot of hiking opportunities. The town was very small with cobblestone streets and nineteenth-century buildings. We are in the jungle again, and it was a big change from just a few days ago when we were sitting on a white sandy beach.

We stayed here for two nights and had a lot of fun. I'm just going to sum these few days up and not give you play by play. Just about anything we could do here, we did it. There were caves to explore that we did as an excursion. The caves had the huge stalagmites and stalactites hanging from the ceiling and sticking up from the ground. There were a few waterfalls and ponds underground that reflected the caves like a mirror. We found several hikes that had waterfalls where we spent a few hours swimming around and jumping off rocks. The town was cool to just see, all the old buildings and cobbled roads. They had a few outdoor cafes that we ate at and just really enjoyed a few days of nature.

On our third morning, it was time to say goodbye to the jungle for now and head back to Salvador. We stayed at the same hostel as the last time. Our next spot on the map was going north to another beach area. It was only a few hours away, and we would be able to catch a bus first thing in the morning. So we lay low that night and actually didn't go out at all. Instead, we brought food and drinks back to our rooms and had a quiet night inside.

The next morning, we were up early and at the bus station to catch the first bus going north. Our next spot was a beach town called Praia de Forte. This was a long beach with a small village and was known for its white sand beaches and was a good surf spot. We all wanted to get in the water and do some surfing. Tanya didn't want to surf, but the other three of us wanted to. We got to the small town and found a clean, cheap place that was really close to the ocean. It was a very open-air place with a common area that faced the beach. It was a very cool place to stay for a few nights.

They rented surfboards all over the place, so that was easy. We dropped off our gear and headed for the beach. The three of us got on board and headed down the beach to a good surf spot, which we enjoyed for hours.

     After surfing, we sat on the beach, and it was great to have people wait on us for anything we needed. If we wanted a beer, all we had to do was raise our hand, and they would bring another. The beers were $1 a piece, so we had a few. The one cool thing was this guy selling fried cheese. He came over to us, and he had a metal circular pan that had holes around the outside. It was attached to a small rope that he held in his hand. He placed about five cheese sticks into the pan and closed it. Then he started to twirl the pan around his head for about a minute or so. He stopped spinning it and opened the pan, and the cheese was now a nice crispy cheese stick. It was so cool, and he showed us how it worked. There were charcoal briskets in the center, and when he swirled it around, it caused the charcoal to get hot and cook the cheese. It was just something different, and the cheese was delicious.

     The third day there, we stayed until the last bus was leaving and enjoyed the small-town atmosphere. By the third day, we knew where everything was, and just when we got comfortable, it was time to go. This is the story of a traveler.

     We left the beach and we were back in Salvador once again. We stayed at the same place, and we did go out that night to try more different styles of Caipirinha at our favorite bar; the wooded one is what we called it. They got to actually know us a little because it was our third time there. We had fun; we didn't get crazy but enjoyed another evening in the city.

     Our next journey, which was leaving tomorrow morning, was to head back to Rio de Janeiro and spend the last week of Tanya and Dillon's trip there. This was a place we were all excited to see, and we knew there was a lot to do, so we gave ourselves plenty of time. The whole thing about this was we would have another thirty-hour trip to get there and a thirty-hour trip to get back. This would be two days plus just traveling, and there was no other way but to fly, and the tickets were not cheap, so we chose the bus and did what we had to do.

The next morning, we were up, had something to eat, and picked up a few supplies for the trip, and just before noon, we boarded the bus for another fun-filled trip. At least we had each other, and we made the most of it. It did give those guys a chance to see what we went through to get here, and of course, the stops were always entertaining. We did the usual: read, watched movies, and slept.

We arrived at the terminal for Rio de Janeiro around midafternoon, and this gave us time to find a place to stay before it got dark. We found a place according to our guidebook that was close to the beach and cheap. It was a dorm-style hostel, and the four of us had our own room. The room held eight people, but we were lucky we had the place to ourselves the entire time. We booked the room for seven nights, which should give us time to see and do everything we wanted. This was one of the main cities on our list.

Rio de Janeiro is a huge seaside city in Brazil. It is the second most populated city in Brazil and known for so many different things. The main attractions are two famed beaches, Copacabana and Panama. It is the home to one of the most spectacular monuments, the Christ the Redeemer. It has world-known slums called Favelas, and this is the heart and soul of Carnival, which is one of the biggest parties in the world. All I knew was we were here, and there was so much for us to do. A day-by-day playback would just be too much. Instead, it is just going to be all our highlights and adventures we had during this week.

Once we had a place to stay, it was all about getting to the famous beaches first and foremost. So we walked a short distance, and we were now standing on Copacabana beach. It was spectacular, and the views from the beach of the city were breathtaking. Of course, we could see the famous statue Christ the Redeemer from the distance and the skyline of the city. We spent almost every day at some point on the beach. We would walk from Copacabana to Panama beach and just marvel at the scenery, the beach itself, the ocean water splashing against the shore, and the people wandering around. The beaches were out of this world.

Like I said, we spent a portion of every day on one of these beaches. It might be for a morning walk or an evening sunset. We surfed a few times, had days where we nursed a hangover for a few hours, or it was time just to watch everyone walk around. The scenery, if you catch my drift, was marvelous. The Brazilian bikini has its own name for many reasons. It was nothing to be in store or business of some sort and not see at least a handful of girls walking around in their tiny bikinis. Thank God for sunglasses, is all I have to say. The first day, we sat and drank on the beach the entire day. They would bring drinks right to us and we had many flavors of Caipirinha. I was sitting on the beach, and this guy came up to me and said, "Can I practice my art by giving you a henna tattoo." I didn't have a single tattoo, and maybe he just thought I needed one. So I said sure, and he proceeded to tattoo me with a scorpion, which is my sign. It was in black ink and looked really good. I asked him why a scorpion, and he said, "It is your sign, right?" Wow, that was so bizarre that I gave him a few bucks for doing this. It made my day, and I loved that tattoo.

On our third day, we did a tour of the Favelas, which was the famous slum called "Shanty Town." We did a three-hour walking tour that took us into the area and gave us a real view of what it was like living in one of the poorest places in the world. It was a type of low-income housing in the city. It is interesting to know that these shanty homes were first started back in the nineteenth century by soldiers that had no place to live after the Canudos war. It has since grown to a city within a city. The name of the one in Rio is called Rocinha, which is on a hillside in the city. It is visible from just about any high structure we went to and very easy to pick out. The Rocinha has little help from the government and is more of a self-governing place.

We walked around on the very narrow streets and witnessed life for these people in person. The average home is no more than a 10' × 10' structure made out of recycled wood, tin, blocks, and tarps. They sometimes will have two to three generations of families living in one building. It is a sea of makeshift structures that would be used to maybe keep farm animals here in the United States. Most of the people we saw looked dirty and malnourished. It is always a thump in the heart when you see babies being raised in these kinds of conditions. It just breaks your heart to see these poor kids being raised in a place that they may never leave.

Unfortunately for these people, they rely on illegal ways of life just to survive. Drugs, theft, prostitution, and other forms of violence are common here and just simply a way of life. We were told the first night we checked into our hostel that Rio can be a dangerous place. Our hostel staff told us not to wear any jewelry at all, stay in a group, and be careful of groups of kids. The kids ages eight to fourteen were known to gang-rob people. If you had a ten-year-old come up to you and say "Give me your wallet," you would just laugh and tell him to go away. Now picture about eight of them, all with knives or guns doing the same thing, and it would be a different story. We were lucky the entire time here, but we always had eyes in the back of our heads.

Our nightlife was always fun, and we tried to do something different every night. After we ate dinner, it would be a walk on the beach, or sitting in a park and watching the world go round, and many nights, we found a club. The clubs in this city were crazy fun. There was loud music, people dancing on tables, bottles of booze being passed around, and everyone was happy. Maybe it was the booze and drugs that everyone was taking, or it could be that Brazilians are just happy people. I think it is the latter of the two because every day, we saw the same thing, and that was a lot of smiles and laughter.

One night, Tanya and Dillon took us out for dinner, and we went to a Brazilian churrasco, which I had never been to. This was a restaurant that had a huge salad bar with everything you could imagine to eat. After you sat down and got your salad, the servers walked around with large skewers of meat. There were some fifteen different cuts of meat that they offered. There was pork, chicken, sausages, beef, and lamb. You just sat there and ate meat that was the best of the best. They would cut you off a piece and then take it back to the kitchen to continue to cook it. I never in one sitting tried so many different cuts of meat. We walked out of there so stuffed that it was the one night no one wanted to drink, and we all went to bed early that night.

It was our sixth night there, and we had gotten word that there was a soccer match that night. It was on the other side of the city, and it was being played in one of the largest stadiums in the world. It was known for hosting the World Cup and Summer Olympics in 2016. This stadium has held 150,000 people on 26 different occasions. It is also the stadium where Pele played his last game. This was enough for us, and it would be fun to check it out. We had seen a match in Bolivia that was unreal, and this one would be the first for Tanya and Dillon.

It was a full-day event, getting transportation to the other side of the city, scoring tickets from a scalper, getting food and drink before the match, and doing a little tailgating on the streets. This was a match between two local clubs, and it was just an average meeting. It wasn't between two countries like the last one. We could buy drinks inside so we didn't have to put the whole booze in a bag again.

The stadium was huge on the inside, the biggest I had ever seen, and it was about 50 percent capacity. We had no idea who the two teams were, so we just cheered on every goal. This way we would not get our asses kicked after the match. It was a great day exploring another portion of the city and being inside a stadium that was once home to the best soccer player to ever play, Pele.

I have saved the best for last, and guess what that might be? You are correct if you said, "Christ the Redeemer." This was a must, and we did this the second day of our trip. This is like the Statue of Liberty to New York City or the Colosseum in Rome. If you are here and don't see this, then you will have missed out on the iconic structure that towers over the city.

Christ the Redeemer is a colossal statue of Jesus Christ that was once the summit of Mount Corcovado. The statue was completed in 1931 and stands ninety-eight feet and has an arm span of ninety-two feet. The statue sits on a base that is twenty-six feet tall, and it is made out of reinforced concrete. The statue is the largest form of art deco style in the world. It is so impressive that words can describe it.

We took a bus up the mountain to where the tourist site is. It was on top of a mountain, so the views of the city were breathtaking. We spent about two hours just walking around and taking photos of every angle we could get. Of course, we all had our photos taken in front with our arms stretched out just like Jesus was doing. The statue was a white color and very well cared for. The entire area around the statue was well kept and very clean. This was Brazil's most famous structure, and they worshipped and cared for it like every single Brazilian owned it. To stand at the base and look up at the massive structure and to see the design in making this was truly a high point in my life. I've been fortunate to see many things that I have already written about in this book. Among all the things I saw in Europe and Japan, this one is in the top three of my all-time list. Still to this day, the Roman Colosseum is the number one thing for me that I have seen.

Like I said, there was so much we did daily here that I will always remember. Watching people play soccer on the beach, our surfing day on Ipanema beach, the many drinks we had on and off the beach, the great people that helped us out, and the fact that I got to see this place with three other great people. I would love to come back here again. I would fly right into Rio de Janeiro, and I would do all the same things again. This was a highlight for all of us, and it was unfortunately time to leave.

On our eighth afternoon, still hungover from our last night out, we boarded the bus back to Salvador. It was going to be another thirty-hour trip back to Salvador, and Tanya and Dillon would be leaving the next day. We had memories and stories to talk about the whole way back; that is when we weren't sleeping or watching a movie. The trip was long, but I just keep telling myself, *You, Stephen Mundy, can now say you visited Rio de Janeiro and did as many things you can do in one week.*

That night, we did have to take time and get all packed up again. We were heading north, and they were heading home. We had made the plan to go to another beach town called Receif, which would get us closer to our destination, which was the Amazon River. That night, we bought a bottle of champagne and had a last salute to everything we had done. It was sad to see them leave. We had a great time traveling with them, but Ronnie and I still had many things to see.

CHAPTER 25

The next day, they left from the bus station on their way to the airport, and Ronnie and I took a bus to Receif. It would take us about nine hours to get to our next spot, which was fine with us. It was weird for the first day not having others with us, but we soon readjusted to it just being the two of us.

Receif is best known for being the first slave port in the Americans. It dates back as far as the fifteenth century. It is now a city known for its large-scale production of sugarcane. We were going there to surf a little and enjoy a few days with not a lot to do or see. About halfway there, it started to rain and never really quit for three days. With this said, we didn't do much at all. We found a cute hostel that had the basics, and we had our own shower. The best thing was the hammocks that were out front of each room. Two big red hammocks were for us to enjoy, and man, did we ever. So the rain started before we even got there, it was raining when we checked in, and it rained for the next two days. So we didn't even go to the beach or walk around the town to see the sights. We found a store close by and got everything we needed to cook ourselves. We stayed at our hostel and ate and drank for two days. The hammocks were our second home, and we spent hours reading and taking naps during our stay. We did have a lot of time for the two of us to just be alone, so we spent many hours just lying in bed naked.

Our next spot on this glorious trip was another beach town of Natal, which is located on the northern tip of Brazil. We planned on doing some surfing and enjoying a few days of the beach before we entered the jungle. This place was another one of those secret gems that offered more than we anticipated. It was a quick five-hour bus ride to get there, and it had finally quit raining.

We got to Natal and scored a beautiful hostel located right across from the ocean. It was another open-air establishment and had nice private rooms, a kitchen, and a pool. We had spent a lot of time on the ocean and sitting on the sandy beach, which was incredible, but here we had a pool. So the first day we got there, which was midafternoon, we grabbed something to drink and spent a good portion of that day enjoying a freshwater pool. We could sit at the pool and look out over the ocean, which is about as good as it gets. The cost for this place was cheap, $15 a night.

The next day, we were enjoying a nice relaxing walk around town, just checking out this cool little beach town, and a guy approached us about an excursion. Natal is known for sand dunes, and he offered us a full-day sand dune buggy ride. The cost was about $20 each, and he would pick us up at our hostel, tour the sand dunes, stop for lunch, and offer a few other things if we wanted. It sounded like a great way to spend a day, and we agreed and got everything set up.

The next day around 10:00 a.m., he picked us up in a dune buggy. It was a blue convertible. It had roll bars, sat four plus a driver, and looked like fun. We got in, and we had to pick up another couple. We were first, so we got the front seats and they had the back seats. There was no bad seating in this thing at all, and the other couple was from England and were pretty cool people.

We set out for the dunes, which took about fifteen minutes to actually get there, and it was on. He left whatever road we were on and started to go up and over all the dunes. There were times that we could not tell what was on the other side, but he went balls to the walls, and we flew over one sand dune after the next. It was scary yet so exciting. Some of the dunes were taller than others, and the tall ones always gave for the biggest drop on the other side. We laughed and hung on tightly for a good hour or so while he navigated the adventure.

After about an hour or so, he told us that he could take us on a little bit more "extreme ride" if we wanted. We were all about it, but the other couple chose to sit this portion out. We dropped them off at a location, and for the next thirty minutes, he turned the level of adventure up a few notches, and it was extreme. When you have all four wheels off the ground and hit the back side of a dune and practically fall out of the buggy, you know it is extreme. This guy had done this before, so we trusted him, but I can't say that I wasn't worried a few times. To launch off a sand dune at 40 mph, not knowing what is on the other side, come crashing down, and get bounced around to the point, you really had to hold on; it just made for a better trip. We did this stuff for about thirty minutes and then made our way back to pick up the other two. They asked how it was, and Ronnie and I just looked at each other and laughed and said it was *sweet*.

It was now time for lunch, and he told us there was this little café, which was out in the middle of nowhere near a freshwater lagoon. We just had to cross this river, and the lagoon was on the other side. We could see the river in the distance, and as we approached it, we could see a raft with a guy standing on it. The driver of our buggy approached the river, and he was not slowing down very much. This was a scary moment because he hit that raft going a lot faster than we expected, and as soon as the buggy was on the raft, he hit the brakes and we were launched from the shore. This was not the first time he had done this, and he knew what to do. For us, we thought we were going to go right off the raft and end up in the water.

We traveled for about ten minutes, and up and over this huge sand dune was this beautiful little fresh water lagoon. It had a small restaurant, and the coolest thing about it was that the tables were out into the water. We walked out into the lagoon, found a table, and sat down with water up to our knees. We spent about an hour here, enjoyed a meal with a few beers, and I fed the tiny fish that were circling our table. The scene was very impressive. It was like an oasis in the middle of the desert. We had sand dunes all around us, a freshwater lagoon, and a cold beer. This was what made for a day that you really didn't know what to expect.

After lunch, we loaded back up and made our way further up the river. We stopped at a location, and here we had the opportunity to zip-line from the mountain down to the river. The zip line was a little on the sketchy side, and it would not have passed regulations in the States, but for here it worked, and we did the zip line about five times each. You sit on a board that is attached to a line, push off with your feet, and fall about forty feet into the middle of the river. You swim back, and they have another swing that you sit in, and it brings you back up the mountain. It was a little scary the first time but fun enough to do it multiple times.

Afterward, we headed out further into the dunes. We came up over this giant sand dune, and we could see what looked like a little adventure park. We could see camels, a big hill, and a little snack shack. So it wasn't really a park at all, just a little place to do a few fun things. We could have paid to sit on a camel, but that seemed a little boring. We did, however, find out what the hill was all about and chose to do that ride. It was a big rubber ball that we climbed into, got strapped to the inside walls, and were pushed down this hill. We went head over heels, we airborne several times, and then smashed into this fence at the end. It was one of those once-in-a-lifetime forty-five-second rides. We laughed the whole way down, and I crawled out of this thing laughing as hard as I could.

It was one of those days that you just didn't know what to expect, trusted the people around you, and had a great day. We got back to our hostel around five, gave the guy a nice tip, and thanked him so much for a fun day. He told us to tell everyone we knew and pass the good word on. We did tell a few people that we had met after this place about Natal and that it was a must.

Our next spot on the map we were headed toward was going to be a long trip, so we soaked up the pool and beach as much as we could. We were headed to Belem, which was the start of the Amazon River, thirty-nine hours away.

We knew it was going to be our longest bus ride ever, but we would be stopping along the way, and we had time. We left from Natal midafternoon, which gave us a few more hours for the pool, and headed north to the promised land. This was my big thing for the entire trip. I had talked about it from the beginning, but spending any time we could in the Amazon was a must for me.

The bus ride was brutal. It was long, and there were not a lot of different things to see. It was just kind of the same thing for a long time. This was our first and last experience of watching it get dark twice. When you're on a bus and you see the sunset twice, you know it is a long-ass trip.

We made it to Belem, which was the beginning of the Amazon River, late in the morning. This was good because we had a lot to do and figure out a few things. First was finding a place for the night, and we wanted cheap and close to the harbor. Well, you get what you wish for, and it was cheap and a little on the scary side. This place, I'm pretty sure, you could rent for an hour if you wanted. Anyway, we found a spot, and now we were making plans for getting up the river. We talked with a guide, and they recommended going to the harbor and talking with captains that were going upriver.

26
CHAPTER

The Amazon

So we walked to the harbor, and really not having a clue what to do, we started looking for boats—not just any boat but one that was big enough to take passengers. We approached a few and eventually found one. It was a rough-looking vessel, about seventy-five feet long, thirty feet wide, three levels, and had not been painted since it was made fifty years ago. The captain was out front, and we asked him how this works. He told us in broken English that we would get a hammock, hang it up on the second level, and that was where we would sleep. We would have three meals a day where we all ate together. There were bathrooms and showers on the boat. Showers are only open for three hours in the morning and three hours at night. We will stop at a few ports along the way, but we could not get off; it was for cargo only. We will be going upriver, so we would at times be very close to the shore for animal sightings and would pass several Amazon villages. The cost for seven nights and eight days was $50 each. This included everything except for drinks that could be purchased on board. We looked at each other, and both said yes at the same time. We handed the captain a $100 bill, and he told us to get a hammock tonight, so we could get a good spot.

We left and went on a mission to buy a cool hammock. They sold them everywhere, so it was easy to find one. We both bought good-quality hammocks that were comfortable to sleep in. They were a lot like the ones we had in Receif, which you could lay in and wrap the entire thing around you. With our hammocks in hand, we headed back to the boat to claim our spot. At this time, there was not another hammock on the boat. We chose the area behind the bulkhead where the helm was located. This boat did have a few state rooms to rent, but they were twice as much, and we wanted to do the hammock thing anyways. So we tied up our hammocks where we were protected from the wind and had a great view. We left them for the night, and the captain assured us they would be safe. He told us the boat would leave tomorrow morning around 11:00 a.m., and we could get on board around 10:00 a.m. It was a done deal, and the next seven to eight days were all taken care of.

We stayed close to our hostel, walked around a little, and picked up things to eat and drink for the next week. We bought a few bottles of booze, snacks, and more bug repellant. We were told to keep bug spray on at all times to avoid getting malaria from the mosquitoes.

So the next day, we were up and made our way with all our gear to the boat. When we got there, we were amazed at how many hammocks now hung on the boat. There had to be at least 125 hammocks hung all over the second deck. The place we had scored now had another five hammocks in just our little area; it was insane. We got on the boat, and we could see a few other travelers, but mostly it was locals. The boat held about 150 people including the staff, and it was about 75 percent local to 25 percent tourists. It just seemed fun right from the beginning. We placed our stuff in our hammocks, tied bags to one another, and tried to keep anything valuable out of sight. It was one of those times when we would just have to trust our neighbors, and I will tell you right now, we lost nothing and never once heard of anyone getting robbed. This made for a great trip.

When 11:00 a.m. came, we all went up to the top level and waved goodbye to everyone below. There was nobody we knew at all; it just was the thing to do. People did the same thing on big cruise lines, and this was just a much smaller and rustic version. We left the dock, the captain steered us out of the harbor, and we were now officially on the Amazon River.

TAKE A DECADE

The Amazon River is over four thousand feet long and had a width ranging from one hundred miles to two miles. It is close to being the longest freshwater river in the world, with the Nile in Africa being right there. It depends on what you read, but some say the Amazon is the longest and others say the Nile. Both rivers are longer than the entire United States. Where we were in Belem, it was extremely wide, and it was about thirty miles upriver from the Atlantic Ocean. The water was brown, and the props turned up the water to make it even a little darker.

We all were up on the top deck, and this was the meet-and-greet portion of the trip. We would all be together for the next week, and we met some cool people. Now they had turned the music on as well, and it was about as loud as it gets. It was almost too loud, but we all were able to talk. We met three guys from the States, four people from England, three local girls, and a bunch of other people. Most of the locals just hung out around the hammocks, and all the people that this was their first time we were on top of the boat, and the party had just begun.

For the next few hours, we had left the city, and it was just jungle all around us. The river was very calm; you could hardly feel like you were on a boat at all. The whole group of us started drinking and getting to know each other. Ronnie and I were two that had been traveling the longest and had the longest trip planned, so we got to share a lot of stories. The guys from the States were very cool, and we got to know them really well. The two hot little Brazilian girls were very nice to look at. The one came up on the deck after we left, laid out a towel, and lay there on her stomach with a thong bikini on, and she had the nicest-looking ass I had ever seen. Ronnie caught me looking about twelve times, but what could she say? The girl was hot.

That night was a blast from the time we left until the time we went to bed. Our first meal came around 4 p.m. and it was cool. They lowered these tables from the ceiling of the second level and we all sat down at these large tables. They had two different seating times and we had the first, which was good because we were hungry. They only had so much room to deal with that they had to break up the meals. We sat at a table with fifteen other people; most of them were locals just going back home, visiting family, or taking care of business. The dishes were all served in a family-style setting. Big bowls of food were passed, and you could have whatever you wanted. The first night was chicken, rice, salad, bread, and fresh tea. It was basic but tasted really good. We all sat and ate, and then it was back up to the top level to see more of the sights.

That night, we danced, drank, and watched the sky full of stars shine down on us. It was a remarkable moment for me that first night. Here I was on a boat, going up the Amazon River; the jungle was close enough to watch it go by, and the sky was filled with bright stars. Just a great night.

It was about 2:00 a.m. when we decided to call it a night, and we made our way to our hammocks, and by now, most people were already sleeping. I had to crawl through three people gently to get to my hammock. I crawled in and I had six people in reach including Ronnie, who was as close to me as possible.

27
CHAPTER

The next day started a bit of a routine for us. We would get up when breakfast was served and then usually lay back down for another hour or so then go to the top deck and stay at the back of the boat because of the loud music and to soak up some sun. There was always someone we knew up there by this point. People would play cards or chess or just relax. The bar was open all the time, and we usually would have a drink around noon and then basically most of the day.

It was the second day when we passed our first Amazon village and it was built right next to the river and had about five wooden structures made out of wood and palm branches. There were kids playing, women doing laundry, and guys fishing from the shore. There were maybe twenty-five people in this little village, and this is where 95 percent of them will spend their entire lives. What a great view, just a little rustic for me. The water was still a brownish color, and I couldn't imagine having to use this water for all of our needs, but they knew how to purify it and use it for their needs.

It was day 3, I think, and we had the chance to see something very unique for the river and not something that everyone gets to see and that was a "Pink Dolphin." We had two of them that swam next to our boat for a few miles. They look just like normal dolphins except they were pink and not the gray color we were used to. It was a rare and exciting sighting for us, and even the captain came over the loudspeaker and announced it.

On day 4, the river had gotten a lot narrower, and the water had turned a more reddish color than it had been. It is the way the

Amazon River is divided, and one side is a reddish color and the other side is brown. We could actually see where it divided, and it made for a great photo. It was this day, that we witnessed something very cool. About midafternoon, we all noticed about four canoes that were upstream and paddling toward the boat. We watched from the side as these kids, ages eight to fourteen, paddle canoes to our boat without our boat stopping at all. It was rather dangerous for kids. As they paddled close to the boat, the person in front would take a hook and get it into one of the tires hanging off the side for fenders and secure their canoe to ours. The kids then climbed on board and sold us stuff. They had fresh fruit, jewelry, handmade bags, and other things to eat. We bought some fruit and watched these little business people make a living. After they were done, they climbed down the ropes back into the canoes and pulled the hook out from the tires to get free of the boat. It was dangerous because if the canoe capsized, it would drag the kids right under the boat and through the props. It was a way they made a living, and it happened several times during our trip.

We found out that this is why they played the music so loud, so vthese people could hear the boat coming and have time to catch up with us. There were several times that the kids stayed on the boat longer than they should have and had to wait for another boat coming the opposite direction to catch a ride back. If this didn't happen, they had a long paddle home on a very dangerous river.

CHAPTER 28

The facilities on board were very basic but worked just fine. We showered every day, usually before they closed it up for the night. It was nice to go to bed feeling clean from sweat and bug spray. It wasn't that we were doing much throughout the day, but it was hot and felt good.

This was the best cruise I had ever done, and I had been on a big cruise ship before. It was just the fact of where we were at and everything we had the chance to see. We were fortunate enough to see pink dolphins, and we saw many different types of monkeys. They would howl at us, and we would howl right back. You can actually have a conversation with a monkey after about ten strong drinks.

We spent seven nights seeing a part of the river that not everyone gets a chance to see. We had times the branches from the trees would scrape on our boat; we were that close. All the meals were good; the beginning meals were a little better, and by the sixth day, it was just the same thing over and over again. We did stop a few times to offload cargo and supplies for nearby villages, but we could just watch what was going on from the boat. They didn't want people getting off mainly because of disease. Not that we would get sick from them, but they didn't want to get sick from us. These villages were really small, and they didn't want outsiders affecting them with something that could destroy a whole family. It was cool with us, and we just sat and watched.

On the eighth morning, we approached the city of Manaus, which was the largest city in the Amazon Jungle. This was the main port for the surrounding jungle area and has a population of 2.2 million people. This was a place that is the center point for all scientific studies on the rainforest and the river. Manaus is called the "Heart of the Amazon" and the "City of the Forest." The city has a free port and international airport, many manufacturing plants, a ship construction industry, and it is also a major export place for Brazilian nuts, rubber, and rosewood oil. From the river, it looked big, but we can only see so much. It was definitely the biggest place we had seen in the past week.

We get to the dock, and the boat is secured. We have our bags packed, and it is time to say goodbye to all our new friends. We get off the boat, and there are people there selling hostels and rides from the ports. All we wanted was a place to stay that had a bed. After a week on a boat sleeping in a hammock with people really close to you, for us, just having a bed that night would be a big reward. A lady there had places to stay, and we followed her for a half mile or so to her spot. It was a hostel, we had our own room, shared bathroom, and had a bed. It had been a week since we had sex. I tried to convince Ronnie a few times, but let me tell you, there was no place on that boat to actually be alone. The only place was the shower, and there was always someone waiting, so that didn't work. Oh well, we had a bed tonight, and things would happen.

That day, we walked around, and it felt good to actually walk on solid ground. We found a place to eat and had a nice meal outside facing the river. It was weird looking at the Amazon from land when we had just spent a week looking at it from being on a boat. This gave us time to plan for the next thing we could do. We wanted to spend time in the jungle, and we found an excursion that would work well for us. It was a four-night, five-day trip that would take us to a different part of the Amazon and more into the rainforest. We found a reliable travel service and booked the trip. That night, we just walked around close to our hostel and took in the sights.

The next morning, we met with a group of people near the harbor. We loaded up on a small boat, about twenty-four by nine feet. It had a small cabin area, and the bow was open. We made our way to the bow and stayed there the entire trip.

TAKE A DECADE

We traveled further up the Amazon and into tributaries of the river. The river had gotten a lot narrower, and you could see nothing but jungle all around us. It took us a good hour of just slowly navigating the river. The crew, made up of three younger Brazilian guys, did a great job explaining what we were seeing and spotting out any animals we saw. Besides monkeys, we hadn't seen much, and this was not out of the ordinary. It was very difficult to see some of the bigger animals that roamed the jungle like black panthers, caimans, tapir, monkeys, and something I wanted to see—an anaconda. Our guide said it was very rare to see one, but you never know.

So after several hours on this boat, we had reached our destination. We would be staying on a floating raft that was anchored about thirty feet from shore. The float house had a roof over the entire area, which was forty feet by forty feet. The main area was completely exposed to the outside, meaning there were no walls, just a roof. There was a small building, which is where a few of the guys slept, and the galley where they did the cooking. At the back of the raft were four small stalls, two bathrooms and two showers. The water wasn't hot, but it felt good each night. We would be out here for three nights and four days.

Once we secured the boat, we disembarked and got situated. We all hung our hammocks up in one row on one side of the raft. It was going to be another few nights of close accommodations. Not as close as on the boat, but we would all be in reach of each other. It was fine with me, and all I knew was we were smack dab in the rainforest.

After we got situated, the guys made us lunch, and we all ate together. It was just chicken and rice, but it was good enough. After lunch, our guide asked if anyone wanted to go piranha fishing. Ah yes, sign me up. So he took me on one of the two long canoes they had. This canoe was extra long and not very wide. It had a small outboard motor with a really long shaft with a small prop on the end. We didn't go fast at all, just cruised around and stared into the jungle. It is something you can't describe in words—the density, mystery, lush green colors, and the sounds. I just couldn't believe we were sitting on a canoe going into the rainforest to catch piranhas.

We spent about thirty minutes making our way back into this remote cove that was completely overgrown with the jungle, and we would have to duck to get under fallen branches and trees. Every tree or bush we went under, I looked for snakes that might fall into our boat. I watched the shoreline for something coming out or going in. The whole place was just what I expected and loved every moment of it.

So we got into this remote cove, and he killed the engine. He handed both of us a wooden fishing pole with just a ten-foot piece of line at the end with a small hook. It was like a fishing pole you would make in a survival situation or as a kid when you were camping. It was just a stick and line with a hook. He then reached into a bag and pulled out a small pile of raw chicken. He too had the same setup, and I followed what he did: Take a small piece of chicken and put it on our hook. Then he tossed the chicken into the water and took the top of his pole and splashed the water with it. This was completely opposite of any fishing I have ever done. Usually, you got the bait in the water and were as quiet as possible. Nope, not here, you get the bait into the water and make some noise in the water. Basically, piranhas are attracted to things that fall in the water. They hunt in packs, and when they feel a vibration in the water, they assume that something has fallen in the water, and that was when they feed. It was so weird, but I gave it a try and it took about three minutes, and our guide caught one. I put more bait on, and as soon as it hit the surface, I had a bite. I yanked the line, and nothing was there; my bait was gone again. I was getting bites but could not get them to stick. Our guide caught three, and after thirty minutes of rebating, splashing, and pulling up nothing, I was out of time and out of bait. I left with my head down and could not believe I couldn't catch one. Our guide said if we had time tomorrow, we could try it again. We did get to eat the piranhas that he had caught, and it was a very good fish. They are small so you need to get a few to have a meal.

We got back and told our fish stories, and nobody really cared. We hung out that afternoon and just enjoyed the scene. Around dusk, one of the guys jumped into the river and swam around. I asked a dumb question: "Is it safe to be swimming in these waters?" I mean we just fished for piranhas, and I knew they were there plus a billion other things that could kill you. They told me that because the house was off the shore, we didn't have to worry about piranhas. However, there are other things that could bite you, and that was just a chance you had to take. Well, I had heard enough and took off my shirt and dove in with him. I can now say I have swam in the Amazon River. The water had this reddish tint to it, visibility was only about five feet, and I could not see the bottom. I spent about five minutes, and then my mind started to wander, and I remembered all the horror movies about the Amazon River and decided to get out. I was the only one of the group that chose to do a once-in-a-lifetime event.

The next morning, we got ready, and they took us on a two-hour jungle walk. Our guide had a machete and just cut his way through the jungle. We stopped at several different areas for him to show us certain things. The first thing was weird; it was a tree that was covered in these tiny ants. There had to be a billion of them on this one tree. He put his hands around the tree, and the ants or bugs crawled over his hand in a second. He then took the bugs and started to wash his hand with them, basically crushing them and making oil out of them. He told us all to do this, and this was a natural form of a bug repellent to keep mosquitoes away. We walked a little further, and he cut down a few vines and we all had a drink of fresh water, which was stored inside of the vines that hung everywhere in the jungle. A little while later, he found this tree that was used in making bubble gum and a tree that produced these nuts. He took a few of the nuts, which were the size of a big walnut, cracked them open and out came these small larvae. They were white in color, and you could see them moving in his hand. They were used as a military survival food for the Brazilian army. The nut was from the coconut family, and it was edible. The larva was also edible, and he offered for us to try one. Once again, no one in the group wanted to try one except for me. I placed it into my mouth and bit down; a burst of coconut flavor was all I could taste. It was delicious, and I ate four of them. We spent about three hours just walking around and always on the lookout for something big.

After our jungle walk, we went to a small village in the jungle. The boat dropped us off, and we all just walked around and talked with the locals about life and living here. This village had about twenty people living here. There were four structures that were used as sleeping and cooking areas. The wood fire was going, and they had a pot of water bowling for their drinking water. The structures were made out of trees, and the roofs were all covered with palm branches. This was living off the grid to the extreme.

After our jungle trip and visiting a local village, we spent the rest of the day on the float house. I got a chance to go fishing again and still had no luck. Those bastards were hard to catch. They had such a small mouth lined with razor-sharp teeth that stole our bait in a split second. Oh well, it was another chance to get out more into the rainforest, and even though we didn't catch one, we can say we tried.

The last night, we had the opportunity to spend the night in the jungle. We were the only two that took this great opportunity. Our guide took us by boat to the beginning of this trail. We started walking and walked about a half mile deep into the jungle. They had this place that they had taken people before, so we weren't the first ones to ever stay there, but we would be the next. The two guides took our hammocks and hung them between two trees and placed a net over them to protect us from the mosquitoes. Then they started a fire for us and prepared our dinner in the open flames. The one guide took a piece of bamboo and carved a small spoon out of it for us to eat our meal. Instead of plates, we used the leaves of the bamboo tree as a plate. The food was okay, but how we were eating it was worth the trip. When you use nature as your plate and spoon, you don't have any dishes to clean.

It started to get dark, and the guides told us not to wander around too much. They told us to stay close to the fire and keep it going as long as possible. They had gotten wood for us, and we got more later that night. They told us that they would be back in the morning to get us and, with a big smile, told us to have a good night. Just like that, we were alone in the Amazon jungle. We had brought a bottle of booze with us, so we enjoyed the fire and had something to drink. Once it was pitch black, the jungle got loud. It was crazy how many sounds we could hear, everything from bugs to monkeys. It was a great night, and we both made the night a little bit more fun by enjoying the use of our hammocks and no one around for miles. I can say one of the craziest places I have had sex is in the Amazon jungle. It was also a fun time to just walk around naked, and this was before *Naked and Afraid* ever was on the air. I can say that I did get very little sleep that night because of the noise. I wasn't worried about animals getting us; it was the loud sounds of the jungle that kept me awake most of the night. I stayed in some very large cities and nothing compared to the sounds of the jungle. The whole night was a blast, and our guides were there to get us the next morning.

It was on our way back the last day that we had a great opportunity to do something that I will never forget. As we were motoring back, a small canoe of three little kids came up to our boat. This time, our boat slowed down and let them tie up to our boat. The one guide whom I got to know the best called me over and said, "They have something for you." I looked into the boat, and this one girl, about ten years old, was holding a three-toed sloth. The boy sitting next to her, who was maybe twelve years old, was holding an eight-foot anaconda.

I said, "Holy shit, this is it." They both got on our boat, and we had the greatest pleasure of holding these two animals. Ronnie took the sloth, and I got a great picture of her holding it, and then I took the eight-foot anaconda and placed it around my neck, and I have a photo of this experience. I did get a chance to hold the three-toed sloth as well, which was such a unique opportunity. Not a lot of people got to handle something like this, and I would never forget it. Just like that, my one thing that I really wanted to see came true, and I was on cloud nine. Both the sloth and snake were pets for the kids, and they took great care of them. The guide said the snake would soon get too big for the kid, and he would have to let it go. The sloth on the other hand could stay with the little girl for a big portion of her life. It was unreal to have a snake, an anaconda, around my neck in the Amazon rainforest.

This was one of the best excursions I have ever done in my life. The whole experience of being on the boat for a week and now another three nights in the jungle, my dream had come true. We spent another night in Manaus, this time at a different place but not much better. The two nights we spent in the city of Manaus were probably two of the worst places we stayed, but it was convenient and cheap. We had now spent twelve nights, thirteen days in the Amazon, and my trip had been completed. Anything from here on out would be just a bonus. From the time we landed in Lima, Peru, until we got to the Amazon, this was the one big thing I really wanted to do. I can honestly say that it met all my expectations and then some.

The next morning, we got on a bus heading north to our next destination, which was Caracas, Venezuela. We had to take a bus to Boa Vista, which was about eleven hours north, and then another long bus ride, twenty hours to get to the city. Besides this being a long trip, we did get to cross over the equator for the first time. We did get a chance to get off the bus on the equator and take a photo of where we were. There wasn't a sign or anything—it was really the side of the road, but we knew where we were.

We had now left Brazil, which had been our home for over a month. If you have ever thought about visiting Brazil, I would highly recommend it, and you won't be disappointed. Brazil is high on my list as one of the best countries that I have traveled through. We did so much and saw so many cool things. I just can't say enough except "Thank you, Brazil."

29

CHAPTER

Venezuela

We crossed into Venezuela just after switching buses in Boa Vista. The border crossing was one of the roughest as far as our crossing had been. It was a dark and dreary experience. There were many more armed guards, and they just looked at us like we were fresh meat. Most of the guards were very dark-complexioned with bloodshot eyes, and all of them were packing a weapon. We did the crossing after it got dark, and I think this made it even sketchier. We did it, however, and were now in our sixth country and our sixth stamp in the good old passport.

Caracas, Venezuela, is the capital of the country and located in the northern portion of the country. Caracas Valley is located real close to the Caribbean Sea. There is a mountain range that does dive the sea from the city, yet there is a river located next to the city called the Guaire River. This city has about five million people living here and is densely populated. We noticed the traffic as we entered the city, and it looked very hectic and very unorganized. There is a fair rate of crime and violence here, which does keep a lot of travelers from visiting. Venezuela is a very big producer of fuel that is used in a lot of our military planes. When you deal with oil or fuel of any sort, you know there is a lot of money behind it. This is a place where the rich get richer and the poor get poorer. The government of this place has had many issues in just the past few years. There was not a lot for us to see and do here. It was more of a layover, and hopefully, we could exchange our US dollars for more than they were worth.

We got to the bus station and used our guidebook to help find a place. It was all about safety here and close to the terminal. We were only planning on staying one night; time to get a shower after a long bus trip and get some sleep. We were planning on leaving for Columbia the next day, which had more things to do. Believe it or not, they said northern Columbia was safer than this city.

After we got our room set up, which was basic hostel living—it shared everything yet was close to the bus station—we headed out into the city. Our plan was to exchange US dollars for Venezuelan money and then exchange it for Colombian dollars when we got there. It was a plan, and if it worked, great; if not, then no big deal. The exciting part of this was we had to go to the sketchiest part of the city. It was called the "black market center" of the city, and it would be here that our exchange would happen. We had no idea what the hell we were doing; it was just an adventure.

We got to a rough area, and I was looking for banks, booths, or stores that would exchange money, but it didn't work like that. As soon as we turned down this one street, we started noticing men standing there on the streets with fistfuls of money. Just about every fifteen feet would be another guy with a wad of money just standing there. So I got the courage to ask one of them if first they spoke English and ask what the hell they were doing. They all spoke a little English enough to communicate with us, and they were the ones to exchange money. There were no banks or pretty little offices; this whole thing was done right out in the open on the street. We asked him what his exchange rate was, and it was not good. So we wandered up and down the street and talked to about ten people. Basically, we had hit it when the US dollar to them was at par. They told us that this week it is at par, next week it could be lower and the week after that it could be higher. It is a market that fluctuates on a daily basis and we just hit it at the wrong time. We did, however, exchange $100 more to just do this illegal thing on the streets of Caracas, one of the deadliest cities in the world. I didn't make any money, yet I can say that I did something a little on the stupid side in a city where we could easily just disappear.

With that done, our next thing was to find an Internet place to touch base with our families. We had contacted them before we entered the jungle, and I told them it could be a few weeks before they heard from us again. This was not what my mom wanted to hear, but she understood the lack of communication. It was good to see all was good back home, and I gave them a rundown of the last few weeks and let them know what was next. We were going to be in Columbia for the next week or so, and that was all we knew at the time.

The next day, we left Caracas on our way to Cartagena, Columbia. This would take us about nineteen hours to get there and would be an overnight bus ride. You just never knew what to expect each day, and each day was just another adventure.

CHAPTER 30

Columbia

It had been about nine hours on the bus, and it was a rough ride. The roads were not the greatest and the traffic was all over the place. It was also time for our next border crossing, and this was a little different. We came to a stop, and within seconds, we had four uniformed armed guards get on to our bus. This was the first time we had been boarded by the border guards, and they looked scary. We stuck out like a sore thumb, and we both just kind of tensed up. They told everyone to get off the bus and go inside with all our stuff. So we left the bus, grabbing our packs from underneath the bus. We lined up and all went in one at a time. They took our passports, and by now, we had a few stamps and a travel map of where we have been. They asked the same questions, and we paid the fee to get into the country, which was about $25. Then they asked to see my bags, and the whole time, they looked at me like I was a drug smuggler. Now I forgot to tell you one thing, and that is the last day we were in Manus, Brazil, I bought five stuffed piranhas for souvenirs and one for myself. They were like $2 apiece and had their mouths open and placed on a piece of wood for a stand. It was one of the coolest things I ever bought traveling, and it is on my computer as I write this book. So they opened my bag, and I had five of these things wrapped in newspaper. They are not that big but take up a little room. So the guy with bloodshot eyes asked me what these were, and I told him.

He opened one up and took a long look at it then turned to me and asked what was inside each one of these. I told him, "Nothing but whatever the piranha ate last." He didn't get my little joke at all. He handed them over to another guy, and he ran them through a scanner, and they could see that there were no drugs in them. He handed them back to me, and I was free to go. I'm sure a lot of drugs cross the border, but I'm not that stupid.

We got back on the bus, and our driver told Ronnie and I that if we got stopped again and we would, one person would stay on the bus with our day bags and the other one would get off the bus and keep an eye on the bags underneath. The reason for this was that the "police" would actually put stuff in bags to get money from the people. It was a very corrupt world here, and we had to be extra cautious. We were now in Columbia, and this was where many people got kidnapped for ransom money. If they did, however, kidnap me, the only thing they were getting was practice because I didn't have a damn thing.

It was about two hours later around midnight, and sure enough, we hit a roadside checkpoint and they came on the bus again. We were able to get off, and I made a beeline to our bags. They checked the whole bus with dogs, and officers asked a few of the local people a few questions and never once asked us for anything. They did notice us; that was for sure. I watched carefully as they moved bags around, but they never did anything to any of them. We stood there for about thirty minutes while this little shakedown occurred, and we were then free to go. It was a little nerve-racking, and this would not be the last.

We arrived in Cartagena safe and sound and happy to be off the bus. The bus terminal had a few people down there selling rooms, and this younger guy found us just what we needed. It was about ten minutes away and close to a lot of things to do. We took him up on this, and he gave us a ride to the hostel. It was on the first floor, a "right off the street" kind of place. We were in a bunk room with a few other people, but the place had a good vibe to it, and he gave us a ton of information in a very short time. This would be a fun place; I just knew it.

Cartagena is a port city in northern Columbia. It is located in the Caribbean coastal region. With the location of this port city, it is used for many different things. The silver that was taken from the mines in Bolivia would have been loaded on ships here to get to Spain. Another thing this place had back in the day was a lot of slaves would have been loaded on boats to get to the northern hemisphere. So this place was invaded many times by pirates. Back as early as 1586, they started to construct a wall that would protect the city from unwanted thieves. The wall is still standing today and serves more as a beautiful piece of architecture than protection. This city was lined with cobblestone streets, and the buildings were painted in very colorful designs. The city was very clean, and the traffic moved at a steady, organized pace. There was a lot to see here, and it was all in walking distance from where we are staying.

We got set up and enjoyed a cold beer with our host. He gave us the lowdown on the place, and there were a few other guys staying here that seemed real cool as well. We had a bit of a meet and greet for the first hour, and we had new friends. After this, Ronnie and I just walked around a little bit and grabbed something to eat. We got back to the hostel, and they were having a little party, so we joined right in. That night, we sat in this court area and told stories with a bunch of cool people.

For some reason, we still got up at a good time and decided to explore the area and see what else we could do. We had heard of a beach that was a few hours away, and it was a rustic living right on the beach. We talked with our host, and he set us up with everything we needed to do this. He had been there many times and told us it would be a vacation for our travels. We got everything set up, and we would be picked up at seven the next morning.

After our day of walking and sightseeing, we found a nice outdoor place to have a romantic dinner. It had been a great day in a beautiful city. It started to get dark, and we made our way back to the hostel. On the way back, this guy approached me and asked if I wanted any smoke. It had been a while, so I bought a bag for like $5. Ronnie didn't have a problem with it, and we had already seen people smoking, so it seemed laid-back and safe. The two guys that I had buddied up with were there and talked about going out that night. I had told them about what I had already got, and we all enjoyed a smoke together; even the guy who ran the hostel joined us. During this time, they told me there was a club they had heard of, and they wanted to go out. I could tell they wanted to "party," and this was the place to do it. I figured with Ronnie, it wasn't going to happen for me, but things do happen. Anyway, I walked back into our room and told her that these guys wanted to go out. She looked at me and said, "Have fun." The sun and heat had taken a toll on her, and she just wasn't into going out but told me to have fun and to remember we were leaving at seven the next morning. I told her we would be out for a few hours and then home and I would be real quiet when I get back. I couldn't believe that I was actually going out alone in Columbia.

The three of us left around 10:00 p.m., and we were told things should be happening by now. I gave Ronnie a kiss and we left. As soon as we were outside, the guys asked me if I wanted to really party, and I said, "Absolutely." It was not just having a few drinks, but Columbia is the cocaine capital of the world, and "when in Rome," have a good time. So we all were on the same page and all wanted the same thing and that was to try and get a little cocaine for the evening. The walk to the place was a good mile, and it went through a few areas that were a little sketchy. It was all good because the three of us were big enough as a group that the chances of getting jumped would have been slim.

We got to the club, and there were people out front drinking and having a good time. We could hear the music from the street, and it was trance music, so this was the place to be. We walked in, and the three of us didn't have a clue on how to get hold of anything. So we headed to the bar and ordered a beer. I asked the guys, "Do you think the bartender would know?" I knew when I've been bartending I get asked for everything. We agreed it was a chance but also a chance to get kicked out right away or even worse. The hell with it and I leaned over to the bartender and asked if he knew how we could get a little something to enjoy a great evening. I was trying to be discreet with my words yet get my point across.

He looked at me and said, "You want to buy some cocaine?"

"Well, yes, we were thinking about it."

He said, "No problem. See that guy in the jacket? Go ask him."

This guy was just a normal-looking guy with a windbreaker on, and as we approached him, he saw the bartender motion him to help us out. He asked what we wanted, and we told him an "eight ball," which is how we buy it in the States. He reached into his pocket and handed us the goods, and the cost for this was about $18, which was $6 each. Wow, this was cheap; the same thing in the States would be $120–$150 easily. With the goods in our hands, we made our way to the bathroom one at a time and enjoyed the purest, cleanest, best cocaine on the planet. This was the motherland for this stuff; it would be like going to Italy and not trying a pizza or going to Japan and not trying sushi.

We partied for many hours that night, taking turns going to the bathroom and smoking a pack of cigarettes. These two guys were single, so I tried to be a good wingman and danced with a few girls that they had met. We partied like rock stars that night, and the night flew by very quickly. It was around 3:00 a.m. that I realized that I needed to get back. Either Ronnie would be up waiting for me and would probably know I was up to something or she would be asleep. *Please be sleeping, please be sleeping.* I told the guys I had to go, and they were not ready yet, so I told them to stay and good luck with the girls and left them with what was left. I then walked the streets of Cartagena at 3:00 a.m. alone and felt like the top of the world. I got back and opened the door real quietly, and thank God she was sound asleep. By this time I was too wired to go to bed, so I stayed up and smoked more cigarettes. It was around 5:00 a.m. when I finally fell asleep, and I didn't get much sleep that night.

Ronnie woke me up at 6:30 a.m., and I could have killed her, but I had to play it off like I had gotten home and gotten a good night's sleep. She asked when I got home and told her just a little after twelve; she told me she hit the pillow and went right to sleep. I know I had lied a little, but sometimes a little white lie is better than a day of getting hell from your loved one.

TAKE A DECADE

With my tail between my legs and every part of my body hurting, I packed up my stuff and followed her out the door. It was going to be a long day but well worth the opportunity. We took a city bus to another terminal and got on a bus, which would take us to Playa Blanco.

Playa Blanco is a white sand beach located near Cartagena and a popular spot for tourists to actually stay on the beach. We took the bus there, which was a long, rough three hours. The roads sucked, and I thought once on the bus I could get some sleep, but that didn't happen. The bus spent as much time off the road as it did on the road. We crossed a river, went through the jungle, and finally we got to the beach.

The beach was beautiful with the blue sea and the white sand beach. This was just what we needed. It hadn't been since Natal that we had a beach and ocean to hang out and relax. The beach wasn't packed at all; actually, there were very few people around. The bus driver told us to walk down the beach and someone would help us out. We walked a short distance, and this little old lady came up and asked if we were staying, and we told her yes. There were about four thatched huts made with just four poles, and the roof was just palm branches. Each hut had two chairs and a small table, and that was it. It was right on the beach, like twenty-five steps away from the ocean. This place was another slice of paradise. She got us all set up with our hammocks and nets hung. She told us that they would bring us three meals a day and anything else we needed. Ronnie was ready to party, so we did ask for a few beers, and she walked to their little house built near the water, which was fifty yards from our spot, and returned with two cold beers. She told us, "Anything you need, just walk over and ask." She was super sweet, and they took great care of us.

So here we were lying in our hammocks under a thatched roof building with no sides and staring out into the blue sea. It was just what we needed, and we drank our beer and I had a smoke. We then both walked into the sea holding hands. The water was warm, visibility was fantastic, and the sand in our toes felt wonderful. We swam around and just sat in the sand and let the water splash over our bodies. After about an hour in the water, I did get a chance to take a nice two-hour nap. When I woke up, I climbed out of my hammock, walked twenty-five feet, and jumped in the sea. This was how life should be for everyone, every day.

That night, just before it got dark, we saw her coming our way with two plates of food. We had fresh fish, rice, some kind of veggie that was good, and a fresh homemade citrus tea. We sat there in our two chairs and small table and enjoyed our dinner. After that, we asked if she had a bottle of booze that we could buy, and believe it or not, she brought us a bottle of rum and two sodas. This would be a routine for us each night.

The only way to really describe this beach is comparing it to a Corona commercial. You have that beautiful white sand, a thatched roof shelter, and a gorgeous blue sea in front of you. We would be sitting there enjoying our day, and the guy who lived with the women would walk by carrying a freshly cut fish and we knew that it was our dinner. It happened two out of the three nights. We had fresh fish, and one night, we had chicken. The breakfast was eggs, meat, bread, and fresh juice, and for lunch, we would have sandwiches, fruit, and water. For three nights and four days we were treated like kings and queens. It was so relaxing and just picture perfect. We hated to leave, but it was time to keep moving, and on the last day, they came to us with the bill. We really never asked how much anything cost, it was just something we were going to do and enjoy it without worrying about money. The cost for this experience was $40 each, and we could not believe it was so cheap and so well worth it.

We stayed one more night in Cartagena at the same place and had a little party that night with a different group of people. We talked with a few people about doing the beach thing and told them it was the best and so cheap that it was a must if you had time. That night, we also had to make a choice on how to get from where we were to our next spot. We had looked into a few options before we left for the beach and had already determined that we needed to fly to our next spot. It was at this time we were leaving South America and making our way north into Central America. We needed to get to Costa Rica in less than four days. Ronnie was flying home, back to New Jersey for three days. They were going to have a memorial for her brother and had to get back for this. We had planned things along the way, and she had already bought her ticket. We figured that by this time, we would be close to Costa Rica and she could get a direct flight to Newark, New Jersey.

The next morning, we took a bus to the airport; it seemed so weird that we would be on a plane and not a bus. It would take under two hours to get there, and we would be flying on Copa Airlines, which we had never heard of before, but it was the cheapest.

We got to the airport, and we checked in our bags. We walked around and used the bathroom before we went through security. We then started our wait though security, and it was just then that I put my hand into my pocket and had completely forgotten about the bag of weed I had forgotten to give away. *Oh shit*, I said to myself, and I told Ronnie what had happened.

She looked at me and said, "Get rid of it," but by that time, we were close to security, and I could not very well leave; it would look way too suspicious. So I just left it right in my pocket and hoped for the best. I approached the security, and they put my bags through the machine, waved me through, and that was it. They never checked my person with a wand or anything, just said, "Have a good flight." I'm not sure if it was because we were Americans or we just didn't look that stupid to try and smuggle drugs out of the country. What they didn't know wouldn't hurt them. As soon as we got on the plane and got ready to take off, I found an open seat and stuffed the bag in the pocket that had all the books. If they didn't search me before the flight, they would certainly search me when we get off. I was an American flying out of Columbia, so I'm sure I would be an easy target. It was all gone, and I had nothing to worry about now. We sat back holding hands and said goodbye to South America, and it was a sad moment for both of us. We had seen and done so much, and we knew that it was coming to an end. Once we left South America, we had about one month left to make it to Cancun for the wedding.

31
CHAPTER

Panama–Costa Rica

We got to the airport. We got our bags, and now it was time to go through security. I was very happy that I didn't have anything in my pocket and really hoped the person that cleaned the plane got a little surprise; I would never know. I approached the security checkpoint, handed him my passport, and they asked the same questions you always get asked. He asked if we were bringing anything, and I told him just souvenirs that we had picked up. They did run my bag through and questioned the piranhas. They took them out and did an inspection on them, but it didn't seem to alarm anyone. He handed me back my passport and said, "Welcome to Panama." That was it—no personal inspection, no strip search, no interrogation with bright lights, no nothing. It was so easy that I regretted throwing away my stuff, but better safe than sorry.

We left the terminal and took a bus to a hostel we had found in our book. It was close to the Panama Canal, and this would be about all we had a chance to see. We did need money and found an ATM at the airport and took out a few hundred bucks. The cool thing was we actually got US currency out of the ATM. We came to find out the US dollar is the same currency that they use here in Panama. This is because we have been a big part of the Panamanians' lives for over a century. We helped build and manage the canal for years. It was our

TAKE A DECADE

money that made the canal possible, and it wasn't until 1999 that the Panamanians took complete control of the land.

We had the pleasure of spending a few hours walking around the mouth of the Panama Canal. We were at the Pacific side, and we watched a bunch of boats either leaving or waiting their turn to enter the canal. The Panama Canal is a waterway that cuts right through Center America from the Atlantic Ocean to the Pacific Ocean. The length of the canal is about fifty miles, and it cost the US government over four hundred million dollars to construct and manage. Jimmy Carter gave the Panama government the right to the canal, which started in the late seventies, and by December 31, 1999, they had complete control. It was an engineering feat to construct this canal, and many men died during the long hot hours it took to complete.

We took pictures of the canal both during the day and a few at night. It was about all we could do. That night, we did nothing except enjoy a good meal and a few drinks. So unfortunately, I didn't have a lot to talk about when it came to Panama. This would be a place that I would return to some day and take a boat from the Atlantic to the Pacific.

We left early the next day for our sixteen-hour trip. We learned one thing about Central America, and that was they didn't have many overnight bus trips. This was for safety reasons, and it could be rather dangerous to travel at night, so we had to manage day trips only.

We were maybe a few hours out of the city when we hit a roadblock. Several uniformed armed guards got on the bus and asked to see everyone's passports. They didn't give anyone a hard time; they were just checking for something, I guess. It is just a little unnerving to have a guy stand over you with a machine gun asking questions. This was one of those times I answered the questions without any smart remarks. It was "Yes, sir, no, sir, thank you very much, sir."

Anyway, we finally made it to San Jose, Costa Rica, and it was already late at night. There were a few people waiting at the terminal for housing, and I really think we got a little screwed on this deal, but we didn't have much of a choice. The guy we decided to go with told us this was the only place to stay, and he also told us he would pick us up in the morning and get us to where we needed to go. The cost of this place was $50 for the night, which was triple the cost we had been paying. We didn't check in until 11:00 p.m. and would leave at seven the next morning. It was a lot of money for a short stay, but we were beat from the long bus ride and just needed something.

That night, we showered and went right to bed. It was going to be a long day for Ronnie tomorrow, and I was going to be on my own for about two to three nights. We slept, and I was not excited for Ronnie to be leaving but completely understood.

The next day, the guy was there on time, which was very nice of him; he could have stood us up and there would be nothing we could do. He was there, and that was all that mattered. We left and took Ronnie right to the airport, and we said our goodbyes for a few days. We were going to meet up on the beach somewhere, and it was up to me to find the way and send her an email on how I got there. That was it, and she was gone. That first hour felt really weird, knowing that I was alone now and it was all up to me to get to my next destination.

I was dropped off at the bus terminal, and I wanted to get to a surf spot called Mai Pais, which was on the Pacific Ocean and known for being a good surf spot. It was a destination and hopefully not hard to get to. Well, it wasn't hard to get to except I had to stay at a small village called Montezuma one night before I could get to the beach. The roads around here were about as rough as it gets, and traffic moved really slowly. Normally, the amount of land we had to cover could have been done in one day but not here. I went out and had something to eat and a few beers, and that was it. I got here in the dark and would be leaving at first light, so there was not a whole hell of a lot to do.

The next morning, I was out of there early, and I had another long ride all the way to the beach. This part of the country is dense with forest and mountains all around us. The trip was beautiful, just not really comfortable. Anyway, I arrived in Malpais and Santa Teresa, which are two beaches that share the same little village. The bus stopped at the only intersection in this entire town, and this was the end of the road. I got off the bus, and there were people selling rooms. I followed this lady to her place, which was really close by and rather cheap. We spent $50 in San Jose, and this place was more like $10 for the night.

This town is extremely small, one dirt road that goes from one beach area to the next. I could have easily counted on two hands the number of buildings. It was rustic, quiet, and secluded. This is a place a big surfer would come for a week or so and just surf day in and day out. I wanted to surf, but that first day it was all about just walking around and checking out the beaches. You could find a place and sit down and not see anyone all day if you wanted. It was just what I needed, and I enjoyed my peace and quiet. They did have an internet café, so I was able to email Ronnie all the details for her to meet me and this is where I would be. She responded later that day and gave me the thumbs up on securing a spot.

That night I spent just walking around drinking a few beers and talking with several people. Everyone was just one big, happy family, and there were several people here from the States that had moved here and created a business. A couple of the guys had opened a hostel, and a guy I met made a living selling breakfast burritos. I bought one from him the second day, and he just walked around with a small cooler filled with burritos. He told me that he made $25 a day, and this was enough money for him to continue to live here and pay his way. He wasn't here to get rich, just here to survive and surf. Certain people that I have met along the way stand out, and this guy was one of them. If more people lived like this, the world could be a happier place.

Now that afternoon, I was walking around, and being as good-looking as I am (ha ha), this cute little blonde came up to me and started talking with me. We hit it off right away and spent a good portion of the evening hanging out. I went from being alone to having a new friend to bump around with. She was a little party girl and found us something to party with. So she and I drank a few beers and partied that night until early in the morning.

It had been three days since Ronnie left, and I knew she was back in Costa Rica, just not sure when she would arrive. Was she going to have to stay a night in Montezuma like I did, or would she be able to go straight through? I didn't know, just kind of waited to see if she showed up. Well, the next afternoon, my third day there, I was sitting with my new friend, and a car went by, and I could have sworn it was Ronnie. I walked to the end of the road, and sure enough, it was her. I was so glad to see her but also a little worried that we would run into my new friend, which we never did. I guess she left that night, and I never saw her again.

Ronnie had gotten dropped off at another hostel at the other end of the beach and paid for a night. I had already paid for my place, so that night, we stayed at my place and had a great night. The next morning, I moved to her hostel, which was so much more fun. This place was an open-air hostel, and he had surfboards to use for free, and the best part of this place was he had a cooler full of beer, and all you had to do was help yourself. You wrote your name down on a piece of paper and just kept track of your drinks and settled up at the end. This was a great place, and we stayed here for three more nights.

I told Ronnie that I had not surfed yet. I waited for her, so that afternoon, we hit the waves and spent a good portion of the day surfing. The waves were a little big for us, yet we managed to find ones that were more our speed. Just sitting on our board and looking back at the land was perfect. With the palm trees cascading out over the ocean and the sight of just a few small wooden structures, it was like we had this whole part of the world all to ourselves.

For the next few days we had a routine: Get up and wait for the guy to stop by with the breakfast burritos, then walk the length of the two beaches, which was like two miles, then surf for an hour and then take a nap. Wake up, have a beer, and hit the waves again, then take a shower and relax at our hostel for the evening. We would grab something to eat and sometimes eat it there or bring it back to the hostel. They had a huge table and a TV to watch movies and enjoy our surroundings.

On my sixth morning there, we left on a bus to get further north in Costa Rica. Our plan was to get to another beach/surf town that was a little bigger and had more to do. It was called Tamarindo, and it would be about a six-hour trip by bus. I would like to tell you the roads were better, but I would be lying. This is a beautiful country, and there was so much to see, but let me tell you, the roads frigging sucked. We were riding on the bus, which was a big bus, and we would hit bumps and rocks and literally get tossed out of our seats. There was no sleeping on this bus, just hanging on. It was a long and painful trip.

We made it to Tamarindo, and it was a much bigger place than where we had just come from. It is not huge at all with a population of about six thousand people. The town was located next to the ocean, and when we got dropped off at the terminal, we were on the only main drag in town. It was basically one road with most of the business on, and it ran right next to the ocean. When you get to a place and get a feeling this is a cool place, it is first impressions that are usually right. I can tell you right now that this was a good place.

We found a hostel to stay at that had surfboard rentals and a kitchen. This place was perfect. Now this place was going to be the last major thing we would be doing. We had to be in Mexico in about ten days. We took a few hours and did a little research that first day to make a few decisions. Do we stay here for a few days and then spend a few days in each of the countries we have to get through, or do we stay here for six nights and then just do a beeline for Mexico? Well, we went to a travel help desk and asked a lot of questions. The big thing was that no buses ran at night, and it would take us a day to cross through each country. There was no way around this, and we understood. We still had to go from here, to Nicaragua, Honduras, Guatemala, and then to Cancun. With the help from our guidebook and the travel agent, we needed four days to make this trip. It would be one night in each country, which meant traveling all day long. Well, we would at least get to see the countries as a whole and not just a city or town. It would be a long four days, but each night, we would be able to get a room, have a meal, and see a small portion of the countries. We had made our minds up, and that was to stay here for as long as possible. This would be our last real week, just the two of us; time to enjoy the beach and surf. It would be our vacation for spending almost 5.5 months on the road.

We had made the right choice because Tamarindo was a cool spot. Located right on the ocean, it had beautiful beaches, good surf spots, an open market for food and gifts, a hotel with a pool, and this place was all about the people we met.

The first day we checked in, I think a whole new group of people also checked in. Some were from the States and some from Europe. They were all around our age, and all were there for the same thing, beach and partying. The first evening, we went to a local store and bought food to cook that night. It was an outdoor kitchen with tables and a place to hang out. This was the heart of the hostel. That night, we met everyone staying there. We cooked our meal, and others did the same. We sat around drinking beers and telling stories. It was a great group with about five girls and four guys. We all seemed to be on the same page in life and all enjoying a nice trip. Of course, Ronnie and I had traveled the most, and we got to share a ton of stories. This made me happy because I did most of the talking. We would eat together and drink together almost every night.

The first day, we rented a few boards and spent a good portion surfing. The surf here was so much easier than Malpais. It was a slow, gentle wave that we could catch and ride almost every try. The water was a crystal-clear blue and had a very warm temperature. The beaches had no rocks, just white sand. We would surf and chill out on the beach. It was like being back home because everyone would stop by, stay for a beer, shoot the shit, and then take off. It was just day 2, and we already knew a few people.

That night, we cooked again and everyone was there, at least nine to ten of us cooking and drinking and having fun. We kept going, and soon, it was close to midnight. One of the girls said, "Let's go skinny-dipping in the ocean."

We all looked at each other and said, "Why the hell not?" So we all took off for the beach, which was right across the street, and once we got to the beach, the clothes came off. There were nine of us that ran into the ocean around midnight, bare ass and all. We surfed in the waves, played chicken with a girl on our shoulders, and spent a good hour having a blast. It was a good night, and Ronnie and I had a good night when we got home.

The next day, there was a hotel next to our hostel, and they had a beautiful pool. We had walked by it a few times and decided to try and see if we could use it. In Hawaii, we were the best of the best in crashing pools, and why not try here? So we walked around to the main area, I grabbed a few towels, and we found chairs to sit on. They had a swim-up bar, a waterfall, a basketball hoop, and guess what, they didn't care if we used the pool or not. So we spent the entire day swimming at the pool and using the swim-up bar for our drinks. We told our new friends about this piece of paradise, and the next day, we went back with our whole group. The bartender loved us because he made good money from us that week. We played basketball in the water and basically took the pool over, and they never said a word. It was great, and this was a great way to spend a few days.

Now Ronnie had been making jewelry this whole entire trip, and she had made a few nice pieces. So one day, we were walking around the flea market area and started to talk with a few of the vendors. We came to find out you don't need any permit or license to sell stuff. With us knowing that and with the help of a few people, we spent a few days hanging out with some of the vendors and sold a few pieces of her jewelry. It was a blast hanging out with the vendors and gave us a chance to meet a lot more people. We would stay for four to five hours, drinking a few beers, and it looked like we lived there and this was our job. She didn't make a lot of money but sold a few pieces, and it made her very happy.

The only bad moment we had this week was Ronnie ended up breaking a surfboard, and the lady who ran the hostel wanted to charge her $100 for the mistake. Ronnie didn't take this well and flipped out on the lady. I thought for sure we would get kicked out, but she did not do this. Even after Ronnie called her a bitch and a cheat, we still had a place to stay. Of course, I did the talking to settle the situation, and we agreed to give her $50. It made her happy, and after a day or so, Ronnie apologized. It was one little mess-up, and it was all good again.

Between the beaches, the pool, the vendors, the surf, the sunsets, and the people, this was a great last real week of our trip. It was a great way to end such an amazing experience. We still had time to get to Cancun, and that would be fun as well, just it would be busy with the wedding and a lot more people around. We took the last night, watched the sunset, and really sat and talked about everything we had done. It was truly an amazing experience, and it was good to be *me*.

On our seventh morning of such a wonderful week, it was time to go. We knew that the next few days would be long and not very exciting. So we were sluggish getting going. We were able to say goodbye to a few of our new friends, and we settled up with our host at the hostel. It was around $20 a night for our room, and this was a great place to stay. We chose the right place, and everything worked out great.

The next four days were all about traveling. It is not enough to separate each place because we really didn't get a lot to do at each place. We traveled all day, and usually, it was around four or five in the evening that we would arrive, find a place to stay, get to a store for food, or find a place close by to eat. It was the same procedure for each day.

We spent one night in Nicaragua, and this was a scary night. When we got off the bus, we could see armed guards everywhere, not just at the bus station but all over the town. That night, we found a pizza place to eat, and when we went there, they had two armed guards at the door. Dressed in full battle gear, they opened the door for us and locked it as we entered. It was not just this establishment, but every place that had money had guards. We finished our meal, and they unlocked the door to let us out. We walked down the street to find a few drinks, and it was dusk. It was at this time that we noticed every business inside and outside closing for the night. It was not safe to be out at night, and we made sure to have everything we needed and spent the evening inside watching TV. Out of all the countries and border crossings, this country seemed the most dangerous of them all.

The next morning, we left for Honduras, and it was all the same thing, the place we stayed, and I can't even remember the name of the town we stayed at. It was as far as we could get that day, so it was where we stayed. It was not as dangerous as Nicaragua, but it didn't have a warm, cozy feel to it either. We ate a quick meal and did the same as the night before, grabbed drinks and food and did what we were told, stayed off the streets.

The next morning, we traveled all day through Honduras and entered Guatemala. I will tell you that each of these border crossings, I had to explain about the fish, and each time, they thought the same thing. It wasn't that I got harassed at all, just questioned, and they looked at them closely. I was waiting to lose them along the way, but each time, they let me go. It was another night close to the station and a quick meal.

The last day, we traveled all day from Guatemala into Mexico. The one thing about this trip was how green and blush the southern portion of Mexico looked. I had only seen it from the northern side, and it was nothing but desert and dry open landscape. Not the southern portion that borders Guatemala. The land was filled with rolling green hills and a lot of vegetation. It just didn't look like the Mexico that I was familiar with. So at least we had something to see for the first part of the trip. As we got closer to Cancun, the landscape turned more into what I knew Mexico to look like.

After about four nights and five days, we had made it to our last destination. It was the last bus trip we would take for who knew how long. It was the end of the trail, and we had three nights here to enjoy my friend's wedding. That night, we stayed at a hostel in town because we had not gotten information from Graydon on where to go. That night, we walked around the old part and the poor part of Cancun. Most people see only the resorts and all-inclusive hotels, but I can tell you there is another part of this beautiful beach destination that is not the same.

The next morning, I had received an email from Graydon, and he told us what resort they were staying at. We really had no idea where we were staying at this time. Would we be able to stay at a resort with them, or would we have to stay in town and come here each day? This we didn't know until we got there.

We walked into the resort after a short bus ride from the main town, and it was beautiful. It was your typical all-inclusive resort with big pools and bars everywhere. We started walking around the pools, and Ronnie asked me, "Is that Jason?" She had never met him, but I had described him perfectly, 6'4", short black hair, and muscular. She pointed to the right person, and just then we made eye contact. He was in the pool with other people who were there for the wedding and yelled out, *"Mundy!"* He jumped out and gave me a big hug, and I introduced him to Ronnie. At about the same time, Graydon came over. The three of us were back together for the first time in a year and a half. It was so good to see my friends that I think I teared up a little. The guys were all set for us and had a plan. We would be staying in Jason's room with him, and they had gotten two extra bracelets for the pool. We all walked up to Jason's room, and once again—I know I'm repeating myself—it was good to see these guys. We dropped off our bags, got into our suits, and headed back to the pool.

Once at the pool, it was game on, and we partied all day long. I did get a good chance to hang out with Graydon and his future wife, Jen. They thanked me so much for making it, and I thanked them for including me in their happy day. The wedding was tomorrow, and it was all set up. They even bought my clothes for the wedding. It was a nice pair of white pants and a yellow Tommy Bahamas shirt. They filled us in on what we needed to do and what time to be there. We were all set and ready to go.

That night, we partied at the pool until dark, and I had a chance to fill them in on our trip. Graydon has always been one of my number one fans, and I feel the same about him. He always told me that I was living life the way it should be and always hoped for nothing but good for me. He is a great person, and I know I mentioned this earlier in the book.

The next day, we started at the pool for the first part of the day, and then everything turned toward the wedding. We got dressed, and everything was right there, so we didn't have to travel anywhere, just be in a certain place at a certain time. Ronnie had brought something to wear as well, and it turns out she had brought a nice yellow top, so it looked like we had planned this a long time ago. It was nice to actually get dressed up a little. For the last six months, it had been about comfort and warmth—that was it.

TAKE A DECADE

The wedding was beautiful, as beautiful as it gets. It was in the gazebo right near the water. Jason, Alex, who is Jen's son, Eric, longtime friend of Graydon, and I stood up with him, all dressed in white pants and short-sleeved yellow shirts. Jen had four of her good friends stand up with her, and we all had the beach look going. At one point, we all put on our sunglasses and posed for a great picture. Jennifer was brought in by horse and carriage, so this was impressive. The whole thing took about one hour, and they said their vows, kissed, and we all screamed happiness for both of them. Her family and Graydon's family were all so nice and made us feel so welcomed. It was a picture-perfect wedding in a picture-perfect place.

After the wedding, we had a nice sit-down meal, drank champagne, and enjoyed a fantastic evening. I do have to mention one thing, and that is Jason and I had been trying to find Graydon's room. It is tradition to mess with the groom a little on his wedding night. He was on to us and would not go to his room unless we were far away. It was this little game we played for several days, and guess who won? Graydon. He was on to us and was not giving up his room number or any clue to where he was staying. We tried to follow him, but he could run faster than I could. It was just fun the whole time.

That night, a bunch of us went out to a big club in Cancun called Carlos 'n' Charlie's. It was a type of place where the DJ got the whole place going with great music and fun games. The place was on fire, and we fit right in. There must have been twelve of us, two cabs, and ready to tear it up. We partied and danced and had drinks poured down our throats and laughed at everything. The boys were back together, and it was another wonderful night out on the town. We stayed there until 3:00 a.m., and by this time, we were loaded. We took cabs back and continued to party in Jason's room, which had a hot tub. How many people can you fit in a hot tub? All of them if you get real close, and that is what we did.

We slept in the next day, and boy, did we need it. Then it was to the pool for one more day of fun and the sun. We did start drinking right after we got something in our stomachs. Jason could not go that long without food, so it was something we all needed badly. Graydon and Jennifer were already at the pool; they had done their own thing last night and we completely understood. It was now Mr. and Mrs. Graydon Ives, and they made a great couple. We joined them around the pool and spent most of the day lounging and drinking but not like the night before. By now, with the wedding over, it was time for them to relax and enjoy this beautiful resort.

The next morning, Ronnie and I packed up our stuff as did everyone else; it was time to go. Ronnie and I had a completely unexpected great time. I mean we stayed at an all-inclusive resort, ate and drank for free, and it cost us nothing. We did buy a few rounds when we went out, but for the most part, it was on Graydon and Jason, and I will always remember this kind gesture. We said our goodbyes and made our way to the airport.

Ronnie was flying back to Oahu, Hawaii. She was starting school in less than two weeks. She had traveled with me for almost six months, and we spent a lot of great moments together. I was going to fly back to Potsdam for a few weeks and spend time with my family, and after that, I really didn't know. I wanted to go back to Hawaii; I just didn't know if it would happen. My plan was to fly home for a few weeks then back to Arizona where I still had a storage unit full of stuff. Would I stay there for a while or what? I really didn't know, so this made for a sad goodbye when Ronnie and I left each other. We both cried and couldn't believe that this journey together was over. We hugged each other and said our goodbyes. Would we ever see each other again? Who knew? It was a sad moment.

32
CHAPTER

Potsdam/Arizona

It was a rather quiet and somewhat lonely trip back home. Ronnie and I had traveled for six months together, and except for a few days, we were together. However, it was still a good feeling going home to share all my stories with my family.

They picked me up in Syracuse, New York, and it was great to give my mom and dad a big hug. It had been tough on them as well having me travel so much without being able to have contact with me when they wanted. Our communication during this trip was strictly done by email. This was the only way to really communicate because phone calls were very expensive. Unfortunately, with e-mail, it was not very personal and lacked emotion in a conversation. It was all done, and we were together now, and everything seemed to be going well.

That first night home, my sister Judy and her husband, Scott, came over with my nephew, Michael, and two nieces, Samantha and Scotlyn. It was the first time in a long time that we sat and had dinner together. Just like anytime I would come home, my mom always made me whatever I wanted for dinner. It was good to be home.

I spent about ten days back in Potsdam. Of course, anyone I ran into got the full story about my travels, and each time I told a story about something, it got better and better. You have to live an experience to be able to talk about it.

That week or so, I spent as much time with each of them as I could. My father is a funeral director, so his schedule can change at a phone call, which he did several times while I was home. He seemed to be doing okay with everything. Now I've mentioned this before when I was in Arizona, but he did have a prescription drug issue, and I was pretty sure he was drinking again. It was not really my place to say anything, just support my mom and hope that she would be okay. Just like in many cases, it is not just the addict that gets hurt, but the people around them as well. My sister, and my mom are very close, so this always helped when I was gone. As of now, things seemed to be going pretty good.

The last night I was home, my mom had gone to bed. My dad walked into the living room carrying two beers. He handed me one, and he opened the other. I was thirty-five years old, and this was the first time I had ever had a beer with my dad. By now, things were harder for him than I had known. The pills alone weren't doing the trick, and he had started drinking again. I said earlier that things were good, but as the day went by, I could tell my dad was not doing that great. His body was shutting down, and only he knew it.

That night we sat in our living room and drank three to four beers each and had one of the best talks we had ever had. We talked that night like two good friends sharing stories. I learned more about his problems and pain. It was a good evening, just sad to know what he was feeling. The one thing for both of us was how Mom was and how she was dealing with everything. He loved my mom and wanted her to be okay even if he wasn't. That night, I had my first beer with my dad, and it would be the last.

Being home is always a great feeling. We have lived in this house my whole life. Actually, my grandfather bought this house in 1928, raised his family of seven, and then my dad and mom bought it from them in 1967. So this house had been in the Mundy family for three generations now, and it truly was a sweet home. So much had been done to the place over the years, and the little trees that my grandfather planted were now 125 feet tall. It was the Mundy residence, and as far as I was concerned, it would always be the Mundy's residence.

TAKE A DECADE

After being home for about a week, I decided to fly back to Arizona. I had a storage unit that I had been paying $75 per month on for almost 2.5 years. It had a lot of stuff in it and personal things that I really wanted. What I would do with everything I wasn't sure yet. Would I stay in Arizona or go somewhere else? The one thing that I was sure about was I needed to make money. My bank account after this great trip was down to about $500, and that would not last long. If I flew to Arizona and had a yard sale, I might be able to make a few bucks to get me to my next spot.

My parents knew that my funds were low and offered to buy my ticket back to Arizona; this helped a lot and gave me a little breathing room. They took me to the airport, and if you had a moment in your life that you could hold on to, this would be one. They both got out of the car, and I gave my mom a huge hug and kiss. I thanked her for everything and as usual she cried. I then went to my father and gave him a big hug and told him that I loved him and it was good to be home. This would be the last time I would see my father alive.

My buddy Murph picked me up at the airport in Phoenix and let me stay with him until I figured things out. Murph and his wife, Kari, had bought a new home near Phoenix, and it was twice as big as their old house. The only problem was it was far away from my other friends, and not having a car would make things tough in seeing everybody, but somehow, I would figure it out.

I spent the first few days making a few calls and getting things set up. By now, I had made my mind up and wanted to go back to Hawaii. I really loved it there, and it seemed the best place to get back on track. If I stayed in Arizona, I would have to get a vehicle first. This would take money I didn't have, and without a car, you can't make money in Arizona. The place is spread out way too much, and the bus system is unreliable. Murph and Kari didn't have a problem with me staying there, but I would want my own place soon enough. This too would cost a lot of money. So it just seemed the best idea was to go back to Hawaii and maybe stay with someone for a short period, where I would not need a car and could make money quickly—at least I hoped.

I contacted Graydon. I wanted to have a garage sale at his place. He lived near a mall and a rather high-traffic area. When we were in Cancun, I had mentioned this to him and he said no problem. So now I just had to get my stuff from the storage unit to his place. That was another phone call and would be an expense. Then I contacted the place where I had lived in Hawaii, and Debra said that someone was moving out in a week and I could have that room. This was about as lucky as it gets. To have a place to move back to and the house that I had left was a miracle in itself. Rooms at this house filled up very quickly because of the location. With this part of my life taken care of, it was a huge relief. I then contacted my captain and told him that I should be back in a week or so and to get me back on schedule as much as he could. Captain Allen told me he would look into things and get back to me as soon as possible. So within just a few days, things were looking good.

After my garage sale, which I made about $1,000, I was able to get a ticket back to Maui for under $400, which left me with a little bit of money in my pocket. Hopefully it would be enough to get me to my next paycheck.

Last night with Graydon, I got to see most of our friends. He had a little party for me, and it was great to give both Jason and him a big hug before I left. I thought both these guys would do very well, and unfortunately, it didn't work out that way. When I gave Jason a hug goodbye, it would be the last time I ever saw him. He went off the deep end with heroin, ruined the business they had been working on, and this put a lot of pressure on Graydon. This pressure and friendship with Jason ended up costing Graydon his marriage and basically went bankrupt.

I spent the last few days with Murph. We would sit outside each night, talk, laugh, and enjoy a few cold beers. By this time, my stress level had declined a lot. Everything seemed to be going well, and my plans were working out. It wasn't until the day before I left that I had received a call from my captain, and he had bad news. The owner of the company didn't want me back. I was blown away and actually hurt by this. I had worked my ass off for this guy for a year and gave him 100 percent all the time. The problem was that when we all worked for him at the same time, we all partied during work, and he found out. So it wasn't just me; it was our whole little group of friends that he didn't want back working for him. It was his company and his decision, so all I could do was thank Captain Allen for trying and told him I would still stop by and say hello. So two days before I left, I found out I *didn't* have a job. It worried me, but there were other boats and things to do to make money. I knew I would be okay, just a pain in the ass for a while. The one thing I have learned is that if one opportunity ends, it just opens time for something else to happen.

    Murph gave me a ride to the airport my last morning, and it was always sad to say goodbye to him. He hoped for the best and told me to keep in touch. With my backpack on, I walked back into the airport for the start of another journey. Stephen Mundy was heading back to Hawaii for who knew how long.

33
CHAPTER

Back to Lahaina, Hawaii

It was the end of August, and I was back in Maui. Once I landed and stepped out of the airport, it felt like I was home again. So much had happened over the last six months, and I was still on cloud nine. It was good to be back, and when my buddy Joel picked me up at the airport, it was good to see one of my friends. There was so much to talk about what I had just experienced, but for now, it was more about hearing how everyone else was doing. Joel filled me in on the way home, and I listened and enjoyed the magnificent view of the beautiful blue Pacific.

I was so lucky to be able to move back into the same house like I said earlier. Debra met me at the door and big hugs all around. The room that was available was the middle room in the hallway, which was small, but I could have cared less. I was back home, and it felt great. It would have been better to come home to a job as well, but that would work out, I was sure of it. We had a few roommate changes while I was gone, and they converted the toolshed into a room as well. This was a separate small building in the backyard that was a 10' × 20' shed. It was used to store tools and stuff people didn't want. It was a cool place, and the rent for this place was only $300 a month. The room in the house was $600, which was still cheap for the area. I had a room, and that was all that mattered.

TAKE A DECADE

There was not a lot going on the day I returned; everyone was working and busy with their lives. So I called Ronnie just to tell her that I made it back to the island and wanted to see how she was doing. School had just started, and she was having trouble finding a place to live, so she was staying at the hostel in Waikiki, Honolulu. It was not easy starting school and living at a hostel, but she was making it work. She said to me, "Why don't you come over here for a few days?"

I thought about it for about five minutes and said, "Why the hell not?" So I unpacked my bags and repacked my small bag and went back to the airport. On the island of Maui, there was a smaller airport on the west side that a lot of the island-hopping planes flew out of, and they had a flight available in two hours. Debra was kind enough to give me a lift, and I was in Oahu in two hours after touching down in Maui. Why not, right? I didn't have a job yet, and it would be good to see her.

I ended up staying with her for about four days. We stayed at the hostel and shared a room with another couple. Ronnie had started classes, and she told me one day to come with her and attend one of her classes. It was a business math class that had one hundred people in it, so they would never know. I actually ended up taking a test the second day and did very well on it for not even being enrolled in the class, let alone the university. Anyway, we had a fun time for a few days and got to see a little more of Waikiki than I had seen before.

We spent some time together, and it was good seeing each other. Her life was different now with school and living on another island. I didn't know what I would be doing, but something would come up. With our lives changing, we had to give each other space, and when I got back to Maui, I considered myself a single man and could do what I wanted. This was easier said than done for both of us.

Back on the rock, and it was now time to see people and get something going. I went over to a buddy of mine, Shawn, who also worked on the boat with me but had left because he couldn't deal with the owner and captain. We had a good talk, and he told me that after we left, a lot of people ended up getting fired or quitting. Now he was working on a house with his brother Drew. Their father had been a contractor, and Drew took over the job when his father had left. I asked Drew if he needed any help, and just like that, I had a job. It was not high paying but would give me something to do and pay rent until something else came up.

We had a great little crew: Drew, Shawn, Josh, and me. The house was a million-dollar home, overlooking the ocean, and they were remolding it. It was fun work, and we all got along great. Drew found out that I could paint, and I did a lot of painting for two months. It was work, and I was making money, and I actually liked to paint, so it worked out great. We would work together all day and then go back to their house and drink beers and play poker. I have to tell you that I'm a better poker player than them, and it helped my wallet. It was all in fun, and we had a great time doing this for about 2.5 months. It was around Thanksgiving that the job came to an end and I was back looking for something different.

The last day we worked together, it was all about just cleaning up and getting our tools out of there. We worked hard that day, and that night, we partied hard to celebrate our job well done. We went to a place called Gabbies, which was a pizza bar that had a pool table and was always packed with people. By now, I had seen most of my good friends, JD, Carmen, Joel, Eric, and the rest of our group. I had not been around the harbor that much, so there were people from there that I had not seen. One guy was my friend Junior, who was a stocky black guy with dreads. He looked like a real brute, but he was so easygoing. I filled him in on my trip, and we got talking. Junior told me he was fishing on a charter fishing boat called *Start Me Up*. He had worked on the boat for about a year and loved it. He was making good money and enjoyed being out on the water. We talked for about a half hour, and he told me they were looking for help. This could not have worked out any better. He introduced me to his captain at the bar, and we talked for a while. He said he would give me a shot, and I was back to work just like that.

Now charter fishing is not an easy job at all. First, you have to be at the harbor by 4:30 a.m., and this was not the easiest thing to do but had to be done. So that next morning with a little bit of a hangover, I met Junior and Ryan at the boat bright and early, and my new career had started. Just a bit of information about starting work on a fishing boat, and that is you don't get paid until you are ready to work the deck by yourself. So I had a job, but the only money I would be making was a few bucks that Junior gave me each day from the tips. It was not easy to survive, and things were tight for a while, but it soon changed.

After working with them for about three weeks, it was the day before Christmas, and Junior wanted the day off. Ryan was cool with me working by myself for the day even though I still needed a lot of work. So that morning, I got the boat set up, and Ryan helped me on the deck as much as he could. He was the captain and really didn't like working hard, not that he was lazy, just he was the captain and the work was for the deck hand. Anyway, we left with our group of people and fished all day long. It was almost the end of the day, and we got a bite. The line went straight down, and we had something big. It took us about an hour, and the fish we had was a 185 lb. yellow fin tuna. This is the big payday fish, and it was so frigging lucky for us to catch this fish. On Junior's day off, we landed one of the biggest tuna caught all year long, and I made some money that day. After everything was said and done, I made $600 in one day, which paid my rent for a month. At this point, I was hooked and fell in love with fishing.

Junior met us at the bar that night and congratulated me on catching a fish he had wanted to catch forever. It just happened one day, and it was awesome. Now I thought things were going good, but about a few days later, Ryan was late to work, his alarm didn't go off, and I didn't call him to wake him up. He was pissed at me, and that was my last day on his boat. He was a tough guy to work with anyway, but I needed a job. Well, the word spread fast around the harbor, and there was another captain that needed help, so I went from getting fired from one boat to getting a job on another boat within one day.

My new captain was John, and he seemed like a nice guy, just very short and direct with his approach. He knew I had only a few months' experience and expected me to do more than I actually knew how to do. It worked for a while but really wasn't fun. At this point, my buddy Joel wanted to get a job on a fishing boat, and I brought him aboard to be my relief guy and give me a few days off. Now Joel had fished his entire life and had a degree in working on diesel engines. He was a perfect fit for any captain with his experience fishing and with the ability to help work on the engines. Well, to make a long story short, Joel ended up taking my place on this boat, and once again, I had no job.

The day John told me that he would rather go with Joel over me, it wasn't a bad thing. He thanked me for helping him out, and there were no bad feelings between us at all. He made the right choice and I didn't blame him. So I left the boat and started walking down the dock. I got to the fuel station, and another captain from the same company was fueling up his boat and we started to talk. I told him that John had decided to go with Joel instead of me, and it was all good. We talked for about five minutes and this is when my career with charter fishing began. Mr. Steve Cravens offered me a spot on his boat, and not only did I start my next career but also start a lifetime friendship with this guy.

Now it is time to tell you about a day-by-day adventure on a charter fishing boat. The company was Start Me Up Sportfishing, and the owner of the company had five boats at this time. Doug, the owner, was a very big guy, like 400 lbs. big. He didn't put up with any shit and ran a tight operation. He hired the captains of the boats, and it was the job of the captain to find deck hands to work with them. SMU was the largest fleet out of Lahaina Harbor and by far the most profitable. The boats were all forty-two-foot Bertrams that were all in good shape. The owner supplied the boat with fuel, ice, and rods and reels and paid for any repairs. The captain and crew supplied all their own fishing lures and whatever it took to catch fish.

So we would leave the harbor around 5:30 a.m. with a group of people, up to six on each boat. We would decide where we would fish based on the weather and day before results. We always said we had a ¼-million-dollar boat with $10K of rods and reels trying to catch a fish of a lifetime for some lucky person.

The fishing part of our day is what kept us doing this day after day. Once we left the harbor and we could see where we were going,

TAKE A DECADE

it was time for me to get the lures in the water. I would get six lines out into the water each based on a certain wave behind the boat. We had the "Long Gone," which was out the furthest from the boat about thirty yards. Then we would stagger the other five lines to the boat, the closest one being just about ten feet from the back of the boat. Each lure would be placed on a wave and would torpedo through the wave on the surface of the ocean. Once the lines were set and ready to go, the waiting game began. We could be out for hours before we got a bite, and then there were days that we never saw a single thing all day. We trolled at about 10 mph with six lures dragging behind the boat, covering as much of the ocean as we could.

This was my job floating around the Hawaiian Islands searching for a big fish. The big fish to catch out here was Pacific blue marlin that could reach one thousand pounds. We also caught mahi-mahi, ono, tuna, and whatever else would go for our bait. For the most part, even the smallest mahi or ono we caught would be the biggest fish that guests ever caught, so it was always exciting to have any fish on the line. We were asked every day if we caught sharks, and the answer was always the same: "If they go for our bait, then yes, we do." In most cases, sharks were caught with bait, and normally, we used just artificial lures. We did use live bait now and then, and yes, we did catch our fair share of sharks.

The fishing was fun, but it is who you work with on a daily basis that makes this job fun. It was always a pleasure to work with Steve. He was 5'10", 170 lbs., with a husky voice and brown hair. He was one of the best liked captains in the entire fleet and had worked out of Lahaina harbor for twenty years. He had worked with other companies and had been working for Doug for a few years when I came along. He was as knowledgeable at fishing as he was in maintaining his boat. He took pride in making sure that he gave each charter 100 percent effort in getting them a fish of a lifetime. It was the Steve-and-Steve team, and we worked great together. Steve was one of the most optimistic, positive people I have ever met. He was the kind of person whose glass was always half-filled. He taught me a lot about whom I wanted to be, and just working with him made me a more of a positive person. His theory was it wasn't what we didn't have but what we did have, and that was all that mattered. I can say that there was not one single day that we didn't have a good laugh about something. To go to work and spend so much time together was what made this job enjoyable for me. We did have our good days of fishing, and we did have our bad days of fishing.

The day was August 11, 2005, and certain dates you just never forget, and this was one of them. We had a private charter that day, a father and his son. The dad was in his late fifties, and the son was mid-thirties. They had paid the $2,000 for an eight-hour trip, which is the cost, brought out beers and food for the day, and were ready to fish. We spent a good portion of the morning just trolling around, hoping for the best. The four of us spent most of the time on the top deck talking and giving them the rundown of the island and living in paradise. It was about four hours into our trip and we had a fish on; it was a marlin because we saw him jump out of the water and started to let out a lot of line. We got the dad in the chair, and he started to reel it in. Marlin are the best fish to catch because of how they jumped out of the water twisting and turning to get that hook out of their mouths. Well, we fought this one for about forty minutes, and we finally pulled a nice 250 lb. blue marlin on the back deck. With that fish on board, we already had a great day. However, we still had about 4 hours to fish, and I got the lines back in the water. One fish is good, but two is always better.

Well, we were back on the top deck, and about an hour later, I was looking back at the lines, which is what I spent most of my time doing, just staring at the lures being dragged behind the boat. Just then, I saw something come up from right behind the boat, and within a split second, we had another fish on. This one didn't jump out of the water; it just started taking the line out faster than any fish before. With all the lines back on the boat, Steve put the boat in reverse, and we started to go back after it. With the waves crashing over the back of the boat and the son in the chair, we had our hands full. The kid lasted about thirty minutes in the chair, and then the dad jumped in for thirty minutes. Once he was tired, I got in the chair for a while until I was spent.

TAKE A DECADE

About an hour and half later, we started to see the fish, but it was going deep now, and that was not good. With a big fish on the line, so many things can go wrong, and luckily for us that day, everything went right. As we got the fish closer to the boat, Steve and I took turns hand-lining the fish a few inches at a time. The four of us all took turns getting this beast back to the boat, and after about 2.5 hours, we could finally see color, and it was close. Once the fish came into complete view, we knew at this time that this was a big marlin. So after about a three-hour fight, the four of us pulled the biggest fish on board I had ever seen. By this time, the trip was up, and we headed back to the harbor with two marlins on board. The one was around 250 lbs., and once we lifted the other one out of the boat with a crane and had it on the scales, we realized we had just caught an 846 lb. Pacific blue marlin. It was 15.5 feet long and made us the heroes of the harbor that day. When we brought fish back, we would hang the fish next to our booth, and this was the best advertising we could do. With that fish hanging there, we had at least one hundred people come to see it. Team Steve and Steve on the *Start Me Up Again* had just caught the largest fish of the season so far. It would be another four months until the end of the year that we had bragging rights for the biggest fish out of Lahaina harbor for the year.

My first year fishing was epic. I caught a huge tuna on day one. We had also caught a big strip marlin earlier that year that was the biggest strip marlin at 130 lbs. and now an 846 lbs. blue marlin. It was a great year, and it was when I got my new nickname for the harbor, and I was now called "Lucky Dumbass." This name was given to me by John, whom I had worked with for two weeks. I loved the name and took honor in having a great first year for big game sport fishing.

Time to just take a break with the fishing. Trust me, there is more to come with that. Besides fishing most of the time, we still had time to have fun. It is great to say that my job was fun except for waking up so damn early, and my personal life was awesome. When I did have time off, it was spent chilling on the beach, hiking, scuba diving, and learning to surf. Every day seemed to have some sort of adventure in it. Don't get me wrong; I did have those days that I did nothing except sleep and prepare for the next four to five days of being out to sea. However, for the most part, there was always someone who wanted to do something. I could get a call from Larry, Joel, JD, Carmen, Eric, Cutts, or someone that wanted to do something. How cool is it that on one day off from work, we could do something in paradise whenever we wanted? Many times, it was just chilling on the beach with a twelve-pack, a football, or a Frisbee, or playing some sort of drinking game. It would work like this: Two people would have an idea to do something, and they would tell one person. That person would relay to another and then to another. It would be nothing to have ten to twelve people show up at the beach with beers to have a good time. When I wasn't out with someone, we always had something going on at the house. With five to seven people living in one house, somebody was always up to something.

This is a little sidenote that I need to mention. When I moved back the first of September, I moved into the small room of the house in the middle of the hallway. It was a room, and I was happy to have it. After about three months living there, the guy who lived in the shed was moving back to the mainland. Debra offered this to me due to my schedule of having to get up so early. I was extremely happy to take the shed. Not only would my rent go from $600 to $300, but it would also give me privacy. It was great to have my own little house. Unfortunately, I would now have to go outside to go inside to use the bathroom and things, but it was so nice to have my own tiny home. Like I said earlier, it was a small shed, and you walked in, and I had a desk to the left, and my clothes were hung on a rod to the right. I had a TV that was possible by running a line from Alan's room through a PVC pipe to my room, so I had basic cable. My bed was at the far end and took up most of the back. It was small, but for me, it was perfect. This would be my home for at least four years and by far the cheapest place anyone could live on the island of Maui.

Back to the house, 795 Wainee, the best place I have ever lived. So with so many people coming and going throughout the day, there was always something going on. The best thing that happened around this time was that my good friend Larry had moved into the house. He had taken Danielle and Jeff's room because they had found their own place in Lahaina and were starting their lives together. I would still see Jeff a lot, which was good because we had become good friends as well. It was nice to have one friend move out and another move in. Larry had been one of my best friends, and to have him live with me was fantastic. We had already done so much together, and this would give us the change to do even more. Everything in my life, living here in paradise was going fantastic.

CHAPTER 34

How Life Changes

There are tough times in life, and then there are tough times. Everything was going great in my life, great job and great friends. Well, every once in a while, life throws you a curveball, and it is up to you and only you to deal with it like you should. My curveball came to me in September.

It was a Sunday, and I had gone to the harbor at 4:30 a.m. as usual to work. We got the boat all set up, and the captain went to get our charter. About fifteen minutes later, he returned with a big smile on his face; the charter had been cancelled at the last minute. I had been working for Start Me Up for about nine months, and this was the first time this had ever happened. It wasn't a bad thing because this just gave us a much-needed day off. So we put everything away, buttoned up the boat, and went home.

It was 7:00 a.m., and I was sitting on my bed watching TV and wondering what to do for the rest of this unexpected day off. At about this time, my phone rang, and I saw it was my brother-in-law calling me from Potsdam. This was kind of weird because he has only called me a few times, and he knew it was early for me in Hawaii. I answered the phone, and a lot of things changed with that conversation.

Scott told me that my father had killed himself in his jeep next to our garage. My emotions took over, and it was by far the worst telephone call I had ever heard. My first question to him was, "How is Mom?" He told me she was pretty shook up and having a hard time with it. Scott told me they were getting me a ticket to come home and get to the airport as soon as possible. Just like that, my world had been tipped upside down, twisted around, and tossed in the wind. *Holy shit, my father is gone.* Certain dates in your life you will always remember, and September 25, 2005, would always be one of those dates for me.

I went inside, and Debra was in the kitchen. I told her what had happened, and she told me to get my stuff and she would take me to the airport. I went back to my room and packed a bag; for how long I would be gone I didn't know.

On the way to the airport, I contacted Steve and told him I might not be around for a while and filled him in on what had happened. Being the person Steve was, he told me, "Steve, you go home for as long as needed and you have a job whenever you get back. Take care of yourself, and I'm so sorry to hear this news." Within one hour of Scott calling me, I was at the airport and a ticket was ready for me. It would be a very long, emotional two-hour wait. I went to the bar and had a few drinks and then called my mom. She was a mess, but Judy and Scott were both there along with my dad's friend Hugh, who worked as a funeral director as well. It was good to hear her voice, and I let her know I was on my way. Coming from Hawaii, it would take an eight-hour flight to Chicago and then a two-hour flight to Ottawa, Canada, which was the closest airport I could fly home to.

After talking with my family, I went back to the bar and had one more for the road. I had also picked up a few minis for the flight because I knew it was going to be tough. Well, the world works in strange ways, and I can honestly say my father did something for me to make this long trip home much better.

We all boarded the plane, and I was in the very back corner and ended up sitting next to a very attractive girl. She was from Colombia, South America, so we instantly had something to talk about. I told her that I was just there about ten months ago and told her all about my trip. Once we were in the air, I offered her a drink on the low-low, and she accepted. She too had brought a bottle of something, and that is what we did. We sat there for the first hour or so talking and drinking, and this kept my mind off what I was going home for. She made me laugh and was a very cool person. About two hours into the trip, we started to get a little closer, and finally, at one point, I just kissed her. From that point on, we had a good time. No, it wasn't a "mile high" experience, but we sat in our seats with a blanket around us and fooled around for a good two hours. We might have made a scene, and at that point, I really could have cared less. All I knew was she was distracting me from my life, and I so appreciated it. After about five hours of drinking and fooling around, we decided to get some sleep. She put a pillow in my lap and lay down and went to sleep. I sat there holding her hand and also fell asleep for a few hours.

When the plane landed in Chicago, we walked off holding hands like we were together and traveling somewhere as a couple. I walked her to her gate and stayed with her until her flight left. It was so weird to actually be sad to see someone go that you had just met eight hours ago. We went from complete strangers to airplane lovers in a short time. When I left her gate and made my way to my gate, I thanked my father for giving me this distraction. I have flown one hundred times, and this had never happened before nor ever again in my life. It was a once-in-a-lifetime event, and I was thankful for it.

So I landed in Ottawa, Canada, and Scott was there to pick me up. I was glad it was just him so we could talk on the way home. He filled me in on what had happened, and it went like this. My parents had a fight that day, and my dad seemed angrier the day before than he had ever been. He was not a man to curse a lot, but I guess the day before, everything was "Fuck that" and "Fuck this" and "Fuck you." The next morning, my mom wanted to get away, so she went up to Judy and Scott's for a few hours. Sometimes, just to get away is the best thing you can do. Well, after a few hours, she went back home, and when she pulled into the driveway, she noticed my dad had parked his Jeep next to the garage in a place he never had parked before. She pulled in and parked her car and she could see him sitting in the driver's seat. She started to walk over to him and knew something was wrong; she went inside and called Judy and Scott to get over here quickly. It took them less than ten minutes, and Scott went over to the Jeep and he could tell that my father had shot himself and was dead.

My dad had used an antique pistol to end his life. He had lost his handguns five years ago because of the possible attempt he had taken back then. It hurt him deeply to lose his guns but never really tried to get them back. He had bought this antique firearm at an auction and was legally able to own it because of the age. Believe it or not, it was a perfect ending for him because he loved his antiques and spent a lot of time selling them for the last thirty years.

Scott had told me that because of the low-caliber weapon, it didn't create a huge mess. My father knew the anatomy of a human, and he had been to many suicides in the past because of what he did. My father knew how to do it, and I know my dad did not suffer.

The first time I saw my mother, there was nothing but tears and sadness. They had been married for thirty-nine years, and he was the only man she really knew. They had raised two kids together, and for the most part, their life together had been good.

We spent the next few days getting all the arrangements made and had a nice service for my father. He had spent time in the military, and we had the local unit do a salute to him as well. I can honestly say the hardest I cried was when they handed me his flag. My mom wanted me to have it, and I still have it to this day displayed in my home.

It was a tough month—that I can say. We spent time together as a family and did everything we could to make it easier on my mom. Judy, Scott, and the kids were there almost every day, and just having her family around was the best medicine for her. My mom and I spent time taking care of his personal matters and getting everything set up for her. My dad was not in debt at all, so he didn't leave her with a financial mess. Thank God for this. Almost everything was in both of their names, so it was just getting his name off certain things and into my mom's. The one big thing we did was take his name off the house and put my sister's and mine on the house as acting owners with my mom having a life estate for the house. For the most part, it was just being with each other that meant the most.

I stayed home for a little over a month. By this time, my mom was back working and ready to move on with the rest of her life and was surrounded with her family and friends. The big thing for me was that my sister was there, and she would do everything to make sure our mother was okay. My dad's friend Hugh, who had lost his wife six weeks before my dad died, was also a big support for my mother. They actually became *real* good friends soon in the future, but I'm jumping ahead just a bit.

My mom and I talked, and she wanted me to go back to Hawaii because she knew how much I loved it there and was doing well for myself. It was a tough decision, but I needed to be happy as well, and I had to move on with my life. I had told her about our Halloween celebration and told her it would be nice to be back for that. With that said, she purchased my ticket home so I could be there with my friends for Halloween. My mom also wanted me to come home for Christmas that year, and we made plans for that as well. It would be hard to take time off work, but family comes first, and they would understand, and they did.

My mom, Judy, Scott, and the girls took me to the airport at the end of October, and it was a tough goodbye all around. There wasn't a dry eye between all of us, and to say goodbye to my mom was extremely emotional. With my arms around her and tears falling down my cheek, I told her how much I loved her and that we would see each other soon.

35
CHAPTER

My Second Home

It was good to be back home, and I was overwhelmed at the support and love that I received from my friends. Most of them I had spoken with while I was home, and they all had wished me the best. It was just wonderful to see them and once again get my life going the best I could.

We did have another fantastic Halloween party, and as usual, we all had great costumes and one big-ass party. Then two days later was my birthday, so it too was another fun-filled day. We spent most of the day on the beach playing drinking games and surfing. These few days were much needed after a long and rough month. Hawaii was my home, and I would stay here as long as I possibly could.

Being gone for a while, I wasn't able to get all my days back right away. Jeff had really stepped up and filled in for me while I was gone, so he had the run of the boat, and I filled in for him when I could. It took about a month or so for me to get most of my days back and back to making the money I was making before. Jeff and I had also set things up for Christmas, and he was not going home, so this worked out great as well. It was back to the normal routine in life and seeing the normal people daily.

The next real big thing for me came just after the first of the year. The owners of the house, Stephen and Lisa, had decided to change things up a little. They wanted to completely remodel the house, and this meant that everyone would have to move out. They had taken a liking to Larry and had asked him to take over the house once everything was said and done. Debra had not been asked to come back, and it had a lot to do with how the place had been run. She was basically making money from all of us and living there rent-free. The only person they allowed to stay during the remodel was Larry and myself. Everyone else had to find a new place to live.

So after the first of the year, it was just Larry and me living there for the duration of the remodel. Now things don't always go as quickly as things might go on the mainland, and this remodel took about eight months to complete. The good thing about these eight months was Larry and I didn't have to pay rent, just basic utilities. However, during this time, we lost cable, a kitchen, and hot water for at least six months. We lived a very rustic life for a while, ate out a lot, and I showered at the harbor almost every day. Larry did stay with his girlfriend, Jamie, a lot, which I couldn't blame him for, but for the most part, it was just the two of us.

It was during this time that I decided to try something different, and I got my real estate license. It wasn't that I wanted to stop fishing; it was just that I wanted to try something that could make a big difference in my life. It was something a little more solid than fishing but would take a lot of work to make things happen. Steve had given me the week off I needed to take my class, and he always joked that he was giving me time off to get another job. I hoped to make millions, but I found out soon enough it was a challenge. Luckily, I still had the fishing boat to rely on and broke my time up between real estate and fishing. The boat was still paying the bills, and I still loved doing it. Anyway, more to come on that, but time to get back to the boat.

Steve and I fished together for about two years until he decided to leave the island and try something else. He had landed a job in the south working as a captain taking crews out to oil rigs. It was sad to see him leave, but it was good for him, and I wished him nothing but the best. We enjoyed a few cold ones that day and a big hug when he left. It wouldn't be the same without him; however, I needed to

TAKE A DECADE

keep fishing and enjoy what I was doing. It was the only money I was making because nothing had really happened for real estate yet.

The very next morning, the new captain met me at the boat; his name was Al Brant. Al was in his mid-forties with blond hair and blue eyes and looked like a surfer dude. He had a high voice that was very distinctive and had been a captain for twenty years. The first day working together, I gave him the tour of the boat and the rundown on our engines and how we had been doing things. The first day, we got to know each other, and by the end of the day, we had become friends. If I had to choose someone to replace Cravens, this was the perfect person. Al and I fished together for about a year and a half. We did have another captain also named Alan and a buddy of mine. We had a great team for our boat, Al and Alan running the helm and Jeff and I running the deck.

So I had the best job for about five years. I fished from 2005 to 2010. I did do a few things on the side during this time, but fishing was my bread and butter. Like I said earlier, in 2006, I got my real estate license and tried to make this happen. It was during a very tough time financially for our country, so it was tough to make a living. I would work at the real estate thing for half of the week, and the other half was fishing. The best thing about fishing was the opportunity to eat fresh fish three to four times a week. If I had some that I didn't want, it was very easy to make a phone call, and one of my friends would take it. This was just one of the perks of the job.

It had been about two years total of me living in Hawaii when I got a call from Julian. We had been in touch a lot during this time, but this call was different. He had gotten all his legal things taken care of and was moving to Maui. This was great, and I was very excited to have him back in my life again. I picked him up at the airport, and he stayed with us for about a month while the construction was going on. It didn't bother me at all, but it did bother Larry a little. He liked Julian, and I thought they would become good friends; it just didn't go that way. Julian sometimes lacked enthusiasm and would rather just party and have fun. Larry always thought Julian took advantage of me, but he didn't understand that Julian and I were brothers and had done so much together. He stayed with us for about a month, and by that time, he had a girlfriend and moved in with her. We saw each other all the time, and he had gotten a waiter job at a restaurant that he had worked at when he lived here many years ago. It was a good job for him except he was always bad with his money. If Julian made $100 that night, he woke up the next morning with $10; it was just who he was. At least he was back in my life, and I was so happy to be able to see him when I could. With my early morning job, and his late-night partying it was tough, but we made it happen.

It was February of 2006, and things had changed for my mother. Remember me mentioning my dad's friend Hugh? Well, after my dad died and Hugh's wife passed away, the two of them had become a couple. Everyone was very happy for them, and it made me feel great to know my mom had someone in her life. It did happen a little quickly, and I can tell you that the first Christmas I went home after my dad had died, they had already started to see each other.

The best thing about all of this was they had decided to come and see me in Hawaii. I had been out here for about 2.5 years, and no one from my family had visited yet. My dad never really wanted to because he was a homebody. Now with my mom with Hugh, they were all about it and we had a blast.

They came to Hawaii in February 2006, and we did everything we could in two weeks. They stayed at the Lahaina Shores, which was right in town. They rented a convertible car, which was something my mom wanted, and we drove all over the island. It was the best few weeks I had while living in Hawaii, and I think it was because I got to show them my new life and introduced them to all my friends. We did it all while they were here: road to Hana, whale watching, horseshoes on the beach, a luau, helicopter ride over the island, and we ate out every night. I had an itinerary for them when they arrived, and we tried to do something every other day. If we weren't out sightseeing, then we were sitting on the beach having cocktails. I tried to get them an ocean view at the hotel, but unfortunately, that didn't happen. This actually turned out to be great because while they were here, the island of Maui was having this huge fire in the mountains. It had been a very dry year, and somehow, a fire started, and it burnt a good portion of the mountains that were basically our backyard.

We would sit in their hotel room and watch the planes fly over dropping water on the fire. It was a spectacular view, and a lot of my friends came over to watch as well. This was when my mom got to meet Julian for the first time, and she fell in love with him right away. He came into the room, put his feet up, and this is when I noticed that I had not lost my good pair of shoes but Julian had borrowed them and was now wearing them. My mom laughed at this, and we still talk about this story today. It was a wonderful week, and it was so good to have my mom see how my life was out here and why I had chosen to come back. She realized at this time that I had made a home for myself and had met some amazing people. She told me when she got back that it made her happy just knowing I was happy and had a family away from my family.

This was one of the best memories I have of living in Hawaii and that was getting my mom there. She had heard many stories and seen a ton of photos, but for her to see how my life was now was the icing on the cake. They enjoyed their honeymoon before the wedding, and on October 20, 2007, I had the honor of walking my mom down the aisle, and she married the love of her life.

Let's take a moment to update you on Ronnie. She had gone to school on Oahu for a year, and we still saw each other as much as we could. After Oahu, she had been accepted to a school in Florida for her doctorate degree in physical therapy. She flew to Maui, and we spent a good week together before she left. It was a fun time and a party time. She had nothing to do except have fun, and I was working seven days a week between fishing and trying to sell a house. It was a busy time, but we had a good week. We stayed in touch the entire time she was in Oahu, seeing each other once a month maybe, but with her leaving for Florida, it was most definitely going to be the end.

It was about at this time that our place had been finished. They had gutted the inside, built new rooms, new bathrooms, and sheetrocked the walls. There was new furniture, a new kitchen, and new roommates. This was Larry's job to fill the rooms, which in Lahaina didn't take long. The first person was Kenny, who was 6'4", 250 lbs., and worked at Moose's as a barback. Then Jennifer, who was from

England and a very cute girl, worked at a bar as well. Then Kenny had gotten his buddy Scotty to move in, and he too worked at a bar. Then this guy Tony, who had moved to the island and worked construction, took the smallest room in the house and turned out to be a great fit. The last room rented went to this girl Silies, who had come to Maui from Oahu to open a new surf store on the island. She was Filipino and very cute. It was at this point that I thought I would take over the place and help the landlords run everything. They liked me a lot, but because of having Julian stay with me under the radar, they chose to have Kenny run the place. They had known him for a while because of where he worked. I really didn't care, and I would have done it, but my plate was already full, and I didn't want another headache to deal with. With the remodel, my rent did go up as well, and now, I had to pay $400 a month. This was still so cheap, and I was very thankful for the place.

So at this time, 795 Wainee Street had a completely different vibe. We all got along great, and it took about a week for all of us to become good friends. Soon after this, Kenny moved a buddy of his out to the island, Joe, who turned out to be a great person and good friend. At this time, Kenny left the bar and started construction with Tony, Joe, and himself. Kenny had also started dating Scotty's cousin Haley, who also was now living with us. and she was a tall, blond bombshell who was very nice to look at. She had grown up near Ottawa, Canada, which is near where I grew up, so we hit it off right away. We had a bartender, construction workers, a retail manager, Haley didn't work, and me, the fisherman. With all of us from different backgrounds and lives, we formed a great family.

It was the end of 2007, and something amazing finally happened, and that was when I sold my first property. It was a very happy day for me. The place sold for $740,000, and my commission check was for $9,990. I went from rags to riches when I picked up my check. It was a good day, and at that point, I figured this is what I would be doing for the rest of my life. I wasn't ready to give up the boat but knew that things might be changing. I knew it took about a year to sell the first one, and I didn't know how long it would take to sell the next one. The economy was not good at all. All I knew was I had money, and man oh man, did I need it.

I contacted Ronnie and told her the good news, and she was so happy for me. She asked what I was going to do with the money, and I told her I wanted to pay off a few bills and try to put some of it back into my business. Now being Ronnie, she had a plan for us. She was finishing up her first semester of school in Florida and really had not planned on going home for the holidays. She asked me if I wanted to go on a cruise. I told her that I would have to think about it for a few days. So about six hours later, I called Ronnie back and told her I was in. "Let's go on a cruise together."

We made the arrangements, and I would fly into Jacksonville, Florida, stay with her for a night, and then drive south to the port and take a six-night, seven-day Caribbean cruise. We would go the week before Christmas, which was cheaper, and then I would be back in Maui for the holidays. We booked our trip, and once again, Ronnie and I were out seeing the world. We left from Port Everglades and went to Key West, St. Lucia, Roatan Honduras, and Belize. It was a fantastic week, and we had a great time. We really didn't do a lot of excursions, just walked around the port towns, found a beach, and chilled out. We spent as much time just sitting around the pools and hot tubs as we could and had a drink in our hand most of the time. We both had money in our pocket, mine from the sale of the house, and she had just received a lot of money for a loan for school. So for a week, we ate and drank whatever we wanted. My bar bill at the end of this trip was close to $800, which wasn't bad, but remember we didn't do a lot except enjoy the ship and each other. This was my second cruise, and I loved every minute of it.

It was just a few days before Christmas when I returned home. I was still working on the boat, and we had been given the opportunity to take Christmas day off if we wanted, and we choose to take the day off. Even though I had just had a good nine days off, it was still nice to have Christmas off. I woke up and opened the gifts my family had sent to me and called home and talked with everyone. It is not the same as being home, but it was good to hear the voices of my family.

Mom and Hugh were together along with my sister and her family, so all was good back home.

It was about a year and a half after Steve left for the oil rig gig, and he had made the decision to come back to Maui. It worked out great because Alan was moving on to another job on a different boat, Al wanted more time off, and Jeff and I worked things out to give each of us enough time on the boat to make a living. Luckily for me, I still had a few bucks in my pocket and was hungry to sell another house. Hopefully it would not take another year, but things were not getting any better for our country, and a trip to Hawaii was definitely not for everyone out there to afford. It was good to have Cravens back, and once again, we had the Steve and Steve team back at it.

I was still doing as much as I could with real estate and fishing as much as I could to keep a cash flow coming in. The days just blended. Steve and I had the month of March where we fished every day except for about five. It was a busy month, and financially, it was a great month. I was always around at night to answer any questions concerning real estate, but there was just not a lot happening.

It was around spring sometime, and JD and Laura came up with the idea of renting a house in Hana and a bunch of us chipping in and spending a few days on the other side of the island. We all thought it was a great idea, and a few weeks later, the group of us caravanned three hours to a beautiful house in Hana. The group included JD, Laura, Joel, Larry, Jamie, Carmen, Justin, Eric, Dino, Cutts, and a few others, friends of friends. We all split the cost equally, and it came to about $200 each, which we figured should cover most of the expenses. JD, Laura, and Joel did a lot of the grocery shopping, and a few of us went and bought the beer and liquor. We had two nights and three days to prepare for, and we bought eight thirty-racks, and we picked up at least four handles of booze for the three days; we thought this would be enough.

To describe this weekend with one word, it would be *laughter*. We had a blast. The house was perfect—no neighbors—the weather was perfect, and we partied the entire trip. We prepared all the meals together, some cooked and some cleaned, and we all ate together. During the day, it was drinking games, card games, walking around, tossing the football, surfing, doing a hike, and like I said, there was a smile on all our faces the entire trip. The crazy thing about this weekend was we were almost out of booze by the next morning. In one day, we went through eight thirty-racks and four handles of booze. Not to worry, we just went the next day and bought more. This was a fantastic time with all my close friends, and it would be something we would do again. Actually, about a year later, we did the same thing, just rented a different house and had more people.

Another very fun experience was with all my roommates. We had made the plan to go to Hana and camp out for the night. It would be the first time that everyone in the house went somewhere together and we had a great time. Kenny, Haley, Dan, Silos, Tony, Jen, Joe, and I plus about twenty other people all made the trip. We camped out at the Seven Sacred Falls, which is a place I had camped out several times. It is this big field near the ocean, and all you do is pick a spot. We had also planned on having an "especially good time" that night because someone had gotten hold of magic mushrooms. It had been a long time since I had done this, but I was completely up to it. We all got our camp set up, and just about the time the sun was setting, we all joined in and all had a good handful of these nasty-tasting things. If you have eaten mushrooms, then you know how bad they taste. If you haven't, then basically you're eating something that grows under cow shit, so you can imagine. That night, we had an absolutely amazing time. We swam at night in the pools, walked around the campsite, and met other people, but the big thing was we played Frisbee with a glow-in-the-dark Frisbee, and if you have ever tripped on 'shrooms, then you can imagine what it was like for twenty-five of us to watch this orange and neon disk traveling in the air; it was the best. That night, we laughed so hard that my stomach hurt the next day. Silos and I had the best time laughing at my little tent, and just watching her have a great time made me laugh even more. It was just another wonderful night in my life.

There is just so much to talk about and so many great times during this block of time. Work was good, and I was surrounded by good people. As far as relationships go, it was a time in my life that it was more about just me. It was a time in my life that I spent doing things for me, and I don't regret it at all. I can say that these three to four years were all about me, and I look back now, and I'm very happy to say that I did this for me and only me.

36
CHAPTER

2008

My life for the past eight years has been something out of a book or movie. It had been a whirlwind of adventure and experiencing things that I had never thought in a million years I would get a chance to do. I have now been living full time on Maui for close to six years. Life here is as close to paradise as you can fathom, and I thank God every day for the opportunity. However, this year was one of the toughest years I had ever gone through.

Everything started out great that year, work was going well, the fishing had been good, and we were making money. I was close to selling another house and hoped it would happen soon. I had finally bought a new vehicle; my car was falling apart. I got a good deal on a Nissan Frontier, which was just what I wanted. So life was good for the first half of the year. The big thing about this year was the damn economy. By 2008, the recession had hit the country hard, and by this time, we could feel the effects on Hawaii. With money being tight for so many, going to Hawaii was just not an option. By the summer of 2008, things had gotten bad.

In July, I sold my second home and made about $6,500, which helped out for a while. I'd been selling real estate for almost two years, and this was only my second sale. With the money I made from this, it really just got my head above water and gave me a little savings account, which unfortunately didn't last long. It was something, and to have a few bucks in my pocket was a good thing. If I could have predicted the future I would have saved more of that money, but I just didn't know.

The other thing that was fun and I will never forget is Silos's birthday party. She wanted to have an Edward Scissorhands party, and let me tell you, this is a good way to celebrate your birthday. What is an Edward Scissorhands party? You take two 40 oz beers and duct-tape them to your hands. You have to drink both of them before you can have them cut from your hands. It is crazy because some people can't drink one beer without having to take a piss. Now you have to drink 80 oz of beer before you can do anything. That morning, Tony and I went to the other side and bought eight cases of 40 oz beers. We had planned on at least twenty people joining us, so we bought what we could. That night, we all formed a big circle, and each grabbed a 40 oz beer for each hand. We then had two people that went around and taped them to our hands. Once everyone had taped up, Silos said a few words, and the drinking began. Remember you can't take a piss, smoke a cigarette, or scratch your ass until both of those beers are gone. We started with twenty people, and by the time the night was over, we had more like thirty-five people show up, all with two 40s and ready to party. It was a blast, and it took me about thirty minutes to finish both. I was the third person to finish; Kenny, our big guy, was number one. It took Silos over an hour to finish, and she almost pissed her pants. So if you want to do something different for your birthday, now you have another choice.

After this ordeal, a group of us went over to Lani for a few nights of camping and having fun. Tony and Dan from the house had not been there before, so we got a small group of people together. That night, we snuck into the pool area and had a blast. We met a group of people, and we started to do races in the pool. We had to be making so much noise but never got asked to leave. Anyway, we were partying and doing races, and something went wrong with my knee, and by the next day, I could hardly walk. I remember waking up and thinking to myself, *Why the fuck does my knee hurt so badly?* Well, it was from kicking so hard in the pool, doing backflips into the water, and drinking a ton of booze. I made it back to the house and kept ice on it for a few days. It did make fishing that week an absolute nightmare. I wore a brace and wrapped it with an ace bandage. It hurt a lot when we hooked into a big fish, but at that point, I could only suck it up and deal with the pain. Steve and Al both helped a lot the next few weeks, and it was bothersome to me for at least three weeks. Basically, the month of August, my knee was an issue and limited me on what I could do.

Just about the time my knee started to feel better, we had a charter, and on this charter was a cute girl. We would get cute girls once in a while, but for the most part, it was dudes and maybe a girlfriend or wife. Well, this charter had a single girl, and that night, I took her out, and she ended up staying with me. She was one of those girls that liked it rough, and rough it was. The big problem happened when she kicked me accidentally in the ribs and literally broke one of my ribs. She felt terrible. We did finish, but the next day, the ribs hurt so badly. It was hard to breathe, and everything seemed to hurt. I had just gotten over my knee and now this. I'm a healthy person and do not get sick very often. I had been out here for a while and never once had a cold or anything. Now I went from spraining my knee to breaking a rib, oh well. I never called that girl again—that was for sure.

Now we were in the first part of September, and the charter business was very slow. The owner of the company decided to pull our boat out of the water and replace the engines. This meant that we would not have a boat for at least two months, which meant no income for a while. About halfway through the month, things started to get real tough, and not just for me but anyone that was working on boats. I made sure not to spend money on anything I did not need. Steve and Jeff were able to spend a few weeks working on the boat in dry dock, but with my knee and ribs, I could not go, which sucked for me.

The only way I was making any money for a good portion of the fall was by running a football pool. It was a $10 winner-take-all each week, and I was getting twenty-five to thirty each week to play. I did win a few weeks myself, and people who won giving me a tip actually helped pay my rent for a few months. Another way I was making money was selling mangoes to the local restaurants and farmers markets. It wasn't a lot of cash, but everything helped. This was a time of life when friends really helped each other out. Julian even helped me out during those few months. He never really had much, but just to stop over with a thirty-rack and shoot the shit for a few hours was a good thing. By this time, I was a homebody and just couldn't do much because of my knee/ribs and money. I can say that I did watch a lot of movies that fall, and it was all I could do.

The big thing, the one thing that really made this year a bad year, happened right before Halloween. Our roommate and friend Silos had met this guy and seemed very happy. We really didn't spend a lot of time with him, but she seemed happy. At least that is what we thought. Well, it was on a Monday morning Haley came out to my shed and asked if I had seen Silos. I told her yesterday I thought I did but really couldn't remember. Haley told me that her job had called and she did not show up for work. Silos was the manager, and it was her job to open the store and get things rolling. We thought that this was strange, but we figured she had taken the day off and was with her new friend. We all just kind of blew it off that day and went about our business. Well, the next day, Tuesday, they called again and she had not shown up for work again. By this point, the roommates, Kenny, Tony, Joe, Jen, Haley, Dan, and I, were a little worried. Silos had come from Oahu to open the first Volcom surf shop on the island and had a great job. Not only did she have a great job, but she loved it as well and was great at her job.

The one thing we had found out through a few people was that the guy she was dating had left her and moved back to the mainland in like forty-eight hours. We had no contact information from him—hell, we didn't even know his last name. It just wasn't like her to get bent out of shape over a guy, but who knew? On the second day of her not being at work, I called the company and talked with her boss, and he told me that the past week, she had been acting differently and she had not turned in a few of the deposits. Silos was not hurting for money; her mom was a lawyer in Seattle and she was making good money on her own. So that night, all the roommates sat around and tried to figure out what the hell she was doing. Her mom had called me a few times, and we all tried to let her mom know that she was probably just off doing something crazy and not to worry. We all were basically waiting to see what happened Wednesday morning. Would she show up for work, come home, or at least something?

Wednesday morning came, and this time we called the shop to see if she had made it to work. They told us she had not shown up again, and they were as worried as we were. It was time to do something, and the other manager at Volcom called the police and filed a missing person report. At this point, her mom was calling me from Seattle with any updates we had, and unfortunately, I had to tell her that we had not seen her and that her work had filed a missing person report. The police stopped by that morning and asked us a few questions about her, and we told them everything we could. The seven of us were now worried, and something wasn't right.

Tony, Dan, and I decided to go and see if we could find her or at least find her truck. She drove a big blue Toyota Tundra, and it was one of the only ones on the island that color. We told the other roommates that we would drive to the two airports and see if we found anything. It was a start, and to be honest, we had to do something. By this point, the seven of us were going crazy and really worried about her.

The three of us left the house, and we had made the decision to first drive to the other side of the island and check out the main airport. It was one of two airports, the main one or the smaller one, which was only about ten minutes away. We decided to check the big one out first, which was forty minutes away. We pulled out of our driveway and made it to the main road. There was only one road on this part of the island that went to the other side of the island. You can either make a left and go the long way, which could take two hours because the road was very narrow at certain points, or turn right and take the easy way, which was how 99 percent of the people would go to get to the other side. We were going to turn right, which only made sense. Just then, a fire truck with their lights on went by us, going in the opposite direction we had planned on. Tony and Dan said, "Follow the fire truck, let's just see," so I turned left, and we could check it out first, then who knew? So in ten minutes we hit the airport, did a quick drive through, and no truck. We decided to see where the fire trucks were going and went from there.

Soon after we were in the area, we spotted the fire trucks and stopped to see what was going on. We pulled over, thinking we would see her truck off the road or something and this was why they were there. They had been called out for a brush fire, and that was it. The three of us sat there for a minute and Dan said, "While we are here, let's at least check out this place called Chutes and Ladders." It was this cliff that you could climb down using ropes and a ladder and spend time in a natural pool that was created by the ocean. We had all been there before, and it was a beautiful place, and it was only about five minutes up the road. Dan had told us that he and Silos had been up there before and she loved it, so it was something to check out. All along this trip, we had been in contact with the roommates and her mother always with the same answer, nothing yet.

We pulled off the road, and there was a short drive to get to the bluff overlooking Chutes and Ladders. I drove down the trail and through the woods, and as soon as it opened up, we saw her truck. "Holy shit, we found her," is what we all said. It was the only vehicle there. We pulled up, and the three of us got out. We walked up to the truck, and she was sitting in the front seat driver's side. She had her head in her lap, so we really couldn't see her face. I knocked on the window, and she didn't move. Tony and Dan knocked on the passenger side window, and she didn't move. The three of us shook the truck with all our force, and she didn't move. At this point Tony picked up a rock and broke the back passenger side window. I reached in and unlocked the door. Tony had gone to the other side, the driver's side, and we opened the doors about the same time. I reached in and put my hand on her leg; it was cold.

Once we had opened the door, we all looked at each other and said, "What is that smell?" The three of us looked at each other, and we knew things were not good. Tony had reached around her and picked her up; just then, we heard what sounded like a breath.

We had to get her to the fire trucks, which were just down the road. Tony carried her to the back of the truck and sat in the back holding her. Dana and I jumped in the cab, and I drove as fast as I could to get to where the fire trucks were. We knew they would have equipment to maybe help her. I pulled into where the trucks were and actually slid in sideways; I was going that fast. They jumped out and realized we were there for a reason. They asked us if this was the girl who was listed as a missing person earlier that morning, and we said yes. They jumped in the back of my truck, Tony got out, and the three of us just stood and watched as they tried to shock her several times without any success.

They worked on her for about ten minutes, and at that point, they came over to us and told us they were sorry, but our friend was gone. Silos had committed suicide and died that night. We knew as soon as we saw her, it wasn't good, but we had that one breath and thought just maybe. Even in the back of the truck, we could tell her limbs had stiffened up and she was unresponsive. They contacted the police and anyone else that might be needed for a situation like this. At this point, we were told not to talk to anyone, so we stopped answering our phones. The police arrived shortly after, and they separated the three of us. The officer that first questioned me told me that due to the situation, he would have to read me my rights. I wasn't under arrest, but because the body was moved, they had to follow procedure. I really couldn't have cared less; my friend was lying in the back of my truck dead. So they separated the three of us, and we all were asked the same questions, and we all answered the same. After about twenty minutes of questioning, they freed us of any charges, and at least we could hang out together. It was a sad moment, and we all showed our emotions.

It took about an hour for the coroner to show up and do what he had to do before a body was removed. They took her out of my truck, and at this point, we were free to go. Once on the way back, I had the guys call all the roommates. We wanted to tell them as a group; we called everyone and told them to be at the house in twenty minutes. Most of them were already home, but a few had to leave work.

We pulled in, and once all the roommates were there, I told them what had happened. There was not a dry eye in the room, and we all felt like we had just lost a family member. The hardest part of this was her mother didn't know yet and was calling me every fifteen minutes. We had been home for about fifteen minutes, and the police showed up, and the detective told us not to talk with her mom. They had contacted a department near where her mom lived, and they were sending a detective with a priest to tell her in person. They didn't want to tell her over the phone, and we were all grateful for that. Could you imagine getting a phone call and someone on the other end telling you that your twenty-eight-year-old only child had just taken her own life? We waited about an hour before we had been told that she now knew, and then I called her.

Her mom was torn apart and was beside herself. *Why would she do this?* was still a question on all our minds. That afternoon, the detective stopped by again, and they went through the truck and found several notes she had written before she decided to take a handful of sleeping pills and drink a half-bottle of vodka. They told us that she had just gone to sleep, no pain at all, and didn't wake up. She had written a note to all her roommates saying she was sorry and loved each and every one of us. She had also written a note to her mom and one to her dad, who lived elsewhere. They would receive those letters when they arrived.

We all decided that day to have a "celebration of life for her." The family wanted to have a small ceremony with her roommates and family that had arrived the next day. The funeral home had contacted me and told me that it would not be a good idea to have an open casket, and at this point, they had decided on cremation. The following day, we all met at the funeral home, and each of us said a few words about Silos and how we would all miss her. This was short and sweet, but we wanted to do more.

Now, not really working, I had a lot of time, so I took the lead on everything. We told her family that we wanted to have a big celebration of life for her with all her family and her Maui family as well. The seven of us put together a fantastic day. We had people play music. We had people who donated vans to get people up to where we had it. We had the celebration at the same spot she had taken her life. Kenny, Tony, and Joe built a cross with her name on it, and they placed it in the ground, concrete and everything. It was really a nice thing to have up there when her family arrived. We had food and drinks, which were given to us from local businesses, and at least fifty people showed up that day.

I started everything off with a little speech about not expecting something like this to happen to such a great person, and from there, many people stood in front of her family and friends and told a story about Silos and what she had meant to them, people whom she had worked with, surfed with. Silos had gotten into capoeira, the Brazilian martial art, and her teacher spoke about what a pleasure it was to have known her. Both her parents spoke and thanked us all for being such good friends to their daughter and how much they appreciated this celebration. At this time, they had received the ashes from the funeral home, and we all got to take a small cup of her ashes, say a few words, and then toss them into the air. She had picked one of the most beautiful bluffs overlooking the ocean on the island of Maui to end her life. She will always be in my thoughts, and I will never forget this wonderful person.

With her death a week before Halloween, it even put a damper on the biggest party of the year. We did celebrate and did something that night to honor our friend even if it was just a shot. My birthday a few days later was real mellow. Just a few friends, Joel, Larry, and whoever else was out that night, sat at the blue lagoon and had a few beers, and I was home by 10:00 p.m.

By the middle of November, my ribs finally felt better, so I went surfing with Larry and we hit some big waves. They were bigger than I should have been surfing, but you only get better by pushing yourself. Well, that day, I had taken a few waves and was held underwater for longer than I liked and had been knocked around the reef pretty good. We spent a lot of time in what they call the "washing machine," which is where the wave holds you under the water, tossing and turning you like a washing machine. It is not fun at all and can be very scary at times. Oh well, we had fun and spent most of the day laughing at each other on how we looked when we would surface gasping for air. Larry and I loved this shit, and it was just a day at the beach. I did, however, cut the top of both my feet on the reef. I sat on the beach and watched my feet bleed until I could get it to stop. I had to use my shirt to stop the bleeding, so there went another shirt. It wasn't like I needed stitches or anything; they were just big scrapes on the top of each foot. Oh well, I would live.

It had been about two months since our boat had been down, and there was no sign of it getting done in the near future. The owner was waiting on parts, and things were just moving real slow on the island. We had six boats in our company, and a year ago, all six would be out on two trips a day. Now we were lucky to get three boats out a day for one trip each, so it wasn't like I could even pick up shifts on other boats; we were all scraping by. By the end of November, things were getting real tight. One good thing about living with a lot of people was the recyclables. Yes, things were that tough that about every two weeks, I would collect all the bottles and cans and take them in for money. I always bought another thirty-rack, and the rest was mine. Believe it or not, I paid for my cell phone, groceries, and gas for my truck all from recyclables. It takes a shitload of cans and bottles, but it can be done, and I can tell you firsthand it helped me out.

You remember those scrapes on the top of my feet from surfing? Well, they were still there. About two weeks after surfing, I could tell that I had gotten a staph infection, and it just made things worse. Now my feet hurt, and it was a pain in the ass just getting around. Staph infection comes from bacteria that are found in a lot of reefs. It is a very common thing out here, and if you are a surfer, you have gotten staph at one point or another in your life. Not having insurance, I had to take care of it myself, keep it clean and keep it dry. It was actually disgusting to look at the top of my feet. Each foot had a circle about the size of a fifty-cent piece of rotten skin. It was like a blister that had broken but had not yet dried up. I would keep a bandage on it during the day, and by the end of the day, the bandage would be covered in blood and puss. The worst part of this whole thing was it hurt to walk, and it didn't go away quickly.

With really nothing going on at this point in my life, I did have the chance to go home for Thanksgiving; it had been a long time since I was home for this holiday. I had told my mom that things were slow, and I had no idea what would happen around Christmas, so I decided to go home for turkey day. Of course, my feet still hurt, and it was rough having to put on a shoe, but I made it happen. This was my first Thanksgiving at home in a long time. I mean after moving to Arizona and then the last eight years traveling, it was all about getting home for Christmas. This year was different, and I had a great time being home. We didn't have to do much except eat and drink. The weather had turned, so there was nothing to do outside, and that was perfect. Honestly, Thanksgiving is one of my favorite holidays. You don't have to buy anything for anyone, just sit around, eat turkey, and drink eggnog.

The holiday season was really quiet on the island that year. The hotels, restaurants, excursions, you name it, they were slower than normal. We all did what we could to keep our head above water, and with me, things had not improved. We still did not have a boat to fish on, and real estate had come to a standstill. I can tell you that around this time, I was living on the dollar menu at McDonald's and drinking one 40 oz beer a day. I would have bread and peanut butter as a backup, but I can tell you my diet was very limited. My big question around the second week of January was how I was going to pay rent. I remember like it was yesterday, the middle of January 2009, I had about $200 to my name. My rent was $400, plus I needed money for food and all that good stuff. Even if I didn't spend a dime, I was still short of rent, and at this point, I had no idea when and how I would make any money. That first two weeks of the New Year were just a continuation of the year before. I lay in my bed, watched TV, and just thought about how shitty this year had turned out. All I can say is life has a way of leading you to the next chapter in life.

CHAPTER 37

One Phone Call

Injuries, poverty, and death. This is how I had spent the last six months of my life, and I was so ready for a change. Life works in strange ways, and my life changed with one phone call. It was the middle of January, and I can honestly tell you that I had driven north to a camping area and come to the conclusion that at the end of the month, I may be living here full-time. I had heard of a few people doing it, and I was two weeks away from this potential life.

It was midafternoon, and my phone rang; it was Captain Al from Start Me Up. When I saw his name, I thought, *Oh, he has a fishing trip and needs help. Great, I'll make a few bucks and spend the day fishing.* "Hello, my friend. How is Al doing today?" was what I said. He said he was doing well, and then he asked what I was doing.

"Absolutely nothing and going crazy," was how I replied.

He asked me if I wanted to help him take a boat from Maui to Oahu. He said, "I'll give you $200 and pay for your plane ticket back." Well, that about floored me; $200 was all I needed for rent, and I wouldn't have to sleep on the beach.

"Hell, yes," I said.

He filled me in on the details. The boat was the *Red Rhino*, which I knew well. We needed to leave tomorrow. "But someone has to sleep on the boat tonight, and I need you at the harbor in two hours." He asked me if I could do this. He knew it was short notice, but he had just gotten the opportunity that day, and he too needed money. I told him, "I'll meet you at the dock in two hours, no problem, and thank you."

I jumped out of bed with a purpose, and my mental state went from depressed and miserable to happy and excited. I grabbed a bag and filled it with a few things—nothing much, just a pair of shorts, two T-shirts, underwear, and my bathroom stuff. I waited an hour and walked down to the harbor. Al got there about fifteen minutes later. He told me that he had gotten a lead from a friend of his that the *Red Rhino* had been sold to an American man living in the Philippines. Al had gotten a hold of this guy whose name was Jim. He asked Al if he could get the boat to Oahu for a two- to three-week wet dock to get the boat ready to make the trip to the Philippines. Al had not met the guy, just talked to him over the phone and agreed to relocate the boat for him. That was about it, and we had something to do.

We got to the *Red Rhino*, which was moored just out of Lahaina Harbor. This boat had been an icon of the harbor since I was there. It never moved and was owned by Atlantis Submarine Company as a boat they could use to work on the sub or was used to dock the sub next to when we had bad weather. Joel and I had also fished off this boat many times, so I knew the boat and always loved this boat.

The *Red Rhino* was an 85' × 35' steel hull catamaran that was built by the US Navy in 1966 as a torpedo recovery vessel. The stern of the boat used to be a ramp that could be lowered down, and with the use of a small crane that was on the boat, they could pull test torpedoes or inactive ones back onto the boat. The back end had been modified so the ramp was no longer there, but the small crane was still on board. So to look at the boat from the water, the boat had a large back deck, like 60 percent of the boat was all back deck. Then the cabin area stood two stories above the water. The helm of the boat was in front of the living quarters above the bow of the boat.

We get on the boat, and we were on the back deck. There were two doors on each side of the boat, and they led down into the engine rooms. This was a catamaran, so one engine was in the port compartment, and the other engine was in the starboard compartment. Once you left the back deck, you walked into a large tool and workshop room. It was 25' × 20' and had toolboxes, cutting tanks, work benches, and just stuff for the boat all over. Then you walked through a steel door, and there was a lounge area with a couch and a few boxes with junk in them. This was about the size of a good-sized living room. Going forward and through another steel door, you reached a small hallway. Off this hallway were three rooms that were basically in the bow of the boat. The first room was a two-person bunk room. The second room was a head with toilet, sink, and small shower, and the third room was another two-person bunk. At the end of the hall was another room that went to the left, and this room was a shower room and was used for diving equipment. Now right across from the second bunk room was a set of stairs that goes up to the next deck. At the top of the stairs was the galley and had several tables for eating. The room was about twenty-five feet wide and twenty feet deep. The galley had a full stove, cupboards for dishes, a small fridge, a stainless-steel sink, and a small island in front of the stove. The galley area had two tables on each side. The one on the right side seated five no problem, and the other one seated three no problem. On each side of the galley area were two more rooms. These were the state rooms, maybe 8' × 6', which had a queen-sized bed, a dresser, a desk, and a small window facing the ocean. Between these rooms and in the middle of the galley area was a door that led to the helm. The helm was twenty feet long and only about five feet wide and loaded with all the electronics and the wheel, and from the helm, you could see the bow of the boat right below you.

Now off the helm was the captain's quarter, which was a small room six feet deep and ten feet wide. It had a built-in bed, a small dresser, and a desk. Everything in the captain's quarters was made out of wood except the mattress of course. Then if you walked out any door from the helm or the galley, you would find a set of ladders that had metal rungs and were attached right to the boat. Climb the ten-step rails and you were now on top of the boat. The entire area above the galley, staterooms, and helm was all just an open deck. From here on top of the deck, you were a good thirty feet above the water, and it had the best view from anywhere on the boat. Well, I should not say that because from the top deck was our crow's nest, which was where all our electronic gadgets were secured. If you're up in the crow's nest, you were now a good fifty feet above the ocean, and from there, you could see the entire boat, bow to stern, port side to starboard side. Another thing about the top deck was that there was a steering station, which was directly above the helm that could be used to steer the boat as well. The only thing about this station was that you didn't have your instruments, just a way to steer the boat and a throttle. It was, however, a great advantage to be able to see your surroundings from this vantage point.

Al and I did a sweep of the boat and checked out as much as we could. It had been held in place by several large chains and ropes. Al had been on the boat the day before, and they were able to start the boat and release the big chains. This meant that the boat was being held by only a few smaller lines and was vulnerable to breaking the lines and washing up on the shore. This we didn't want to happen, so someone would have to spend the night on the boat alone just in case. Guess what, I volunteered for this, and Al gave me a quick overview of starting the engines if something went wrong. I did stop at the store on the way down and bought a few things to eat and drink. I didn't know what to expect and wanted to come prepared just in case we were on the boat for the day, which turned out to be the night.

After about an hour or so, Al left and told me he would be back first thing in the morning. It would take about ten hours to go from Maui to Oahu, and we wanted to make the crossing during daylight. This was the safer and easier time to go. With that said and done, he left, and I had the entire boat to myself.

That night, I went through every cupboard, drawer, and shelf, under the mattress, through each toolbox, in and out of each engine room, and walked the entire boat at least twenty times. It was a lot of fun. I enjoyed a few beers, ate my food, and slept that night in the captain's quarters. It was so beautiful to sit on a boat and stare at all the lights on the island. It was so peaceful and quiet out there. All you could hear was the waves crashing against the hull, and the boat just rocked me to sleep. This was the first night on the boat, and I thought it would be the last, but things changed quickly.

The next morning, I was up early and waited about an hour for Al to show up. I could see him in the dinging making his way out to me. He had brought coffee and donuts for breakfast, and he was as excited as I was to get going. We did our engine checks and fired up each engine—so far, so good. We checked all the fluids and figured out how to get the generator started and functioning. With everything a go, he pulled forward, and I threw off all the lines. The *Red Rhino* was actually moving and would be gone forever from the waters off Lahaina.

Once we were underway, we kept an eye on all the gauges, did engine checks every hour, and took turns at the wheel. For the most part, we sat at the helm and just shot the shit and talked about how miserable our lives had been for the past few months. He had also been out of work and getting a few charters here and there, but for the most part, it had been a rough few months for him as well. We talked about the fact that this boat was going to cross the Pacific Ocean and that he might be going with them. The owner had mentioned something about Al making the trip with a group of guys. The owner was going to fly a crew from the Philippines to Hawaii, and they would take the boat back to the Philippines. As soon as he told me this, I told him that if they needed an extra hand, I would go. I had got nothing going on right now, so why the hell not?

We had a very smooth crossing, and after about ten hours we had approached our destination. It is such a fantastic view when you approach Oahu. You have Diamond Head, which is an inactive volcano, and the skyscrapers that line the beaches of Waikiki, and as we passed the downtown area, we could see the Pearl Harbor Memorial and the start of the naval base that had a lot of huge-ass boats. Our new home for the boat was Pier 43, which was in the industrial part of Oahu. We had everything entered in our GPS, and with the help of our electronics, we found the pier without any problem. Once at the dock, we got the boat secured to the side, and at this point, I thought our job was done. We just had to wait for the owner to show up and we would be done.

TAKE A DECADE

Jim arrived about an hour later. He was about seventy years old with a crew-cut hairstyle that was gray and white. He was about six feet tall and about 225 lbs. He looked like a hard-ass from first sight and someone you just would not mess with. He got on the boat and introduced himself, and it turns out he was a very nice guy. We talked about the boat, and he thanked us for delivering it from Maui. He told us what his plans were for the boat. He owned an oil and natural gas business in the Philippines, and this boat was going to be used to lay cable on the ocean floor searching for natural gas, and it would also be used to take crews out to his bigger boats. He owned about four boats; most of them were 250- to 300-foot oceangoing boats. He himself had been in the Navy for four years as a young guy, originally from Florida. He had spent time in Southeast Asia and fell in love with the people and the islands. So he had spent a good portion of his life living and working in the Philippines. He had no children and had recently gotten married for the first time to a much younger Philippine lady, whom we met later. Her name was Mia, and when Jim told us about her, he said *Mai* as in "mine." He was a very straight shooter and had my respect after about two minutes of conversation.

Jim told us his plan and said this boat needed a lot of work before he could send it across the ocean. It had to have inspections and paperwork done. Jim did not know anyone on the island and was doing all of this for the first time. So he asked Al and me if we wanted to stick with him for a few weeks and help him get the boat ready. He asked how much we would have to get to make it worth our while, and we came up with $175 a day. With this, we would be able to sleep on the boat, work eight to nine hours a day, and make some money. Al and I agreed to his terms, and just like that, I had a job. It might only be for a few weeks, but it would take care of the situation I was in at that point. That night, Jim took us out for dinner, and we started a game plan of what we needed to do. It was a lot of stuff, and we would need help. Jim told Al to hire as many people as we needed and gave us money to get started. He did also pay us for the delivery that day, so I now had $200 in my pocket, and it felt good.

The first morning, the three of us walked all over the boat and started a list of things that needed to be addressed. We had to turn fresh water holding tanks into tanks for fuel, weld up portions of the doors, get all the proper safety equipment, install more electronics, secure everything on the boat, and work on the engines and generators, and this is just the beginning of what we needed to get done. So after about three hours of going over the boat, Al and I jumped right in and started to go to work.

We spent the first four days cleaning, organizing, and doing whatever we could to make progress. There was so much to do, and we were not moving fast enough for Jim's standards. After one full week, with just the two of us plugging away with what we could do in a nine-hour day, it was time to get some help. First, though, each night around 6:00 p.m., we would stop work, make a drink, and Al and I would go over what we had accomplished that day and tallied up all our receipts. Jim had given us $2,000 on day one to use for whatever we needed. He had also given us sheets of paper to keep track of what we were spending money on. We had a marine store right next to the harbor called Gander, and this is where we spent a lot of time and a lot of money. The first week was fun, just the two of us most of the day. Jim and Mia would stop by each day and check with the progress.

Now Jim lived in the Philippines and basically lived a better life than most. They had a person who cooked and cleaned for them, a driver, and other people who assisted with his daily life. The one thing Jim didn't like to do was drive. With this said, I became his driver, and whenever he was ready to come to the boat, he would call and I would pick them up at their hotel. During our drive back, I would fill him in on what we had done and where we were at with certain projects. It was during this time that I started to let him know that I would be very interested in working with Al to get the boat to the Philippines. I wanted to go real bad and made it very clear.

We had engine issues, and we needed a mechanic that could help us out. Neither Al nor I knew anyone on the island of Oahu that we could trust and would want to help us out. So I mentioned to Al that my buddy Joel was a diesel mechanic and good with boats.

Al knew who he was but didn't really know him. I told Al he could help, and he gave me the okay to contact Joel. Joel wasn't working at this point either, so he agreed, and he also mentioned that JD was available; he too could help out. I told Al about JD, and he told me to get both of them here tomorrow. They were on the first flight out of Maui the next morning, and I picked them up at the airport. Once on board and after a quick tour, Joel proved his worth in the first fifteen minutes on board by getting a generator going. The fuel had been shut off, and he figured it out quickly, and I knew right then that I had made a great recommendation to get him here to help.

The next week, the four of us worked all day every day and made a lot of progress. We all had our jobs to do and spent every working hour busting our asses to get things accomplished. It was about the middle of the second week that we needed an electrician to wire up a bunch of stuff. Again, not knowing anyone on the island, Al came up with the idea of flying his buddy Brian from Iowa to help us out. At first, I thought it was crazy to spend money to fly someone from the mainland to help with our electrical matters, but Jim didn't have a problem with it, and the next day, Al contacted Brian, and in two days, he was on the boat helping out. Brian was 5'8", 160 lbs., and a good old boy from the farm. He was the same age as Al, mid-forties, and they had grown up together. We now had a crew, and we all worked great together.

By this point, we had a busy operation going on. Jim had rented one truck to get us around, and it was not enough, so I ended up renting another truck in my name, which was absolutely needed. Joel would be working on something, or JD and I would have to run to a parts store to get whatever we needed, so two trucks was a must. With so many things being worked on at one point and a lot of cash flying out the door, I became the accountant for the ship. Jim would give me $2,000 at a time, all cash, and each night, I would collect receipts from the guys and give them money as needed. Between being Jim's driver and the money man, I also took care of one big project, and that was converting a 4,000-gallon freshwater-holding tank to become a fuel tank for the journey. I can tell you I spent days in a very dark and nasty place with a bucket of water and a bilge pump cleaning and removing some of the nastiest water I had ever dealt with. Joel worked on the engines and helped with some of the welding. JD worked on a number of projects that were needed for the inspection and safety of the boat. Brian worked each day on all the electrical issues, and he too had done some welding, so he was helpful in this area. Al worked with Jim to get all the paperwork and new electronics for the helm.

We worked our asses off for a total of about three weeks. With this said, it was nice to have money in our pockets, and each night, we would order food, grab drinks, and have fun. We worked nine hours a day, and at 6:00 p.m., it didn't matter what you were doing; it was time to stop. We all met in the galley, grabbed a cold beer, and would discuss the day's accomplishments. At this time, I would collect all receipts and take care of the money. I can tell you that by the end of the three weeks, Jim had spent about $20,000 on just getting the boat ready to go.

It was a great three weeks, and I had made more money in three weeks than I had made in the past four months. I went to the bank to make a deposit. This will tell you how broke I was. My account had been negative $150 for two months, and they had actually closed my account. This really sucked because the only way to pay my bills was from this account. So I spent about two hours one day with this banker, and he finally was able to reactivate my old account, and I was able to deposit about $2,000 to bring my account back to life. It was a great feeling to spend an hour and pay some of my bills that were by now months overdue. I felt like I had won the lottery.

It was the beginning of our last week working on the boat. We had our inspection and just needed to fix a few last-minute things. Everything was up and running, and all our safety equipment had been bought and installed. Jim called and asked Al to meet him at his hotel. I thought that Jim was going to give Al an earful for all the money we had spent. I mean Mai was giving me $2,000 a day, and we were spending it as quickly as we got it. You know what BOAT stands for, and that is "bust out another thousand," and that was exactly what we were doing.

TAKE A DECADE

So Al left, and he was gone for about an hour. We saw him pull up next to the boat and told everyone to meet him in the galley. We all walked up, thinking we were going to get our asses chewed out, but that didn't happen. Al told us all to grab a beer even though it was midafternoon and we still had three hours to work. Al told us that he had just talked with Jim and Mia and they had changed their minds. Instead of Jim flying out a crew from the Philippines to take the boat back, he had offered the five of us the job to deliver the boat. Jim would give us $30,000, split equally to make the trip. This would be $6,000 each. We would get $2,500 before we left and $2,500 when we got there. The other $1,000 would be for us to fly home, so basically, he paid us to get there, and we would have to pay for our return flight.

This was cool with me and sounded too good to be true. I got a huge smile on my face and was the first to raise my hand and say "I'm in." Al knew I wanted to go and had already told Jim that Steve would be the first to say yes, and I did not disappoint. Al, of course, was in, and it was now up to the other three to make their decision. Brian said yes, but he didn't have a passport, which would be required. Al told him that they could pay extra and get one done in about three days, so with that info, Brian was in. Now it was Joel and JD's turn, and both of them had issues. Joel had a girlfriend, and would she be okay with him being gone for three to four weeks? So he left the room, and about twenty minutes later, he came back up and said he was on board; his girl was cool with everything and gave him the go-ahead. There will be more to come on this later, so just remember his girlfriend said it would be okay. Now the last person was JD, and he had the biggest thing going on, and that was Laura, his wife, was four months pregnant. He left the room and was gone for about thirty minutes. He came back up to the galley with a smile on his face and told us that he was in as well. With that said, we stopped work early that day and celebrated this opportunity. I could not believe this, but I was going to cross the Pacific Ocean on this boat.

Al told us what Jim had also said. He told Al that he was very confident in him to captain a crew on his boat to make this journey.

Jim told Al that he was confident that if we got into any problems, I would be able to talk my way out of it; this made me laugh. He told Al that he was happy with the work Joel and JD had done and confident that if we had engine problems, Joel could figure it out. He told Al the same about Brian and his electrical abilities. He had praised us all and had made the right decision. Al then gave us all official titles, which would be used on all the paperwork. Al was the captain. I was first mate, second in charge. Joel was chief mechanical officer. Brian was chief electrical officer, and JD was named navigational officer. It was so cool, and all we could do that night was laugh and talk about what could happen.

The next week was all about finishing the boat and taking care of a few personal matters. We all had to fly back to Maui and get whatever we might need as far as clothes and any other personal things we concerned. Joel, JD, and I flew over first for a night, and when we got back, Al and Brian flew back. This was so we would have someone on the boat at all times.

When I found out we were going, I had done a little thinking, which usually just gets me into trouble, but this was something good. If I had a one-way ticket to Southeast Asia and would have money when I got there, why not extend this trip a little? I had decided to stay about a month after we got there and travel around Southeast Asia for a while. *Why the hell not?* is what I thought. There was nothing going on around here, and I had a few bucks in my pocket, and how often would an opportunity like this come up? So I decided to rent out my room to a friend, which would save me money for a few months. My truck payments had been made, and except for a few other bills, everything was in order. I packed up my big backpack and made plans to be gone for a few months.

That night in Maui, I called my mom and told her what had happened. I'm sure I started the conversation with something like "Mom, I have this opportunity to do something that is different than anything I have done before. I'm going to cross the Pacific Ocean on a boat, and it could take up to a month to do this. Oh yeah, we won't have service to contact you, so I will call before I leave and call you when I get there. So what do you think? Mom, Mom, are you there?"

TAKE A DECADE

She didn't know what to say. I filled her in on all the details and told her about the money and the chance to travel a month or so in Southeast Asia, and I don't think she was as excited as I was. My mom is my number one fan, and I knew she would be worried, but I had already done a few crazy things, and what could she say except "Be careful, call when you can, and I love you"? I told her I loved her and would be calling her in less than a week before we left.

We had a few things to still do on the boat before we left, so we worked at it until everything was done. That is when we had our last inspection and had been given the green light to leave. The next big thing we had to deal with was our fuel. We had a long way to go, and we would go through a lot of diesel. Jim had first mentioned about us getting to Guam, which was about 75 percent of the way, and refueling there. However, he found out that because we had a personal vessel, they would have to refuel us out to sea. We would not be able to pull into port and refuel that way. Guam is a military island, and no personal boats are allowed in the harbor. He also found out the cost of doing this was extremely high, like triple the normal cost. So he decided that we would have to take all our fuel on board before we left Oahu. They had done the calculation, and we figured we would need at least twenty thousand gallons of fuel to make the trip. This would give us about thirty days. If for some reason we needed more, then it would be up to us to figure that out.

With this decision made, Al found six 500-gallon fuel bladders that were delivered to the boat. These were big-ass rubber balloons that would expand when fuel was added. They were heavier than hell, so even to get them on board, we used the crane. We also loaded about ten 55-gallon barrels of hydraulic fluid and oil for the engines. It was the last day we were there, and they came with the fuel, which cost $20,000 and was paid in cash. I can tell you with all this fuel on board, our boat sat pretty low. This was a lot of weight, and we would feel it.

The best part of getting things ready was when we all went shopping. The five of us went to Costco, and each grabbed a cart. Jim gave us $2,000 to buy food. He told us he wanted us to eat well, get steaks, burgers, chicken, and whatever else we wanted. So the five of us spent all of that easily. We bought meats, breads, cereals, snacks, puddings, milk, powdered milk, eggs, bacon, and the list goes on and on. We also had to buy a lot of fresh water for the trip. We figured we would need at least five gallons of fresh water a day for the five of us, so we got twenty 5-gallon bottles of water. We spent everything Jim had given us, and we had two truckloads of food. It took us about two hours to get everything put away. With all our food on board, it was now time to get our booze. Jim had no problems with us having alcohol on board; he told us that he would not go without a few bottles at least. With that said, we took the trucks back to the store and bought about $1,000 of beer and liquor; this was out of our pockets, but who cared? We also stocked up on smokes and dip. I had also managed to get an ounce of weed on Maui and stuffed it down the front of my pants for the plane ride back. So we had food, booze, smokes, dip, weed, and a bunch of fuel. We had everything we would need, we hoped.

The last night on the boat before we left, we decided to have a little party. It was Al's idea, and he had something special for us. Once we were done with whatever last-minute thing we needed to do, we showered and ordered a few pizzas. Al had also taken the liberty in getting us some entertainment. At about 8:00 p.m., a car pulled up, and out came this stripper. She was 5'5", 120 lbs. with a nice body, longer brown hair, and was dressed for the part. She was okay-looking, not drop-dead gorgeous but cute. She was someone that would be willing to do this on a boat in an industrial harbor, so what could you expect? Anyways she was a female and would be willing to take her clothes off in front of us. This would be the last female we would see for who knew how long. Anyway, we got her all set up on a table, and she did her thing. We sat there groping her, drinking shots of booze, pounding beers, and having the time of our lives. We laughed so much that night we could have been heard a mile away. It was a blast and a great way to spend our last night. She did end up spending the night and sleeping with Al, so that made the captain a happy man. The next morning, he called her a cab and she was gone. We all laughed and thanked him for a good night.

TAKE A DECADE

This is a good time to talk about our gifts to each other. Al started it by buying all of us a watch. He wanted all of us to have a watch on so we could determine time and set up a schedule for driving the boat. We had our watches set at Hawaiian time and never changed it the entire trip. My gift to everyone was a dirty magazine for each of them. Joel, JD, and Brian all bought us stuff as well, and I remember getting a hat and a book. I know that Al had bought me a copy of *Moby Dick*, which was very kind of him. Anyway, we all took the time to think of each other and knew that for the next month, it was just us. I had also bought a BB gun for something to do. I thought we could set up targets and practice shooting. We had a month, and we needed to come up with things to keep us occupied. We went to a secondhand shop and bought some cheap clothes for the trip, and we also bought a couch that we used the crane and put it on top of the boat. JD and I had also brought hammocks and had them hung out on the top of the boat. We were going to be living on this thing for a month, so why not be comfortable?

The day had come, February 17, 2009, and we were scheduled to depart around 2:00 p.m. We had to return the trucks. They gave me a hard time about a scratch, and it took me a good hour to convince them it was already there and really pissed me off, but I won, and that is all that mattered. We tied up any loose ends. I booked a flight back to New York to see my family after I returned, which is something my mom wanted. We also got completely unpacked in our rooms. Joel and JD took the two bunk rooms on the first deck, Al and Brian had the staterooms, and I had the captain's quarters. These were the rooms we had all been staying in during the wet dock, and we were all comfortable, so we all just stayed put. Before we left, we all took pictures, a group photo in front of the boat, and pictures of each other. I had bought a new camera for this trip, one that had a disk and a view window to see how the photo came out. It was a $200 camera, and I wanted to capture this trip the best I could.

Jim and Mia came down to see us off and gave us $2,000 to keep in the safe just in case we had any emergencies. This was very nice of them, and we just didn't know. Around 2:00 p.m., Al fired up the engines, and we did our last inspection of the boat. Once our last check was done, it was time to set sail. Jim threw me the bowline, and JD took the stern line. At this point, Al put the boat in gear, and we were on our way. Jim and Mia waved goodbye and told us, "Safe travels and we will see you in about a month." The *Red Rhino* left the dock of Oahu for the longest journey of its career.

CHAPTER 38

The Red Rhino

The five of us made our way to the bridge for one last look at land, and we all just stood there with a big-ass smile on our faces. We were now on an epic journey together, and the real fun had just begun. I haven't mentioned this yet, but this trip would cover around 5,300 miles of ocean; that is like going from the west coast to the east coast and halfway back but all ocean.

Before we had lost all communication with civilization, I made a few phone calls. The first was a short and sweet call to Ronnie to let her know we had left the dock and I would not be back to Maui for a few months. The last call I made was to my mom to let her know that we had left and would be in touch with her as soon as we could. I did tell her that I had booked my flight home for when I returned from this epic trip. This made her very happy, and it would be nice to see everyone after I had successfully made this crossing. It was when I was on the phone with my mom that I lost service, but I had already told her that I loved her and would be in contact as soon as possible. We had a satellite phone on board, and besides calling the owner every day around twelve noon, we had set up a plan for JD to call his wife once a week and give her an update on how things were going. Once JD contacted Laura, she was going to call all our families to let them know we were okay and making progress. Once the phone went dead, I made my way to the bridge and notified everyone that we were now out of service and that our new life had just begun.

The one great thing about this trip was that I had all my worries and concerns taken care of before I left. My financial situation was a whole lot better. I actually had a few grand in my account, which would be needed when I got back. This took a lot of pressure off this trip because I knew that when I returned, I would have the means of getting started again without being completely broke. My relationship with everyone was good and left behind no worries about anything. To have stress about your personal life could have made this a longer trip than it was, but not me. I had all my ducks in a row and one of the best things to have, and that was a peaceful mind.

We just couldn't believe this was actually happening. I went up to the bow of the boat and stood and stared at the water for a good fifteen minutes. Just staring out into the open ocean, the blue color of the water just sparkled from the sun, and the heat from the sun made it a perfect day. I stood there and looked all around to see the waves crashing against the hull and was about as happy as one person could get.

Then I went back to the stern of the boat, and Joel and I watched the island of Oahu get smaller and smaller. It was about two hours into our trip, and we had lost all sight of land; all we could see 360 degrees was the beautiful blue Pacific Ocean. Once land was out of view, I went up to the helm, and Al asked me how we should set up our wheel watch. We talked about it and came up with four-hour intervals. We had five guys on board, but Brian had never operated a boat in his life, so he was out from driving the boat. So we all had our watches, and we would switch every four hours. Al started, and he drove until he didn't want to anymore, and then the rotation started—Al first then JD then me and then Joel.

I'm going to give you a basic overview of our plans for this trip. We left from Oahu and our first point of destination was to Johnston Atoll, which is a Naval/Air Force base in the middle of nowhere. This would be our first bail-out place if things went wrong. After Johnston Atoll, we would head west the tip of the Marshall Islands. We didn't have an exact place for emergencies, but it was a land mass, and we should be able to at least have radio contact. After we passed the Marshall Islands, we would make our way toward the southern part of Guam. After we passed Guam, the next stop would be the Philippines. We had thirty days of fuel and plenty of food, so we hoped it all would work out great.

After about our first three hours out to sea, Joel, Brian, and I grabbed a couple of beers, took chairs out, sat on the back deck, and watched the horizon of the Hawaiian Islands disappear. We were now done with work; it was all about just getting this boat safely to its new home. Jim had told us not to do anything at all with the boat, just maintain it and keep ourselves safe. When the boat made it to its new home, it would be completely gutted and remodeled to fit his needs. So it was time to sit back and enjoy our new surroundings.

Al came down from his wheel watch, and he had turned the wheel over to JD. Al asked me to come with him and walk around to make sure the boat was running okay. We started with the starboard engine room, and with earmuffs on, we went down to the engine and looked for any leaks or anything that might be wrong. We spent a good fifteen minutes checking everything, and it was all good. We then made our way to the other engine room, and the engine seemed to be doing great, running well and no leaks. Then we walked around where the generator, transformer, and fuel tank was located, and we instantly saw a problem. We were losing diesel from the tank. At the top of the fuel tank, there was a missing weld about eighteen inches long and about one inch wide. Every time the boat hit a wave, we saw diesel fuel was spilling out of the tank. This was not good because it was splashing on our transformer, which created power for our instruments, lights, and everything else on the boat. Al looked at me and said, "Go get Joel, and tell JD to throttle back and slow the boat down." I ran up the ladder, yelled at Joel to get down there and then ran up to the helm and told JD to slow the boat down, keep us going into the waves, and try not to make the boat move from side to side.

I get back down in the portside engine room, and Al and Joel were trying to put something in the gap to stop the leak. They tried diapers, a piece of wood, and plastic, and nothing was working. Al was five minutes away from telling JD to turn the boat around; we had to get this fixed. Joel spoke up and said, "We can fix this. If we go back, it could take a week to get this boat out of the water and repaired. We can figure this out, let's just think." At one point, I was standing on the transformer trying to push something to fill the hole, and diesel fuel was running down my arms and down my back. I wasn't the only one covered in fuel; Joel and Al had also been soaked by now. Here we are standing on a power box and saturated in diesel. If something had ignited the fuel at this point, we all would have been burnt to a crisp. This was not the way I want to go out.

Finally, we had a plan, and we had one of the fuel bladders that were only half-full. If we could pump the fuel out of the tank back into the bladder and lower the amount of fuel in the tank, this just might work. We had practiced getting fuel from and bladders to the tanks, so all we had to do was reverse everything. We got all the hoses and pumps ready and started the process. Brian was on the back deck and gave us the thumbs-up that the bladder was expanding. The tank held about eight thousand gallons, so we took it down to six thousand and stopped to see if this worked. We watched carefully for about ten minutes, and the problem had been solved. We now knew to only fill the port side tank to six thousand, and it would give room for the splashing around, and nothing would leak out of the opening. We had our first major situation for the trip, and we were only about four hours in. We worked on the problem and solved it as a team. Man, that was close because we didn't want to turn around and go back. After this little ordeal, I headed straight for the shower and got all that diesel fuel off me.

Now it was back to my beer and time to chill out. About this time, we were all hungry, and I made the first meal of the trip. We had sandwiches and chips, nothing fancy but much-needed. After lunch, it was my turn to take the wheel for the next four hours. Al and JD both gave me an overview of what to do. We had a GPS on board, and Al had programmed into the GPS our first day destination. So basically, it was just following the line on the screen and keeping the boat moving forward as best we could. It was the ocean, and we had waves four to six feet tall, so the boat got rocked around and could get off course with just one wave. We used a small joystick to actually control the rudders, which would move the boat back and forth. So I stood and watched the waves, moving the stick a few clicks to the left and then a few clicks to the right. Our other instruments were radar to see if any other boats were near us and a depth finder, but we knew the ocean was deep, so we didn't use that as much; however, it did come into play down the road.

So I was now the captain of the boat. Whoever was driving the boat became the captain as soon as they took over. It was fun but a little stressful to keep the boat on course and keep it from getting smashed by a wave. During the day, we could always see out and predict what a wave was going to do and sometimes be able to steer out of something. Then there were times that we just couldn't avoid a wave, and everyone on the boat felt it. If you were at the wheel and a wave hit us hard, everyone else would yell "What the fuck was that?" or "Are you awake up there?" and you really didn't want to hear from the crew. Anyway, my first wheel watch went by rather quickly, and by now, it was dark. With the way we had things set up, we would have four hours at the wheel and twelve hours off. We did this day in and day out for many days. My first shift was 6:00 p.m.–10:00 p.m., and my next shift would be the next day from 10:00 a.m. to 2:00 p.m. Then my next shift would be from 2:00 a.m. to 6:00 a.m.

So let me take you through a typical day once I had finished my turn at the wheel. Grab a drink, take a shower, and spend time somewhere on the boat. At the beginning of the trip, we loved being on the top deck. I would go up there and lie in my hammock, and with the rocking of the boat, my hammock would swing without having to do anything. We would spend a few hours up there and then get bored with that and walk around the boat. Just the view was wild because all you could see was the ocean. There were no birds, just the open ocean that went on forever. It was so surreal those first few days. No matter what window you looked out, it was all the same, water everywhere.

About the third day on the boat, Joel came up with a great idea. We had brought with us a few big fishing poles. Now it would have been tough to have someone sit next to them the entire time and watch for fish. So he hooked up the lines to an alarm system, so when we had a fish on, the alarm would go off. This was ingenious, and if you were at the wheel and heard the alarm, your job was to throttle back and slow the boat down. Then whoever was closest would run out and start fighting the fish. We caught at least one fish a day and sometimes more. We had a lot of food on board, but I would say that at least one third of our meals involved some sort of fish. We caught a lot of mahi, ono, and we even landed a few marlins. We had hoped to catch something we would not catch around Maui, but we never did, just our basic fish and that was enough.

We ate a lot of fish almost every day, and it was always right out of the ocean, as fresh as you can get. Between the four of us, we could prepare fish 101 different ways. We baked it, broiled it, and sometimes we ate it cold and raw right off the bones. If we had landed a mahi that day, between the five of us we would eat half of the fish; the other half was packaged up to date and put in the freezer. Jim had told us how much he liked fish, so we figured we would get the boat to him with a freezer full of fresh fish. This was just a little gift for him, not like there were any stores out here to buy anything, ha ha.

It was day 4, and we would be approaching Johnston Atoll, which is a small group of islands that is home to nothing more than a small Naval and Air Force base. We had not seen it all day but knew it was getting closer. We would only skirt and island, maybe see a light in the distance, but we had to keep our distance. Anyway, it was my shift from 6:00 p.m. to 10:00 p.m., and at about eight o'clock, it would be dark. Al had set the GPS that day for our course, and I was doing everything I could to stay on it. Well, at about 9:00 p.m., I looked out the window and saw a few birds. We had not seen anything for the past four days. We had been so far out to sea that it was too far for birds to fly. I thought it was really cool, and as I was driving, I just watched them fly around. I keep my course and motoring along at about twelve knots. Just then, Al came into the helm and asked me how deep we were. We had not even turned on the depth finder once on this trip, and I didn't think to turn it on and check the depth. He looked at me and said, "Those birds came from land, so land is close. We need to see how deep we are." He turned it on, and we had gone from one thousand fathoms to about thirty-five feet real quickly. At about this time, we could now see lights in the distance from the island. It was still twenty-five miles away, but we could see it. Seeing we had gotten close to land, the depth of the water had changed and changed quickly. Al throttled back the boat, took over the wheel, and steered us back out to deep water. He kind of yelled at me but understood I was just following the GPS. If we had continued on that course, we could have hit shallow water, hit a reef or something, and we could have destroyed the boat. By this time, everyone was in the helm, and we all got a lesson real quick. I was so damn lucky, and thank God Al was paying attention. After this shift was over, I had an extra-large cocktail, Black Velvet on the rocks.

By the next day, we had passed Johnston Atoll, which would still be our bail-out place for the next few days. It was now day 5, and so far, so good. It was around this time that we got our weather fax set up. This would give us our forecast for future weather. We had checked before we left and knew we had a good week of weather, but by now, it was time to look ahead and keep track of our future. This was set up in my room, so I kept track and got a report each day—so far, so good.

After a good week on the boat, we had a system down that worked pretty good. The four of us drove the boat, cooked all the meals, and cleaned the dishes. Now I said the four of us and there were five of us on board. We are not sure how, but once we left the dock, Brian went on vacation. He told JD, Joel, and I that he was here to fix any electronic issues and that was it. It was our job to do everything else. We spoke to Al about this, and all he could say was "Oh well, can't make him do anything," and he did let us know that Brian was in constant pain with his legs, so we cut him some slack.

He did help with refueling, which had to be done about every third day. It would be at this time we would move fuel from the bladders on the back of the boat into the fuel tanks. This task took about an hour and required us to pay close attention to a lot of moving parts. Someone had to be down in the engine room, one person holding the hose, another one at the bladder in case something went wrong, and someone working the switches. This really was about the only thing we really had to do. We still were checking the engine all the time, and that usually was done before we took our shift or right after.

Each day on this boat so far had been great. We would drive for four hours and party for the next six or so. We did have a TV with movies we all brought. Joel brought two seasons of *Californication*, and we would have date night once in a while. JD would be driving and Al and Brian would be sleeping, so we would watch a few episodes every couple of days, and we made the two seasons last the entire trip. It was our little thing to do together, and we would make a drink and sit back and relax. Another thing we did almost every night was play poker; it usually was when Al was driving, and we would play poker for a good two to three hours every night. It was fun, and by the end of the trip, I was the big winner. I had this cloth bag that I kept my change in, and by the end of the trip, it was almost full. I loved playing poker with Joel and JD.

Remember my BB gun? Well, about six days into our trip, I set up a little gun range. I hung bottles and cardboard around the back off the boat, and we would take turns seeing how many targets we could hit. JD and I had fun with this, and every few days, we would see who was better that day; it was just something to do. Every day so far had been okay weather-wise. The seas were five to seven feet, not a lot of wind, and everywhere on the boat was comfortable. This would definitely change, but I'm jumping the gun.

We were almost at this time about twelve days into our trip, and we had a major problem. We had run out of booze. The $1,000 of beer and liquor we had bought was almost gone. I had bought two handles of Black Velvet and thought it would last longer than it did. I was not alone, and we had all drunk our liquor and all the beers. It was a dark day for us when we realized what had happened. We all had several drinks every day, and like Brian, who was drinking all day long, it just didn't take long. It sucked, but I still had a little weed and a few cans of dip. What was worrying me was my dip supply was low. I had brought with me twenty cans, and I thought this would be enough, and it too was low. I realized that I would definitely not have enough and the day would suck when it was all gone. There was nothing I can do about it at this point. I was not the only one low on

TAKE A DECADE

supplies, and Brian, who was a smoker, was running low on smokes as well.

Al called all of us to the helm one day and told us he had a plan. We were going to travel by the northern part of the Marshall Islands, and we would be very close to the Bikini Atoll. We had not heard of the Bikini Atoll, but I did like the name, and he told us that we might be able to take a day and possibly stop by and check things out. Al then told us about this atoll and how it was the place for the hydrogen bombs that were tested back in the fifties. It was the place they tested the bomb that made that big mushroom cloud. It seemed interesting, and maybe we could restock on a few supplies like dip and smokes. It was a shot, and we made the decision to check it out. We were still a few days away, and it wasn't really off our course that much, and we would make up the time later.

Around day 14, we approached the atoll, and it was the first real land we had seen in two weeks. The Bikini Atoll is a coral reef in the Marshall Islands consisting of 23 islands surrounding a 230-square-mile lagoon. After the Second World War, the inhabitants were relocated, and this was the site of twenty-three nuclear tests done by the United States until 1958. At this time, the US and Russia were competing to design a weapon of mass of destruction. Operation Crossroads started in July 1946 and continued until 1958. They determined that the largest and most powerful explosion was one thousand times more destructive than the bomb dropped on Japan at the end of WWII. So this place had a lot of history, and we were actually going to be able to see it.

We found a way into the lagoon, and Al steered the boat slowly with all of us on deck in different places watching for reefs, rocks, or anything we didn't want to hit. The islands were low lying with plush green vegetation, and the water was as clear as it gets. This place looked amazing; it almost looked like a painting or something made up. It looked fake to a certain degree, but it was a real as it gets.

We made our way into the lagoon, and now we were surrounded by the small islands, and in the distance, we saw one island that looked like it had a light on. We knew nothing about this place, so we made our way toward the one island that looked like it might have something on. We got closer, and we could see a small house and what looked like a truck. Al got us as close as he was comfortable with, and we lowered the anchor. We then used the crane to lower our small dingy that we had on the top of the boat into the water. Al and I got in the boat and told the other guys to hang tight. We took the boat and headed to shore, which took about five minutes.

When we stepped on land, we both looked at each other and said, "This feels weird, solid ground, wow." We then walked up to the house and knocked on the door—nothing. We knocked a few times and still nothing. I then looked through the window, and the place was empty, not a stick of furniture anywhere. Then I walked over to the truck, and the keys were in it, so I jumped in and tried to start it, but the battery was completely dead. We could also see a small hanger in the distance, so we walked over to it. We stepped inside and yelled, "Hello, anybody around?" Nobody responded, so we walked into the hanger, and it was filled with parts for just about everything. It had big equipment parts, filters, belts, nuts, bolts, and everything was in order, still in packages. It was just a big building that was used to service equipment and hold supplies. Still, there were no people.

We walked out the door and saw another group of buildings, and we figured that everyone must be there, so we walked a short distance and approached a door going into the building. We knocked, and no one responded, so we opened the door and walked in. This was a dormitory room with bunk beds and dressers. The entire hallway was littered with papers, posters were half hanging on the walls, it was a complete mess and we knew that nobody had stayed here for a long time. We kept walking and found what looked like a nurse's office; it had some medical equipment, and the floor was covered in expired packages of medicine, aspirin, stomach stuff, and your basic needs. It too did not look used in a long-ass time. We then found the galley, and this was the weird part. There were tables and chairs and each table had salt/pepper shakers and other condiments on top, but the weird part was that vines had grown up all over the tables. The vines had started from the ground and made their way up each leg of the chairs and over to the tables, and even the ketchup bottles were tangled with vines. It seriously looked like something out of a Stephen King movie. It was really eerie, and Al and I looked at each other and said, "There is definitely no one home." We walked back to the boat and went out and got the other three guys. We walked around the island and showed them everything we had seen. It looked like the people had just up and vanished without a trace.

We spent about two hours walking around. Joel, JD, and I walked around the entire island in thirty minutes. While we were walking around, I found a glass-blown fishing float that was nothing like I had seen before. It wasn't round but more oblong. It was about ten inches long and three inches thick. It was very cool, and I still have it today. Anyway, we spent time checking out the island and soon realized that we were not getting any supplies here. We joked that the store was closed; we would have to check out the next one. Ha ha.

As we were walking back to the boat, we noticed a concrete structure that we had not seen yet, so we all walked over to it. This was a 20' × 20' steel and concrete building with 4" concrete walls. The only openings were small little windows that allowed a small amount of light. It was then that Al said, "This is where they filmed all of the nuclear blast." When you see those old pictures of the huge mushroom cloud caused by a nuclear explosion, this was right where those photos were taken. This was probably the most unique out of the ordinary places I have ever been. I've seen a lot in my life and spent time in some crazy places, but to say that I stood in the concrete bunker that was used to photograph something so powerful was mind-blowing. The five of us can say that we are one of the few people to see this, and it is historical.

We got back to the boat, and Al suggested we stay here for the night, do an oil change, which was needed, and leave first thing in the morning. This would give all of us a break from constantly moving and time to take care of a few things around the boat. Joel had disappeared and returned with a special treat. He walked into the galley carrying a thirty-rack of beer. "Holy shit, Joel, what is that?" I asked. He told us he had hidden this for a special occasion, and the fact that we were where we were was about as special as it gets.

That day, we got the oil changed, transferred fuel, and did so while drinking beers. The sun was hot, and not moving made things warmer, so the beers went down nicely. We each had six to drink, and after we got done with the boat, I started fishing off the boat and catching fish right away. In the lagoon, the fish were twice as big as the ones in Hawaii. They were the same reef fish, just twice as big, and we feasted on them that night. It was good to eat something besides mahi and ono. Just before it started to get dark, I started to get a headache from hell. All six of my beers were gone; we had walked around the island, worked on the boat, and spent the entire day in the sun. I had not drunk any water and was just dehydrated. Anyways, my head hurt, and I did miss something fun, which pissed me off. Joel and JD went snorkeling and found a bunch of lobsters. They brought back six lobsters that had to be three pounds each. They were amazing and that night not only did we have a different fish to eat, but we also had the best lobster I have ever had. We all sat around the table together and enjoyed a great meal.

This place was untouched, and very few people came this far out in the middle of nowhere. We found out later that after the nuclear test, sometime in the early seventies, they did send scientists to do research on the aftermath of such a powerful explosion. They spent several years collecting data and doing research. It was at some point the island was going to get hit with a really bad typhoon, so they evacuated everyone. After the storm had passed, they realized they had collected enough information and spent enough money on the project that they didn't send any one back. That is why the place looked the way it did. One day, there were a few dozen people working and researching the effects of a nuclear blast, and in one day, they all were flown off the island for their safety, never to return. This place had given me bragging rights to a very unique place on this planet.

The next morning, we pulled out, and in a short period, land had disappeared again. The seas were okay, not great, six- to eight-foot waves, and the wind had picked up a little. After we left, I had until 6:00 p.m. before it would be my turn at the wheel. I checked the forecast, and it didn't look good up ahead. I found Al and showed him what I saw. It looked like high winds and high seas. Now we also could get information from our radio. We were still connected to the United States via weather and any other information. The problem with the weather forecast was that they were giving it to a certain location but not really out where we were, so we had to plan things accordingly to keep us safe. It looked like we were headed right into the middle of a typhoon. To classify a typhoon, you had twenty- to twenty-five-foot seas and wind blowing thirty-plus knots. It would not be good. The other thing that was not good, not good at all, was I was out of dip. Brian was out of smokes, and JD had brought a few cans, and they were gone. Al's few cigarettes that he brought were gone. Basically, we were out of all tobacco items. Like I said, this was bad.

Just a little sidenote, I wanted to tell you my sleeping arrangements because things did change. Up until now, I slept more nights on the top deck than I did in my room, either sleeping in my hammock or sleeping on the couch we had moved up there. To lie there and look up at the stars was about as good as it gets. Some nights, I would be up there, and whoever was at the helm would come up and drive from the station on the top deck. It was a great way to see all around you even at night. When we would drive from up top, we didn't have our GPS or radar, so we relied solely on the stars. We had been heading due west for the most part, and as long as we kept Orion's belt just off our starboard side, we could stay pretty close to keeping on track. This was such a relaxing way to guide the boat. Just keep a group of stars in sight and go that way.

Back to the weather, Al made the decision to try and skirt the storm as much as possible. If we changed course and headed more southwest, we might miss the major part of it and just have to deal with the end of it. We would see.

On day 3, after leaving Bikini Atoll, we could tell that things had gotten a lot worse in a short period of time. The swells were pushing fifteen feet, and the wind had picked up enough to show spray off every wave. At this point, we closed all hatches and buckled down the ship as best we could. We had gone through half of our fuel on the back deck, which meant we were now sitting higher in the water. This boat was just one big square red box on top of two pontoons. It was big and heavy, and it was about to test its true strength.

When the storm first hit, we could hardly walk around the boat at all. You basically had to be hanging on to something at all times. Going upstairs, walking through the galley, and standing at the helm were all a challenge. The boat would go up a wave, sometimes at a forty-five-degree angle and then back down the wave, smashing the bow into the sea, causing waves to go over the entire boat. At this time, due to the size of the waves, our anchor, which was attached on the side of the bow, was now slamming into the hull on each and every wave. It could be heard banging against the side off the boat from every part of the boat. It was loud, and I don't know how Joel and JD slept in their bunk rooms with that pounding right against their walls. It was getting bad and would not let up for a while.

By the next day, we were smack in the middle of hell. We had twenty-five- to thirty-foot seas, blowing thirty- to thirty-five-knot winds, and we were this tiny-ass boat out in the middle of the Pacific Ocean. We knew—and we did mention—that if anything went wrong, there was no way in hell they would get to us in time. We all did a little praying at this time. The boat was rocking and rolling side to side, up and down for days. It was like living on an extreme roller coaster that just would not stop. Like I said, we had every door, porthole, and opening locked and sealed up. We still had to do an engine check during this ordeal, and we always made sure at least two people went together. One wave could easily hit us, and if someone was on the back deck, they could be swept off the deck in a split second. We had to be extra careful with every step, every movement we made.

We still had to eat and sleep during these five days of hell. Yes, for about five days, we dealt with Mother Nature like I had never seen before. To look out the windows, especially at night, and see these waves bigger than our boat at times, wind howling to the point we could hear it through the windows, was very unnerving and downright scary. When we ate, we held on to our plate with one hand and ate with the other. We got a drink after eating because there was no way a cup would have lasted long on a table. Now for sleeping, this was exciting because we were in constant motion even as we slept.

TAKE A DECADE

I stayed in my room during this, and I would roll from one side of the bed to the other. My head would come off the bed and then slam back down. At times, my head was higher than my legs, and a split second later, my feet would be higher. Like I said, it was a constant roller coaster, and trying to sleep on a damn roller coaster was tough.

As far as your wheel time in the helm, it was a white-knuckle ordeal for four straight hours. Just to hang on in the helm was a challenge, and to try and keep the boat on course was truly difficult. At this point, you had four other people that were at your mercy and their lives as well. To have the boat go nose up and then get swallowed by a wave was not fun. Each and every wave knocked us off course without any order. To spend four hours dealing with this shit was draining and took a toll on our body and mind. After our shift was up, we would just sit there in a daze for an hour to get over the stress. We dealt with this for five days and five nights; we were in the middle of hell and could get out.

On about day 6, things started to relax and settled down to the point we could finally open the boat up and get some fresh air. I remember going up top for the first time in a while and just thanking God that we had made it through that mess. The sun was shining, and the heat from the sun felt so damn good. The boat had gotten worked over hard, but it stayed in one piece, and we were so thankful for that. We did have to transfer fuel because we had not transferred any during this storm, which was definitely needed. It was just so good to be outside again and not see huge waves. Don't get me wrong—the ocean never was a glassy, easygoing body of water, but anything is better than a typhoon.

Our next point of contact was Guam, and we had been on the boat for about twenty days. We could see the island on our GPS and radar, but we stayed far away. The only things we saw of this island were a few lights that night in the far distance. It was just a small glow, and that was it. We did pay close attention to our radio during this time in case they had us on radar and wanted to know what we were doing, but we never got any contact from them at all. Guam came and went in one day, and our next real stop would be the Philippines. Once we passed Guam territory, we had lost all communication with the United States of America. From now on, any communication would be through Tokyo, Japan. So I had to change our station with the weather fax and redo all our connections with the States. We were now tuned into Tokyo, and it gave us a new element of concern for the last part of this trip. This meant that if something went wrong, the US coast guard would not be coming to our rescues; it would be the Japanese.

Let's talk about time for a minute. We had crossed the international time line and at least five other time zones by now. We still all had our watches set to Hawaiian time, but it changed on a daily basis. The one thing we did this entire trip was contact the owner at some point. Either Al or I would call Jim at twelve noon our time. We did this every day, and for us, it was always around twelve noon; for Jim, this could have been 6:00 a.m. or 4:00 p.m. We didn't know, but he wanted an update each day. This was also a safety measure we put into place before we left. If he didn't hear from us in one day, he would not panic. If two days went by, then he would call the coast guard to set up a search, so we made sure to contact him every day. We would give him our coordinates and fuel supply so he could monitor and record our progress. After we passed Guam, it meant we were getting close, but still had a good week at least before we saw land.

This was another really cool thing we had the chance to do, and I still have never met anyone that has had this opportunity. Once we passed Guam, we went right over the Mariana Trench, which is the deepest part of any ocean on the planet. Once we were over the trench, we all stood in the helm and slowed the boat down to get a more accurate reading. Our goal was to stop over Challenger Deep, which is the deepest part of the trench, hence the deepest part of any ocean on the planet.

We spent about an hour moving slowly until we were directly above Challenger Deep. Al put the boat in neutral, and we all looked at each other and said, "Let's go swimming." We all left the helm, and I went right to the top of the boat. Joel and JD were the first to jump in, and from the highest part of the boat, I did a swan dive right into the ocean. The water was warm and really good on the body. Now it was not a good thing to have all our crew in the water at one point, but we were careful. We made sure we had a way back on to the boat and didn't go far.

Here were five Americans out in the middle of the ocean, all swimming in the deepest part of the ocean. We swam around, laughing and joking. I would look over someone's shoulder and be like a tentacle from a giant squid or joking with each other that something had my leg. We laughed, and it was a blast. We swam around for ten to fifteen minutes, then I grabbed a mask and snorkel, and we checked out the bottom of the boat and just did a little inspection of the props and rudders. From what we could see, everything looked good.

After we checked the boat out, I floated away from the boat and started to look down into the abyss. Here I was with 36,000 feet of water beneath me, which is almost 7 miles. This was so cool and something I will never forget. If you think about it, a plane travels above the planet at around 35,000 feet, then you have sea level and then another 36,000 feet of water below us. I spent about ten minutes swimming around, and then my brain went to work, and I started to think about how many creatures and big-ass marine life were swimming below us. They were swimming in the depths looking up and thinking, *Oh, there is a good meal.* So I made my way back to the boat. The entire swim back, I just waited for a big-ass tentacle to wrap me up and pull me under to my death. Well, I safely returned to the boat and made it out alive. We had just swum in the deepest part of the ocean on Planet Earth; this was a big deal.

After our little adventure, it was time to throttle up and time to keep moving. I had time before my wheel watch, which wouldn't be until two early in the morning. I had time to sleep, eat, and work out. Oh yes, I forgot to tell you I had created a little gym on the boat. I had made weights out of engine parts, a steel bar, a few ropes, and a piece of wood for a bench. I was planning on traveling for a month after this was all said and done, and I needed to stay in shape. For the most part, we really didn't have a lot of exercise. It was just a lot of sitting around, eating, no drinking at this point, but we had two weeks of that, and I could feel my body getting weak and sluggish. I made a little gym, and each day, I tried to spend thirty to forty-five minutes lifting weights, jumping rope, and doing pull-ups. All the guys at some point joined in, but for the most part it was my little thing to do, and after our swim, I got a workout in.

After we ate dinner, I took a good nap, and had my alarm set for 1:45 a.m., which would be time to relieve JD. I was never early to my watch, and JD could account for this. I would usually say hello, go get something to eat and drink, and be ready to go five to ten minutes later. He would bust my balls on this, but hey, I needed time. Anyway, my alarm went off, and it was time to go to work. I walked out of the captain's quarters and told him I would be right back. I went in and grabbed a few puddings, which was the only thing we had that was a treat. There was no more dip, so I had to take my mine off that with a pudding and a drink. I made my way back to the helm, and JD told me he was going to take a shower and then to bed. By this time, everyone else was sleeping, and it would be up to me to run the boat for the next four hours.

This is where my book started; remember page 1, and what a way to start this *Take a Decade: A True Story*'s amazing journey. It was 2:00 a.m., and I had just taken over the helm of the *Red Rhino*. I had been at the wheel for about fifteen minutes, enjoying a chocolate pudding, and just like a switch was thrown, I lost all power in the helm. I lost my lights, GPS, radar, and rudder control and was instantly in the dark. It was at this point I throttled back the engines, and within thirty seconds, I turned around and Al was coming into the helm. "What the fuck just happened?" he said. At this point, we were a sitting duck without any lights or controls. The waves started to hit and rock the boat from the side, and we started to get pounded pretty good. He told me to take the wheel; we did have an actual wheel in the helm. We had nothing to go by, and I did whatever I could to get the boat going forward. At this point, about two minutes after this happened, everyone else was in the helm. Brian and Joel had both woken up with the sound of the boat throttling down, and JD was just getting ready to take a shower.

The problem was our battery bank for the helm had shut down, and we needed to get another source of power. This was an electrical situation and time for Brian to go to work. We found the problem, and we had to get a new battery into the helm ASAP. We had one, and it was at the bottom of the boat, three decks down. Joel, JD, and I managed to pull up this battery that was 3 feet long by 2 feet wide and weighed at least 150 lbs. We used ropes to pull it out of the hull and then attached straps around it to get it up the stairs. The boat rocked from side to side, up and down, and we were trying to carry this 150 lb. weight. If it dropped, we would have been in a lot of trouble, not only losing our power source, but the battery was filled with acid and could badly hurt us. This whole process took about an hour, and it was a scary moment. Well, after an hour of pure stress and agony, we had fixed the problem. Brian rewired from the old battery bank to the new one, and when the light came on, we all screamed, "*Yes!*" It was back to the wheel for me, and the rest of the guys went back to bed.

Al looked at me when he left and said, "Don't break anything else. Ha ha." For me, this was the scariest time on the boat. The storm was bad, but to lose everything just like that in the middle of the night was probably the craziest thing that has ever happened to me in my life.

When 6:00 a.m. came around and Joel walked into the helm, I wished him well and walked right out. This night was tough, and I was so glad it was over. I showered, ate, and slept for eight hours. Just the stress of the early morning ordeal was exhausting, and my brain was spent.

After this night, we figured we should start seeing land in five to six days. Now I loved every minute of this trip, the good, the bad, and the ugly, but man oh man, it was going to be great to actually complete this mission. We were all getting tired, and every day, someone mentioned either beer or smokes or, by now, women. It would be good to see other people, have a drink, and smoke a cigarette or something else.

Well, about five days later, Al was at the helm, and he blew the horn. We all ran up, and he said, "Look, guys, do you see that?" It was land—it was the first land mass of the Philippine Islands, and it was a speck in the distance, but it was land. Wow, we were almost there, and we all got excited at this point because we were so close. It did take a full day, twenty-four hours, before we could see the islands and actually see civilization.

As we approached the island, JD was at the helm, and we had discussed that once we got close to the island, we needed to have two people on watch at all times. This area was known for pirating and would be the time we would be the most vulnerable for the entire trip. It was one person at the wheel and the other person keeping an eye on the back of the boat for anyone approaching from behind. JD and Al took the first watch, four hours at the wheel and four hours standing guard. This meant that Joel and I would take the next eight hours. So I left and made my way downstairs and fell asleep; Joel went into his room and crashed as well. I can't say what happened because I wasn't there, but JD and Al told us that they went through one of the worst sections of water we had gone through the entire trip. They said it was like a huge washing machine with areas where the ocean had created whirlpools, and the boat was a bitch to get through. I can't say much for this time because I was sleeping, but when Joel and I made our way to the helm for our turn, you could tell that they had worked hard and were both beat from the stress of this ordeal.

It was now our turn, and by now, it had started to get dark. We would spend the next eight hours maneuvering through the islands and avoiding a collision with any other boats. Once we got to the islands, we could see hundreds of other boats, fishing boats, charter boats, and boats carrying cargo. Now JD and Al might have had a tough time with their shift, but I can tell you that Joel and I had our hands full. We had slowed the boat to just ten knots and for the next eight hours, we maneuvered around at least five hundred other boats. Most of these were fishing boats, and they paid little attention to us and would race in front of us, come up on our sides, and basically make our lives miserable. When I was at the wheel, Joel had the walkie-talkie and would be like, "You have a boat approaching portside, go right." Or "There are four boats dead ahead. Turn starboard hard, or you'll run them over." We must have gone through at least fifty sets of lines that these guys had in front of us, but there was nothing we could do but go forward. It was about six hours into our shift, and Joel was at the wheel. It had gotten foggy, which made things even more challenging, and without any warning, we had a ship about the same size as us dead ahead. I radioed Joel, and without much warning, we missed this boat within inches. They had a crew on the back deck yelling at us, and I turned and yelled right back. We were inches from a head-on collision that would have sunk the boat right then and there. Well, we had our hands full for most of the day, and by this time, we had only about twelve hours to our destination.

We spent that last night motoring on, and by now, we were all a little delirious from everything we had been through. That night, we ate our last meal, which was steaks saved for this special occasion, and talked about what we were going to do when our feet hit land. We all agreed on cold beers and whatever tobacco we could get our hands on. We also could not wait to see a female. This was the main thing for all of us. I was going to find a girl and love her for a long time.

That night, most of us really didn't sleep; we took shorter times at the wheel and spent most of that night hanging out in the wheelhouse. We had calculated that we would arrive earlier than expected, like 6:00 a.m. or 7:00 a.m. We had originally planned on closer to noon, but we were making good time. I called Jim, woke him up, and told him we were early and asked him if he wanted us to slow down and stay out until noon or is the dock ready for us at any time. He told us to get there when we could, and he would meet us at the dock.

It was about 7:00 a.m. The harbor was in sight, and Al took her in for the final leg of the trip. As we approached the dock, we could see Jim, Mia, and about five other guys waiting for us to get there. We pulled up, threw the guys our lines, and got the boat secured to the dock. At this point, Jim got on board and walked up to each one of us and shook our hands. Al had left the helm for the last time, and we were now all standing on the back deck. Jim had his guys bring down this cooler; he opened it up and gave us all a cold beer. "I bet you guys could use this by now," he said and also opened up a case of cigars and handed each one of us a big, fat stogy. At this point, he said, "You guys are now completely relieved of anything else on the boat, and job well done." We sat there for about thirty minutes drinking beer and smoking our cigars, laughing and telling Jim all about our trip. It was at this point he told us to use the satellite phone and call each one of our families.

I went to the top deck and dialed a million numbers and heard my mom say, "Hello."

"Hi, Mom, we made it," and I had a tear running down my cheek. She was so happy to hear my voice, and I told her we were safe and sound and I would be in contact soon to talk more, but for now, her mind was at ease and happy to hear her son's voice.

We had spent 28 days, gone over 5,200 miles, burnt through almost all our 3,000 gallons of fuel, made it through a typhoon, stepped on land that many have never heard of (Bikini Atoll), swam in the deepest part of the ocean, and did all this without killing each other. Once again, I can say that my life has been absolutely amazing these past eight years, and what more could I do? All I knew was that Mundy was in the Philippines, and for me, it was just the start of another adventure.

39

CHAPTER

Southeast Asia

We sat on the back of the boat talking with Jim and Mia about our adventure. We showed Jim the freezer of fish we had for him, which was now about half-full, all labeled. We drank cold San Miguel beers one right after another in thirty minutes. There are times when a cold beer tastes good. Spend twenty-eight days crossing the Pacific Ocean, and they really taste good. However, before we could step on land, we had to wait for the custom and immigration officer to show up. They had to check our passports, give us our stamps, make sure we had not brought anything illegal with us, and ask how long we would be staying. It was just basic questions for a border crossing except this was done on a boat and not a car or bus. Of course, we all were good; we received our stamps in our passports, and we were free to leave the boat.

Before we reached the dock, I had taken time to get my bags all backed up. All I had was my big backpack and a small day bag. One thing that I asked Jim if I could have was a small porthole window that was on the boat. He said absolutely. It was a little on the heavy side, so I persuaded Joel to take it back with him so I didn't have to carry it for a month or so. I think we all took something from the boat as a reminder of an epic adventure.

When I was finally standing on solid ground with my bags on my back, I took a moment to turn around and say goodbye to the best boat I had ever worked on. It was a little sad to actually be done with the delivery. We had accomplished our mission, and now it was all over. Don't get me wrong; I was very excited to be on land and for the ground beneath me to actually not be moving. It was just such a rewarding and thrilling opportunity, and it was now over. Once I did that first step onto the dock, I was officially in Southeast Asia.

The five of us loaded up in a van that Jim had hired to transport us around, and at that point, we watched the *Red Rhino* disappear in the distance to never see her again. We all yelled out, "We love you, and we will miss you."

Jim had set us up in style at a hotel near the bay. He had told us that he would pay for the first two nights, and after that, it was up to us to take care of the bill if we decided to stay. At this point, none of us had airline tickets to go anywhere, which was something that would get done ASAP. The hotel was about a twenty-minute drive, and we all said how strange it was to be riding in a car down the road. This was the Philippines, so the road was rough, and the place looks nice, just a little rundown, and it was a third-world nation, so we could not expect too much. Subic Bay which is an extension of the South China Sea was formerly the site of a United States Naval Base, now it is known as Subic Bay Freeport zone. The area is known for an industrial and commercial area, this is not a tourist trap by any means.

We get to the hotel, and it was a five-star resort for the area. For us, it would be more of a three-star, but right now, it was more like a ten-star as far as we are concerned. Jim had gotten each of us our room, which had a bed, dresser, desk, AC, and our own shower. We got checked in. We all enjoyed our rooms for about five minutes, and then all met up in my room to take care of something very important, the money.

The five of us sat in my room, and Al counted out twenty-five $100 bills for each of us. They were crisp, clean, and looked like they had just been made. It was a great feeling to have $2,500 in my hand and it would go to a great use, more traveling. After we were all rich again, we went to the front desk, and we all were able to keep most of the cash in their safe. We were told it would not be wise to have that much money in our rooms, so we listened and kept most of it in the hotel safe; we were high rollers. First time and last time I've ever needed this service. The front desk of this place was great. We asked for beers; they got them for us. We asked for smokes; they got them for us. We were treated like kings while we stayed here, and it was so appreciated. The hotel had a pool, so after "the business" was taken care of, we all spent the next few hours swimming in the pool, drinking beers, and acting like five-year-olds who had not done anything like this in our life. It was strange to be at this point when just twenty-four hours ago, we had just approached the islands.

After we were all cleaned up and put our best clothes on, we headed out for dinner. Now Jim had hired this guy to transport us anywhere we wanted to go. We had no clue about anything, so he also turned out to be our tour guide. We took us to an outdoor venue with tons of different food all over the place. That night, we all ate a big-ass steak with all the fixings. We didn't have to cook or clean up at all, and to be waited on was priceless.

After dinner, it was around 8:00 p.m., and our driver took us to a place that one of Jim's friends own. Jim had given the driver instructions on where to take us that night. We got to this group of buildings, and it looked rundown from the outside, but this was not Vegas or a real fancy place, so it was what it was. We walked in, and there was a long bar with guys and girls all over the place. We found 5 seats in a row and belled up to the bar. Before we could even get our first beer, we each had at least one girl on us like peanut butter on bread. It was great, and my girl was a cute little Filipina girl who was twenty-two years old. As the beers came, we were all in seventh heaven. We looked at each other and made a toast with our beers while holding on to a female. Just the touch of her skin was all I needed to know that I didn't want this to end anytime soon.

Our little group sat and drank for about two hours; by this time, I had kissed my girl and touched every part of her body I could without being a jerk. I was good but didn't let her go for two hours. We bought the girls drinks, and our driver/guide came in and told us that for "real fun," we had to go next door.

I walked in, and this place was filled with women; most of them were half-dressed or wearing something very sexy. There was a dance floor in front of me, bars all over the place, dance music playing loud, and the lights were dim with neon lights illuminating the entire bar. As I walked in, I could see the four guys sitting around this rounded couch with a big table in the middle. I started to walk over to meet the guys, and this beautiful girl walked right up to me and gave me a big hug. Her face was gorgeous. She was about 5'2" with long, black hair and a beautiful body. She said to me, "How are you doing? I'm your new friend."

I looked at her and said, "You're the best friend I have ever had." She smiled, and we walked over to the table holding hands.

The guys were having a blast. There were the five of us and about eight other girls that were all over the place. Joel was getting a back massage, Al had some girl sitting on his lap, Brian had two girls treating him like he was the most important person in the world, and JD was being good, just talking with a very attractive girl. My girl went to the bar and brought me back a beer and a shot for all of us. Beers cost $1, and shots were $2, and each of us had a pocket full of money. My girl was now sitting on my lap, loving my bald head and telling me everything a guy wanted to hear. "You are so strong, you are so cute, and you are so smart…blah blah blah." Anyway, they were doing their job, and we were enjoying every minute of it.

For about five hours, we drank beers, did shots, and got to know our new friends. We had the owner of this place join us for a few hours. He was friends with Jim, and he told me how this bar works. If you see a girl that you like, you can take her home with you…only if she wants to. These girls were not hookers or prostitutes, just hardworking girls. My girl was actually going to college, and a few of the others were doing the same. So if you and a girl liked each other and they decided to spend more time with you and if they left with you, the establishment got $30. I relayed this information to the other guys, and they all said the same thing: "Thirty dollars, that's it?" You gave the money to the girl, and she gave some back to the bar and kept the rest. Hey, it was a tough world, and they had to make a living as well. Anyway, after sitting there drinking for hours, we all started tearing up the dance floor. I can say that tonight, we were the big rollers in this place and the only white guys. So we had the bar and the girls at our beck and call. We said we were going to party like rock stars, and this is exactly how it felt.

After more drinks and more dancing, my vision and balance was getting the best of me. I asked my girl if she wanted to escort me back to my room, and with a big smile, she said yes. I paid my tab and told the guys that I was heading back and she would be going with me. They were all still having fun, but it was 2:00 a.m. and time for bed. We go outside, and the driver is ready to take me back. He dropped us off at the hotel and went back to get the other guys when they were ready.

My new best friend went upstairs. We took a shower together, and let's just say we had a great evening. It had been a while since I had seen a naked female body, and she was beautiful. I don't think she put her clothes back on until sometime the next day. That night was fantastic, and I treated her with the utmost respect and made sure she had fun too. We fell asleep, and that night, I slept like a baby except the bed was not moving side to side, so that did feel weird.

We woke up the next morning, and it felt like we had known each other forever. We lay in bed and had sex again that morning, and after I asked if she was hungry and she was. We got dressed and went downstairs to the small restaurant and had a nice breakfast together, talking the whole time. She was a smart girl who just had to do what she could to make a living, and she was very good at what she did. Anyway, after breakfast, we went back to the room, and I asked her if she wanted to fool around again, and she said, "No more boom boom," as she grabbed her crotch. She had had enough, and I didn't push it, so instead, we lay there holding each other and watched cartoons for an hour or so. It was really a very nice night, and I had a girl tell me "No more boom boom," which is something I had never heard; it was great.

Just before noon, I went to JD's room, and he was up and ready to go do something. I knocked on Joel's door, and he had some company as well; in fact, he had a lot of company. "Holy shit, Joel, how many girls did you bring home?"

"Just three," he said. I laughed and told him to get ready. Then I went to both Al and Brian's room, and they too had a special guest that night. Well, we all met in the lobby, and the girls had called for a ride, and they sent a van to pick up all the girls. It was a night to remember, and after they left, we all stood there laughing and joking around with each other. My new friend left with $100 in her pocket, and we both wished each other the best when she left. It was a once in a lifetime night.

After the girls were gone, we all walked to the beach and found a place to have lunch. We started with cold beers and ordered our food. At about this time, we had been spotted, and the beach vendors started approaching us. It felt like Amazon had showed up, and we had the opportunity to buy just about anything from clothes to jewelry, cologne, sunglasses, jerseys, and watches. I ended up buying a Rolex watch for $25 and a few new T-shirts that were needed badly. Now I knew the watch wasn't a real one—I'm not that gullible—but it looked and felt like a real one, and it looked cool. I could say that I bought a Rolex watch on the beaches of Subic Bay. We all got something that day; it was hard to say no to the cheap prices, and we all had money in our pocket.

After lunch, we found an internet café and spent time getting in touch with family and friends, and this is when I booked my flight out of here. The other four got their flight as well, which would be in two days leaving from Manila, the capital of the Philippines, which was about two hours south. My flight was out of a smaller airport about forty-five minutes away.

That night, we had lost our driver and guide, so we relied on information from the front desk. They told us that there was an outdoor concert going on, and it would be fun. So we all went to this event, and it was perfect. Once again, being the only white guys around we were popular from the beginning. I sat down next to a group of girls, and the guys joined in. They were all about us and took to us just like the girls had the night before. The difference here was they were not getting paid; it was because they just wanted to meet us and find out our story. That night, I met another really nice girl. We talked most of the night, I bought her a few drinks, and she bought me a few drinks. I told her about our trip, and she told me about her life. She had a two-year-old son, who was with her parents, so she could take a night and enjoy time with her friends. She did spent time with her friends, but I would say more time with me. We sat there until at least midnight, and once again, the beers and shots had taken their toll. I told the girl I was heading out and it was nice to meet her. She looked at me and said, "Aren't you taking me with you?"

I looked back at her and said, "Yes, I am. Let's go." This was more like going to a bar and getting lucky that night, and lucky I got. She was a perfect person, and she probably would have married me that night if I had asked, but that wasn't happening.

Our third and final night at this hotel, and our third and final night with all of us was spent hanging out at the hotel. We had drunk ourselves silly for two nights, and we all were just beat from walking and hanging out. It was a quiet and relaxing evening. We all got our bags together, and I gave Joel a few things to take back for me. One was the porthole window, and I also gave him some of my cash to deposit into my checking account. I didn't want to carry $2,000 around with me for the next month or so, so I kept $1,000 and had him deposit $1,000 in my account. Once there, I could use my ATM card and get money that way.

The last night in our rooms was mellow. I spent time researching my *Lonely Planet Guide of Southeast Asia* and started to come up with a plan. I didn't want to plan too much until I got there just to keep my options open. My first step was flying from the Philippines, which was going to be from a small airport called Los Angel, to Kota Kinabalu, or KK for short, which is in the Sabah region of Borneo, Malaysia. Malaysia is a country that is separated by the South China Sea. Part of it is called Peninsular Malaysia, which is located north of Singapore and south of Thailand. The other portion of the country is located across the sea and is referred to as Malaysian Borneo, which is north of Indonesia. This was going to be the start of another epic adventure.

The next morning, we all met up for our last meal together. We ate breakfast at the hotel then settled our bill with the hotel and got our bags ready. It was going to be sad to see these guys leave, and after all we had been through, we had such a bond now. During breakfast, I gave the guys a quick overview of where I was going and told them that they could all go if they wanted. JD was ready to get back to his pregnant wife, and he missed her a lot. Brian was going to stay with Al for a week and check out Maui a little. Al was ready to get back and find a job for his next chapter in life. Joel would have gone with me except his girlfriend wanted him home. This backfired on him big-time, and he wished he had gone with me. The day he got back she broke up with him. Her reason was that their relationship was a little rocky going into this, and he should have stayed home to work on it. He had asked her before we left, and she had agreed to let him go. If it had been that big of a deal, then she could have said something sooner, but she waited until the first day and broke up with him. I wasn't around, but he took it hard and was more pissed off than anything. I found this out about two weeks into my travels. What a bitch and trust me, he is much better off now that he isn't with her.

Jim had sent his driver to take us to the airport, and he came with him to wish us well and thank us again for what we had done. He had already enjoyed some of the fish, and he found the BB gun I had brought. He asked me where the bottle of BBs were, and I told him in the captain's quarters in the drawer. I knew I wanted to take that with me and actually forgot about it. He told us that it worked great to keep the damn monkeys out of his yard and needed more ammo to teach them a lesson. We all laughed when he told us this and said they were a pain in the ass and would steal or destroy anything they got their paws on. I was glad to help him out, and we all thanked him for such a wonderful opportunity and the money he paid us. It was truly appreciated and one of the biggest experiences of our lives.

We got to my airport first, which was a small airport near Angeles, Philippines. It was about a forty-five-minute drive, and the guys and I talked about what was next for all of us but especially what was next for me. None of them had ever traveled alone before, and they found it crazy that I was going to do this by myself. I had traveled alone before when I was in Europe, so I wasn't scared at all, just excited to see and do more fun things.

We got to the airport, and everyone got out. We all took a moment to say a few things, and there were big hugs all around. I thanked each of them for one hell of a journey and thanked them all for their support. For me, it was a tearful goodbye, which was something I always did when saying goodbye. I don't know why, but I think it is because of my mom. She always cries when saying goodbye, and I'm a lot like her. The guys wished me well. "Be safe, Mundy, and keep us posted."

"I love you guys," was the last thing I said and then turned around and walked toward the terminal. I turned around, and they all were waving goodbye, and just like that, I was now alone.

40
CHAPTER

Southeast Asia: Solo

The airport was in the middle of nowhere. As we were driving, I could tell that this airport was away from any stores or places to eat. I figured when I got there, I would get checked in, have something to eat and drink, and then maybe take a nap somewhere. I did have eight hours before my flight. It was no big deal, and I would be fine.

I looked at the airport, and there was one small terminal; it was a small airport that didn't get your 747 or 777 big planes, and that was for sure. As I walked toward the building, I could see people sitting in the lawn/field area everywhere. They were using luggage as pillows or chairs, and at first glance, I could tell that I was the only white man around. I was 6'2", bald, and carrying a backpack. This was one of those times that I felt one hundred sets of eyes on me and me only. It was a little unnerving at first, but I would soon get over it. All I wanted to do was get inside and find a place to chill out for a while.

So I got to the main door, and there was a guy standing there, fully armed with dark skin and bloodshot eyes. As I approached, he noticed me and came right up to me. I told him, in English of course because I didn't speak any Filipino, that I had a flight to KK. He spoke a little English, which was good for me, and told me no entry until thirty minutes before the flight. "You have got to be kidding me," I said to him, and he shook his head and pointed to the sign that said, "No entry until thirty minutes before flight." Well, that sucked, and this was not at all what I had planned on, but oh well, guess I had to deal with it. This is why I had seen about one hundred people all sitting outside in what was more of a field than a lawn.

Well, I took a quick look around and saw a piece of land that was near people but would give me a little space. I walked over to my new little piece of paradise that I would be at for the next seven hours at least and get set up. All the while, I could tell people were looking at me like *Who the fuck is that and where the hell is he going?* Most white people would be flying in and out of Manila, not this tiny-ass airport going to other portions of Southeast Asia. Well, guess what, people? I'm going where you're going.

I would like to tell you that the next seven hours or so were fun, but I would be lying. Nobody said a word to me, and I just kept to myself. It was hotter than hell that day, and all the shaded areas had been taken, so I was fully exposed to the sun, and it was hot. I had one small bottle of water and nothing to eat. Time went by very slowly. I would check my watch and think an hour had gone by, and it would have been more like fifteen minutes. It was a long wait and very uncomfortable. I thought of the guys who were probably bellied up to a bar drinking a cold beer and eating a delicious sandwich. Here I was sitting in a field with a bottle of warm water and the sun pounding down on me. When the doors opened and I started to see people make their way to the building, I didn't hesitate for a minute.

Once inside, I realized this was not your average airport. They had a few vending machines but no real stores. I did grab more water and a few snacks. We had picked up some local currency while shopping, so I did have a few bucks to get something. Everything was moving quickly, and people were running around everywhere. I found my gate, and they were already getting people on the plane. I wasted no time and got on board as soon as I could. I had a window seat next to an older woman going back home to Borneo. It was about a four-hour flight, and thank God they served food on the trip. It wasn't much, but anything at this point was better than nothing. At one point, I used the lavatory on the flight, and this is when I realized that I was the only white person on this flight. This was not the first time for me, but each time it happens, I always think of the international travelers that come to the States, and they too are the ones that look different and get all the stares. It is a humbling experience.

We arrived in Kota Kinabalu, which is the capital of Sabah, Malaysia. The city is located on the northern part of Borneo, and it is on the coast of the North China Sea. When we landed, we were out of the city and had to take a bus to the main square of the city. Once at the main square, I was now in a place like I had never been before. KK is a large city with skyscrapers, big roads, and a lot of people. The area that I was in was more laid-back, easygoing, and had more of a third-world feel than a city would have.

According to my book, there was a good hostel called Lucy's. It was highly recommended in the book, and the price was right. I knew my dollar would go a long way here, and it did. It was basically 1–3.85 ringgit, and the hostel charged about 16 RM, which meant it would cost me less than $5.

So here I was walking down the streets of KK. The buildings were very basic, some two to three stories but painted with ocean colors. There was nothing fancy about what I was seeing, and yet it felt comfortable and safe. I passed an area that was a huge tent with at least one hundred tables under it. I found an ATM and got some local cash, passed a small store, and bought something "good to drink," and after about a mile or so of walking, I found Lucy's Hostel.

The hostel was known for a friendly environment, cooking facilities, and a veranda that was outside and a great place to hang out at night. I walked in, and she was sitting behind this desk, which was right in the middle of the room. I asked her, "Are you Lucy?" and she responded with a yes. I told her I needed a room for a few nights, just got in, and hopefully she had something available. She had a room, dorm-style, ten to a room, and this was perfect. I got checked in and had already seen about six to eight other people that were all where white and traveling like I was. I picked out my bed, which was one of three beds available, and it was a top bunk. Not really my favorite choice due to the bathroom in the night and moving around a lot, but it would work, and I was happy to have it.

Once I was settled, I wanted to find an Internet café and touch base with my family. Everything was within walking distance and rather convenient. The area that I was staying at was more of a beach town but had a city close by. Anyways, I found an internet café, contacted my family, and let them know I was here, and it was day one of another major adventure. All was good back home, and I did start right then looking for flights back to Hawaii in a month or so. From Bali, which was going to be my last stop to Maui, it was around $800. Hopefully, the price would come down a little, but at least I now had an idea. We had $1,000 for our flights, but if I could get in cheaper, it meant more in my pocket; we would see.

I got back to the hostel after grabbing something quick to eat and made my way out to the veranda or patio, however you wanted to call it. Outside, there were about six people all talking and hanging out. I went outside with my bottle of booze and said hello to everyone. They started asking the basic questions, "Where are you from?" and "Where are you going?" I struck up a conversation with at least five people and at that time offered them a drink, and just like that, I had new friends. It is amazing how many friends you can get at a hostel and especially when you have something to drink. We spent the next few hours talking about places they had been and where they were going. I told everyone that I had taken a boat across the Pacific and flew here from the Philippines. I can say that my story was better than anyone else's. They all were amazed how I had gotten here. All of them had flown on a plane from their home country, and that was it. Anyway, that night, I sat with about five others; we got to know each other and learned about the area.

I did also talk with Lucy herself; she too was excited to have her first person ever stay here that lived in Hawaii. I felt like a rock star all over again. Lucy did fill me in on things to do in the Sabah area. The first thing she told me about really got my attention and that was a rehabilitation center for orangutans. This place was in the northern part of the country in a town called Sepilok. She gave me the rundown on how to get there. Lucy also mentioned the southern part of the country was known for its diving. Borneo was also well known for its jungle environment, and there was plenty to see there. With those few ideas, I had some planning to do; it all sounded like fun.

My first day in KK I spent walking around with a few guys, just checking out the sites. We stopped into a few places for a drink and a bite to eat. I had made the decision to head west toward Sepilok and check out the orangutan place. I booked my ticket for the next day, six hours, and it would cost about $9. With this all done, my plan was set, and now I would spend one more night here in KK and see how the nightlife went.

That night, about six of us from the hostel all went out for dinner together. There was this fish market they had told me about, and it was the place that had all the picnic tables under the huge tent area when I first got there. It was dark when we got there, and the place was packed. There were at least one hundred tables, and it took us a while to find an empty one. This place was really cool and a lot of fun. We sat down, and at the end of the table was a cooler full of fresh fish. Each table had someone that would help you with whatever you wanted. You could get any kind of seafood you could imagine. I picked out this whole snapper, about two pounds and it looked good. We all chose something, and they took the fish and cooked it on a big grill. There had to be at least ten big grills, the person would take it to the closest one near us, and the guy running the grill cooked our fish. I asked for a beer, and off my little lady went, and within sixty seconds, she handed me a beer. The six of us sat there with at least five hundred other people all dining on fresh fish, cooked right on the grill next to you. My snapper came with potatoes and corn on the cob. It doesn't get much better than this. The entire experience was remarkable. The place was loud and full of energy. The food was absolutely delicious, and for less than $10, I had a great meal and a few beers.

Our little group of people walked around that night and checked out a few bars, but basically, we all just went back to the hostel and sat on the patio. We had all picked up something to drink and sat outside, shooting the shit and enjoying a few cocktails. It was a great night and the best meal I had had in a few days.

TAKE A DECADE

I want to answer a question right now, and that is "Why Borneo?" What was it about this place that I chose to travel around here? Well, let me tell you, Borneo is the third largest island in the world. The island itself is about 287,000 square miles and has everything you could want from beautiful beaches to dense rainforest. The island is owned by three different countries, Malaysia, Indonesia, and Brunei. The island was once completely covered with rainforest, but with deforestation, the island's rainforest is a fraction of what it once was. Much of the rainforest is being cut down for timber, pulp, rubber, minerals, and palm oil. There was also a threat to the wildlife that inhabited the island. The animals have been killed due to fires but also illegal wildlife trafficking. This island offers a lot as far as wildlife goes and I guess that is what really attracted me to coming here. This is not my first time in a rainforest, but this area is just different.

The next day, I was on a bus for a six-hour trip through the northern portion of the island. It was my first glimpse at how much of the forest had been cut down. There were so many acres being used to grow palm oil; you could see the fields and large piles of the leaves on their way for processing. Now don't get me wrong—it was still jungle all around me, just not first-generation jungle. That had been cut down decades ago, and now, new growth had started the next phase of the growth. The one thing that I had read about before getting here, and Lucy also talked about it was the orangutans that lived on the island. For me, these are one of the coolest animals on the planet. I had seen them in zoos but wanted to see them in the wild if I could. The Orangutan Rehabilitation Center there took care of injured and orphaned orangutans, and this was where I was going.

We got to the small town near the center. I found a place to stay, Sepilok, B & B. It was a dorm style accommodation for 27 RM, about $8. It was cheap, clean, and had a nice feel to it. Really, I didn't meet anyone staying there, just kind of did my own thing. After I got set up, it was all about getting to the center. They had buses running quite frequently, so I took the next available one. I get to the Center around 2:00 p.m., and I was lucky. They were having a feeding session in one hour, so I should be able to see them up close. I took an hour and just walked around the park. They had nice wooden walkways that went all around the area. I was here to see one of the great apes of the jungle, but let me tell you, the plants, fauna, and botanical gardens were very impressive. To be honest, I saw plants and flowers that I had never seen before. As I was walking, I finally spotted the first one. It was not real close, but I could see it. How could you miss a big orange ape? They really stick out once you have seen one.

Orangutans are called "the man of the forest" and are derived from three species: humans, chimpanzees, and gorillas. A mature ape can weigh up to two pounds and stand five feet tall. It is their long arms that have always attracted me to them. An orangutan can live into their forties, and some in captivity have lived into their fifties. They feed on vegetation, make a nest in trees to sleep, relax during the day, and take very good care of their young. An orangutan can have children as young as eight years old, but they really can't take care of them until they are in their teens. So when they are young and have a baby, another older, more mature ape will care for the baby and help raise it. They are so cool-looking with the reddish-orange coloring, hairy faces, and long arms, and they have this human look to them that is amazing.

At three o'clock, I was at the place that would give me the best view of them. The worker came with a basket full of fruit and bamboo and crossed over to where they would come out. These great apes are smart and know when it is time to eat. As we watched the jungle, we would see the apes making their way toward the food. The first few that came out were the big ones, fully mature and hungry. I was about ten feet away from one of the biggest. He took a piece of bamboo, moved over to where I was, and sat and enjoyed his meal. I'm just standing there in awe looking at him, eating and watching me. After the bigger ones came out, then we had the absolute great pleasure of watching a mom and her little tiny baby feed. The mom would eat, break off a small piece, and hand it to her young. The baby was just like a human baby and was all over the mom. Up one side and down the next, sit on the mom's head, and for a split second actually touch the ground, only to go right back up to mom. We were so close to them that I could hear the crunching of the bamboo and hear them grinding on their dinner.

I sat and watched them for a good hour. Even after they were fed, some stuck around and watched us, watching them. I wonder if they do the same thing we do. "Hey, in a while, let's make our way to the clearing and watch those stupid humans watch us eat." They probably thought we were the simplest creatures on the planet. *What is their obsession with watching us eat? Don't they have anything better to do with their time?* They were the Man of the forest, and for me, it was a special treat to see them so close.

After I had seen what I wanted to see, I made it back to town for something to eat. While sitting outside enjoying my chicken, rice, and cold beer, a guy approached me with another potential experience. He was selling this package deal that was a stay for two nights and three days in the jungle at a jungle lodge. The price was rather cheap at 330 RM, about $34, and that included two nights' stay and three meals a day. We would spend time in the jungle and on the water. This trip was all about seeing wildlife in the untouched rainforest.

With my plans set for the next few days, I spent the night just walking around and checking out the sites. The town was small, and there was not a lot to see, but I was just walking on dirt roads along the jungle, taking my sweet time, and always looking for something to see. At night, I was smart and stayed inside due to the nature of the jungle and that there are dangerous animals that like to eat meat, and I would be a good snack for some black panther or something else.

The next day, I took a bus from Sepilok to meet up with other people to enjoy this jungle adventure. The drive there was rough, the roads were not the greatest, and we moved along at a nice easy pace. There were times I could see the jungle and times we passed huge fields of palm oil. You know palm oil is used in so many things, everything from chocolate, ice cream, shampoo, to lipstick, which makes it a valuable commodity. This is why they cut down the rainforest and planted fields of this stuff. It is sad, but unfortunately, this is not the only place in the world where this is happening. Again, it is not a bad thing to look at; the fields are amazing to see these beautiful trees growing all over the place.

After about a six-hour trip, we got to the meeting location for this trip. There were about fifteen people that I would be living with the next few nights. A family of four (mom, dad, son, daughter), a group of five from Denmark, a single girl, and a few other guys. We all met up and started talking about what we were getting ourselves into. Everyone was happy-go-lucky, and of course, I had my eye on the one single girl.

We got to the banks of the Sungai Kinabatangan River, which was the longest river in this area. It was a wide and rather muddy-looking river. There was no real desire to swim in this river, and we never did. We all got into this eighteen-foot-long aluminum boat. The helm was in the back of the boat with nice, comfortable chairs in the front. We had about fifteen people, and the boat was pretty much filled. The guy driving was from the Philippines and worked for the WWF, World Wildlife Foundation. This guy I will remember forever because he was about five feet tall and missing his two front teeth.

Once we were on our way, he started to tell us about some of the wildlife we could see—orangutans, about ten varieties of monkeys, many types of birds, bearded pigs, crocodiles, and pygmy elephants. He was very knowledgeable and excited about the wildlife, which got all of us pumped to see stuff. The boat moved along at a good speed with the jungle all around us, the brown, muddy water that was warm to the touch, and the never-ending potential to see something. Before we even made it to our camp, we stopped and watched a group of monkeys playing in the tree. It had already been a good choice to do this, and it was already paying off.

We get to the camp about fifteen minutes later. We were on the other side of the river, and I could tell the camp was surrounded by jungle. We pulled up to the dock, and the first thing we saw was this twenty-foot fence that went all around the camp area. We were met by two women, and they escorted us up to the camp. I could see three to four buildings on the left side, a few little cabins on the right side, and a main little house with an open patio with benches and tables. The entire camp area was about a half-acre at most, and this huge-ass fence went all around it.

We are taken into the main house, and we all sat out on the patio at the tables. They introduced themselves and gave us a quick overview of how this place worked and what we would be doing. They told us mealtimes; they talked about our excursions by boat and at night on land and the most important thing, the fence. They asked us why they had a fence, and almost everyone assumed it had to do with keeping animals out. We were right, but it was not the monkeys and cats but the elephants. They told us that if one elephant got in this area, it could destroy this camp in a matter of minutes. They were strong and showed no mercy, so that was why there was a huge electrical fence around the camp. We were given specific instructions not to go outside the fence unless we were with a guide. Also, don't touch the fence because it was like 220 volts, which was needed to keep out such a large animal.

Once our orientation was over, we were given our rooms. I had a dorm room that slept six people, and when I went inside, the entire room was filled with one group, the kids from Denmark. The one guy left as soon as I walked in, and I was thinking something was wrong. He came back with a staff, and she asked me to come out; she had made a mistake. The group had been told they would have the entire place to themselves, so with all the other beds filled, they gave me one of the single cabins, which had its own shower. This was what they called a jungle upgrade, and I was happy to have it. It was my own little house. I had two full beds, a desk, and my own bathroom. This was great, and I was happy they made a mistake.

Once we got all set up, we ate lunch, which was a good-sized sandwich, chips, tea or water, and cookies. It was filling and hit the spot. Then we all went back to the boat and loaded up for an hour-long tour. We did the boat tour every day, three times a day, so I'm just going to sum up what we saw along the river. The thing we saw the most was monkeys: howlers, southern pig-tailed, gibbon, and the proboscis monkey. This monkey is the one that is a red and dark color with long arms and a long tail, very cool-looking. We did see a few crocks sunning themselves on the riverbank but none in the water. We also on the second day ran into a few wild orangutans, which was a great thing to see. We were not as close as I had been a few days ago, but to see them in the actual wild was fantastic. It was on our second day that our guide got a call from another group, and they had spotted the rarest thing and that is the pygmy elephant. So we motored to them, and there were four gigantic beautiful elephants eating near the shore. We stayed back and joined two other boats doing the same thing. We just floated around the area and watched these massive animals—two had tusks—forage through the trees for something to eat.

We watched them for about thirty minutes, and our guide told us he was going to beach the boat, and maybe we could get out and get closer photos. He pulled up to the beach, and the bow of the boat was on land. He gave us the okay to get off, and I went first. Well, I took two steps off the boat and went right up to my knees in mud. I took another step, and it went past my knees. I looked back in the boat, and everyone was looking at me. "Hey, Steve, is it a little muddy?" my guide said, and all I could do was laugh and say just a little. Well, this basically stopped anyone else from getting off the boat. I was already covered in mud, so I kept going. About fifteen steps later, and I was now on dry land. The elephants watched me watch them, and I got as close as I felt comfortable. They were about thirty yards away, and I took one more step, and the big one turned and looked right at me. He was basically saying, "Take one more step, you idiot, and I'm going to squash you."

At this point, the guide said, "Far enough, you might want to get back in the boat," so I listened to him and did just that. I had mud past my knees, which gave everyone a good laugh. It didn't matter to me because I got the closest to an animal that could destroy me quickly.

So anyway, our boat rides were fun and exciting each time. We would just sit back and enjoy the wildlife. Our guide did a great job on the water and really went out of his way to find as many things as possible. There was the tiger that lived in the jungle, and he had been doing this for a while and still had not seen one. He told us that if you actually got to see a tiger, then you were actually in danger at that time. The tiger would see you long before you see it, and when you saw it, well, it could be too late. We still looked but never saw one.

At night, we all hung out around the main area and had our dinners, which were really good. They served us chicken, fish, pork, rice, salads, and always something sweet at the end. It was fun all of us sitting around the tables, eating, and they did have beers we could buy, so about six of us enjoyed that little aspect of the lodge. To just sit and watch the river flow by around sunset was always beautiful. The rainforest, the river, and the sky would always change colors of some sort each night.

Once it got pitch black out, we would take a nature walk in the jungle. They gave us these long boots to wear and a long-sleeved shirt, and we all brought our flashlights. The entrance into the jungle was in the back of the camp. The guide would open a section of the electric fence, and we would all leave the camp together. He had a bright spotlight, and we walked each time about a mile or so through the jungle searching for more wildlife. We saw more monkeys, a few bats, and a couple of huge-ass bugs. Walking through the jungle at night was fun; however, we saw more from the boat during the day. After, we would return each night, we had to do a leech check on each other. This was the reason for the boots and long shirts. In just an hour or so, I could have five leeches on me at any given time. You didn't even feel them get on you; it was just from walking though the dense jungle, brushing up against leaves and other vegetation that they just stuck right to you. A leech could make you sick, so it was in our best interest to make sure we got them off.

So I spent two nights and three good days living in the jungle. For the amount of wildlife, we saw this trip was so worth it. The people who ran the camp and my fellow guests were great as well. If only that girl had been single—she did have a serious boyfriend—I might have given this trip a 10 out of 10.

On our last day, we went for one more boat ride; we saw a lot of the same thing, which really never got boring. I can sit and watch monkeys play in a tree for hours. They are the best things to see for sure. After lunch that third day, we loaded up our gear and made our way back to civilization. We got dropped off at the same spot we had originally met at. My next spot on the map was heading to the ocean, which was in the southern part of the Sabah region. I had looked into maybe doing a dive in one of the best places on the planet to scuba dive.

So we got dropped off, and my bus was leaving soon, but I had no idea just how soon. I wanted to grab water and something to eat on the bus. The bus stop area had a few outdoor stores, very basic but useful. I was getting my drink, and I watched this bus pull out and leave the area. I went up to this guy and asked, "When is the bus to Semporna?" He looked at me and said that the bus had just left. "What the fuck? We just got here like three minutes ago."

He told me, "Next bus is tomorrow at the same time." He said there was nowhere to stay the night. He could tell I was shit out of luck and said, "Come with me, we can catch it." So he put me in his car, and we pulled out of there with the tire spinning. He drove really fast, and soon enough, we could see the bus. The guy pulled up along the side of the bus and yelled for the driver to pull over. Here we were driving alongside this big bus, the wrong side of the road, and going 60 mph on a shitty-ass road. Well, we get the driver's attention, and he soon pulled over. The guy jumped out and went over and explained how I missed the bus. They both had a good laugh at my expense, and with my tail between my legs, I got on the bus. Some of the people who were with me at the jungle lodge were on the bus, and they started to heckle me and laugh. We all had a big laugh on Mundy's account, and I laughed right along with them. I thanked the guy and the driver for making this happen.

Once on the bus and avoiding what could have been a long night sleeping at that bus station, I sat back and enjoyed the ride. We were now headed to a town called Semporna, which was on the southern portion of Malaysia but still on the northern part of the island. This town was the gateway to get to a few small islands off the coast that was world renowned for diving and snorkeling. It would also feel good to jump into the sea.

We got to the small town, and the water was right there. This was a beach town, and it felt like home. Once I was off the bus, I headed right for a dive shop to get any info I could. The guy was your typical surf dude; he spoke English and filled me in on everything I needed to know. The boat to Mabul Island left in the morning around ten. I had missed it for today, but he told me of a hostel to stay at. I asked about the diving, and he would put me on a waiting list because right now, it was full. This was about all I needed. He also informed me that there were no ATMs on the island, so get cash before. After my information session, I made my way to the hostel.

It was so nice to see the ocean again. I was off the northern part of the island on the coast of the Celeb Sea. The water looked blue and very inviting; unfortunately, this would have to wait until morning. I walked along the water and crossed over this small bridge. The hostel, Dragons Inn, was right there, and I walked in. They had room, and I got all checked in. The rooms were all dorm-style, so I picked out a bed that was free and unloaded my backpack from my back. The room was rather empty at this time, but there were people staying in here. The cool thing about this place was you could look through the boards on the floor and see the water beneath you; I thought it was cool, and it was cheap by the way, $5 a night.

After that was taken care of, I wandered around this beach town. Everyone was walking around in board shorts, bikinis, and sarongs. It made me feel at home. I enjoyed a good meal and a few beers while watching people just mingling around. I didn't know a single person, and not a single person knew me; it was great. After I had something in my stomach, I decided to go to the ATM, get some cash, and then walk around for a while. So I walked around the streets, and I noticed this long line for something. I figured it was a show, a sale, or something; boy, was I wrong. The line I saw with about thirty people in it was for the damn ATM. Holy shit, this was crazy, but I did need money. I go to the back of the line and started my wait. I asked the person in front of me, who looked to be from here, why the line was so long. He told me that the signal for the ATM went out all the time, and when the signal was working, everyone waits. The other problem they had in this remote area was that the ATM ran out of money because so many people use it at one time. Well, this was not good, and all I could do was hope the signal stayed and they didn't run out of money. My plan to quickly grab some cash and then walk around soon changed. I stood in line for two hours until it was finally my turn. Luckily for me, the signal was still transmitting, and they still had cash. I took out about $50, which would be equal to 1,500 RM. This would be plenty for the next few days.

After this ordeal, it was getting late, and I decided to just grab a few beers and head back to the hostel. I got to my room, which would sleep about ten people, and one guy was in there; his name was Seth. He was from the States and a real cool guy. We started talking, and we were both going to the same place for the same amount of time, three nights and four days. We sat around and had a beer or two together and got to know each other. Seth was 5'8", a skinny guy with brown hair. He wasn't a ladies' man kind of person but a really cool person.

The next morning, we got up and made our way down to the harbor, which was the center of the town. We purchased our boarding passes and loaded up on the boat. It was a twenty-six-foot open-bow ferry boat that had a great view from wherever you were. Seth and I found a spot near the front and waited for everyone to get seated. The weather was beautiful, sunny skies and eighty degrees. The seas were easy going, and we had a great two-hour trip to the island.

Where I was going were these two islands off the coast. The first one was Mabul Island, which up until the nineties was basically a fishing village. However with the popularity of its neighboring island, Sipadan, which was a famous scuba diving spot, the island of Mabul also became a tourist destination. However, the main source of income for most of the residents on this island was still fishing.

We got to the island and were offloaded on a beach near the main area. I could already see that this island was small and had a lot of small houses on it. We had checked out a few places to stay and left the beach in search of our next home. The island was so small that you could walk around it in twenty minutes. Now there are about two thousand people living on this island, half of which are children under the age of fourteen. With this many people on this island, it would either take a large or very tall building to accommodate everyone. This was not the case; the people all lived in what they called longhouses. So picture seeing this island from the sky, and all you would see is homes built over the water with long walkways out to each of them. There were plenty of buildings on this island, and most were small shacks made of straw, wood, and tin.

We walked down through the houses, and we were looking for this specific number for the longhouse that served as a guesthouse. We walked ten minutes halfway around the island, and we found the spot. We walked out on the wooden walkway, and a guy was sitting in a chair. He was next to a building that housed his family, very poor, I can tell you that. We asked if he had room available, and he had one room left, which had two beds. This was perfect, so Seth and I agreed to stay here. We could share a room, no big deal. He showed us the room, which was another twenty-five steps out further from the shore to another set of rooms. He had four guest rooms, and past that, on the end of the dock or walkway was a patio with four tables and an awning. One more step past that and you were in the sea. Our room was right on the end, and we were now out above the sea about two hundred feet from land. Our room was basic, two beds and that was it. You could look through the boards on the floor and see the water beneath you. This time, the water is a lot closer to the floor, and I was sure on a stormy day that this room would get wet. The place was so unique and perfect for our needs. Now the deal with this guesthouse was you got a room and three meals a day for 50 RM or about $15 a day. Where in the world could you get a room and three meals a day for $15?

We got there around lunchtime and got to meet some of the other guests. We had a young couple, two younger guys there specifically for the diving, two older ladies from Germany, and the two of us. The girlfriend in the relationship was drop-dead gorgeous with blond hair, blue eyes, and a beautiful body. At least we had something to look at. Anyways, we all sat down at the tables, and the sea was right there five feet away, and we could at any time jump in the water from here and swim around. They brought us all a plate of food, fish, rice, beans, and a drink. We sat and got to know everyone, and the couple and Seth and I hit it off right away. We talked about what they had done, and they had just gotten there the day before and not really done much except for swimming around here. We talked about snorkeling later, and we got some information from our host.

After we ate and talked for a while, it was all about getting in the sea. We all suited up and jumped in right from our longhouse. Now one thing that we noticed right away as soon as we stepped on the longhouse was the amount of trash in the water. It was horrible, and it was all over the island. Once you walked out to the end of each longhouse, the water was clear and garbage-free, but along the coast, it was bad. This island's population was primarily made up of Filipinos who were Muslim living a nomadic lifestyle. They really didn't have residency in the country and lived off the land. Now the fact they didn't have legal residency meant the children were not allowed to go to school. About 60 percent of the children on this island never got any formal schooling. They were educated by their families and that was it. Like I said, the place was poor and so interesting.

I stood at the end of the longhouse and dove into the sea. The water was warm and felt so good. I did have a snorkel and mask that I had brought from the boat. No fins, they were way too bulky. Now I lived in Hawaii, but the water here and the corals that we saw in a very short time were way better than anything Hawaii had to offer. In just five minutes underwater, I felt like I was inside a tropical fish tank. The coral was bright colors and alive. You could pass your hand over a section, and a portion of it would disappear, and a minute later, it would reappear. There were tons of reef fish, some I had seen before and some that were new to me. This place was a marine life sanctuary and amazing.

After a good hour-long swim, we got out, and I went looking for something to drink. I asked our host about getting a bottle of booze and a pack of smokes. He told me, "No problem." He left and ten minutes later returned with a bottle of rum, a few Cokes, and a pack of smokes. The four of us enjoyed a drink or two and talked about renting a boat to take us to another reef. I did have my name in to possibly scuba dive at Sipadan but wasn't counting on that.

At night, we would all hang out at the end of the longhouse and watch the sunset over the sea. There were certain nights during all my travels, and these three nights were top of my list. It was just perfect: the sunset, right next to the sea, music playing in the background, and good people to hang out with.

The next day, we snorkeled at two different spots. The first one was by boat with a local guy who we got hooked up with through our host. He took the four of us off the coast to a well-known reef that was teaming with fish and coral. Once again, my mind was blown away with everything I was seeing. Now I don't know why, but for some reason, in this water, I could hold my breath longer than I had ever done before. At this point in my trip, I was smoking a pack of cigarettes a day, and still I could hold my breath longer than the other three.

We spent three hours that afternoon with our guide, snorkeling and loving every minute of it. When we got back, we had a meal, and we were told of another place on the other side of the island that was also a great place to snorkel. Now it took twenty minutes to walk around the entire island, so it wasn't far. We found the place, and it had this overhanging deck that you could walk down a few steps and jump right into the sea. It too was amazing and had more structure, so there seemed to be more fish. I saw my first rooster fish and several three- to four-foot barracudas. These fish had teeth and were attracted to anything shiny, so you don't want to wear any jewelry, watches, or rings. There can be a single barracuda or there could be one hundred barracuda around this area at any given time. This place was as good as the reef and would be a place I would spend more time.

That night was another very cool night, and the reason for this was it was Green Planet night. The plan that night was everyone would turn off all their lights, and we would all sit in the dark. When the time came, all the lights went off, and we all sat on our deck with nothing but candles. The longhouse next to us had someone that played the guitar, and we sat and listened to music, which made the night perfect. Once the lights started to come back on, we chose to keep ours off and spent the entire evening with the sea in front of us and the blue sky above us.

The next day, I went snorkeling by myself. So I left with my stuff and walked to the other side of the island, the same spot as before. I jumped in and instantly saw a bunch of fish. I just swam around checking out the scene, and I saw what looked like a snake on the bottom of the water. So I dove down, and sure enough, it was this six-foot-long sea snake. I know it was six feet because it came to the surface, and at one time, I was rather close to it, and it was the same size as me. Once it hit the surface, it disappeared, and I continued doing what I was doing. Well, an hour went by, and I was ready to get out, so I swam over to the dock and started to get out. As soon as I hit the first step, I was startled by what I saw. There all coiled up was a sea snake, so I avoided it and kept going. Just then, I noticed another one, and now I stopped in my tracks to see just how many there were. I stood there and counted twelve snakes. Some were on the steps, and some had even climbed up the post holding the roof and coiled up in the rafters. When I went into the water, I didn't see a single one, but one hour later, this place was covered in them. Just writing this makes my toes curl up. So I walked very carefully and quickly to get out of this area. When I got back to the longhouse, I told the host about them, and he told me to stay far away from them because they were very poisonous and I would be lucky to survive a bite here. He told me that they had a very small mouth and could only bite a human in a few spots. The one spot was on our hand, anywhere between our fingers that has loose skin. The other part is our ears because of the cartilage. Well, I had swum right next to one not knowing this and then stood with fifteen of them all around me. Well, I guess I got lucky this time and would take more caution next time.

So we stayed here for three nights and four days. It was relaxing, enjoyable, and downright one of the coolest places I had ever traveled to. It was such a unique experience to stay in a longhouse over the water and something I will never forget. If you're in the area, you have to stay here; just watch out for the sea snakes.

The fourth day, I got a few hours to snorkel around, and then it was back to the boat and the mainland. We stayed one more night in the same hostel and went and had a good meal together. He was heading in one direction the next day, and I was heading back to KK to continue my trip. By now, I had decided to fly from KK to

TAKE A DECADE

Singapore. It would be a ten-hour bus ride back to KK, spend one night at Lucy's, and then to the airport for a flight to Singapore. My plan was set for my next destination and my next country.

After a long trip back to KK, one more night at Lucy's. I was able to tell her about my trip, and she was so happy to hear I had a great time. Most of the people were new by then and sat on the veranda and made new friends. Everyone was all about where they had been and where they were going. My story was a little different, and each time I told how I got there, everyone was impressed.

The next morning, I took a bus to the airport and waited a few hours before it took off. At least here I could wait inside and have a drink. I had done some research the first few days and found a ticket to Singapore for $73 one way. It was on an airline I had never heard of, but as long as they got me there safely, I could care less. With that said, I was done with Borneo and off to Singapore.

We arrived at the Singapore airport at midday after a wonderful flight. We were fed and had drinks and a little nap on the plane, so when we landed, all I needed was a place to stay. With the help from my book, I found the cheapest place available and asked at the airport how to get there.

Singapore is a first-rate country with all the fancy things we have in the States and maybe even a few more things. Singapore is a very unique place. It is considered a city-state with a population just under six million. The area of Singapore is about the same size as Portland, Oregon. So with this many people in one area, the rules are very strict. The city is called the "Fine City," and there is a reason for this name. They believe in very strict laws for many different occurrences. For example, it is illegal to have chewing gum in this country. My bags were searched at the airport for just this one thing. With gum outlawed, there is no littering of this and helps keep the city clean, which is why this city is the cleanest I've ever seen.

The term Fine City is just that: They believe in heavy fines for many things. Not only is it a monetary penalty, but they use physical punishment as well. If caught stealing, you could lose your home and also be whipped many times. Eating on the subway, jaywalking, littering, and smoking near a building can all end you up in jail with possibilities of several lashes with a cane. All I knew was that I did what I was supposed to do and paid close attention to the law.

The cost of visiting this place was much different than any other place in Southeast Asia; it was pricey. That is why I chose the cheapest place to stay. After a twenty-minute bus ride from the airport and a short walk, I found the place, which was right in the middle of the city. I made my way in and found the front desk. The lady informed me that they had rooms available, inside rooms and outside rooms. The price was $25 for inside and $8 for outside. Now for the big question: What do you mean outside? She informed me they had beds set up on the rooftop, and I asked to see them. We took the elevator to the roof about thirty floors and walked out. They had about twenty beds set up under an awning with lockers for each and a shared sink. The showers and toilet were located on the floor below us. Well, for me it was perfect. I paid for three nights, and luckily, they sold beer at the front desk. I stood there looking out over the city and thought to myself, *What an amazing view I have, best ever*. I spent about an hour, enjoyed a cold beer, and got a basic idea of what to do.

After a quick shower, it was out and about for me. That first night I spent walking the nearby streets and getting a feel for the area. All the restaurants looked way out of my league, so most of my food was bought from street vendors and small stores. I never once ate a meal in a restaurant, too expensive. The big thing that night was figuring out the mass rapid transit, called MRT, for the next few days. It was rather easy; I took a quick ride to just check it out and something to do. The cost for about one mile was $3.50, so going anywhere was costly. You actually had to pay $4.50, and when your ride was over, you inserted your ticket and got a dollar back. This way, no one was discarding used tickets in the trash. Once again, smart move keeping things clean. I had figured it out, and that was all I needed to do.

Back to the "rooftop," I brushed my teeth and stared out over the city at night. Wow, it was beautiful. However, it was time to sleep and get ready for a busy day tomorrow.

It felt good to sleep in a little. The breeze was cooling, and with the sound of the city around me, I got a good night's sleep.

TAKE A DECADE

The next day, I was off to see what brought me to Singapore, and that was the port area. The Singapore Port was one of the busiest ports in the world. Due to its location, basically smack dab in the middle of the world, it had more cargo come and go through here than anywhere else in the world. I didn't think I would be able to just walk around the port, so I found the highest peak in the city and climbed to the top. I had stopped and bought a sandwich, chips, and a few drinks to just enjoy a few hours watching the port in action. At one point, I had counted over a hundred boats, coming, going, and some just waiting their turn. It was amazing and just what I wanted to see. Mission accomplished.

The rest of my time in Singapore, I visited their version of Chinatown and Little India. Both places provided me with good, cheap food, fresh off the street. I did buy a pack of cigarettes, and it cost me $10 for a pack. The only reason I mention this is that on each pack of cigarettes they had a picture of a tumor, lung cancer, open heart, or just something disgusting. It was a means of getting people to quit.

My last day was spent on Sentosa Island, a man-made island with imported sand. It was a relaxing place to enjoy the sea, get away from the hustle and bustle of the city, and just relax. This place was cool; it had a Luge Ride at $11, and I had to do it. I watched many people go down and finally decided it was my turn. It was a three-minute ride that was well worth every dime; what a blast.

Singapore was brief. I wish I had more money, but it was awesome. I'm sure I walked at least fifty miles in these three days. You can't always see everything, but something is better than nothing.

41
CHAPTER

Indonesia—a Tough Road

My alarm went off at 6:00 a.m., which was the earliest I had been up in a long time, and got ready for my day. I stood brushing my teeth at the sink overlooking Singapore for the last time. My rooftop accommodations turned out to be a wonderful place to stay while I was here. I had a nice breeze all night long, and besides a little traffic, it was extremely quiet. Today would be the beginning of a rough few days, and I had no idea.

The MRT was on time and dropped me off at the boat terminal with twenty minutes to spare. The terminal was clean, well-organized, and a super happy staff. The lady who helped me gave me perfect instructions on where to go and what to do. It was so nice to have a smiling, helpful person at 6:30 a.m. The best information she gave me was to get Indonesian currency before I left. The terminal I was going to on the island of Pulau Baton didn't have an exchange office, and the exchange I would get at the terminal would not be a very good rate. So with this information, I transferred what I could and was able to get Indo money from an ATM. Now that I had Indo cash on me, it was time to get on the boat. The ferry was two stories, open air on the top deck and protected on the lower deck. It was about forty feet long and twenty-five feet wide, made out of mostly wood. It looked safe, and it was my choice to take a boat rather than fly. I was being really cheap right now, and it might come back to bite me in the ass.

We left the terminal, and I was sitting on the top deck taking in all the boats around that I could see. Once we were off the coast, I got a good look at the port and could see things were busier than ever. I do have to mention that out of the 125 passengers on board, I was the only white guy, and I stuck out like a sore thumb. Oh well, I found a spot and sat back and took in the waterway around us and enjoyed a nice two-hour boat ride.

We get to Pulau Baton, and I could tell right away that I had gone from one environment to another. It was like cold to dry or up to down. Pulau Baton is described in the book as "multinational industrial plants, sweatshops, and sweaty businessmen going crazy at girlie bars." If this is something you're into, then spend the night; however, for most, it is a quick stop over to catch another ferry to Sumatra. This was my plan: Get off this ferry, go through customs, get my ticket, and get on another ferry, hopefully right away. Well, let's just say that changed.

The terminal was dirty. The few people besides the ones on the boat with me looked rough and not happy at all. I got inside and first went through customs, paid my fee, and got another stamp in the passport book. The customs agents just looked at me, I'm sure thinking what the fuck this white boy is doing here, dumbass. They really didn't give me a hard time; they asked a few questions and were kind of rude. I then found the terminal for Sumatra and asked for a ticket to Pekanbaru. The girl looked like she hated her job. She didn't speak English except for a few words, and she told me, "Tomorrow." I asked again for one ferry ticket, pointed to the name of the place, I wanted to go, and all she said again was, "Tomorrow, the ferry just left."

"You have got to be joking. They said it left once this one came in." Well, they were wrong, and once again, she said the one word, and that was it: "Tomorrow." Well, that sucked, and now what do I do? The ticket agent was no help at all, so maybe I could find someone to help me find out what I could do.

I walked outside, and there were several taxi cabs waiting. The guy got out and asked me if I needed a ride. He spoke a little English, enough to get by. I told him I needed a place to stay for the night close to here so I can catch the ferry in the morning. He told me there were no places to stay near the terminal, but he knew a place, and he would take me. I asked how much for the ride and the room. He told me about $5 for the ride and the room he didn't know. Well, I really didn't have much of a choice; I was kind of at this guy's mercy, and I decided to go with him.

We got in the car, and this car smelled worse than any NYC cab I had ever been in. He was smoking, which didn't bother me—I was smoking at the time—it just reeked of smoke and sweat. We pulled out of the terminal, and I was hoping this was a quick ride—well, it wasn't. We drove for twenty minutes to the other side of the island, and at one point, I wondered where he was taking me. My mind started to play games, and I was thinking, *We are going to pull into some warehouse, and that would be that, no more Mundy.* This was all I could see: big warehouses, industrial factories, and a rather poor area.

Well, we got to this town of some sort, and he pulled up in front of a hotel. The road was about a half-mile long and had a row of buildings on each side. The street was in the middle, and I didn't see a single person. It was early, but I saw no one. We got out of the car, and the first thing I noticed was the smell of the air. It smelled like rotten meat, burning trash, and sweat. It was really bad.

The guy went in with me to make sure they had room, and they did. I paid him and thanked him for not killing me—just kidding, but that is what I was thinking. Anyway, he asked me if I wanted him to pick me up tomorrow morning to go back to the ferry. I told him yes, and he said, "I will be here at seven a.m."

The hotel was rough-looking, and I just didn't get the warm, fuzzy feeling that I had hoped for. The girl showed me my room. It had a bed, a chair, a bathroom (with a shower), and a small TV. She gave me the key, and I thanked her. This was a rough place. I looked out the window. I was on the second floor and right in the middle of this street. I looked one way and saw twenty or so buildings all attached to one another on one side and the same on the other side.

TAKE A DECADE

The street also had fifty-five-gallon barrels like every fifty feet or so; I counted like ten on one side and twelve on the other side. Once again, I really had not seen too many people yet, a few people walking around but not many.

All I knew at this point was I needed a beer and it would be well deserved. I walked down to the front desk and asked about food and drinks. The best thing and the only good thing about this place was she sold beer and other drinks right from the front desk. So I grabbed a couple and went back to my room.

The TV was small and only got a few channels, but at least it worked, and there was a soccer game on, so I sat back and watched it for a while. Then I started to get hungry and made the choice to venture out and get food for the entire night so I would not have to go out again. The girl at the front desk was gone, so she would be no help. I hit the street and looked one way and then the other way. It was a fifty-fifty shot at which way to go. I turned left and started down the street. The buildings did not have a lot of signs on the outside to let you know what kind of business they were, so I just kept walking. Across the street, I noticed a police officer, so I figured he could let me know of a store to get food. I crossed the street and walked up to him. "Excuse me, can you tell me of a store to buy food?" I said. He didn't speak any English at all. He was about my height and weight with dark-brown skin and bloodshot eyes, and he was not my friend. I put my hands to my mouth, the universal code for food, and he said something and then pointed in a direction. I thanked him and walked away. The direction he pointed me seemed to be leaving town. This was weird; there had to be something around here. Well, in the distance, I saw what looked like a fruit and vegetable stand, so I did walk over to it. There was a guy sitting behind his little cart with about twenty items to choose from. Most of the products looked rotten, had flies all over it, and not even an apple looked good. So I turned and walked away.

My only chance of finding something was on the other side of the street. I walked out of my way to avoid the cop; he was not my friend and had basically given me shitty information. I crossed the street and walked along the building looking for something that sold *fresh* food. Well, about halfway down, I saw what looked to be a grocery store. It was on the second floor, so I walked up the steps, and I could see things for sale through the window. Once again, there really was no sign or advertisement for this place. The door was open, so I walked in, and I could see a few people shopping. Okay, this would work, and I started walking down the rows of stuff. This place was not like any grocery store I had ever been in before. Most stores have sections for certain things—the bread is with bread, fruit is with fruit, and clothes are with clothes. Well, not this one. I walked down one row, and it was like this: socks, bread, detergent, beans, towels, meat, lettuce, hangers, shoes. There was no order for anything. You had to go up and down each row to find stuff. I grabbed a small loaf of bread, a small jar of peanut butter and jelly, two bananas that didn't look great, and a big bottle of water. This would be what I would eat until tomorrow. So I checked out and make a beeline for my room. By this time, it was late afternoon, and I didn't want to be on the streets at night.

I got to my room and also grabbed a few more beers for the night. I locked my door and put the chair under the knob just in case. Well, it was home for the night, so I would make the best of it. I had a sandwich and continued to watch the game on TV.

Around 10:00 p.m., I started to hear more noise on the street and looked out the window. Half of the big barrels now had a fire going in them with people around them partying. What really caught my attention was the sound of dirt bikes and mopeds; this is what I first heard, and when I looked out the window, the streets were lined with bikes of all different sizes and shapes. This is when things started to look strange. I really had not seen a lot of people all day, and now the streets were packed with kids and adults standing around the street partying.

Okay, have you ever seen the movie *From Dusk till Dawn*? This is what it looked like. At this point, I would not even stand by my window. I sat on the floor and peeked out from the bottom of my window. At this point, I shut my lights off and just left the TV on for light. I also took some empty beer cans and put them right next to the door. This was in case someone tried to get in. Of course, I still had the chair under the doorknob and whatever else I could do to booby-trap my room.

In the next few hours, the place got rowdier, and more of the barrels were now burning. The stench in the air was now in my room; the smell of burning garbage was everywhere. I would assume that this is what they were burning and that was their trash for the day. Anyway, it was awful and just added to a strange night. Every once in a while, I would sneak on the floor and look out. I didn't want to make eye contact with anyone. I didn't want them to see me and decide to drag me out of my room and turn me into a vampire. So to be honest with you, I didn't get a lot of sleep that night. I even had my little knife under my pillow as I lay there, staring at the door and listening for a mob of people coming to get me. Well, I'm still here, and I still love the sunlight and garlic as well.

I'm not sure when I fell asleep, but all I know is that when I woke up, it was light; thank God I made it through the night. It was a little after six, and hopefully, my taxi guy would show up; if not, I would have to figure something out quickly because I would not stay here again.

Luckily, about ten minutes before 7:00 a.m., he arrived. I made my way down to the lobby, turned my key in, and went outside. "Thanks for being here" was all I said. He gave me a lift back to the ferry. I was on time to catch the next ferry in twenty minutes, and I was getting the hell out of *hell*.

The lady at the counter was the same unhappy person who was there yesterday; she remembered me. She sold me the ticket, about $30, and I asked her how long the journey would take. She told me, and I heard her very well, three hours by boat and then three hours by bus. That was how long she told me the trip would take. Okay, we would see.

Now I was going from a small island south of Singapore almost due south to get to the island of Sumatra. My destination at first was the middle of the island, a place called Pekanbaru. There was not a lot to see here, but it was halfway to where I was trying to get, and that was a city called Bukittinggi. This was a city on the south side of the island, and it was the place to go to climb Mount Marapi, which was an active volcano and my destination.

We loaded up on the ferry, and I chose to stay below in the cooler shaded area of the boat. The ferry was about the same size as the other one and laid out about the same. They did serve food and drinks, so this was a plus. Once again, I was the only white person on the boat. At this point, I couldn't care less; all I knew was I was tired and just wanted to sleep.

We left the dock, and I was so glad to be on this boat and away from Batan. I had found a wooden bench seat for my trip. I took my big backpack and placed it on my lap and was able to lay my head on the bag and go to sleep. I would wake up now and again, check my watch, waiting for three hours to go by, and three hours did go by, and we were still moving. Four hours into the trip, I went and asked someone how much longer. The people selling food didn't speak English. I went to one of the workers. He didn't speak English. Finally, I went to another crew member, and he took me to another crew member that did speak a little English. The young boy was about fifteen, but he was my only hope. I asked, "When are we going to get to the end?"

He looked up at me, and all he said was "Not yet." I tried to ask more questions, but he didn't understand. Well, he said not yet, so I hadn't missed anything, I hoped.

It was frigging six hours before we got to the end. We had traveled from the open ocean up a tributary; sometimes the width of the river would only be fifty feet wide, and by the time we got to the end, it was really narrow. The land was almost all tall grass around the water with forest in the distance and dark muddy water around us. It was a real scenic trip and definitely longer than three hours.

The boat stopped, and there was this old, beat-up bus that I hoped was not mine. Guess what, it was. We got off the boat. They rushed us to the bus, grabbed my bags right off my back, and before I could say anything, they had tossed it to a guy standing on top of the bus putting all our gear on top. Oh well, at least I didn't have to deal with it on the bus. We were pushed onto the bus, which was all this was, an old school bus. It had the same straight-back seats and no bathroom. This would suck, I was sure of it. We were not on land for five minutes and we were off like a bat out of hell.

It only took about two miles for me to realize that the roads were horrible. The bus driver was spending more time off the road than on it. I was sitting toward the back of the bus next to some guy who never spoke. The bus was packed, and at least half the bus was smoking. There were a few small families, older, younger, and all native to the area. Then there I was sitting there among these people, dealing with the same conditions they were.

It was about two hours into the trip, and the driver pulled the bus over. We had a flat tire, and he would have to change it. At least I could get off and find a place to take a piss. Trust me—I wasn't the only one. Even the old ladies wandered into the forest to relieve themselves. It took the guy about an hour to complete the change. I just walked up and down the dirt road we were on, looking into the jungle, hoping to see a Sumatra tiger. I knew they were here, but the chance of seeing one was slim. Oh well, it gave me something to do.

At our three-hour mark, there was not a building in sight, not a light, sign, or nothing. All we could see was the jungle on both sides of us, and that was it. I guessed we were running a little behind schedule. All I can tell you is this bus ride might be the worst one ever.

Four hours went by, and we stopped at a roadside stand area to use the facilities and get something to eat. The place had two little buildings—well, three-sided structures—with a few things to get. I got a few pieces of fruit and a bag of nuts and another pack of smokes. I did ask the driver how much further, showed him my ticket, and told him my destination, which at that point was a hostel in the city called Poppie's. Someone had told me that the guy who owned the place spoke English and could help me from there. Well, my driver didn't speak English. He looked at me like I had two heads, and all he said was "Not yet." I had heard this before, and it was not good.

Well, my three-hour trip turned into a full six hours, so I had spent six hours on a boat and now six hours on a bus. Once we had reached the city, I could tell this was not a tourist trap at all. Pekanbaru was a modern industrial city. It was the helter-skelter oil capital of the island. It was a loud, disorganized place from my view. As we drove through the city, all we heard were horns beeping, and traffic was all over the place. There was no sense of traffic order at all; just go and honk your horn.

The bus came to a stop on the corner of three major roads. There was no "bus terminal," nothing. I was thinking, *Why are we stopping here?* Well, the bus driver stopped, and he pointed to me, then he pointed to the door. He said something in Indonesian, and I couldn't make it out, but someone spoke up and said to me, "Your stop." So I grabbed my bag and told him as I was getting off that I had a bag on top. He shook his head up and down, and just then, I saw a guy climb off the top with my bag. Okay, this didn't look right, but what could I do? Nobody else got off at this spot, just me, and that worried me.

Now was when the scariest time of my traveling experience began. I got off the bus, and the door shut, and the bus pulled away, beeping his horn along with everyone else. Here I was standing on a street corner, and all I saw was traffic, large buildings, smokestacks from industrial buildings, no signs for information, people walking past me, and just a few feet away was a group of men standing on the street. I start to walk down the street, wondering if Poppie's was close by and that was why he dropped me off here. I only walked a few feet when this group of guys all came over to me. They surrounded me, and I thought this was it and figured I would have to fight to stay alive. They all had dirty clothes on, stained teeth, and dark eyes, and they were not people I would hang out with. One guy asked me in very broken English, "Where are you going?

I told him, "Poppie's Hostel."

He stood there for what seemed like forever. All the other guys just stood there staring at me, and he said, "I know, I take you." Before we moved, I asked him how much. He told me seventy thousand rupiah, which was Indonesia's currency. I did some quick math and realized this was about $8, which was cheap enough, but it still seemed high.

Well, at this time, I didn't have a lot of options and told him okay. I had my big pack on my back and my day pack in front. He told me to follow him, and as I left our little group of guys, they all just stared at me like they wanted me dead. We walked down the sidewalk, and I was looking for a car. Well, he didn't have a car; it was a moped. *You have got to be kidding me. I'm going to have to ride on the back of this moped close to him.* It was not what I wanted at all, but what could I do? He took my day bag and put it in front of him; he got on, and then I got on with my backpack on my back. He took off, and we were zigzagging in and out of traffic. We were speeding down the road between cars, buses, and trucks. If that wasn't bad enough, it started to rain a little, and the road would be getting slick. This did stop him from moving along at a nice little clip. I had no idea where we were going, and just then, the guy turned back to me and said, "Are you my friend, or are you my enemy?"

Without any hesitation, I told him I was his friend—and a very good one at that. What a question to be asked on the back of a moped, driving through traffic like a madman. At this point, I thought for sure I was a dead man. After he asked me this question, I unbuckled my backpack just in case he stopped and I had to run. I would leave my bag in an instant to save my life if I could. In the strap of my backpack was where I kept my knife, and I should be able to grab that if I needed it. The guy never said another word. It was scary and not a fun time at all.

We drove for about twenty minutes, and by this time, I was thinking, *Where the hell is this guy taking me?* Well, just then I saw the sign "Poppies" and had never been so happy to get to my destination. We pulled up, and I told him I needed to make change. I went inside and asked if they had room, which they did. Just then, I saw this guy walked by, and I hoped this was Poppie, and it was. I asked him real quick how much a ride should cost from where I got dropped off to here, and he told me no more than Rp 25,000. I told him this guy wanted 75,000, and he told me that was way too much. With that information, I went back out and handed the guy Rp 25,000, and that was it. He jumped off his moped and started yelling at me in his language. I just turned around and walked back into the hostel. They took me to my room, and I looked out the window, and the guy was sitting there in a chair waiting for me to come back out. I wasn't going anywhere anytime soon. He finally left after a half hour, and I never saw him again.

I went and found Poppie again, who was an older Asian man with gray hair. I asked him if he could help me and told him where I wanted to go. He said he would get me a ride tomorrow morning, and that was it. He left, and I never saw him again the entire night. I wanted to ask him so many questions but got just one in, and that was it. So much for waiting to have an English conversation with someone; that would have to wait.

My room was on the first floor overlooking the street. It was about an hour after being there, and I heard this loudspeaker sound off, and all I could hear was someone praying. Sumatra is a primarily Muslim community. Here I was, an American surrounded by Muslims. The prayer could be heard all over the city. I waited until it was complete, which took twenty minutes or so, and decided I needed food and something to drink. I wanted a beer real bad after my day of hell.

I ask the girl at the front, but she spoke no English, and I decided to just walk around and see what I could find. There were a lot of outdoor markets around where I was staying. All the food was stuff that I was not used to, and nothing looked good. I walked up to an outdoor stand and asked for beer, no luck. I check out another stand, and they didn't have any either. It took me going to about five different places before they had beer. It was warm, but who cared? While I was waiting, the lady who ran the little stand went into the back and brought out her entire family, two kids, grandma, and her husband. They stood and stared at me and laughed a little. They may not have ever seen a white man before. There were no other white people that I had seen so far; it was just me, and I was all alone.

It seemed rather safe but just had uneasiness to this place. While I was walking around looking for food, most of the people looked at me, smiled, and kept walking. This was a very Muslim place; the women all had the entire head-to-toe black garments on. Some just had their eyes showing, and that was it. The men all dressed in dark colors, and a lot of them wore hats. This was my first experience being around a religion that we as Americans were taught to dislike.

They were nice to me, and I had a group of kids stop me to take a picture with them. This made me feel like a rock star and also an easy target.

Well, I found this sidewalk vendor serving what looked like chicken and rice in a leaf or something. I stood back and watched for a few minutes and decided why not; it would be something in my stomach. So I walked up and pointed to what the person had just got, and he scooped this stuff into a banana leaf and handed it to me. I had my beers and something to eat. It was dark by now, and I just wanted to get back. As I was walking back, the loudspeakers went off again. This time, I was on the street, and I stopped and watched many people lay their little towel down, get on their knees, and start praying. I found out that the mosque, of which there were several in the area, sounded off the prayer throughout the entire city using speakers that looked like ones used for weather emergencies. They prayed five times a day, once before the sun came up, then three times during the day, and then once after it got dark. They did these 7 days a week, 365 days a year.

For me, it was very cool to see and witness society worship the way I had only heard of and seen on TV. It was something to see so many people stop and pray right in front of me. Just another first for me and I was taking it all in.

I got back to my room and ate my food. The banana leaf was used as a packaging item and not to be eaten. I didn't know this at first and tried to eat the leaf. It tasted like grass, and I spit it out. It would be later that I found out about the banana leaf. The banana leaf was just that and used here to wrap food in; it was their version of Tupperware. The banana leaf is biodegradable, so it is better for the environment and cheaper. So my banana leaf was filled with rice and some sort of meat. They did not have any utensils, so I used my fingers and ate it that way. Later, I found out this is the way they ate all their meals, with their fingers. I had seen this before but never had to do this myself. At least I was in my room by myself, so all the things I was doing wrong, no one would know. The food was filling, but I can't say it was good, just for the record. If you asked me what

I ate, I would not have a clue. All I know is that others were eating it, so it had to be safe.

Before the sun came up, the mosque sounded out the first prayer of the day and scared the shit out of me. Here I was sound asleep. It was still dark out, and this thing went off. It got my heart beating, that was for sure. The only thing about this one was a little girl or a lady with a high-pitched voice singing the prayer. It sounded beautiful, and I just lay there and listened to this soft voice do the morning prayer. Of course, I had no idea what they were saying, but it sounded nice. After it was over, I went back to sleep for a few hours until it was time to get going. Poppie had left a message for me that someone would pick me up and take me to Bukittinggi, which would take about six hours. They would get me around noon, which would get me to my spot around 6:00 p.m., which meant it would still be light out, and that was good.

Noon came, and I heard a horn beeping outside. The girl came and told me they were here. She said this in her language, but I knew what was happening. The guy had a van, which was better than a moped, and it was rather full. He took my bag and put it in the back and got me a seat. The price for this trip was around $15, which was fine and looked like a better ride than the bus. It was a van that held about ten people. The driver did speak a little English, enough to tell me we would stop for lunch halfway there. That was great. I gave him money, and we were off.

Once we left the city, the jungle was once again all around us. It was nice to look at and much nicer to look at than the dirty city. It was about three hours later that the driver pulled into a place for lunch. There was a huge open-air building that was made of wood and had a thatched roof. No walls at all, just a big deck with tables for eating. There was also a bathroom, which I used first, and next to that was a place they could pray if the time came, in which some of the people stopped and did their thing. Everyone in my van went inside to eat. The driver told me to sit here, which was right in the middle of the restaurant. The table was set with four small dishes for sauces, and it had two cups of water as well. I sat down, and a waiter came and gave me a menu. It was not in English, so it did me no good. All I could say was *pollo*/chicken, and he understood. He asked if I wanted rice and something else, so I said yes. After he left, I took one of the cups of water and drank it. The water was warm but something wet. Just then, I looked around, and I saw all the other people were using this water to wash their fingers. They ate with their fingers, and this was used to clean them. I just sat there and thought to myself that I had just drunk some nasty-ass water. Who knew what was in it? The thought of it made me sick to my stomach, and I hoped like hell it would not give me some parasite or some flesh-eating disease. Nothing I could do about it now.

My food came, chicken and rice, and there were several sauces that he poured out into the tiny bowls. He also brought me a fork to eat with. I watched everyone else, and they would take a small portion of rice, roll it up with their fingers, dip it into a sauce, and then eat it. I used my fork to eat with and ate the entire meal. He did bring me drinkable water as well, and it was much appreciated because a few of the sauces were spicy.

After we all ate and used the facilities, it was time to get back on the road. It was another three hours before I started to see buildings and the city of my destination. I had read in my book about a hostel with a German guy who spoke English. This was where I wanted to stay for the night, so hopefully, it was not hard to find and he had room. The van stopped at an intersection, and we all got out. This was much better than the last stop when only I got out; this time, we all had reached the end. I thanked the guy, grabbed my bags, and started walking to find this hostel.

It had been a very long few days, a tough night on a sketchy island, a long boat ride, the worst six-hour bus ride, another long night in a Muslim country, and another long bus ride to this city. All I wanted to have was a conversation with someone who spoke English, a bed, and a shower.

Bukittinggi was a cool, quiet market town located on the western side of Sumatra. This was a main destination for outdoor extremists with volcanoes, canoe trips, and off-road 4WD adventures. The town seemed to have just about anything I would need. The center area was very compact, and within just a short walk, I passed restaurants, shops, and outdoor food vendors. The name of the hostel I was looking for was Hotel Rajawali, which was owned and operated by a German couple. The hotel was easy to find, and I was excited to have a comfortable place to sleep tonight.

I walked in, and the owner, a German guy, greeted me at the door with a thick accent, but he spoke English, and this was great. He told me he had a room for me and showed me to it. The cost was great too, about $6 for my own room with a bathroom. As I unloaded my pack, he asked me what I had planned on doing while I was here. My plan was to climb Mount Merapi, and that was about it. Then I told him I was making my way toward Bali, which was my final destination. He did ask where I had started from, and I gave him a rundown of how I got to this point, and he was impressed. I would be the first person to stay at his hotel from Hawaii, which made him feel pretty good. It was always nice to be the first.

So we started talking, and he told me about Mount Merapi. It was about a six- to eight-hour hike, and the cost of hiking the volcano was about $20 for a pass. This was more than two nights' stay here and was more than I was thinking it would be. He told me that I was in luck and that tonight, the pass for entry was waived. Once a month, they had a free day so that locals and lucky tourists could see the beauty of the mountain for free. Now for the kicker and that was we had to leave in one hour. He had three other people that were doing the hike tonight. They were going to hike all night and get to the top of the volcano for sunrise. He told me that this was the best time to see the view from the top, and that was when the sun was just coming up. This meant that after the long few days I had had, I would forego a relaxing evening and instead hike all night.

I took my day pack and packed it with whatever I felt I might need. He told me that it could be cold at the top, so bring warm clothes and a flashlight. The only thing I really didn't have was water and food for an overnight hike through the jungle. My best new friend told me he would stop at a store and give me a chance to get a few things. The plan was to leave the hostel at 8:00 p.m. It was a thirty-minute drive, and if we started hiking around 9:00 p.m., we should have plenty of time to be at the summit by 5:30 a.m. or so to watch the sun rise. It was going to be a long night, but hey, this was one of those opportunities that you could plan yet take full advantage of them when they arose.

I met my travel buddies, a guy from France who was mid-twenties, a tall, good-looking guy, and two girls from Poland that were around the same age, not really attractive but seemed very nice. We loaded up in our host's jeep, and he did stop real quickly for us to get supplies, and we took a nice thirty-minute ride through the jungle to get to the start of the trek. This gave the four of us time to get to know each other, and they all seemed very cool and excited to be doing this trip. I was excited as well; I just wished I had one day to plan for it and get some rest, but hey, I was tough and ready to go.

The starting point was at this small wooden building that had a small sign telling you about the mountain. We all went inside, and we had to give them information on where we were from. They took our passport numbers down and used these to make sure we would all come back safely. We were given a few directions, to stay on the trail and stay together, which was our plans anyway. With this said, we all left with our headlamps on and started our trek through the jungle at night.

Mount Merapi, also known as Merapi or Berapi, is a complex volcano in Sumatra, and its name means "mountain of fire" and is the most active volcano in Sumatra. It is 9,485 feet above sea level, so it is going to take some time getting there. This is why I was here and why I put myself through pain and suffering to get here. Oh well, it was time, and we were off.

The four of us started hiking, talking as we went, and sticking together as much as we could. We were literally walking through the jungle at night without a guide and, most importantly, without a weapon. There were animals in the jungle that fed primarily at night and could have us as a snack, but hey, here we were. The one thing we all noticed right away was the amount of trash on the trail. It was like we were walking on a layer of garbage, but it did help define the trail. It being night, we could really only see as far our light would shine. We did have a beautiful clear sky with a ton of stars shining, which made for an incredible night.

We hiked for about three hours and came across a group of local kids who were sitting by a fire enjoying a beautiful night. They were so amazed to see us, and they all took pictures with all of us. They just didn't see a lot of foreigners, and we were a treat for them to see. We stayed and talked for about fifteen minutes, giving us a water break and time to eat something. It was a lot of fun talking, and getting our picture taken made us feel like royalty. After our break, we continued, and the hike was a gentle incline for most of the way.

It was around 2:00 a.m., and we had come to the base of the volcano. From here it would be the hardest part of the hike and would take a few hours to go a short distance. We all just pulled together, got some food and water in us, and started the last and hardest part of the hike. Once we got on the mountain, the vegetation disappeared, and it was mostly loose rock. By this time, we had all stopped talking and doing everything we could just to keep going. I could take about twenty-five steps and then take a break. We still were all sticking together; the French guy was leading the pack, then me and then the two girls. It was tough, and this was no joke. I've hiked a lot of mountains in my life, and when you have to walk for six hours before you even start going up, it can make it a long trip.

Well, it was about 4:00 a.m., and we were real close. It was still dark out, and besides what was around us, we couldn't see much. We could, however, start to smell the sulfur in the air, and this was a sure sign of a volcano. At this point, we decided to hang tight, relax for an hour or so, and when we saw the first hint of light, we would make the last push. By now, the temperature had dropped, and it was getting cold. We had sweated for the past seven hours, and now we were not moving, and the chill went right through us. So here we were on the side of a volcano. The mountain was at a forty-five-degree angle, and you had to watch your step or you would slide down due to the loose rock. I found a large rock and used my foot to keep me from sliding down. I had a light jacket, a long-sleeved shirt, and a poncho in case it rained. Well, I put all these layers on, including the poncho, braced myself against the rock so I didn't slide down the mountain, and used my day pack as a pillow. I got as comfortable as possible, and by now, I was exhausted and it had been a long night. I closed my eyes and actually fell asleep for about an hour. This was how I now knew that I could actually sleep anywhere. If you can sleep on the side of a volcano when it is cold and braced up against a rock, then you can sleep anywhere.

Just as the light peaked over the horizon, our French guy made the announcement, and we all packed up and made the final push to the top. We all congratulated each other and stood there and watched the sun rise over the jungle. Here we were at the rim of a volcano. The smoke was rising out of the bottom, the smell of sulfur in the air, and the sunrise was spectacular. Just to stand on the rim, look down to the bottom of this massive natural wonder, and then stare out over the jungle was amazing. We stayed there and enjoyed the sight for a good hour, took photos of each other, and enjoyed the fact we had successfully climbed one of the most famous volcanoes in all of Indonesia.

After we were done, we started the trek back only to be very careful walking down the mountain. The rock was so loose, and every step was sketchy, so we had to be careful. It took about an hour to get to the base, and from here on out, it was smooth sailing. Now we could actually see more of the jungle around us, and it was dense and beautiful. We made it back to the entrance at around 1:00 p.m., and our guy was sitting there waiting for us. He had done this trip many times and knew the time frame very well, and it was nice to not have to wait to get back. We once again congratulated each other and thanked our guide for making this happen. By now, all we wanted was a hot shower, and I wanted to take a nap.

We got back to the hotel/hostel, and we all went to our rooms. Now I had spent about five minutes in my room, and that was about it. I saw that I had my own bathroom and assumed it had a shower. Well, this was when things got different for me. The bathroom had a toilet, and next to the toilet was a 2' × 2' tile basin that had a PVC pipe dripping water out of it. In the small basin was a scoop that looked like the Big Dipper. *Is this my shower?* I asked myself. It couldn't be, so I went out and found the host and asked him where the shower was, and he started to laugh. He told me that the shower was in the bathroom; you used the scoop to get wet, soaped up, then scooped water over your body to rinse off. This was an Asian-style place, and it was what it was. So I went back to my room and took a very cold, very quick, first-for-me shower/bath. There was a drain on the floor, and all the water went down the drain, and it was what it was. Well, it wasn't the hot shower I wanted, but it felt good to be clean. After my "shower," I lay on the hardest bed I had ever had and finally got some well-needed sleep.

So the next day, I walked around, and I spent time talking with our host on getting to my next spot. I had to take a bus from here to another city, Padang, where I was going to fly from there to the island of Java. After talking with my host about the island, I made the choice to not go to Jakarta, which was the capital of the island. He told me that it was just a busy city and not a lot to see. However, Yogyakarta, a little further, has more to do and see. So with this information, I booked a flight from Padang to Yogyakarta. With this next step of my journey booked and ready to go, I was able to spend my last day enjoying this quiet, relaxing, and mainly Chinese-run town.

The next day was all about traveling. First, I had a 5-hour bus ride to the city then a 4-hour wait for my flight then a 2.5-hour flight to Yogyakarta. When I got out of the airport, I found a ride to get me to the main drag of the city. It was by moped, and if you remember, my last moped ride was a nightmare. This one was cheap, and he knew the right place to take me. It was a cheap way of getting around, but riding on the back of a moped in a city with very few traffic rules can be a little scary. Well, the guy got me to my destination, which was a hostel near the main street called Malioboro. The place was clean, colorful walls and was run by a nice local couple. My room was very basic, but they did have an outdoor common area that was nice to sit and watch people walking by and enjoy a beer or two.

After I got situated and did a little research, I was out and about to see more of the city. Yogyakarta is the second biggest city in Java and is loaded with history and culture, and it seemed to be a fun place to visit. After leaving the hostel, I was going to make my way to the Kraton. The Kraton was a city within a city. It was home to 25,000 people and seemed to be the thing to see while you were here. This was the home of royalty and the home to Ratu, who would be

TAKE A DECADE

the king or queen at the time. It was supposed to be this amazing royal temple and something to see. The Kraton was located at the other end of the city, which was fine because it gave me a chance to see more of what the main street of Malioboro had to offer. Well, I can tell you this street had everything you would want. It had a ton of shops, cafes, internet cafés, clothing stores, outdoor vendors, and a ton of people. Just walking around the streets was entertaining enough with so much to see. The locals were pleasant, a little pushy about buying things, but for the most part, it was nice.

I continued my mission that day and just walked and walked. Once I had left the main area for all the shops and business, the city just became more of a city. As I was walking, I could see this guy in front of me; he was wearing a pair of white pants and a white shirt. I didn't know if he was going the same direction until we got there. The wall of the palace was about twelve feet high, so it was tough to see anything else. I watched the guy in white in front of me and kind of followed him to see what he came up with. As he was walking around, he stopped, and I think he was waiting for me to catch up. I walked up and asked him, "How do you get into this place?"

He told me what I thought he would say, "I have no idea." Well, at least now we could try and find it together. His name was Brian, and he was from England. Brian was in his early fifties and traveling around just like I was. So right then and there, we became friends.

We walked around the outside and finally found a way into the palace. Now this was not a big, fancy place like you might think. It had beautiful buildings, all glittering with gold, but it also had a lot of basic accommodations for the many people that live there. We did check out the fancy parts, and once inside, we started to run into a few people that helped out with locations of things to see. This place was huge. Remember, it is home to 25,000 people, so it is not just a one-block area.

So after a few hours of walking around, Brian and I decided it was time to have a beer together. We walked back toward the main street and found a cool place to sit and get to know each other a little. I found out he was staying at the same place as I was, and he too wanted to check out the Hindu temples close by. We also talked enough to know he liked to party, and Brian had been to a few other Indo islands, like Komodo and Gillies, which are supposed to be really cool. I would not have time to see those islands, but it was nice to hear about them. I filled him on Sumatra and my ordeal getting there. We had a good conversation, and he would be cool to hang out with for a few days.

We got back to our hostel, and we stopped and bought some beers. We got back and talked with our host about trips to the temples. They got us in touch with a tour guide, and for 60,000 RM ($7), we now had a plan for the next day. That night, we walked around the streets, and both of us liked to smoke, so we had a little plan to try and find some weed. It didn't take long, and it wasn't expensive at all. We got a small bag for like $5 and found a place to kick back. It had been weeks since I had smoked weed, and it made for a great night.

The next morning, I came out to the common area, and he was up with coffee. I'm not a coffee drinker but enjoyed a cup that morning with him. Our tour started around 11:00 a.m., and we had a short walk to get there. It gave me time to grab a few pastries along the way from a great little bakery that I found. The food was good, fresh, and rather cheap, which was a trifecta in my book.

We got to our tour area, and we were loaded into a small van. There were about fourteen people in our group, and the plan for the day was to spend time at two of the most famous Hindu temples in Java. It took a good hour to get to the first one, and we were now outside the city, and the landscape had opened up to more jungle and mountain feel.

The first one we stopped at was Prambanan, which was amazing from the first sight. The temple was the largest Hindu temple in Indonesia and the second largest temple in Southeast Asia; Angkor Wat was the biggest. The whole area had many temples, all built with the same material, stone. The tallest one was around 154 feet tall, and it was just like the others, tall and pointed architecture. In 2006, some of the temples were damaged during an earthquake, so we could not go into any of the temples; we could just see them from the outside. This was fine with me because the creativity and designs of the building were impressive. They used gems to create eyes in some of the stone sculptures that were on the outside of the buildings. How the hell they made these things back in AD 860 was beyond me. All I knew was it was something cool to see.

The second one was Borobudur, and this was actually a Buddhist temple, not a Hindu temple. It too was created around the same time in the ninth century, and it was stunning. The temple consisted of six square bases with three circle ones on top of them. There were 432 Buddha images in chambers around the terrace, and on the upper circular terraces, there were 72 more Buddha images. The tallest structure stood about 115 feet above ground and was just something amazing to see. Around the outside of the main structure, it looked like these huge bells were made out of stone, and I'm sure if they were ever lit up with lights, it would make for a special attraction. Anyway, I have not seen Angkor Wat, but I have seen these two, and I feel like I have seen a great example of Hindu and Buddhist cultures.

My last day in yoga was spent getting plans set for my next trip. I wanted to make my way to Bali the next day, so I'd have plenty of time to check it out. At the same travel station that Brian and I got the temple tour from, they had another one that worked great for me. It was a two-day trip that would leave from Yogyakarta to Mount Bromo to Lovina, Bali. This trip would get me from one island to the next and give me a chance to see more.

That last night, we sat at our hostel and drank beers and booze for a long time. It was late when I finally went to bed, and it was one of those nights that my head hit the pillow and I was out, clothes and all. The thing that sucks about drinking so much the night before is the morning after, and I felt like shit. It was going to be a long day, but I did have a long bus ride before Bromo, so this would give me time to shape up and get my act together. Brian and I said our goodbyes, and I was off to my next spot.

The eight-hour bus trip from the city to Mt. Bromo, my second volcano, gave me time to sober up and get a little more sleep in. Once I got to the mountain, I knew there would be some walking, so I wanted to be ready. This was a good thing because we did have to walk.

We got to the top of the mountain, as far as the bus could go, and we stayed at Yoschi's guesthouse in a mountain village of Cemoro Lawang. It was a basic accommodation used for tourists traveling to the volcano and perfect for the night. Almost right away, we were on a trail toward the site. It took a while hiking, and by now, I was feeling much better. If I had to hike six hours ago, it would have sucked, but it was good now. We spent about forty-five minutes walking through the jungle, and it did take a bit of energy to get to the top. Mount Bromo was an active volcano, 7,641 feet tall and one of the most visited sites in south Java. The last time this erupted was in 2004, and two people died from falling rocks. The smell of sulfur and the steam coming from the crater was very much like Mount Merapi.

We spent a while walking around, and there were other people with me; just today was all about hanging out with me. This gave me a chance to sit and just stare at the beautiful landscape and watch the steam roll out of the mountain. We stayed up there until the sun set, which gave for a beautiful sunset over the jungle. I had seen the sunrise on Merapi and now the sunset on Bromo, which was perfect.

That night, I walked around the small village, found things to eat and drink, and that was it for the night. It had been a long few days, and we were leaving the next morning early, and I wanted to be ready for that trip. I would be taking a bus to the coast of Java, which would take four hours or so, then a one-hour ferry ride across the strait to Bali and then another bus to Lovina. So the next day was a travel day, and that was about it.

The bus ride was fine, and once we got to the water, the landscape changed from jungle to beach in a short distance. The beach, ocean, and palm trees were a great sight to see. It had been a while since I had been on the beach, and all I wanted to do was find a place in the sand and soak up some rays.

The bus got to Lovina beach later in the afternoon. The beach and ocean had been in sight for some time now on the bus, and it looked so good. It was just another tropical paradise on the planet, and I was going to spend a few days doing nothing except relaxing on the beach. Once we stopped at the station, it was time to find a place to stay. There were several options, and the one I chose was perfect. Lovina was a beach bum magnet filled with surf shops, bars, restaurants, and beautiful beaches. My plan was to stay here for three nights and just enjoy the ocean. I had spent the last three weeks or so in a mountainous jungle environment, and now it was beach time. Lovina was located on the northern shore of the island, and the town was perfect, not too big and not too small.

After getting situated in my room, it was a short walk to the beach, and I was a happy person. I found a place to drop my stuff and walked into the warm blue Bali Sea. With one dive, I was underwater, and the whole world stopped around me. The feel of the waves along my body and the taste of the salt in the sea made me think about Hawaii, and I would be home soon enough. After a good swim in the sea, I went up to the beach and laid out my towel. It was about this time that the people started asking me if I wanted to buy stuff. I can say that in about two hours of sitting on the beach, I had twenty people come up to me and offer me anything from food, drinks, massage, drugs, and women. Now I did have food and drink brought right to me, and this was great; it is just not relaxing when every five minutes, someone is trying to sell you something. All you can do is be polite, tell them no thanks, and that is it. Well, it was the start to a lot of soliciting while on the island.

That night, I just walked around the cool little town, got some food, had a few beers, and checked out as much as I could. There were a few bars, but nothing was exciting to me that night; it was just nice to be here. This was my last island and almost the end of the trail, so I wanted to enjoy things as much as I could. That night, it gave me time to find an internet café and catch up on what was going on elsewhere. All was good back home, and everyone back on Maui was going about their daily routine. It was just nice to hear from a few people. Of course, the boys had checked in with me a few times just to see how things were going, and it was good to hear from them.

So Lovina was there for three nights and it was all about the beach and sun. Now I would be lying if I didn't tell you that the topless girls on the beach were also a wonderful thing to see. For the most part, I kept to myself, swam, soaked up some sun, had beers throughout the day, and wandered around the town at night. After the first day of people asking to sell me stuff, I became used to it, and it didn't bother me as much. The food and drinks on the beach were awesome, and that never stopped. Got done with a beer, raised my hand, and in five minutes, I had another. This was the life I liked and could get very comfortable with it. However, on day 4, I set out for my next spot.

I took a bus from Lovina to a town on the east coast of the island called Tulamben. The reason I had chosen this place was to possibly do some scuba diving. The town itself really had no appeal, but this was a place to dive. The bus ride was rather nice, going from along the beaches to the jungle and back to the beach. It was nice to have a variety of things to see when you are traveling.

This town was small, and I found a nice family-owned hostel close to the water. It was my own room and bathroom with a shower. Once I got settled, I explored the area and talked with a few people about diving. I learned there was a shipwreck dive right off the beach and not expensive at all, less than $10 for a tank. Now I met this guy at his place of business, asked about diving, and never once did he ask if I was certified or even knew how to dive. I talked with him for about ten minutes, and we got things arranged for the next day but no mention of PADI or anything. Maybe tomorrow, he would ask more questions.

The beaches were nice but not as nice as Lovina; it was a little windy that day, and that made for a short time on the beach. It was another day of walking around, getting used to my new location, and getting ready for the next day. You see, traveling so much, you do have to work. Every three to four days, I had to get used to a new place. You had to figure out the cafes, bars, Internet, ATM, housing, and food. Think about having to find a place to eat that is completely different than a few days before. This does take time, and it is work at some points.

The next day, I was at the beach around 10:00 a.m. and the place I was diving from was right on the beach. The same guy was there, and he had all my stuff ready to go. He would be going with me to guide me around, which was good. At one point, I thought I would be doing this solo, which is not a safe way to dive, especially when you don't know the area. But he was going with me, and we got all suited up and walked to the beach. Just to let you know, he never once asked for certification, PADI card, or anything; it was just the money he wanted.

We hit the beach, got our flippers on, and double-checked our tanks. He told me that as soon as we got into the water, just a short distance out, there was a quick drop-off, and on the edge was the shipwreck. So we walked into the water, got wet, went under, and I checked out all my equipment. This guy had checked it, but I wanted to check it myself. Well, it was all good, and we started out. It was about two minutes of being in the water that I first noticed the wreck. It was so close to shore but underwater enough that you couldn't see it from the beach. We swam out to it, and it was impressive. Here was the USAT *Liberty*, a 360-foot supply boat that had been hit with a Japanese torpedo during WWII. The boat was resting on a ninety-degree angle and is still intact. We swam around the entire boat, inside and out for the length of my dive. It was so cool to see so much coral and fish that now called this place home. The structure was still there, and you could see many different parts of the boat all the way from the bow to the stern. The props for this ship were still on the boat and had coral and fish all over it. I've done a lot of diving, but this one was my first ever shipwreck, and it was a good one. To be able to walk off a beach and not take a boat to the wreck was perfect. It was cheap and easy, and I had a great dive, one of my best.

After my dive, it was time to eat, and it was time to set up the last leg of my trip. I was going from here, the east coast of Bali, to the southwest coast, a place called Kuta. This is where I would spend my last week of this trip. Kuta was known for surfing, beaches, entertainment, and a crazy nightlife. For me, it would be my vacation after a long trip.

First, I had one more night of peace and quiet. The town really didn't have much going on, and my place had a nice outdoor area, so this is where I spent most of my time that night. It was an early night and time to get all packed up again. This was another thing; all

I owned was on my back, and each place I have stayed it was unpack, find what you might need, and then repack everything for the next spot. Once in Kuta, I would find one place, stay there the entire time, and not have to move my stuff for a while; it would be nice.

The next day, I was off and running and on my way. We left the beauty of the beach, and once again, I was in the mountains. This trip gave me a great view of the interior of the island and a view of the mountains/volcano that were on the island. It was so quiet and relaxing compared to Kuta. Once we got close to the city, the vibe and energy increased a lot. The place was packed with people, a beach place, with everything from five-star resorts to basic hostels. The streets were lined with shops selling clothing and souvenir items. It was like going from one extreme to the next. Lovina and Tulamben were small beach towns, and Kuta was a busy city. At least I would have plenty of options of places to stay and to eat. We would see how this went.

I got dropped off at an intersection, and almost instantly, I was being solicited for everything. Now I had a place in mind to stay from my book, and that was where I would check first. I was walking down the street toward my destination, and I was asked if I wanted clothes, drugs, women, or taxi, and that was just the beginning. "No, no, no, I'm good," was all I could say. They did speak English, so this was a plus. Of course, their English was only good to a certain point. If it had money involved, they understood. If not, then you were on your own.

Well, I found my place, and it was perfect. They had single rooms with a bathroom and a shower. The place was a big courtyard with small bungalows as rooms. It was about $15 a night for a private room, and the location was perfect. The guys who checked me in seemed nice and rather helpful. They had room for the week, and this meant that I had found and secured the last place I would stay in for the rest of my trip. It was so nice to know that I had a week here, and it was time to see the beach.

The walk from my place to the beach was about ten minutes; the only problem was I had to walk by a lot of shops. Each one wanted me to come inside and see what they had. Each store had the best deal, and they would take good care of me. Each store had the same damn thing, and for the time being, I was all set. Now I had decided to pick up a few things while I was here. You could get surf clothes for a fraction of the cost in the States, and I had told myself that before I left, I would spend a few bucks and get some new clothes. This was just day one, and all I wanted was the beach.

I stopped at a store on my way and bought a few beers. The beach was huge; it was as long as I could see in almost both directions. The city of Kuta was on the beach, and this was why people came here. I walked out onto the beach, and right away, I could tell this was a topless beach. So I walked around and found a nice spot with a good view and close to the water. I lay my towel out, cracked open a beer, and began my vacation. At about this time, they started coming over and asking if I wanted a pillow, massage, or food. I was all good, just relaxing. Well, this went on for about thirty minutes, and I think everyone who had something to sell on the beach hit me up. After saying no to all of them, they finally got the picture and left me alone. I sat there for three hours, in and out of the water and enjoying my beautiful view; the ocean was nice too.

That night after I took a shower, I was walking around the streets and met this dude from the States. He could tell I was from the States, and he too looked like an American. We started talking and ended up going to a bar. We walked in, and right away, these two girls came over to us. They were local girls and seemed to be really cool. They invited us to sit with them, and I already had my hand on my girl's leg. She was very welcoming and not shy at all. We talked with them for a good hour, and we were all getting a little saucy. Well, about two hours later, I was pretty sure this girl was going home with me, which would be great. At about this time, my girl crawled under the table and proceeded to start throwing up. Her friend helped her, and at this point, our date was over. The friend told me she was sorry but had to get her out of the bar. Yes, I agreed 100 percent, and just like that, they were gone. We stayed for a bit, waiting to see if we could meet anyone else, but it never happened. We left the bar and called it a night. The one thing that sucked was this guy was leaving the next day, and he would have made a great wingman, but that was it.

    Okay, I can sum up the next four to five days in one paragraph. My day would start around 10:00 a.m. I would find a place to eat, and most of the time, it was a donut or a pastry from a store close by. Then I would pick up a few things for the beach, beer, and a snack; find a good place to sit with a good view; and get all set up. Then for the next thirty minutes, I would fight off all the solicitors until they gave up. I would stay on the beach until 2:00 p.m.–3:00 p.m., about the time I was getting hungry and my beers were gone. I had found a few places to get quick food, and it was always good, so I refueled with food and beers and then went back to the beach for another two hours. About the time it would be getting dark, I would make my way back to my room and shower and relax for a bit. After this, it was time for a meal, and I tried a few different places out. One steak house was my favorite, and I ate there three nights, I think. After dinner, I would walk around and say the word *no* about a hundred times. It was a little on the annoying side, and for those that have been there, you can understand. Some people would grab my arm and actually pull me into their shop. They were aggressive and wanted my money.

    So this was just about the same thing every day. I wanted to surf, but the waves were not that great, and the tide was so extreme. I was out in the ocean once, and the horn blew for everyone to get out. The water was up to my hips, and it was a struggle to get back to the beach. Many people had nearly drowned here and had to get saved by lifeguards here every year. The riptide in Kuta is no joke, and make sure you pay attention to the lifeguards.

    I thought for sure I would meet other people, but almost everyone was with others, and there were not a lot of solo people around. The bar was fun the first night, but it was expensive to drink out, and the money thing was an issue. With this said, I stuck to myself and enjoyed time to do whatever I wanted.

    It was the sixth night and my last night here. The next day, I would be flying from Bali to Maui, and I could not wait. It was now the first of May, and I had been away from Maui since the middle of January. It was time to go home, and I was ready. That last night, I spent time getting my bags packed and ready to go. I had all my personal things in my day pack, and my big bag had clothes. I did make one shop owner happy and spent $50 on new clothes. My day pack had everything I would need for the plane ride. While I was packing, I had gotten a small bottle of booze and was sipping on it. By midnight, I was feeling pretty good, had everything organized, both packs next to my bed ready to go. It was time to get some sleep because I knew it was going to be a long day.

Around 2:00 a.m., I got up to take a piss, and once I turned the bathroom light on, I noticed that my front door was opened. Well, I finished peeing and went over and double-checked, and sure enough, the door was open just a bit. So I shut the door and turned toward my bed. This was when the nightmare started. I looked, and I only had one bag there, my big bag. My day pack was gone, and it had been stolen right out front underneath me. Well, my panic level went about as high as it had ever gone. I ran outside, hoping to see someone with my bag, no luck. I went across the courtyard and saw two girls sitting there and asked if they saw anyone and told them what had happened, no luck. Then I went to the front of the building, and four guys were sitting there. The one guy had checked me in, and the other three I had seen just hanging out. I told the four of them that I had just been robbed. They sat there and said nothing. I looked at the main guy and told him to call the police. He told me they wouldn't come; we would have to go to the police station. I yelled at him and told him to get his ass up and take me right now. The guys just sat there and really didn't say much, but something wasn't right.

After a bit of swearing and threatening, he finally told me to relax and he would take me. So I went back to my room and made sure the room was locked, then I met him out front, and he had a moped to take me to the police station. Along the way he said nothing to me the entire fifteen-minute ride. We got to the police station, and I asked for an English-speaking officer. Guess what, they didn't have one. So my driver, the guy who ran the place, after everything that happened, I think he knew who did it.

Here I was at three in the morning and giving my statement to an Indonesian police officer who was translating with the guy who might have robbed me. All this did was piss me off more and more. The officer took down a lot of information. I actually still have the report he wrote. My guy told me the officer would keep an eye out but didn't think I would get it back.

Okay, here is what was in the pack: clothes, money, my wallet with credit cards and debit card, my Rolex watch, and do you remember me a while ago talking about journals that I had kept along the way? Well, my South American and Southeast Asian journals were gone. I brought the one from South America because I thought that maybe I would start my book. Well, it never happened, and now it was gone. This was six months of backpacking through South America, and it was all gone. So this is a little sidenote that when I did start to write this book, it took me a few months just to recreate the time frame with the help of a new copy of *Lonely Planet South America*. It took time and many hours to make sure I didn't miss a thing, and thank God I have a good memory. So that was gone, along with my copy of *Moby Dick* that Al had gotten me, and finally, the biggest thing gone was my passport. This I needed the next day, actually now hours away from leaving, and without this, I could not fly, which meant I could not leave. It was the roughest night of all my travel experiences. I had been robbed before but not like this.

We got back to the hostel, and as soon as we were off the moped, I let the guys have it. "I know you know something and are not telling me the truth. I should just kick the shit out of each one of you!" Let me tell you, I went off. They just sat there and said nothing. I left and went to an internet café close by and spent the next hour trying to cancel my cards. It took time, but finally, I was assured they had been closed and could not be used. Then I pulled up information on the closest US embassy near Kuta and found one about thirty minutes away. As I walked by the guys, I told them that my credit cards had all been canceled so they wouldn't get anything from them, and walked away. After getting all that stuff done, I went back to my room and just lay on my bed, and I'll tell you the truth, I cried. It was such an emotional roller coaster that I just needed to let it out. In all my travels, this country was number 32 on my list where I actually cried because of what had happened.

After I had settled down a little, I went back up front to the guys and told them they were giving me a ride to the embassy and I needed to leave in one hour. By now, it was 6:00 a.m., and the embassy opened at 8:00 a.m., and I wanted to be there first thing. The four of them just looked at me, and I reiterated they were paying my way. All my money was gone, so they would not get paid for the room either. This was a little white lie; I had stashed money in my room just in case something like this happened, but they didn't need to know that. I'm surprised they didn't just kill me, to be honest. I stood over all four of them and yelled at them, called them thieves, and told them that the embassy would shut this place down. I went from being sad to angry just like that.

Now it got interesting. I went back to my room, got my stuff together, found the money I had stashed in the curtain of my room, and packed up the few things I needed. I made my way back up front, had my big pack on my back, and that was it; I felt naked not having my day pack in my front. I looked at the guy and said, "Let's go—now."

Just then, one of the other guys walked up to me and said, "Are these yours?" It was my wallet and passport. The guy had it in his hand and told me he had found it in a bush down the road. My first emotion was of joy; I will give you that. With my passport, I could go home, and I so wanted to. Without a passport, I would have had to stay for who knew how long until the embassy could grant me a new one, could have been a day or a week.

I grabbed it out of his hand and then got angry. "If you motherfuckers have this, then you have it all." My passport and wallet were in the back pocket of a pair of jeans that were at the bottom of my bag. I had put them there because I would change into a pair of jeans when I got to the airport. I like flying in jeans because you never know how cold it is. So in order to find them, they had to have gone through the entire bag, and why would they give me back two of the most important things? Well, this was a question I was still asking myself, but for real, they just wanted me gone and didn't want to stir up any questions with the US embassy. At this point, they realized I was not playing around and would make a scene for the entire situation.

It was now 7:30 a.m., and I wanted out of there. The guy actually had the balls to tell me that now that I had my wallet, I needed to pay for the week. I told him that now that I had this, I could relax for a while in my room and would be back later. Well, I walked around the corner, out of sight from the guys, and hailed a taxi to get me to the airport. *Fuck those guys, they are not getting a penny more from me*, and that was it; I was out of there.

My flight home was not for eight hours, but I had no problem waiting at the airport for my flight. If I had stayed there any longer, someone would have gotten hurt. I should have fought for the rest of my stuff, but I told myself right then and there that it could all be replaced. The journals would be the hardest, but let me tell you, honestly, with the right research and great memory, I believe I did a great job remembering some great travel experiences.

I sat at the airport for eight hours waiting for my flight, and the time had finally arrived. Once I got to my seat and the plane took off, I had this sigh of relief that it was all over. I will tell you that the eight hours at the airport were nerve-racking because I thought the guys at the hostel would contact the authorities and tell them I had walked out on my bill, so when we took off, it was a big relief because I knew it was all over. It was time for a drink, and they served me free drinks for the next few hours. It was much needed and time to relax.

After a few drinks, I sat and forgot about the last part of the trip. I took the time to think about the entire journey. In the middle of January, I received a call that saved my ass. This call turned into a wonderful opportunity that led me across the Pacific Ocean, where I stood in a bunker used to film one of the first nuclear explosions and swam in the deepest part of the ocean. I had seen orangutans in Borneo, Malaysia, spent time in the jungle, snorkeled in some of the best water ever, seen the big port in Singapore, spent the night in *hell*, traveled as rough as it gets, climbed several volcanoes, visited ancient temples, dove a shipwreck, swam in beautiful seas, and met a lot of people. The past 3.5 months had been a spectacular time, and thank you to all that made it happen.

CHAPTER 42

No Place like Home Times Two

I'm starting this chapter the same way I ended the last chapter. I just have to say how lucky and how happy I am to be on my way back. Traveling is part of my life and a big part of who I am now. There is nothing like seeing the world. Pictures and movies just don't do certain things justice. To see these wonderful places with my own two eyes is fortunate. Not a lot of people get to say yes to traveling, but it is something I know everyone thinks about. However, there is no place like home.

I still had another portion of my adventure, and that was going back to Potsdam for three weeks. It would be the longest I had been home since my dad died. There was nothing I had to get back to Maui for, and I knew this would be a good time to spend some quality time with my family.

So this chapter is about flying back to Maui then to New York and then back to Maui. It was the third portion of the trifecta of this adventure.

The plane touched down in Maui, and it was a beautiful sunny day. Joel picked me up at the airport, and it was so good to see him. We had a good thirty-minute ride home to catch up and get all the gossip about the island. He was now single and so pissed about his ex. He could have done this whole trip with me. Oh well, things happen. It was just nice to have a conversation with someone due to the fact the past month or so were all foreign countries. I filled him in on my last night in Bali, Indonesia, and like anyone who has heard that story, it sucked, and there was no way around it. However, it has made for a great story, and I've told it a bunch of times.

Joel hung out for a bit, and I got a grasp on just being home. Kenny, Jenny, Joe, a new girl, and a guy who was renting my room were all home when I got back. Once again, it was so nice to see my friends. To be around people that I know and care about is a great feeling, and most people take this for granted. Like I said, "There is no place like home."

That first night, I went out and saw as many people as I could. The main people to see that night were Julian and Larry. I had been in touch via email, but it was good to see both of those guys. We sat and drank a few beers and gave them the rundown of my trip. It was the first time I was able to tell the whole story from the boat to Southeast Asia. We had a good time, and both guys were doing well. Julian was working and staying at a friend's house; his relationship had ended as well. Larry was working on the zip lines and living with Jamie. They had a nice condo in Kahalue with two of her friends. So everyone was well and seemed happy. I can tell you I was happy to be back.

The next day, I did something that I regretted for a few days. I was so hungry for a cheeseburger at McDonald's. The big thing about McD's was that it was right next door and you could almost smell the burgers in the air. So I went over and got three cheeseburgers and ate all three of them. Now for the past three months, I'd been eating rather healthy. We ate well on the boat, a lot of fish, and while traveling, it was a lot of chicken and rice. The burgers tasted so good, and I enjoyed every bit; it was about three hours later that my life sucked. My stomach started to hurt, and by 5:00 p.m. that night, I was in bed. This is basically where I stayed for three days. I wanted to see more people and do something, but my stomach didn't like the burgers like I did.

With the help of my roommates and a few friends, I did survive. They made me soup and bought me what I needed. It was a rough three days, and I was just lucky to be fine by the time I left for Potsdam, which was the next day. Sorry to say, but I do like McDonalds and that had never happened before, but my body just wasn't expecting that, and I paid for it. This was the only time, except for injuries, that I was sick while living in Hawaii. Never did I get a cold or the flu or anything like that, just a few injuries that lasted for four months and now this.

The next day, I was packed up again and ready to travel for the entire day. Joe dropped me off at the airport, and I thanked him sincerely for helping me out when I was down and out. Like he said, "That is what friends are for, and we do it for any one of us." This was for sure, and I have definitely paid back that same favor from time to time.

In just five days, I was back on a plane and headed west. From Maui to New York was the destination, which was easier said than done. No, I had made these plans on a boat as we pulled away from the dock, so I didn't pay real close attention to how I was getting there. Okay, we left Maui and flew to Dallas, Texas, and had a two-hour layover then from Dallas to Boston with a two-hour layover and then from Boston to Saranac Lake, which was about 1.5 hours from my home. It was a long day, but you make the most of your situation. How I did that was easy. I had a Kona Lager beer in Maui, then in Dallas, I had a Lone Star beer, and then in Boston, I had a Boston Lager. Hey, it was beers around the States flight, and I had a blast.

My mom and Huge picked me up, and it was so good to see her. It had been the longest away ever. It had been over a year, and I hated to go that long without seeing my family. They were doing great and very happy being with one another. My mom had been put through hell and back, and it was great to see her so happy. Hugh was a great guy and treated her like a princess. He also loved Samantha and Scotlyn and treated them like his own granddaughters. Huge was a good guy, and I'm so happy he is treating my mom like she should be treated.

That night, it was late when we got home, and you know how I said it was good to be home—well, Potsdam, New York, is and will always be home. Just to walk into our house is such a calming feeling for me. This house has been in our family for three generations, and it truly is home.

The next day, I got to see my sister, Judy; Scott; and the two girls. It was amazing how quickly my two nieces were growing, and both were beautiful girls. We hung out, and I got to tell my story for the third time since being home. It was fun to share my stories because they knew where I was and kept track of my journey. There is nothing better than family, and it is the best thing anyone can have.

The next few weeks were very enjoyable. I got to work around the house, mow the lawn, eat my mom's home cooking, play with my nieces, and we did some camping. The one thing that was something I had not been around for in years was Mother's Day. I had been away for this date for twenty-plus years. I would send flowers and always call her, but to be with her was priceless. That day, we cooked outside, all sat around the table, enjoyed a few beers, and really spent time with my family. Most of the time home was around holidays or a week at Memorial Day, and things were rushed and busy, not this time. This time, it was laid-back and relaxing for everyone.

The three weeks being home flew by, and it was great to see everyone. I had been in touch with the guys on the boat, Cravens and a few others. My plan when I returned was to try and get back fishing and start making some money. It had been almost six months since I had worked. The boat went down and then the economy and then my health, so it had been a while. Cravens was back on our boat, and according to him, the trips had picked up, and they were at least getting one every day. I asked him if he needed help, and he said, "Yes, we could use you." This was a big relief, and at least I would have a job to go back to. The other issue I was facing was my room. It was the cheapest place on Maui, and I did love it; however, having to go outside to use the bathroom or the rest of the house was getting old. I had lived in this shed for four years, and it was time for a change.

The greatest thing about Maui was the coconut wireless communication system that we have. All you needed to do was call one or two people about something and everyone finds out. So when I was home in Potsdam, I got a call from Larry, and they had both of their roommates moving out. This worked out great, and I made the choice to give up my place for good and move into a nicer place. Of course, it would cost more, but I would be living with Larry and Jamie again, and we always had a good time. So I was six thousand miles away, and I had a job and a new place to live. This was excellent and two big things off my shoulders.

The last few days at home were just spending time with my family. Each night, we would have a nice dinner and sit on the back porch and talk about everything. We would always have our nightly cocktails and laugh at the world. It was great to be home, and it was sad to say goodbye, especially to my mom, but it was time to figure out the next chapter in my life.

It was the first of June 2009, and I was back on the rock. It felt good, and this time it would be for good, at least that is what I thought. Larry picked me up this time, and we got a chance to discuss the move and plan something fun. He had been living with three girls, and it was a girls' house; now I was moving in, and our buddy Dino would take the third room. Poor Jamie went from her friends to boys, which she was fine with. We had been together for years, and we knew each other well. It would be fine, just a little different.

My first night back home, I did get to stay at 795 Wainee Street in the shed one more night. The guy who was taking it over was gone for a few days, and this worked out perfectly. I got to spend one more night with my roommates, and it was tough leaving this place. This had been my home since I had moved to the island and met some of my best friends from this house. I had gone through the remodel, a bunch of roommates, and a lot of parties. It was a very emotional night for me. This place would always be one of the best places I have ever lived.

The next morning, I said my goodbyes and drove fifteen minutes north to my new home. Kapalua was the name of the town, and it was all residential with a few businesses. The condo was on the side of the mountain, and we had a small view of the ocean from the kitchen. My room was small, but just outside my door was the bathroom, and it was awesome. I didn't have to put my slippers on to go inside and take a shower. The place was new, wall-to-wall carpet, plenty of parking, nice breeze going through the windows, and they had everything we needed. It was just different not being in the center of Lahaian, and from now on, I would have to drive to go anywhere. This was not a problem, and we did have a bar at the end of our road, which became our new hangout.

So I got moved in, and it was time to start work again. Cravens had called, and I had three days on his boat and maybe a day or so on another boat. I owed him big-time for this, and the next morning, it would all start. It started at 3:45 a.m. the next day, and this was not something I was looking forward to. Getting up when it is still dark out sucks, and I never got used to it.

I got to the boat, and Steve showed up soon after. We had not seen each other in seven months, and we had so much to catch up on. I tell you, just stepping on the boat was a great feeling. This was a cool job, good paying, great people, and a chance to catch a big fish. We got all set up, got our charter, and before the sun popped up, we were out on the ocean. The ocean breeze, blue water, the island of Maui, and Cravens at the wheel—let me tell you, it was one of the best mornings ever!

The day was spent catching up with my friend on everything that had happened in the last six months—a lot of adventures and a little bit of change. It was so good to be back!

My life got back to normal, a routine if you call it, and things were going well. I had been back for a month and Julian informed me he was moving back to Alaska. He had been struggling with keeping a job and paying for a place to live. Unfortunately, he had burned a few bridges, slept on everyone's couch, and he needed a change. Our friend John bought a dive shop and wanted Julian to help him out. It would be good for him; I was just going to miss him not being around. Even with work and everything, I would see him three to four days a week. It was sad, but I did understand, and we would still keep in touch. The next week, I drove him to the airport, and we had our sad goodbye. He hated to leave but knew it was the right thing. I was going to miss him borrowing things and never seeing them again. I was going to miss him using my truck and returning it on empty. He was one of a kind and one of the best friends I had ever had. When I dropped him off at the airport, I never thought in a million years, but it was the last time I saw my friend.

It was around the end of August, and I got more news about someone leaving; it was Larry. He and Jamie had decided to go their separate ways. They had both been seeing other people, and it just wasn't going any further. Larry also had plans on going to New Zealand at some point in his life. He wanted to go back to Connecticut and spend some time with his family.

Before he left, we all chipped in and got him a room at the Westin Hotel, which was a great place to hang out. That day, we partied all day by the pool, a bunch of people showed up: Carmen, Justin, Joel, JD, Laura, Dino, and a bunch of others. We had a great day and a great night. Only Larry didn't stay the night; he went home, so I decided to stay and had the whole room to myself.

A few days later, I drove him to the airport and cried most of the way. It would be different not having him around. I had said goodbye to a lot of people, but this one was tough. He was a good person, and Larry went back home for a few years and finally made his way to New Zealand, which is where he is still living. Larry and I are still good friends, and we talk when we can. Each time we talk, memories of Maui come up in every conversation.

Things happen for a reason, and in mid-October we found out the landlord of the place was moving into this condo. We had to move out, and we had two weeks to find a new place. Jamie was moving in with her new boyfriend, and Dino was getting his own place near Carmen and Justin. I had to decide what to do.

This would be the first time you have heard this name in a while, Ronnie, and yes, we were still in contact. She left Florida after she graduated and moved to Seattle with her boyfriend. By now, I had dated others but really had been single for two years. With everything that had happened for me, it might not have happened if I had been with someone. So Ronnie and I would talk from time to time and keep in touch the best we could. Once I got back to the island, we started talking more. She had been in Seattle for six months, and her relationship was not doing well. It was about a month later, and she moved back to Oahu to live and work.

TAKE A DECADE

We were on the phone one night, and it was about a week before we had to move out. Ronnie asked me, "Why don't you move over here?" It was something to think about and would be a change. It was great being back on the island, but I wanted more like I said. JD and Laura had bought a house on the other side of the island, and I saw them a lot less. Justin and Carmen had bought a house and were busy with their lives and expecting their first child. Joel and his girl were living together and doing well. It was a time with a lot of changes, and after a good talk with Steve, I decided to give it a shot. Like I told him, for Ronnie and I me, it would be the test to see if we were meant to be together. The other thing was Oahu was a busy place and had a lot more options and opportunities to make a good living. I had been on Maui on and off for eight years, and it was time to try something else. I could always move back if things change and would always have a place to stay.

One of the last big things that I did experience on Maui was turning forty years young. I arrived on the island when I was a young thirty-two-year-old adventurer. Now I was eight years older, and I can tell you I have had the time of my life. I didn't feel any smarter or wiser, just lucky I guess.

The night of my fortieth, a bunch of people met up at a local bar, and it was a blast. When it is your birthday, you don't pay for drinks and are treated like a rock star. It was great to see all my friends show up; however, this night was not just about a birthday but also the fact I was moving. It was a great night and also a sad night.

It was my last mourning on Maui, and I hoped this was the right choice for me. I wouldn't know until we tried, and all we could do was hope for the best. I stopped on the way to the airport and said my final goodbyes to a few people. Then I had my last drive down the coast of Maui for a while. The stretch from Lahaina to Kahului, right along the ocean, was breathtaking and never got old.

I dropped my truck off at the harbor filled with everything that I own, did all my paperwork, and was told it would take a few days before it arrived for pickup on Oahu. Then I took a taxi from the port to the airport; they were like three miles apart. I got dropped off, and it was really kicking in that I was leaving. It was surreal standing there and just thinking about what it was like eight years ago when I first got off the plane and didn't know a single thing about this island. Now I was standing there, and I hoped someone else got to enjoy this place as much as I did. Who knew? That day, someone else might have been just getting off the plane and ready to start the next chapter in their book, and for me, it was time to close this chapter and start another.

43
CHAPTER

Love and Live

We had talked many times before this actually happened and tried to get things arranged as best we could. She was living in a small efficiency apartment in Waikiki, Honolulu, and had about two weeks on her lease. Her place was big enough for one person, and that was about it. Knowing this before I got there, I had made plans to find my own place for a few weeks. I found a place that was $225 a week and was just outside of Waikiki. This is where I would stay until we found something big enough for both of us.

The plane landed in Honolulu, and I was now home; it was day one of my next adventure. Ronnie picked me up, and she looked great. We had a big hug, kiss, and a big hello. It had been over a year since we had seen each other. We had talked many times, but it was the first time being together in a long time. It was weird, but it felt like I had just seen her the day before; time just didn't matter, and we were back together. We got to her place, and it was the size of a big bedroom and that was everything: a single bed, a small place for a hot plate, a small fridge, a tiny bathroom, and that was it. This was the tiniest place I had ever seen, and it would be so tight for two people. We hung out, went and got something to eat, and walked around Waikiki for a few hours. We stayed at her place that night, and we had a great night. It felt so good to be with her, and I really hoped things worked out for us.

I had been in Oahu for about six hours when my phone rang, and it was the port telling me my truck was ready to pick up. That was really fast, and we went to pick it up. Not wanting to leave my stuff in the back of my truck, we took my stuff to my new place. It was a section 8 house, which meant most people who lived there were disabled or just not right in the head to hold a job. Most of the people here had their rent paid by the state or government. So you can imagine what this place looked like. It was an old motel converted into a home for low income. I got to the front desk and told the guy who I was; we had spoken on the phone. He looked seventy years old and probably was younger than me. As soon as we walked inside, the smell of stale cigarette smoke lingered in the air. I would have a small room about six feet wide and twelve feet long. It was all wood with a small bed, dresser, and chair. I would share a common area with five other people that had a sink, fridge, and small stove. The place looked like hell and smelled so bad, but it would have to do for a short period. Anyway, we unloaded my stuff into my room, got my keys, and I spent the rest of the night at her place.

The first day I was there, we realized that neither one of us had a lot of money. She had come to Oahu with money, but she had not worked since getting here and had just started selling these nutritional supplements. Ronnie had a doctorate in physical therapy but didn't want to do this anymore. She was going to make money doing something else, which never made any sense to me, but I'm not her. I had less than $1,000, and this would not last long, so we had to be smart with our money.

My first full day on the island, I grabbed a paper with ads in it and two beers; I let Ronnie work and I went to the beach. The beaches on Waikiki are beautiful and world-famous. You could sit on the beach and see Diamond Head on your left side and the big city of Waikiki behind you. The sand was warm, the water was warm, and the beach was full of people. There was a light breeze coming from the ocean, and for me, it was a perfect day. I sat there for about four hours, just looking through the paper for any ideas on work and enjoying a few cold beers.

TAKE A DECADE

    Now I have to back up a little and tell you that when I first decided to move over here, the job I wanted was selling beach umbrellas on the beach. I had told a few of my friends and Cravens that I wanted to get off the ocean for a bit; I wanted to sit on the beautiful sandy beach, wear a big hat, and sell beach umbrellas. This was my dream job. Of course, at this point, I would take anything I could get as long as it was outdoors.

    On my second day on the beach, I decided to just walk up the beach and see what I might find. So I left from the main part of the beach and walked along, just getting a feel for what might be out there as far as beach jobs were concerned. It wasn't far up the beach when I saw this small stand; they sold a bunch of things like sunglasses, surf lessons, beach toys, and umbrellas. So I went up to the desk, and this guy asked how things were and if I was enjoying my day. I told him it was as good as it gets, and before I knew it, he had handed me a pair of sunglasses to try on. They were Maui Jims, and the lenses in these things are the best of the best. The cost of the pair I was wearing was $250, which was way out of my budget.

    So I started talking to this guy, Drew, about a job. I asked him right off the bat, "So are you guys hiring?" I told him that this was just what I was looking for; I had sales experience and loved people. He told me that the manager would be back in two hours and to stop back and talk with her. This was great, and I had my first lead, which made me feel a lot better.

    So I spent the next two hours walking up the beach. When you leave the main area of Waikiki Beach and head north, it is a great walk. There is just sand for a while, and then you reach this boardwalk that takes you by all the great hotels in the area. You pass the Sheraton, Outrigger, Trump Towers, about twelve other big ones, and end at the Hilton. The beach starts out narrow, but by the time you reach the Hilton, the beach is wide enough to play a football game on. The ocean is right there, beautiful beach, and a lot of girls walking around in just a tiny bikini. This was a beautiful place, and I was very excited that this is my new home.

    How about a little Hawaiian island lesson? There is a lot about these islands that most people don't know. The islands were named the Sandwich Islands by Captain Cook, who first found the islands in 1778. There are eight main islands: Hawaii (the big island), Maui (the Valley Island), Oahu (the Gathering Place), Kauai (the Garden Island), Molokai (the Friendly Island), Lana (the Pineapple Island), Niihau (the Forbidden Island), and Kahoolawe (the Target Island). Oahu is the third largest and has the largest population of all the other islands. According to the 2010 census, there were 954,000 living on this island, which means that two-thirds of the entire population of Hawaii live on this island. It is not the biggest but by far the most populated. Even though there are only eight main islands, only six of them are actually accessible to live on. Niihau is a small island from Kauai, and only about two hundred locals live there. It is not an island that even tourists can go to. It is an island for just Hawaiian people, and it is respected in such a way. The island of Kahoolawe is uninhabited except for animals. This island was used as a target for years from our military. They used it for bombing practice, and because of the unexploded bombs that might be on the island, nobody can go there unless you have a special permit from the state. So we are down to just six islands, but the Hawaiian island chain actually consists of 137 different islands. This is a great trivia question: "How many islands make up the Hawaiian islands?' Most people would sit and count the main ones, but they would be wrong, so it is not 8; it is 137.

Okay, back to getting a job. I was back at this booth in two hours, and Drew introduced me to Joni, who was the manager. She was mid-forties with blond hair, a nice-looking lady, and she was in charge. I told her a little about myself and that I had just moved here and wanted to have a job right on the beach. The only problem—and she made this very clear right from the beginning—was they really weren't hiring. She oversaw two sections of beach, and right now, she told me she was good with staff. She did tell me that things changed quickly and to stop back in a week or so, and like she said, who knows? I could tell she saw something in me and didn't just tell me no, but give it a week, and who knows what could happen? Well, I stopped back every day from that day forward. On the fourth day, she told me that she might be able to get me one or two days at the other location. This was what I needed to hear and was ready to go.

That day, Joni walked me up the beach to the Outrigger Reef location and introduced me to the assistant manager, whose name was Steve. He was a young college kid, who was doing a great job and very responsible. So Steve and I met, and he told me that he could get me one shift a week and this was being a "beach boy." My dream job had come true; I was going to be selling umbrellas on the beach. The only thing was one day of the week would not cover the bills, but hey, it was a start. So it was at this time that I became an employee of Beach Activities of Maui, or what we call BAM for short. It was just the beginning of a great job.

I went back to Ronnie's place and told her the great news; I had a job, just not a lot of hours. It was a start, and even though it was not a lot of money, it did take a little stress off my shoulders. That night, we did go out and have a plate of nachos and a few beers; we had to celebrate. It was also that night we realized how bad our money situation was. Ronnie had not made any money with her new thing yet; her bank account was down to less than $100. My account would not last long, and that was for sure.

From the second night on the island until about the sixth it was rough staying in my place. It was a hot and dirty environment. The people staying in my area were all individuals that had a rough life. Some were veterans, and others were people that had breakdowns of some sort and just not all there. Everyone was nice, just not the people I would hang out with. At night, I would put a movie into my laptop just to have some sort of entertainment. It was a place to stay for the time being but not an enjoyable place to live; that was for sure. Each day, Ronnie and I would spend most of the day together, have our meals together and stuff like that. I was still job searching, and she was trying to make contacts with her new business.

The fourth night in Waikiki, I parked my truck on the Ala Wai Boulevard, which was a free parking street along a canal that ran a few streets away from the ocean. The street was a main place for residents who lived near the area to find a place to park for free. Parking in the city was a challenge. Ronnie was paying $700 a month for her tiny efficiency apartment and also paying $350 a month for a parking place, which was five blocks away from where she was living. This was a normal thing in the city, pay for a place to live and pay for a place to park. Well, I was not paying for parking and I would find a place along the Ala Wai. Well, that night, they cleaned the streets, and I didn't move my truck. Guess what? I got towed. The next morning, I went looking for my truck, and at first I thought it had been stolen but soon realized it had just been towed. This mistake cost me $185, which really hurt the wallet. I had been here less than a week and now this.

Well, it got better about a week later. It happened again. This time, I had parked in a construction zone, which was not marked out very well, and boom, another $185 out of my pocket. By this time, I was not a happy person and was running out of money quickly.

After six nights of staying at my own place and after the first towing expense, we decided that at the end of the week, we would live together in her tiny place. It would be cramped, but this would save us $225, which would help our cause. We needed money, and we needed it badly.

The second to the last night at her place, we ordered a pizza for dinner, and when the pizza delivery guy showed up, I asked about working there. We had ordered Domino's, and the guy told me he made $100 a night easily. So with that information, the next day, I went and applied for a job. It took two days, and by the third day, I was in training. I wore the whole Domino's Pizza outfit, shirt and pants, put the sign on my truck, and was now a pizza delivery guy. It was so helpful to have this, but it did not solve our problem of finding our own place. The average cost of an apartment was $900–$1,500 for a place in Waikiki. To get a place, it was first and last month's rent, which would cost us $1,800–$3,000, and we did not have the money.

Well, a friend of Ronnie's, she and her boyfriend had a place on the north shore of Oahu, and they told us we could stay with them for a few weeks until we could get our own place. They were a couple that I had met before; they came to Maui with Ronnie one time, and I showed them a great time. It was their time to repay us for a fun weekend, and they allowed us to sleep on their couch for a few weeks until we got on our feet.

This was not an ideal situation, but we had no choice. So we moved from Waikiki to the north shore, which was about a 1.5-hour-long drive for me each morning. I went from walking to work to driving in the worst traffic I had ever dealt with in my life. Here I was living on an island in the middle of the Pacific, and I was dealing with rush hour driving like I had never had before. On a good day, I could drive from the north shore to the beach in forty-five minutes; this was without traffic. At 7:00 a.m. to 9:00 a.m., it was rush hour, and the trip would take me 1.5 hours each way. So I was getting up at 5:00 a.m. to be there by 7:00 a.m.

Now when I first got my job on the beach, it was just one to two days a week. Well, my first week, I worked four days, and the second week, I worked six days. It was easy picking up shifts from other people, and I was willing to work as much as possible. It was the three-hour commute that was tough to deal with.

Enough bellyaching about the drive; I had a job and was making money. My job was just what I wanted except harder than I thought it would be. I would get up around 5:00 a.m., leave around 5:15 a.m., and drive through traffic; even on the island of Oahu, they had highways. I would take small roads for the first fifteen minutes of the drive then get on one highway to get to another. Once on the 101, it would be bumper-to-bumper traffic until I took my exit toward Waikiki beach. Once I was close, it was all about finding a parking place in a parking garage that was still three blocks away from the beach. Once I found a spot and turned my truck off, my stress level would decline. Then I had a three-block walk to get to the beach and get punched in before 7:00 a.m. Once this was done, I could relax and start my job.

What does a beach boy do on Waikiki beach? Well, I can tell you they work their asses off for the first few hours. Our section of the beach took care of two big hotels. We had the Outrigger reef and the Trump Towers to accommodate. The hotels were near each other, and both had a contract with our company to take care of their guests. So at 7:00 a.m., we would all get started. We had two booths set up for the two hotels. The Outrigger reef booth was made out of wood with an awning over the top. It was the bigger of the two at about eight feet long and five feet wide. It was set up right on the beach, made of wood, and had big umbrellas that shaded it from the sun. The booth that took care of the Trump guests was really small, just big enough for one person to be in at one time. It was basically just a booth with enough room to display sunglasses and lotion. The two booths were maybe forty yards apart, and we shared this section of the beach.

    The beach boys would get the chairs and umbrellas set up, and the salespeople would get the booth set up with sunglasses, lotions, and beach toys. Being a beach boy was not as easy as I had thought. We would dig a hole and put in the umbrella, which had a piece of wood attached to it to help keep it anchored in the sand. We would put the wood piece that was attracted by a small rope to the umbrella into the hole and then bury it. Then we would grab two chairs and two cushions to put under each umbrella. It was a physical job until you got everything set up, which could take two to three hours before everything was filled. It was tough work, but hey, I didn't have to wear shoes, and the ocean was right there. Once everyone was set up and situated, we had a good portion of the day to sit back and relax. Then around 4:00 p.m., we started to break down everything and get it all put away. This was the worst part of the job because by now, we had been in the sun for most of the day and were just beat from the heat. It had to be done, and this is what we did.

    So I was a beach boy for about three weeks and got five days of work each week. Now each day, the salespeople would take their lunch, and we would fill in for the hour they were gone. It was up to us to keep things going as far as selling the chairs and umbrellas was concerned but also the merchandise we sold to keep our business going. The big thing was the Maui Jim Sunglasses and this lotion that was only sold in high-end places called Absolutely Natural products. Well, I was a salesman and always have had the gift of gab. One day, the regional manager from Maui was over to make sure things were going smoothly, and during my one hour of relieving the salesperson, I sold two pairs of sunglasses for $550. He watched me do this and realized that I had sales ability. Seeing the girl who was working the sales booth that day didn't sell a single thing and I sold two pairs in one hour did help me out a lot. Well, by my fourth week working for the company, they had promoted me from beach boy to salesperson. They fired the girl and gave me her shifts. This was great, and it was then that I started to make money. I could sell the sunglasses and sold more lotion on that beach than anyone else. I went from making $150 a day to $300 in a short time. I can tell you that selling sunglasses, lotion, surf lessons, snorkel gear, and blow-up rafts on the beach was one of the best jobs I had ever had. I was good at it and loved my job.

The only thing that wasn't great at the time was our living situation. The couple we were staying with were great people and very understanding of our situation. It was just not the ideal place to be living. Well, after working five days on the beach and three to four nights delivering pizzas, we had saved enough money to get our own place. Well, it wasn't really our own place; Ronnie found a B&B on the west part of the island called Kailua. This was a good place for me because even though I had started delivering pizzas in Honolulu, they had asked me to help around MCBH, which was a marine core military base. I had been working over here for about two weeks, just a few days a week, and it was good money. Even though I felt I was better than a pizza delivery person, I could say that it was not a bad job at all. On average, I would make $100–$125 cash every night. It was good money, and we needed it. So when Ronnie found a B&B for $600 a month, it was a done deal.

The B&B was nice. We had our own room and a shared bathroom. The unfortunate thing was we could not use the kitchen, so our meals were limited and costly. I can tell you that the days I delivered pizzas, we had pizza. The other days were sandwiches and food we could buy and eat in one day. We did have a small refrigerator in our room so we could keep drinks and a few things cold, but for the most part, it was eating what we bought that day.

Ronnie and I had been back together for two months now, and things were going good. I was working six days a week and had Sundays off to sleep in and relax a little. She was working on her job still, but nothing major had happened. The bills were being paid by what I made, and it was still tough to do anything fun. With working six days a week and five of them on the beach in the sun, all I wanted to do on my day off was lounge around and do nothing. Ronnie was pretty good about this, but she was in the room seven days a week, and when I was home, she wanted to do something. We were living two different lives, and it was tough at times.

So for the next few months, it was all about working and making money. For me, it did not really bother me; you just get into a routine and work with it. It was a lot like fishing and working twelve hours a day: Come home, do your thing, and do it all over the next day. This is how it was for me, and as long as I was making progress, it was worth every hour of work.

After two months of this, we had saved enough to get our own place. Ronnie found a one-bedroom place in Waikiki. It was in a building right on the Ala Wai, which was a good place to live. We would have a view and be close to work for me. The condo was on the twenty-second floor of a thirty-two-floor building. It would be living life like I had never lived before. It was not a house or an apartment, but we would be living in a skyscraper as far as I was concerned. The rent was $1,250 a month, which included everything except our cable. The first time we went there, it was kind of cool. The building had security to let you in, take the elevator to the twenty-second floor, and walk down an outside hallway from which you could see the ocean. The unit was a good size; I walked in and to the right was the bedroom—there would be room for a queen-sized bed easily. Straight across the front door was the bathroom with a tub, sink, and toilet. Then to the left was the kitchen and living room. The best part of this place was the view. We had the best view of the Ala Wai Canal and the mountains in the background. These were the same mountains that I had to drive over each day, and now we only had to look at them. The place was perfect, and we moved right in.

The name of the building was Aloha Lani, and it would be home to us for a while. The building had security, one parking stall for one of our cars, a pool on the seventh floor, a laundromat on the seventh floor, and a postal service in the lobby. It was different for me

TAKE A DECADE

growing up in the country and even living in Phoenix. I only stayed in small two- to three-floor buildings. Now here I was, a big shot living on the twenty-second floor in a building in Waikiki, Hawaii. I really loved this place, and we set it up so nicely with plants and colorful cabinets.

About this time, things really started to come together for us. We finally had a place of our own, which was so needed—you have no idea—and work was going great. As a salesperson, I was selling my fair share of stuff and making good money in doing so.

Once we got moved in and situated, I received another promotion within the company. The guy Steve who had been the assistant manager on the beach was leaving, and they made me the new assistant manager, which was five days a week and more money. It was at this point that I gave up the pizza delivery job and stuck to just one job. I was now making more money in five days than I was in six days, and two days off a week was needed by this time.

Around this time, I received a call from Julian, who was now living back in Alaska. "Hey, Mundy, how the hell are you?" he said.

"I'm doing great, just moved into our new penthouse apartment in Waikiki."

He was excited for me, but I knew something was wrong just by the tone of his voice. "Well, I got something to tell you," he said. He proceeded to tell me the story. He had hooked up with this girl about a month ago; it was a one-night stand, and guess what? She was pregnant.

"Wow" was all I could say, and of course, I asked if she was going to keep it, and the answer was *yes*. Holy shit, Julian was going to be a dad. Well, he was not as excited as some expecting fathers. It was a one-night stand, the girl was young, and like he told me over the phone, she wasn't the greatest-looking. "Well, dude, you will have to do your best, and when the baby is born, it might just change your life." He was not really feeling this at the time, but things did change. I couldn't believe my buddy was going to be a dad. I was excited for him because I thought this would be something to change his life around. We would see. Jullian and I talked at least once a week, so I would see how he reacted to this new life once it happened.

For the next six months, my life was right where I wanted it. My job, which I loved, was going well. Who would not want to have a job on the beach, twenty-five feet from the ocean, looking at beautiful women all day, working with cool people, and making $250–$300 a day. Each day was the same, but now that I was a manager, things were always changing, and this was exciting. I now had control over hiring, firing, and schedules, and I had the pick of the best days to work. To go to work and the first thing I do is kick my slippers off and feel the sand on my feet is a good day in my book.

After work, I would stop at the store located at the bottom of our building and get a can of dip and something to drink. Ronnie and I would make dinner, watch a movie, and just relax and enjoy the evening. Once I was making a few more dollars, we had the ability to eat out once a week and explore more dining options. Don't get me wrong; we were still just getting by, but we did get one night a week to enjoy something different.

Ronnie was still trying to get her business off the ground, and she still refused to find a job in her field, leaving me with the major burden of the bills. I'm a worker and always have been, so the work part didn't bother me; however, we did have discussions on cleaning, laundry, and shopping. I guess these are just things that all couples deal with, and we worked them out the best we could.

Here I was working on the beach, living in a large building and for the most part very happy. Things got better when I was made the full-time manager of the Outrigger Beach Services. This gave me a chance to make more money and have more control over the beach. It had only been six months, and I had been promoted three times within the company.

It was around the end of summer. I had been running my section of beach for three months as the manager, and Dave, the vice president of the company, came to Oahu, as he would every couple of weeks, and wanted to talk with me. We went out for lunch, and as Dave put it, opportunities came up once in a while, but great opportunities only came up a few times in your life. They wanted me to take over the largest property they had on Oahu. It was the Sheraton Waikiki, which was a much larger operation than where I was now.

TAKE A DECADE

At the beach I was working at now, I had a staff of about eight to ten people. We would have two salespeople and three beach boys a day, so each day, I had about five people to worry about. The beach was small, so we could mingle easily, and it was rather nice to have everything in one place.

The Sheraton would be a much larger operation. They had a staff of about thirty-five, two pools, two sections of the beach, three different locations on the property, and a much bigger hotel to deal with. The Sheraton Waikiki was the second largest hotel on Oahu, the Hilton being the first. The guy who was managing the property was leaving the island, and they wanted me to take his place. So Dave asked if I would be interested, and of course, the pay would increase. We enjoyed a meal and a drink, and I basically told him right then and there that I would take the job. Starting pay would be $52,000 plus a bonus opportunity. It would be a lot more work, but hey, I was excited for the challenge.

That night, Ronnie and I celebrated and it was a fun evening. She was excited for me and was so supportive of anything I did. This made life a lot easier, and I told her it would be more hours, but hey, more money. I had worked for this company for around nine months now, and this would be the fourth promotion I would receive.

When I first took over as the department head of the Sheraton, our first big thing that occurred was the fact that Oahu was hosting the APEC meeting. This was the Asian Pacific Economic Cooperation, which meant that all major heads of each country would be here in Oahu. The Sheraton was going to be the main meeting point. The Sheraton would accommodate the president of China, Obama was staying at the Hilton, and our building would be on complete lockdown during all of this.

The first agenda for me taking over this property was preparing for POTUS, President of the United States. This was a big deal, and it was very exciting. *Don't fuck this up, Mundy*, was all I told myself.

Those first two weeks were extremely busy, the hotel preparing for such a large and important meeting. Major heads of state would be here, and the hotel would have security like no other time. I had to make sure all my staff was identified. I did background checks and made them aware of the importance of having such a major event. I was the department head of the pool and beach services, so we were not expecting to be busy during this time, which we were not. However, with security all over the building—I'm talking DEC, ICE, local and state police, DEA, secret service, coast guard, and snipers on the roof—we were ground zero for security.

It was exciting, and the week went well. I did try and see President Obama but was politely denied. It was a shot, and I was willing to give it my best. They brought him underground in a secured elevator; he did his speech, and he was gone. I could, however, hear him from one room that I managed to get into. It was a crazy and exciting day. The coast guard had patrol boats out front and snipers on the rooftop; it just didn't get any better than that.

After this ordeal was finished, it was back to just a normal routine. I would get there around 7:00 a.m., meet my four sales staff, and get them situated on the day at 8:00 p.m. I would have six pool staff show up to watch the pools when they opened and get my three staff members set up on the beach. Once that was all set and going smoothly, we would have our meeting and plan for upcoming events. After the meeting, I would check out each location and make sure things were going according to plan. Then I would spend time talking with the "first-class guest," whom I was given information on each day. My phone rang fifty times a day, and I was on the go from the beginning to the end of each day.

The job was so me, and I loved what I was doing. It was an important job, and it came with respect. We were able to go to the Governor's Ball; we attended the New Year's Eve party and had the pleasure of dining out once in a while with other department heads. It was also nice to have an expense account that I used to take care of my staff.

Ronnie and I got to stay at the hotel one night. We had a room bigger than our apartment, free meals, drinks, lounge chairs by my pool, and anything else we needed. The cost for our one night would have been around $750, and it cost me nothing. Just a perk in the business, and we loved every moment of it.

It had been nine months since Julian had told me his news, and guess what? He called to tell me he had a baby girl. Mom and daughter were doing great, and he seemed very happy. After the baby was born, they tried to be a couple, but it didn't work out, and he had gotten his own place. He had his daughter a few times a week and was taking great care of her. Julian was working with John from the oyster farm in Alaska at a dive shop that John had bought. They were doing certifications, rentals, refills, and everything that went along with being a diver. Julian had received his certification to train other divers, and he loved it. I talked with him every couple of weeks, and according to him, it was all going good. Each conversation ended with "Love you, man," and we both meant it.

I had been working a lot, and things at work were always busy. This hotel was always at 95 to 100 percent capacity. We had events one right after another, everything from APEC, big business, Mary Kay, teachers' union, to big weddings (two-million-dollar weddings), and we even hosted the farmers' union. It was always crazy and always busy, and the time flew by. One month turned into six months, and six months turned into a year.

It was around the end of March, and we had heard of this sandbar that people partied at. So we packed a cooler and drove to find this place. We found the harbor, and I asked a guy to take us out to the sandbar; he agreed. We got out there, and the sandbar was underwater. So here we were standing in water up to our waist, holding our bags, and we were in the middle of the ocean. We found a boat with people on it, and they allowed us to hang out. It was one of those days that could have been horrible but turned out to be wonderful. We met new people, and it was a blast. Unfortunately we had timed it poorly and missed the low tide to expose the sand. Oh well, it was a great day. We had so much fun, and I definitely drank my share, so before I would drive, I took a little nap. However, Ronnie had other plans, and we ended up fooling around in the parking lot then a side street close by. It was a good day, and we both needed it. I was working sixty hours a week, and she was trying now to write a book. She was busy just not making any money; oh well, we were in love.

We had a great day at the sandbar; it was the first time in a while we had the chance to get out and do something. That is a strange thing about life: It seems when things are good, something bad happens. We had just got home, and my phone had gone dead during the day, so I got it plugged in to see how things were. Hopefully, the hotel was running okay and nobody got hurt. It is sad to say, but if no one got hurt that day, then we had a successful day. This was the gauge of my job, and I really didn't like it, but it was the truth.

So I got some juice on my phone, and I had a message from a number I didn't recognize. I listened to the message and started crying. Ronnie came into the room and asked what was wrong; I could not even answer her. I told her I had to make a call and hit redial on the number; it was John from Alaska. He knew it was me and said, "Hey, Mundy, I have some bad news." John went on to tell me what had happened. He had gone to pick Julian up for a dive class. Julian was going to be teaching ten people the basics of scuba diving. This was how they were making money and building the business. He went to get Julian, and he had been up all night doing lines of cocaine. He was a mess, and John was so pissed at him. They had to be at the shop, give a class, and make some money. Well, John got Julian into the truck and hoped like hell he would straighten up before the class. John told me that once they started driving down the road, he could not help himself but to yell at Julian. John said, "I was so mad at him and just let right into him. You have a daughter and a good job. Why the fuck are you screwing this up?" John told me that without a moment's notice, Julian opened the truck door and jumped out; he was driving about 55 mph. John said that before he knew what happened, he looked in his rearview mirror and saw Julian tumble down the road. He hit his brakes, stopped the truck, and ran back to Julian. He was not that bruised up or cut anywhere major, but at that point, he was unconscious. John called 911, and Julian was airlifted to Anchorage, Alaska. Once there, John was told that he would never wake up and be the person he was before. They put him on life support until Julian's older brother could get there and make the decision. His brother got there a day later, and they made the call to unplug him and let him go out in peace. Just like that, one of the best friends I had ever had was gone. Julian was dead, and I would never get a chance to talk to him again. I was devastated for a while after this. He was a good person and had treated me like a brother from the first time we started to talk. The memories of Yosemite, Alaska, and part of Hawaii were all about him, and now that was gone.

I still miss my friend today. Time goes by, and people meet new people, but for me, Julian was one of a kind and will always be a part of my life. About three years later, I found this small Bengal tiger. It was just a little animal statue. The reason I kept it was it reminded me of Julian. It had the same green eyes that Julian had. He was a strong, brave, and good-hearted person. I picture this tiger walking through the jungle alone making his life any way he wanted it, and this was my friend. It was a tough time to know he was not coming back.

After this happened, I had decided to take a few days off and talked with Ronnie about going somewhere. We talked one night and said that neither one of us had been to Kauai, the garden island. It would be nice to get away, and it was not that far, so the next day, she found airline tickets and booked a mini vacation. Now working at the Sheraton, they got me a room on Kauai for a fraction of the normal cost. It was perfect and just what we needed.

So we flew to Kauai and got a lift to the hotel. It was on the south shore of the island and a remote location. Well, I would like to say we saw a bunch of things and explored the island, but I would be lying. You know what we did; well, we did as little as possible. We lounged by the pool, drank a good portion of the day, ordered food right out at the pool, and had sex two times a day. We did as little as we could do, and let me tell you this, sometimes little is good. We stayed there for two nights, and I needed some serious R & R and we got it. I can now say that I have had sex on all the six major islands. People talk about their accomplishments in life, and I can add this one to my list.

Here is another great accomplishment in my life. We had the opportunity because of where I worked to go about three miles off the coast of Oahu and experience a shark cage dive. We left from a local harbor and took a twenty-minute boat ride. There was this platform in the water, which was a floating dock, and they secured the boat to this platform. The cage was suspended in the water with large floats on the top. The cage looked to be about twelve feet long and ten feet wide, all made out of steel. It was so cool; I couldn't wait to jump in. Our guide gave us the rundown. Each group will have about fifteen minutes in the cage to get pictures and enjoy the experience. We were told to keep all hands and legs in the cage, duh.

Ronnie, I, and two others were the first to get in. Now they had started to chum the water as soon as we got there, and we could already see a few sharks swimming around near the surface. It was nothing like when we finally got in. I was the first to enter and told to go up as far as possible, Ronnie right behind me. As soon as my head was underwater, I could see at least fifteen sharks. It was amazing, and I loved every second of it. The sharks were right in front of us, like almost touching the cage. They swam around us and enjoyed the free snack from the chum going into the water. They would swim by us, mouth open, teeth showing and just fantastic. Now I had seen plenty of sharks in the ocean at aquariums around the world, but this time, it was different. They were so close, and we were in their environment. At one point, I counted over twenty-five sharks, ranging in size from three to twelve feet. We saw black tips, white tips, bronze whalers, and one tiger shark. It was so much fun, and I stayed in that cage for a full fifteen minutes; actually, I went back in after everyone had a chance to try it. A few people got nervous, so I took their time as well. It was awesome, and I highly recommend that if you get a chance to try this, *do it*.

There were so many things to do and so little time or money. Unfortunately, it usually was about the finances. Ronnie and I had been living together in Oahu for about a year and half. I had moved over here with little money, and we had to suffer for a while until things got going. The problem was that I was still the only one making money. Ronnie had spent time trying to get her business going and writing her book. The problem was I was making more money than I had ever made and I was still living paycheck to paycheck.

TAKE A DECADE

    The financial aspects hurt both of us. Ronnie did start working at Starbucks, but that money all went to a loan she had for school. So that left me with the full brunt of the bills; it was tough. After a year and a half of working five to six days a week, busting my ass, at the end of the week, I still had nothing. This took a toll on us; we both felt it, and after a big fight one night, Ronnie decided to move back east. She was just so dead set against physical therapy and would rather leave the island and leave me to avoid it. Well, by this time, I was just tired and wanted more from my life. I know she didn't want to go, but at this point, she needed to go for her own well-being.

    At the end of February, she had made her mind up and was leaving. It was a very sad day from the last morning to the airport and to say goodbye. We had been through a lot together, known each other now for nine years, spent time traveling together, and I know we loved each other. When she left, there were no bad terms; it was just something that needed to be done, and we realized that we were just not meant for each other. It was the hardest goodbye of my life, and I cried for two days. I wanted Ronnie to be the one for me, and for me at the time, she was the one. For her, she didn't know what she wanted, and it would be up to her to find her happiness; it just wasn't with me. I said goodbye that day and never saw her again.

    So after Ronnie left, life was different. I was working six days a week now; they fired the regional manager, so I had to pick up her slack. It didn't matter because work was my life at the time; it was fun for me and I talked with people all over the world every day. It just became a routine for me to get up, go to work, work all day, come home, make dinner, have a few drinks, and go to bed. I wasn't into meeting anyone special. I actually got used to having my own place, and my time was spent doing what I wanted. It is a rare opportunity to have *your* time to do what you want. In most relationships, it is give and take at times, and sometimes you find yourself standing in a shoe store on your day off, and this is the last place you want to be, but you're doing it for the one you love. Now that I didn't have this, my time was for me and me only, and I enjoyed it.

    Around Memorial Day weekend, I had made plans on going back to Potsdam for a vacation. With my job, I had two weeks off, and I ended up taking this time to get home for a bit. It had been a while, and it would be great to see everyone. Now this was not just going to be a fun time; we did have a major thing to accomplish and that was redo the roof. My mom had problems with leaking, and the roof needed to be done, so this was the plan: spend ten days with the roof and take four days and go camping.

My mom and Hugh picked me up, and it was great to see them both. Hugh had an issue with his lung; they had to remove a piece of cancer, but he was doing okay. Now he was in his mid-eighties, and I could tell he was failing a little and not quite the same person. They were still very much in love and did everything for each other. It was just good to be home; for some reason, this time meant more than other times.

We had a family project, and it was to fix the roof. We had my brother-in-law Scott, my nephew Michael, my cousins Dan and Patty, Hugh's son Lucky and his daughter Vicky, Judy, Mom, and me. We had the whole team, and it was time to get to work. After our first day, we realized how much work it will be and ended up hiring a few Amish guys to help out for a few days. It was a tough job, and we worked our asses off. Scott, Dan, Michael, and I worked on the roof; everyone else did something on the ground, either picking up old shingles or bringing up supplies to us. My mom would be cooking for a big part of the day, and each meal, we would sit around, laugh about the day, joke, and have a wonderful time. At night, we would drink some beers and plan ahead for the next day. We busted our butts to get this done, and we did it.

Now it was time to camp out and lick all our wounds from the roof. Our backs, legs, and hands were all sore, and let me tell you, a few nights around a fire under the stars was all we needed. The girls planned great meals, and we ate like kings and queens. It was Higley State Park, so we had about five families and everyone was there. Adam and Robin, Chris and Heather plus girls, Tim and Karen, and all of us were up that weekend, and we had fun. The weather was perfect, warm enough to enjoy the lake and play around on the jet skis.

Being home this time, getting quality time to spend with everyone, especially my mom, got me thinking. I had many talks with her, and it was a lot about how Hugh was failing. He had been diagnosed with Alzheimer's and dementia. He was still there but not the same person. This was hard on my mom, and I could tell. She had the house to take care of. Scott did a lot for her; however, he only had so many hours in the day, so he could only do so much. It was just a lot for her, and she made it clear to me while I was home. This was my family, and this was our family home, which both meant the world to me. This got me thinking.

That plane ride home, I did a lot of thinking. Here I was living in Oahu with no one really. I had a few friends, but they were all work buddies, and we really didn't do a lot together. My job was taking a toll on me, and I knew I couldn't do this for much longer. I liked the job, but to have the only thing that matters each day is that no one gets hurt is just not very rewarding. The job—it had been a year since I took over the Sheraton—was starting to act like a "groundhog" day, and this was not the way I want to live. There was so much to think about, and was it time for a change in my life?

The next few months, I tried to come up with ideas of what I could do. I could move back to Maui and get a job with the same company, just not as stressful a position. I thought about moving to Colorado, which had always been on my radar. I also thought about North Carolina; however, moving back home seemed to be the thing to do. The conversation with my mom at least once a week was about Hugh and the house. She was getting overwhelmed, and I could hear it in her voice that she was tired.

I'm sure I don't have to tell you my decision, but I will anyway. I had made the choice to go back to Potsdam and help out my family. It was not an easy decision, but it was time. The only thing about this would be leaving Hawaii, and that would not be easy. I kept this to myself until the end of August. At that point, I contacted my mom first and told her what I had been thinking about. "Mom, I'm moving home." And that was all she needed to hear. I told her it wouldn't be until the end of the year, but I would be back before the holidays.

The middle of September, I told Dave when he came over what I had decided on doing. I told Dave that things were tough for my mom back home and it was time for me to step up and be a good son. He completely understood, and they appreciated the month-and-a-half notice. My plan was to leave Oahu, fly back to Maui, and enjoy one more Halloween, spend a week or so seeing everyone, then fly to Vegas for a few days, try and see Murph in Arizona for a bit, and then fly to New York.

My last few days on Oahu were packing and shipping a few things back. It cost a lot of money to ship stuff six thousand miles, so I only kept the things I could not replace. All my travel things and photos were the first things shipped. I could carry on a bag and check in up to two more bags, so I had to make some choices with a lot of my stuff. I tried to have a sale and sell stuff online, but besides my bike and a few other things, a lot of my stuff was just given away. It is the same way I had accumulated so much stuff in ten years; people had moved and gave me things. Now it was my turn to pay this stuff forward, and my friends got wet suits, tools, furniture, you name it. All I knew was that I could get all this stuff again; it was not worth the cost to ship it home.

On my last night on the island, my friends had a nice send-off for me, and I drank way too much tequila. I can tell you that my last night on Oahu, I slept in my bathroom. Yes, I did, and when I woke up on the cold tile floor, I knew I had had a great night. You don't sleep in your bathroom unless you have had the time of your life, and it was not the first time, nor would it be the last.

The next day, I flew from Oahu, and Laura picked me up at the airport. JD and Laura lived close to the airport and told me I could stay with them until I left. This was perfect because Joel was also living there, and I would get to spend time with two of my best friends. Joel and I went out for Halloween. I was a pirate, and Joel was the Macho Man Randy Savage. He had a great costume and stole the show on Front Street that night. He had let his hair grow out and just looked the part. We partied that night with a lot of people and crashed at Big E's place. It was great to be back "home" even though I was leaving again.

For about ten days, I saw everyone I could, played a round of golf on my forty-second birthday with Joel, spent time on the beach, and just soaked up the island as much as I could. During the day, I would meet up with whoever was around, and at night, we would have a few drinks at the house. It was just great to be around my friends. I had been in Oahu for two years, and some things had changed, but for the most part, everyone was still the same. It was a great ten days, but the time had come to say goodbye.

Joel took me to the airport, and I would be lying if I said I didn't get choked up. He gave me a big hug and wished me well. I knew he would miss me because we had a lot in common, and Joel and I had done a lot together during our time, so it was tough to say goodbye. I had left the island before but always knew I would be back. This time, it was different; this time, I would not be returning.

44
CHAPTER

On My Way Home

The flight from Maui was one of the saddest flights I have ever taken. It was hard to believe that my time was up in Hawaii. It had been an amazing time; ten years of my life was spent in paradise. I knew I needed a change; it was just who I am. It seemed that no matter where I went, after a time, I got restless and wanted something new. Going back to Potsdam at this point in my life would be new even though this is where I grew up. I left at an early age and was now returning as a grown man.

Lucky for me, I had a few stops on the way and a bit of time to myself. I was flying to Vegas, which is a place that always makes me happy, win or lose. It would be the first time that I spent time in Vegas by myself. It was kind of exciting to think I could do whatever I wanted on my schedule, and this was a good thing.

We landed at the airport, which is close to the strip. The only thing that I was not looking forward to was carrying my bags around. I had two suitcases, one box, and a day pack. So I was loaded down and didn't want to walk that far. So we got to the airport, and I got my bags. Now it was time to find a place to stay. I thought about booking something before I got there, but it never happened, so now was the time. I sat down in a chair and used my phone to find a cheap place. According to what I found, Circus Circus Resort was the cheapest, $23 a night. Now what was the best and easiest way to get there? I'd been to Vegas many times, and I knew that this hotel was at the other end of the strip, which hopefully wouldn't take a lot of money to get there. Well, it did. My cab ride there cost $40, which was more than one night's stay; oh well, it had to be done.

That first few hours of being in Vegas, it was time to just unwind and relax. I took a hot bath, which is something I hadn't been able to do for six months. I just had a stand-up shower, so a hot bath felt great. I took this time to check out for any deals going on and set up a game plan for the next three days. I was staying here for two nights, leaving on the third day, and meeting Murph in Laughlin, Nevada.

After a hot bath and a few beers, I was ready for the strip. The first place I wanted to go was Caesar's Palace and play some good old-fashioned Texas Hold 'Em. So I left the hotel and headed up the strip. Now Circus Circus was at the far end of the strip near old town, so it was a walk to get there, but hey, I was in Vegas, baby. Now I did have a budget, and that was $1,000, which was more than I had ever brought to Vegas, but this may be the last time in a long time before I get back. It was my reward to myself after working my ass off for the past two years and the fact I had left Hawaii.

So I started at Caesar's Palace and lost $100 in thirty minutes. I did have a few drinks while I was there, and I was just getting warmed up. It was going to be a long few days, and I wanted to pace myself with gambling. Now Vegas is entertaining from the moment you get off the plane until you leave. There is so much to see with all the casinos and the people. Just walking around the strip is fun in itself, and you can drink on the streets. I'm pretty sure I had a drink in my hand for a good portion of this trip. I gambled in about ten casinos, walked from one end of the strip to the next, enjoyed several buffets, and had my fair share of drinks. By the time I left Vegas, I was up $200 and happy to be ahead. At one point in the night, I was down $500 and got a lucky run with blackjack and recouped. It was a blast from the time I got there until the time I left. Nothing beats this city.

One fun thing I did that didn't involve gambling was a visit to the Pawn Shop. If you watch the show, you will understand why I wanted to see it. So my second morning, I woke up, got ready, and walked to the Pawn Shop. It was at least a 2.5-mile walk; it didn't look that far on the map, but man oh man, it was a trek. But I got to meet Chumlee, who was one of the main guys. The shop was smaller than it looked on TV; they had a lot of stuff for sale but nothing that excited me. So all I bought were a few T-shirts and took some pictures and walked back. It was cool to meet Chumlee, so it was all worth the trip. I also saw a section of Vegas that I had never seen before, and it was not a really nice area, so I didn't need to do it again.

It was time to leave, and I had a van that was going to take me from Vegas to Laughlin. It would take about three hours, and I looked forward to the ride. It had been a long time since I had seen the open desert, and it was spectacular. There is something about the vastness, the lack of vegetation, and the mystery about the desert that is so intriguing to me. This was also the first time in a long time that I was able to take a long drive in one direction. If you take a three-hour trip on the islands, you drive in a big circle and arrive home. This trip was windows down, staring into the desert, and each mile was different. This was just one of those trips I remember like it was yesterday.

The plan to come to Laughlin was set up by Murph. He and his buddy had been coming up to this place for a while, and they had accumulated a lot of points. This meant they had free rooms and free buffets, which was perfect for me. The plan was to stay here for two nights and then drive back with them to Phoenix.

It had been five years since I had last seen Murph. I stayed with them after South America for a week, and that was the last time. Now things had changed for him a little; he had gotten divorced yet was still good friends with his ex-wife. They just came to the understanding that they loved each other and just didn't want to be married. I thought the world of Kari, and Murph told me she was coming over to see me when we got back.

Anyway, I got dropped off, and Murph told me he would be in the lobby waiting. I walked in, and this guy came up to me and said, "Are you looking for Murph?"

"Well, yes, I am," I said. This was Murph's friend, and he knew who I was; guess Murph described me pretty good. Murph was at the counter, and I went right up to him and gave him a big hug. It was so good to see my friend. Murph and I had met in Baltimore, Maryland, and moved out to Phoenix, Arizona on a Greyhound bus. It took us fifty-two hours going from bus to bus to make the trip out. It took us time to get all set up in Phoenix, and he has now lived there seventeen years. I had 7.5 years in Phoenix, and well, that is where my story started. Murph is a great person, and once again, we were going to be able to spend time together.

We had a blast in Laughlin, which is the first city over the Nevada border that you can gamble. It is located right on the Colorado River, and it is much smaller than Vegas and much more relaxed. Three of us drank, ate, and gambled for a good two nights.

It was fantastic—two nights in Vegas and two nights in Laughlin. I mean I was at a table for at least nine hours each day, and I ended up losing $300. This was very good because I was down a lot more than that and happy to have only lost $300. However, if you take into consideration my rooms, food, transportation, and drinks and only spent $300, that was for everything. With this in mind, I had a hell of a good mini vacation.

We drove back to Phoenix, and the drive was still so much fun. I felt like I had never seen this before, the cacti, rock formations, land as far as you can see—I was just taking it all in. We got to his house, and it was different not having Kari around, but we got situated, and Murph showed me my room. Murph's main place to hang out was out on his porch. He smoked, and this was where he spent a lot of time. He had a small pool with fake grass around it. His backyard was fenced off with a concrete block wall that was about eight feet high. There were neighbors on each side and a road in the back, yet he had his own piece of paradise all to himself. It was small and perfect for him; I loved the backyard at night.

I stayed in Phoenix for about three weeks. During the day, I would take the new train system and check out some of our old spots. Murph would be working, so the days were mine. I did help out his friend by tearing down this brick wall, which he paid me $800 to do. It took one day and gave me something to do. At night, we would either cook something on his grill or go out for dinner and drinks. All I knew was it was good to be hanging out with some of my oldest and best friends in the world. Even though a lot of people had moved on, I got to see the ones that were still there. Kari came over several nights for dinner, and the three of us sat in the backyard talking story and reminiscing. This is what you do when you get together with friends: laugh about the past and contemplate the future.

Another thing I got to do while I was back was drive to Pine Top and visited my friends Scott and Rica. Murph let me take his truck, which would be the first time in seven months that I actually drove a car. The drive from Phoenix to northern Arizona was picture-perfect. The canyons, mountains, open roads, and then the pine trees you saw along the way were only seen here in the southwest.

I had met Rica when I first moved to Phoenix; we worked at the same pizza place and became great friends. She introduced me to her boyfriend, Scott, and we hit it off right from the beginning. They had moved around several times—Phoenix, South Korea, Guam, Florida—and now they were back with their families. They have two children now and were living the family life. It had been ten years since we had seen each other, and after those first five seconds, it was like we had never left each other. I spent Thanksgiving with them, and we had a wonderful time catching up on everything and filling each other in on life stories. Of course, my travels were a big part of the conversation; they too had new and exciting things happening. Rica had opened a fancy restaurant that was doing great, and Scott loved being a father to his son and daughter. They had a big family, so it was great to see everyone, and this family knew how to cook, that was for sure.

It was now time to get home and see my mom. The time had come for the last part of the trip and the beginning of a new world. Even though I had grown up in Potsdam, there was so much about the area that I had not seen. Potsdam is at the base of the Adirondack Mountains. The Adirondack Park is a six-million-square-mile state park. It is the largest park in the country.

On December 9, 2012, I made my way home. "Hello, Mama, I'm home." It was an exciting time, and I could tell my mom was happy to have me home and this time for good. It is also time to close the book on this chapter in my life. I've said it once, and I'll say it again. I'm a very fortunate person to have accomplished everything you just read about. Thank you all from the bottom of my heart. It was so surreal that I had traveled around the world and was now home; I mean I was actually *home*.

Roman Colosseum Rome, Itlay Europe trip 2000

Nikko, Japan The Shinto Shrine Japan 2000

TAKE A DECADE

Mexico "Dude Rance" A local cowboy and myself. Riding a house named Gringo

Yosemite National Park Myself with Half Dome in the background.

STEPHEN MUNDY

Yosemite National Park The Giant Red Woods

Alaskan Shrimping boat "The Winning Hand"
Jullian and I with a 200lb Halibut

TAKE A DECADE

Shrimping in Alaska

Hawaii April 2003, "week one and I'm surfing"

STEPHEN MUNDY

Hawaii back deck of the Start Me Up Again, best boat ever.

Captain Steve Cravens, First Mate Steve Mundy 846# 15.5 ft tall Pacific Blue Marlen Largest fish Lahaiana harbor 2005

TAKE A DECADE

Peru, South America: Machu Picchu

Boliva, South America Uyuni Salt Flats

STEPHEN MUNDY

Boliva, South America Outside of Silver mine,
Holding Dynamite and High explosive

South America Baby Alpaca and her caretaker

TAKE A DECADE

South America Ronnie and I on a epic Dune Buggy Ride

Brazil, South America. Christ the Redeemer Statue

STEPHEN MUNDY

Amazon Jungle- Piranha Fishing with private guide

Amazon river 6' Anaconda Snake around my next

TAKE A DECADE

Costa Rica Selling home made jewelry with locals

JD and Joel, Bikini Atoll, March 09' Photo taken by me Stephen Mundy

The Red Rino, 85'x40' catamaran. Oahu, Hawaii to Subic Bay, Philippines 5200 miles

Me at the helm of the RED RINO

TAKE A DECADE

Cartagena, South America- Playa de Blanco beach 3 days of R&R

Nick Kim, myself, Nathan, Ryan.... Love of my life and Family

STEPHEN MUNDY

My mom, Marie Mundy-Storms, My number one fan

Epilogue

My name is Stephen Mundy, and this is my book. In my earlier thirties, I was a financial representative for a large financial company. I started traveling and fell in love with the world, quit my job, and spent a decade fulfilling my passion. At this point in my life, I have traveled to thirty-two countries, crossed the Pacific Ocean, worked on a shrimping boat, worked for a hot-air balloon company, spent time in Yosemite, lived in six states including Alaska and ten years in Hawaii, and met so many wonderful people along the way. There has been sadness, death, financial worries, injuries, and tough times. With everything said and done, I have lived a blessed life to have had the opportunity to do as much as I have. It was also the love and support from family and friends that kept this passion going for me, and I thank you all.

I would like to think that my life has been a continuous adventure with so many future memories. Six months after being home, I met a girl named Kim Moffitt, and we have been together ever since. She works with children and started a very successful real estate business. Being with her has made me a better person, and she, too, wants to see more of the world. I couldn't have met anyone better to fulfill the next chapter in my life. She has three boys, Nick, Ryan, and Nathan, and they are now a big part of my life. I have met the one I will spend the rest of my life with, and I can tell you that I am happy. I have my family all around me, and life is good.

All I can say is I thank each and every one of you for reading this, and I hope in some way I may have inspired you to take that chance and just say *yes*. This is Mundy, signing out, *peace*.

About the Author

Stephen Mundy was born in Potsdam, New York, to Jim and Marie Mundy. He has one older sister, Judy. After a few years in Utica, New York, with an attempt at college, he left New York and started his journey in Baltimore, which is where he lived for three years. After that, he proceeded to move out west to Arizona, which he called home for seven years. During this time, he became a financial advisor for a large mutual fund company. After a trip through Europe, his life changed. It was at this point that his life changed forever and why this book was written. A snowball effect took place, and the adventure began. This book tells of the tales, the adventures, and the many places he travels to during his decade-long journey. With seven states he has called home and over thirty countries traveled to, he is now considered a worldly man.

Stephen Mundy has made a full circle in life. Leaving his home at the age of seventeen and returning to northern New York at age forty-two has made him a successful person in his own way. He wanted to see the world, and he has accomplished so many of his dreams. He has seen a lot, but by no means is this guy done. Stephen met the love of his life after returning home and has been with Kim for ten years now. His time with his mother and family at home has been extremely special. Stephen has been working at a family-owned garden center with Kevin and Jennifer Blanchard called Willow Tree, and he loves his job. He has not stopped exploring and has since became an Adirondack 46er and so much more. I guess he will just have to write another book